Crisis of Capitalism

Studies in Critical Social Sciences

Series Editor
David Fasenfest
Wayne State University

The titles published in this series are listed at brill.nl/scss.

Crisis of Capitalism
Compendium of Applied Economics

Luciano Vasapollo

Haymarket Books
Chicago, IL

First published in 2011 by Brill Academic Publishers, The Netherlands
© 2011 Koninklijke Brill NV, Leiden, The Netherlands

Published in paperback in 2012 by
Haymarket Books
P.O. Box 180165
Chicago, IL 60618
773-583-7884
www.haymarketbooks.org

ISBN: 978-1-60846-239-1

Trade distribution:
In the US, Consortium Book Sales, www.cbsd.com
In Canada, Publishers Group Canada, www.pgcbooks.ca
In the UK, Turnaround Publisher Services, www.turnaround-psl.com
In Australia, Palgrave Macmillan, www.palgravemacmillan.com.au
In all other countries, Publishers Group Worldwide, www.pgw.com

Cover design by Ragina Johnson.

This book was published with the generous support of Lannan Foundation
and the Wallace Global Fund.

Printed in the United States.

10 9 8 7 6 5 4 3 2 1

Library of Congress Cataloging-in-Publication data is available.

CONTENTS

PART THREE

A CRITIQUE OF ECONOMICS AS APPLIED TO THE
STRUCTURE OF MANAGEMENT: THE ENTERPRISE
SYSTEM AND THE PUBLIC ADMINISTRATION SYSTEM

PART FOUR

A CRITIQUE OF ECONOMICS AS APPLIED TO
ECONOMIC SYSTEMS: REGULATION AND PLANNING

PART FIVE

A CRITIQUE OF ECONOMICS AS APPLIED TO THE
WORLD SYSTEM: OPEN ECONOMY AND IMPERIALISM

PART SIX

SCENARIOS FROM THE SYSTEMIC CRISIS AND
THE VALIDITY OF MARX'S SCIENTIFIC ANALYSIS
FOR THE CRITIQUE OF APPLIED ECONOMICS

PART SEVEN

CAPITAL AGAINST NATURE

PART EIGHT

CURRENT TRENDS: FROM QUANTITATIVE GROWTH
TO THE STRUCTURAL AND SYSTEMIC CRISIS
OF CAPITALIST PRODUCTION

ACKNOWLEDGEMENTS

This book is intended as a compendium of the more exhaustive, organic and articulated *Trattato di Economia Applicata* (*Treatise of Applied Economics*), with the difference that this volume presents adjustments, adjournments and a whole new section that focuses on the problems connected to the contradictory relation of capital to nature—a relation that is intrinsic to the conflict between capital and labour.

The author's acknowledgments are due to all those people who offered their various contributions to the development, systematization and editing of the *Trattato* (H. Jaffe, J. Petras, A. Micocci, B. Borretti, just to mention a few), and in particular, Esteban Morales of the Centro de Estudios sobre Estados Unidos at the University of Havana. Efrain Echevarria, Head of the Department of Marxism at the Universidad de Pinar del Rio (Cuba), Hugo Pons, at the University of Havana's Centro de Estudios Económicos y Planificación also made important contributions to the argument advanced in this book. In addition, I would like to acknowledge the valuable advice of Joaquin Arriola of the University of the Basque Country (Spain), in the general planning of the book and Alessandra Barbato for the translation into English.

In addition I would like to acknowledge the contributions of Henry Veltmeyer and his two graduate student assistants—Mark Rushton and David Martin—for the editing and reformatting of the English edition of the book.

This volume would not have been possible without Rita Martufi (socioeconomic researcher, in charge of the Scientific Committee of CESTES Studies Centre, and editor of PROTEO and NUESTRA AMERICA) and her constant help, solicitations, priceless additions and commitment.

I would also like to thank Rita for contributing a scientific mutual exchange, that strengthens our wonderful collaboration and the political-cultural debate we have been having for years now through our academic undertakings and, more generally, through our research activity at the CESTES Studies Centre. More importantly, I am deeply grateful to Rita for her true friendship.

ECONOMICS BETWEEN SCIENCE AND 'NON-SCIENCE' IN THE CURRENT CRISIS OF THE CAPITALIST SYSTEM

One day I said: 'I became a revolutionary in this university' but it was because I came in contact with those books. Well before I had committed myself, without having read any of those books, I was questioning capitalist political economy. Even at that time, it all seemed irrational to me; and I took a political economy course during my first year, held by Portela, 900 mimeographed pages, really difficult, almost everyone failed. That Professor was terrifying.

It was an economics that explained the laws of capitalism and examined the various theories about the origin of value; it also mentioned the Marxists, the Utopians, the Communists, in short, every economic theory. But once I began studying the political economy of capitalism, I began having great doubts, I began questioning all that.

– Speech delivered by Fidel Castro Ruz, President of the Republic of Cuba, in the Aula Magna of the University of Havana on November 17, 2005, at the Commemoration of the 60th Anniversary of his admission to the University of Havana.

Political Economy, "in a wider sense, is the science of those laws that regulate production and exchange of material means of life in human society" (Engels). It studies the system of laws that regulate production, distribution, exchange and consumption of material goods. The economic relation is a practical and productive one, for which individuals or social classes achieve their purposes by means of the product of their work. These kinds of relations define who regulates the whole production process, what are the goods that have to be produced, how to produce them, who and how many people will be able to access the market and under what conditions. Therefore, political economy should be considered as the analysis of the set of social laws that regulate a socially determined production and distribution system.

It is often thought that the substitution of political economy with so-called "economics" occurred at the end of the 19th century. *The Economics of Industry*, the work of Alfred Marshall and his wife, is regarded as the first treatise about this subject. It actually is relevant for us to briefly comment on this work's premises, especially from the standpoint of the development of science. Modern empirical science, which started to develop during the 16th and 17th centuries in Renaissance Europe, constantly employs idealized representations of reality as foundations of experiments, reasoning and projections on reality. Working with these idealizations is not objectionable, and it constitutes a fundamental instrument for scientific work in natural, mathematical and social sciences.

As far as social sciences are concerned, the attempt to convert these idealizations into widely shared projects of perfect societies which we should slowly try to resemble represents a problem. This kind of utopian belief plays a central role in neoclassical thought, and seems to be a peculiarity of the sciences of modernity. Perfect competition, freedom of access to the market, free trade, general equilibrium, the theory of strategic market planning, functionalism with its proposal of balanced institutionalization, and many others assume the hypothesis of a perfect estimate (omniscience).

In the 19th century positivism, the idea of "tangibility" and "formalized realism" are considered as the main evidence of science. The presumed virtues of differential and integral calculus, with the form of a mathematical model, contributed to build an environment of scientific fundamentalism, a kind of metaphysics which replaces theoretical models for the concrete reality of the world and of everyday life.

Neoclassical thought brought deep changes into economic methodology, which begins to be characterized by the denial of the theory of social division of labour, followed by the refusal of the law of value, the abandonment of the theory of economic surplus and, thus, of the analysis of class contradictions. It also introduces a market-centered vision, where perfect competition is the unit of measure and regulates the whole of human interactions.

The neoclassical economist's denial of the theory of value constitutes a relevant digression. As long as the economy had been thought of as part of the human reproduction sphere, the theory of value seemed to be adequate in order to carry out such an analysis. But this element disappeared as soon as economics, intended as bourgeois science, turned into the *administration of scarcity*.

To consider scarcity as economic theory's main subject means to develop economics on the basis of supply and demand. This is the reason why Neoclassical subjective theory of value bases itself, first on utility value, and, secondly, on the empirical simplicity of deriving prices from supply and demand, which results in the derived concepts of competition, scarcity, etc.

Despite the Neoclassical denial, we should not forget the class nature of Marx's analysis. According to Knut Wicksell (1851–1926), the theory of labour value seriously concerned neoclassicists, because of its potential of turning into a terrible weapon that could damage the existing order. If labour was the only source of value, then every other factor of private production was to be considered as a parasite of the production process itself, and their retribution as theft with labour being the one and only element with a right to remuneration.

The "Austrian school" and the school of Jevons, in England, were created independently. They were followed by Marshall, Walras and Pareto, members of the so-called "Lausanne School," who built the fundamental basics of the marginal approach to economics. This school, which was defined by "marginal utility," reflects the displacement of supply and cost towards consumer demand, transforming utility into an instrument of analysis of economic decisions. These categories did not result from a real cost, but from the subjective marginal utilities of goods. Such ideas were subsequently refined, until they could demonstrate that it is not the total utility that determines prices, but the utility for the last purchaser. This interpretation avoids the danger of contamination by the Classics and eased the use of mathematics.

Production factors began to progress autonomously so that the value of each factor could stand as a function of the prices of the goods it produced: this is what started the theory of marginal utility. During this phase of economic thought the production cycle commenced to be presented as something that had its origins in the consumer's decisions and not in the need for capital self-increase.

In his book, *Economics*, published in most of the world's languages, Paul Samuelson defines economics as the study of how people and society end up choosing, with or without the use of money, employing scarce productive resources that could have alternating uses in order to produce various commodities over time and their distribution for consumption, now or in future, among various groups in society (Samuelson and Nordhaus 2001:25). Notice how the object of study changes in regards to the cost-benefit analysis of the improvement in resources' distribution.

So the production and the reproduction of the process of economic life are replaced by processes of selection and calculation that are

aimed at narrowly delimited results. For the Neoclassicals, the object
of economics is the best allocation of resources to improve the yield.
Therefore, the reproduction and accumulation of capital correspond to
the need of such an economic rationality.

Critiques of this interpretation of economics were soon put forward. Sismonde de Sismondi (1773–1842) complained about how
British political economy, wrapped up in obscure calculations, was
becoming progressively cryptic, and about the necessity to come closer
to life and reality. He warned of the generation of ideas that encourage the loss of sight of the facts, while considering public welfare to
correspond with an increase of economic wealth, and ignores human
beings' pain.

It became clear that the economists were on a wrong path that led to
a point of no return, where science was characterized by the disregard
for real problems. We could mention many other scholars, such as
Leontief, Robinson, Galbraith (Assman 1997: 93–193) who criticized
economic science's persistent indifference to practical application and
the explanation of facts. Currently, there are entire branches of economic theory that are a sort of immunization to critique, leading to an
ideological denial of critiques.

Still, the attitude of the so-called "Classical economists," which outlines the very beginning of the history of this pseudo-science, was
everything but technical or dogmatic: the works by Marx, Malthus,
Ricardo, Smith have little in common with these abstractions or mathematical models. They rather favoured comparisons of historically
determined phenomena that marked the age and country in which
they occurred, such as the long lasting cycle of growth in Europe and
the US, during the 19th century. Only a very little part of this lesson on
realism remains in contemporary economic science, where models are
often required to include, without verification by the reality of things,
its dangerous ideological deviances. Ideological beliefs can exist only if
adapted and used as the basis for the "rules of the game".

According to Robinson (1959:362), though many of the premises
of economic theories cannot be proved, they have the ability to provide hypotheses that can be used to orient the economic actions of
countries and enterprises. Such as it is, economics assumes the ideological bases of the bourgeoisie as the dominant social class. From this
point of view, the necessities of the Italian academy do not derive from
any judgement of value, because judgements of value, ideology and

political doctrines are generated by subjective conditions of capitalist science.

On the other hand, the ideological predominance in the critique frequently leads to total denial. As Joan Robinson suggests (1959:362):

> We need to admit that each economic doctrine that is not trivial formalism, contains political judgements. But it would be naïve of us to choose those doctrines we want to accept because of their political content. It is foolish to reject an analysis because we do not agree with the political judgement of the economist that supports it. That is why the "non-science economics" makes the economist that hunter who catches ants even if he thought he was hunting elephants...

It is clear that the Marxist critique of political economy and Neoclassical thought has different ideological and scientific premises. But they do not necessarily exclude one another (Figueroa 2004:198–9). These two points of view have to coexist and diverge in order to explain today's economic reality. This coexistence is part of the dialectics of scientific thought: the administration of scarcity is a product of the instrumental dialectics of means (Marx 1976: III, 49). The labour theory of value is a theoretical result of the logic of reproduction at the base of human life.

To accept the labour theory of value does not mean rejecting the other theories. The supply and demand law, for example, provides a series of useful indications about the fluctuation of prices. There should not be an attempt to eliminate it, but rather to integrate it as part of the essential vision that illustrates at what level, determined by the theory of labour value, prices fluctuate. Marx stated that if the wage, the surplus value, the necessary and the additional labour of a capitalist nature are abstracted, then the foundation that is common to each social type of production will persist. Therefore, both analyses are necessary and legitimate, and a synthesis that outlines the reasons why they are in conflict and what social interests are involved, is required in teaching and research.

From an academic, scientific and practical perspective, the relationship between the Marxist critique of political economy and neoclassical thought do not have to absolutely exclude each other because it is necessary to take into account that Neoclassical thought itself is composed of multiple schools and tendencies that often times diverge. The acceptance of an unique economic idea is useful exclusively from its general political perspective because its application in various capitalist models cannot be always the same, nor have the same results.

The Marxist critique of political economy is both science and critical ideology at the same time. Paradoxically, it has limited its own development by defining itself as the only science, and in doing so it paralyzed and ignored some precise realities in the name of a preconceived truth (Hinkelammert 1997; 2001). A critique cannot aim at transforming science into an absolute power. In Marx's work, the critique of the thought that preceded him led him to a construction based on synthesis.

The economic kind of rationality has to be connected to the social rationality of the model and not the opposite: in other words, social rationality needs economic rationality as its premise, but the economic rationality does not automatically express the social kind of rationality. It is neither a matter of quantity nor a matter of quality of goods and services, but rather of the manner in which they are created and the long term social relations that derive from that production method.

This work has limited purpose space and time. It is not an exposition of the so-called "pure economics" (assuming this has a scientific stature, not only in a formal sense, but in a more "explanation of reality" sense). Nor is it a theory of the capitalist production in its forms of movement, law and period-related tendencies. Here, we intend to offer a guide to understanding the *current phase of globalization* of production and social reproduction in the capitalist form, referring to the theory of the capitalist production as a process. In this sense, we are dealing with applied economics, but not with the academic distinctions that determine the various kinds of applied economics, e.g. environment, engineering, sociology, etc.

To present a comprehensive, but necessarily not exhaustive, critique means indicating possible research horizons by dealing with empirical material or examining aspects only mentioned in this work, and developing conceptual findings proposed here, that have sometimes been simplified for a didactic and pedagogic use of the text.

The Marxist critique of political economy involves the laws and categories that regulate capitalist production and the dynamics of its intrinsic contradictions. Political economy does not involve "production," but the relations between those inside production. No human community can be such, without operating within or by working on the surrounding nature, since production always stands for reproduction of a community, that without working and producing would immediately extinguish itself (also self-sufficient farmers base their economic relations within the family dimension).

To minimize political economy to the production without taking into account the relations of production, not only generates Robinson-like ideas, which had already been pointed out by Marx, but it especially leads to the "naturalization" of the economy, as occurred in the remarkable works by Ricardo, who considers all those relations he conceptualizes (such as capital, labour, land) as natural and eternal. However, the bourgeois economists consider these economic categories as natural categories of production that can be modified.

The Marxist critique of political economy deals with the analysis of the phenomena of capitalist society, revealing the laws and categories of capitalist production as a reflection of the social relations of production, and therefore the class relations of capitalist society. So the object of political economy, the "relations of men in the context of production," *is always the production and reproduction of human society*, though relations and conditions are determined by the historical circumstances. The specific method in which the living labour and the so-called "dead labour," that is, the means of labour and, more generally, the "means of production" where previous labour is stored, defines the fundamental images of the production and reproduction of human society, that is, the *methods of production*. In the capitalist method of production, living labour is in the wage earning workforce form, the "dead labour" is in the capital form, and production occurs because, during its process capital embodies living labour, as it is going to be further explained later on in the text.

Globalization in this context is a financial goal (i.e. the instantaneous movement of capital, monetary competition and conflicts between currency areas). Moreover, globalization of goods can only be partially carried out.

The labour aspect, which is empirically presented as the access of millions of individuals to wage labour, in a directly or a more or less disguised way, is completely different. Since these masses of individuals coexist for capital both on a global and local scale in zones and territories of individual countries, this aspect has the practical effect of segmenting the working class into strata identified by different levels of exploitation, systematically competing against each other (examples include the externalization, delocalization, the increase of precarious work, stagnating unemployment, as part of the processes of the generalized social factory). But this means, (a) continuity of production (i.e. production and reproduction, since if hypothetically a community's activities came to a perfect standstill, even if just for a month, everyone would die). It therefore means (b) labour, and therefore production, always operates within precise relations, called the relations of production. Again, this means, (c) that the productive forces of the community, both human or machines, exist, modify, develop and perish, too, within a determined set of relations of production. As a matter of fact, "productive forces" paralyzed in their abstraction, without those relations in which they operate and develop cannot exist without the production process (e.g. old iron tools that rust will brought back into the natural cycle.

The current economy has to be contextualized within its historical cycle. This cycle begins in the 1970s with a major and still lasting capitalist structural crisis of accumulation and overproduction, and is characterized by the ability to generate huge structural transformations, such as the redistribution of wealth and poverty. Nowadays we are experiencing an increase of poverty in rich countries and an increase of wealth in some layers of the population of poor countries.

If global competition rules the system, then so does the concentration and centralization of capital, as they also generate the daily evolution that typifies capitalism. Also, the present-day process of flexible accumulation means ever larger concentration and centralization. Concentration involves, because of this accumulation process, a growth in the size and power of capital. Small enterprises that cannot reach a sufficient level of concentration are not efficient, and sooner or later they end up under the control of large capital, represented by multinational corporations. In the process of centralization, "big fish eat little fish," that is, capital grows more concentrated not only because of its internal dynamics, but also because it pulls together other capital through mergers and acquisitions. We are currently experiencing this rapid process; for example, the automobile, pharmaceutical and banking sectors are rapidly centralizing, creating huge chains, which not only diversify but spread all over the world.

In a few years, almost every sector of the economy will be dominated by just a few enterprises on a global scale. This process reached such a point that international trade is now subjected to those flows that are determined by large enterprises as they act on their strategies of global localization. Finished products exchanged between countries is slowly giving way to trade between subsidiaries of companies, placed in different countries, through production delocalization and the imperialist use of direct foreign investments and of foreign trade.

After the industrial era and the following post-industrial period (or the information period), we can now state that we are living the post-information phase, or a phase of deviant communications, that has also been called post-fordism or the knowledge economy. Information is now very personalized, in the sense that messages are not addressed to masses anymore, but tend to meet the requirements of ever smaller groups of people, or to reach the single individual and then extends to entire social enclaves. We are now living in an epoch of global competition, but within the sphere of individual production and social loneliness.

Therefore, the enterprise system should mix the different kinds of communications, in order to obtain from each type of information, the commercial and social results required by the company: the recipient is the entire society, conceived as a whole composed by isolated individuals, unable to organize their dissent toward the empire of capital, and for whom the control of information has a techno-social domain.

Communication does not only conform itself, but tends also to conform time and space to make them more functional to its needs. As a matter of fact, the capitalist conception considers leisure time as wasted time, no matter whether it is spent in resting or for intellectual work (real and independent intellectual work is now denigrated since it does not produce anything material). Thus, capitalist-oriented communication encroaches on one's own private sphere, endeavouring to spread the word of consumerism, a world in which it has become essential not to be excluded and that does not allow anything else, since "non-conformed" people are dangerous "freaks" and have to be excluded and subjugated.

On the other hand, present-day capitalism is characterized by the hegemony of financial capital. The banking system, that represents the heart of the international financial system, is fundamentally a mechanism of centralization (but not concentration, because this results from the accumulation carried out by each enterprise). By means of its clients' money, a bank can convert liabilities (deposits) into assets (credits). For example, the workers of an enterprise deposit their salary in their bank account. The bank lends that money as credit to the enterprise, which invests in new technologies, which, in turn, causes a mass layoff of the workers. Is this development? Is this economic democracy?

Nowadays, mass communications collaborate in this new phase of capitalism by reproducing itself and by communicating nothing but the culture of profit. It seems to be turning itself into a nomadic, deviant, absolute, and global communication system that can be simply defined as goods. These strategic goods transmit the culture of the empire of capital in a globalized market, where a crisis exists of an overproduction of goods and production factors, but also supports the crisis of the social distribution of goods, income and socially fulfilling wealth.

During this decades-long process, the triple command over wage labour has changed and strengthened.

First command: capital, by giving precarious work, or simply by asking workers to consider themselves useless (that is, asking them to die), chooses at any moment among the many workers of the segmented, stratified, available mass, which and how many of the workers should join the production process or should be discharged.

The second command of capital is the one wielded by production process itself. Since a product is to be or a service is to be provided, capital makes sure that the techniques, the organization of work, the innovations of process, and the product that make possible the manufacturing of such goods in a specific period of time, look as if they were its own force of production.

The third command of capital consists of the fact that the product (good or service) is a commodity, so it has to be sold. Through this sale capital's valorization is actualized. So the entire production process of goods is regulated by the strict rules of the valorization process.

In a developed capitalist market, some production sectors (and in perspective the whole market) pass through an overproduction crisis as soon as the technologies used, the workforce employed and the organization of the labour process allow the production of such a huge quantity of goods that the market is not able to absorb them (unless prices are so low they cannot even reach the valorization level): supply exceeds what little demand exists, just the demand is inferior to the supply. This does not mean that goods are not demanded by any consumer, since often an overproduction crisis coexists with widespread poverty in advanced capitalist countries as well as all over the world, but it simply means that those goods can be sold at such prices that no valorization would be possible (i.e., the positive closure of the valorization cycle of the capital invested in their production). This means that the capital spent to produce them has been wasted, not valorized, and not only it does not increase, it does not come back at all.

So, it is not a matter of quantity of goods produced compared to people's real requirements, but it is a matter of goods that cannot be sold at their "value". This is why products and techniques will be adopted or discharged based only on their valorization. Therefore, both the individual and collective work is subjected to its own work, in order to not only increase the society's wealth, but to increase the valorization, that if not fulfilled causes the loss of the enterprise's basic purpose, profit.

Capitalism is a form of social organization, whose intrinsic dynamism and ability to change have a strong unity in terms of the laws of motion of the capitalist production itself. But this unity is difficult to understand both for the economists' theoretical analysis and the other social scientists, who only recognize partial aspects of the process or phenomena analyzed through their mathematical or statistics models, which are isolated from the context from which they arise.[1]

The present text does not pretend to reveal any secrets; nor does it present a final interpretation of such a complex system as capitalism. We shall propose some reflections on some of the main theoretical elements of the study of capitalism, whose comprehension is basic in order to develop concepts that will later be applied to the reality in which we live: workplace, consumption space, international relations, family context and personal, cultural and social relationships, factors that determine the social conflict with the capital-labour conflict at its core, which is now being joined by other contradictions such as

---

[1] "Economists, in particular, have major responsibilities for the good or for the evil: politicians' actions will be all the more effective the more rigorous and realistic are the analysis that must be prepared. And here we are faced with the problem of economic theory' condition. As I tried to argue in this book, these conditions are very unhappy: the basic structure of dominant theory is static just when innovations play a major role, transforming and sometimes disrupting the economic life, indeed the whole society. Dominant theory in dynamic analysis is precluded or fed through devices such as assuming displacement of curves that are static and hypothetical; but assumptions are not explanations. In the prevailing theory mathematical methods are largely used, which normally provide a guarantees of rigour. But rigour is only one of the two conditions of scientific propositions, the other being relevance. When both requirements are present a proposition becomes effective interpretation, which after all is what counts in any science." See Sylos Labini (2004: 114–115).

capital-science, capital-gender, capital-environment, and capital-rule of law.

We have discussed the role and the development of economic production processes, including the dynamics of the so-called information capital and the capitalist models from the modern corporate sciences' standpoint in previous scientific works. The same themes have been examined in a political-economic interpretation (see my books published by Jaca Book since 2003, in collaboration with J. Arriola, H. Jaffe, J. Petras). It is useful now consider all those issues in terms of a critique of applied economics, explaining and determining the trends that are taking place in the capitalist world, in order to understand the current phase of global competition. The present approach is different, and often opposite to the analysis of some other authors. References to such authors are used to give a brief overview of other and "opposite" standpoints, that is, to the positions that do not hold our Marxist approach, but share the analysis of a counter-trend in capitalist projects.

If the analysis proposed in the present text refers to Marxian theory, precisely to Marx's critique of political economy, this path is not chosen for ideological proselytizing or cultural and political sectarianism; it is because only through Marx's analysis is it possible to grasp and critically examine the rules and contradictions of capitalism and its methods of production.[2]

While, on the one hand, in recent years in Italy, the studies about Marx and his theories have gained ground, thanks to the spread of an up-to-date literature in various disciplines,[3] on the other, in the academic environment, there is still a radical ostracism, especially when Marxism is developed as a critique of political economy and applied economics.

---

[2] It is difficult to pick up the thread of a discourse on Marxist theory and analysis in the present time, often characterized by cultural obscurantism, historical simplification of the labour movement and of Marxist and Marxist theory, which constitute a fundamental part of the scientific society built in the nineteenth and twentieth centuries. We seem to be living in a time of true cultural and political apartheid against Marxist thought, reaching so far as to exclude Marxist theory from the scientific and academic fields. We are witnessing the attempt to implement an annihilation project of the scientific diversity of approaches; and a cultural homogenization to a sort of neoliberal "unique view" in its different variants, excluding non-conforming scholars, and expelling them from the official science.

[3] We refer, only citing a few, to the books by Fineschi (2001), Carandini (2005), Gattei (2005), Mazzone (ed. 2002, Musto (2005), Vasapollo (eds, 2002, 2003, 2005), Vasapollo, Petras, Casadio (2004) Vasapollo, Jaffe, Galarza (2005).

The marginalization, or rather the expulsion from the academic field, of Marx's critique of political economy and Marxist political economy itself, pushes us to develop a new perspective on the methodological, conceptual and ideological functions of the Marxist critique of political economy and applied economics.

In what follows, a critique of applied economics is suggested. The prevailing economic theory considers and spreads patterns of reduction in production costs, by laying off and making precarious the positions of more and more workers, no longer useful to mechanized productive world. This is the main rule of the so-called post-Fordist flexible accumulation, which does not need the laid-off workers to re-enter again in the production cycle. Temporary unemployment is usually considered as a conviction, a condition of helplessness and uselessness, not a time to live and provide educational enrichment, and overcome the alienation due to impersonal, enslaving, but productive work. Therefore, unemployment is regarded as a burden on society, something totally useless, not a chance that can be taken to prepare oneself for a new position, requiring improved training, and to ensure income while allowing the unemployed to choose the desired forms of social life, including spare time. The unemployed condition must be completely subservient to capital, without resistance, even at the point of exclusion, despair, and social suicide.

During long periods of unemployment, potential workers live in ghetto conditions, locked in a desperate economic condition. How could it be otherwise, if they are not producing? If there is no boom or urgency, some precarious workers will fill the slums of the world, not the world of work, but all the others will be ruined as well. The lack of medical care, inadequate diet and strong competition for limited resources are the sacrifice's tools. Like the workers in the fields, the United States' industrial reserve army is mainly made up of minorities. From a Conservative point of view, it was necessary to install new markers to the boundary between the "shadow economy" and economics. The references to the restoration of family values are euphemistic appeals in order that the horror of the sacrifice is rejected in the darkness of deflection. "Family values" are a euphemism for the militant reoccupation of the visible part of the forces of social order, and they are not to be interpreted as demands for abolition of the shadow economy. On the contrary, this representation is just another spectacular way to identify and monitor the shadowy border between the two economies (Critical Art Ensemble 1998: 89).

The strongest contradiction of capitalism is the despising of spare time out of the logic of capital and its intellectual and practical enrichment. Unemployment and the increasing job and survival insecurity in Western societies is the mirror of the historical limit to which capitalist production has reached. Facing this limit, manipulated communications are used to make the more apparent victims, that is, the unemployed, the precarious, compatible to the system, destroying any possibility of rebellion.

The present text is focused on how the empire of capital project is manifest in the actual globalization process and how capital has managed to identify the ways of deciding, communicating, and, thus, dominating the values in the social sphere with the logic of the market. In order to achieve these goals, capital takes the form of enterprise, which is the generalized social factory, and the form of state, which is the "Profit State." While capitalist models may be different and complex, they all represent the features of the neo-liberal, post-Fordist model, characterized by the immaterial resources of information and communications.

This model focuses more and more on the search of flexible accumulation forms, based on production flexibility, work and life precariousness, the exploitation of new and manipulated communications, an ability to impose the cultural dogma of trade, profit, and social life based on the principles of enterprise. A form of genuine cultural totalitarianism emerges and uses uniform intellectual human capital for its achievements: the intellectual becomes an organic function of the Profit State's dominant class, subservient to the needs, the values and the logics of profit, market, enterprise, and attempting in every way the social and cultural destruction of the "rebels," the non-approved.

On the contrary, a simple approach is suggested to face a complex world. More than a membership, this is a choice in life, the strong unification of theory and practice in an attempt to contribute to criticism and overthrow the capitalist production model. Such a 'style' of life was realized by great revolutionaries, such as Che Guevara.

On October 7, 1959, Fidel appointed Che as the head of the Department of Industry of the National Institute of Agrarian Reform. In this period, the budgetary system was conceived and applied only in the industrial sector of the Cuban economy. This system was the base of state's economic organization of Cuba in the industrial sector, with the centralization in a single fund for all incomes of firms belonging to that Department, while the resources for management were taken from the same fund according to a budget and annual programs. Between 1961 and 1962 the budgetary system was applied to eliminate anarchy and to strengthen the revolutionary state, using advanced forms of control, accounting and planning production utilized by some foreign firms in the country with a centralized system. These forms of economic management, from a technical point of view, were taken from the place they were most developed and then were adapted to the new society. The structure of the system was based on:

- Advanced accounting techniques that allowed more control and efficient centralized management;
- Calculation techniques applied to economics and management, such as mathematical methods applied to economics;
- Techniques in production planning and control;
- Techniques for budget as a tool for planning and control by finance;
- Techniques in economic control; Experiences from other socialist countries.

In this system the company had no cash in an account, and delivered all to the national budget and spent all the necessary resources without using credit. Che himself acted as a critic of the budgetary system, especially of the aspects related to the role of the middle managers for the faults in the administration, to the quality control, for the lack of supplies and effective inventories, for the problems in optimal factories size, among others.

After that, the work organization, the labour standards, the remunerations and incentives, the strict costs and process controls, from the Ministry to the smallest factory, were established. Financial discipline, respect for the contract discipline and compliance with quality standards were also required, including in these processes a wide participation of workers and unions, to organize the preservation of national resources and make decisions to improve processes in Cuba. The construction of socialism and communism is considered as a production, organization and consciousness phenomenon. It is not just an administrative-technical-economic task, but an ideological, technical, political and economic work. This is the synthesis between theory and practice!

In the following pages, the economic arguments are examined from this standpoint.

So, there are essentially two ways to grasp economic reality. The first considers only the reality that can be measured in goods and prices. According to this view, the economist's task does not concern the economics of living, work and of civil life, but, instead, it is to the study the aspects which have monetary expression (for example, according to this conception, the task of applied economics is to determine the main accounting relations: supply and demand, import and export, incomes and outcomes, amount of money and production quantities, etc.). This viewpoint, prevailing in the modern neoliberal paradigm, is based on the idea that people are programmed to act, according to rational and systematic self-interest. Any other relational, ethical, and ideological drifts are not considered not relevant to the practice of economic analysis (Ormerod 1994, 1998: 44).

The second perspective takes into consideration, in addition to the reality of goods and prices, a wider economic framework, an economic and social structure, including the world of prices as one of its several subsystems; it corresponds to the reality of values. According to this view, monetary phenomena closely interact with economic phenomena, not expressed in the form of prices, but originated mainly from work.

These phenomena acquire social, relational, behavioural connotation, integrating and expanding our consideration of monetary facts. For example, this viewpoint regards the exploitation of wage labour as a first level economic phenomenon, and argues that a merely technical approach to economic problems does not permit long term solutions.

In this text, the qualitative difference of capitalism is analyzed in relation to previous economic systems, because it is a system that focuses on the role of money in the accumulation process and the commodity features of money and labour. Therefore, some basic notions of economic theory about investment, employment, trade, international relations, the economic role of State, will be introduced, to show how these concepts are translated into the historical dynamics of capitalism. So, we discuss the concept of quantitative economic growth, technological revolution, neoliberal globalization, the role of transnational and multinational corporations,[4] without omitting the

---

[4] Although later in the text the term "multinationals" will be used, we have to clarify that in this enterprise the parent company has a dominant role in strategic decision-making, while transnational companies combine coordination needs with the needs of autonomy of the whole experiences by their branches, addressed to the dynamics of integration and aimed at the exchange of knowledge, products, services. The transnational company gives branches abroad the right to decide on critical

analysis of territorial and geographical imbalances and the way these are affecting the peripheries of the capitalist world. To carry out this investigation, the fundamental notion of "economic crisis" and the theories of crisis are to be introduced. The importance of international trade and the global characteristic of productive capital, which are more and more influenced by the choices of financial capital, are stressed, providing a description of the main international relations operating in economics.

The structural dimensions of the economic policies currently applied at a global level will be explored through the presentation of the concept that lies at the basis of structural adjustment programs and neoliberal proposals in education, labour market, financial system, sectoral policies and public sector reform.

The above statements point out the objective of this work and the categories that are used to conceptually express masses of data and widespread partial representations of the process (as 'enterprise culture', 'social culture'), that, because of their partial nature, impede understanding rather than facilitate it. These unilateralisms claim to be total, regarding partial moments of the process as a single truth (financialization, culture, technological progress, use of science, the culture of enterprise, English, informatics).

If the above-mentioned assertions are left out, the current process of capitalist globalization cannot be understood. For this reason, in several attempts to construct both a science of economics and a critique of the economy, a partial knowledge of capitalism leads down the wrong direction. A substantial part of the problem is the lack of understanding the rules of the game rules in a society where power is distributed according to how much money people have, generating at the same time an ideology claiming that power is distributed according to the innate abilities. For this reason, economists of the "partial phenomenon" are experts in explaining what has already happened. They hardly examine what is happening and are unable to predict what will happen in the future and this is even more evident in the analysis of the capitalist crisis, which is a structural and systemic crisis of the capitalist mode of production, unlike what prevailing economic theorists assert.

---

business functions, which are different from country to country. The classical multinational, however, not only exports a product, but also a cultural and behavioural system, which is rigidly imposed unlike transnational firms that follows the strategy of adaptation and integration in the macro-environmental host context.

Mainstream economics, and, in general, conventional theories including the Keynesian approach, regard the crisis as an anomalous and extreme event, not only for its rare frequency but because it presupposes a macroeconomic model of equilibrium and a system supposed to be regular and predictable both in a trader's behaviours and in the systemic structures. In this sense the crisis is a kind of sickness of the system, which needs a response each time with "medicine," referring to the type of crisis itself, in order to solve the handicap system and continue the dynamics imposed by capitalist production. Within this logic, a clear separation between the real economy and the financial economy is supposed, considering the construction of the balance sheet of budget in which material assets are to be kept separate from financial ones; therefore, the financial crisis is supposed to have its own dynamics, followed by a possible crisis of fundamental economic elements, as the laws of capitalist production have imposed.

This approach is often claimed by many economists who label themselves as Marxists and have put down the "Marxian toolbox" to carry out theoretically unfounded but politically rewarding operations of the so-called radical left, reconciling Marx and Keynes, but really only referring to Keynes (both to the social and military Keynesianism and its other possible variants) and confusing strategy with tactics, so that tactics is used as a strategy both in political-economic terms and, more closely, political levels.

Such more or less unintended confusions have to be stopped, and it is important to explain clearly why faith in Keynes is demonstrating that the left, including sections of the radical left, is subordinate to the ideas of political and economic democracy imposed by capitalist production. The expected solutions to the crisis are all compatible with the reproduction and continuation of the capitalist system itself.

In what follows, we refer to our own works and those of a few others, such as Alessandro Mazzone, Guglielmo Carchedi, Gianfranco Pala and many others from Latin America, from Osvaldo Martinez and Attilio Boron, in which it is claimed that neoliberal globalization is the current stage of capitalist globalization and the current form of imperialism, and, from a Marxian viewpoint, the "normality" of the crisis has assumed all the characters of a structural crisis of accumulation and enhancement of capital for 35 years.

a) the current crisis is a structural crisis of the system that has been extending from 1971 when the Bretton Woods system was broken up;

b) the current financial crisis is thus a consequence and even an appendix of a more general structural crisis;

c) the economic crisis, with more or less strong characterizations of recession or structural collapse, is not subsequent to the financial crisis, but it is its mother;

d) there is not a productive, "good" capital that pursues the realization of productive investments, as opposed to the so-called "bad" financial capital that operates only profit and speculation, and therefore the first has to be pursued and the second has to be saved;

e) therefore there is not a 'good' capitalism with more a moderate and social character as opposed to a "bad," more aggressive and wild capitalism, but there are various forms of capitalism living in different places and areas, depending on the socio-economic production context and the cultural traditions of the place. In any case, they pursue the laws of capitalist production that is only one and is based on the law of value and surplus value, from which the capitalist law of exploitation originates.

The concept of 'normality' is used because Marx wrote clearly about the cyclical nature of the capitalist system that has economic crisis and peak growth as its phases. Through the crisis the system regenerates its equilibrium by destroying productive forces, labour and capital. The crisis is therefore a destructive regularity necessary to achieve a new phase of economic growth by rebuilding what had been destroyed earlier, and realizing the desired rate of profit, by means of unemployment, precariousness, no man's lands, but also destroying businesses, creating mergers, destroying productive and technical capacity, destroying fictitious capital. Recalling, however, in this last case, the destruction of financial capital, for example, through stock market crashes, does not mean destroying real wealth. The stock exchange does not 'burn' wealth because it does not make real wealth, but, in a sort of zero-sum game it moves fictitious capital by some operators (i.e. all those are losing financially in that particular time) to others who in that particular stage of speculation realize gains.

Only when the themes touched on above are developed, the reader can find the specific aspects of the capitalist globalization process in its current stage and the arguments that explain the links and the characteristics of the structural and systemic capitalist crisis, in a kind of research and culture where the real needs of people are at the centre.

The growth of institutions specifically structured to enhance the knowledge (universities and research centres) is already an integral part of industrial relations and transforms their thought workers into salaried workers submitted directly to capitalism, obligated to guide their mind and consciousness to a knowledge production capable of rapid commercialization or, if they are part of public institutions, submitted to a series of pressures and constraints (financial, political, media, career) so that the knowledge production process fits the needs of capital accumulation. This is why political economy and its appurtenances (applied economics, economic policy, etc.) are to be considered non-sciences.

In general, in countries with mature capitalism, the defeat of the European Socialist bloc continued to justify the idea of capitalism as the only horizon of humanity and affirm in economic studies, as well as in the universities, the absolute dominance of neoclassical thought in the analysis of macro- and micro-economics, and other disciplines in applied economics.

Never before, however, does Marx's critique of political economy and an updated analysis of the Marxist critique to applied economics seem to be more necessary for its timeliness and scientific ability of interdisciplinary analysis in the new conditions. For this reason this text deals with the critique of political economy and is meant to represent a critique of applied economics since Marx and Marxist economics, also recognizing its limits and errors.

The possible construction of an authentic participatory democracy is the basic idea that runs through all these pages, but in order that universal citizenship becomes a law as well as a representation, there is a long way to go. The real universal citizenship is opposed to the perversity of capitalism, which grants the power of money only to those who already have and use it with the goal of making more money to obtain more power. In the so-called "market society" system, society is submitted to the market, and the capitalist market is a tool to dominate the citizens.

History teaches us to distrust political, social, economic, academics trends that have a short life. Many neoliberal texts, and also those related to liberal progressive left currents of thought, express the condition and illusion of the richest countries in the world about the present and the future. The real literary landmarks dedicated to the construction of social knowledge, however, may be temporarily forgotten but they continue to resist. They do not cause a furor, nor a sensation. They make other contributions, slower, less spectacular, less scenic. Even, many times, they pass from hand to hand almost in a clandestine way. When a work has a real ability to explain and understand social processes, it continues shining despite the years, with a strong persistence. It resists the waves and trends and becomes an instrument of cultural, political and social training.

This book tries to give this context, with trepidation. It deals with a reflection on the national, regional and global economic framework, in which militant cultural activity is developed. It does not offer instructions, but rather indications and guidelines, in order that the reader's work could be carried out with deeper and broader lucidity, in their sociocultural dimensions (students, researchers, academics, trade unions, political parties, cultural associations, international solidarity, etc.). The hope is that the reading of this text becomes a study that could suggest the idea of the need, and the real possibility, of overcoming of capitalist production, through culture and hard work for and in the new international workers movement.

Here again the example of Che Guevara who in Discussions are collective, decisions and responsibilities of one man, in Economics, wrote: "Theory and practice, decision and discussion, direction and orientation, analysis and summary, are the dialectical opposites which must guide the administration revolutionary." Reinforcing this belief, giving a broad scientific value to this claim, is the ultimate goal of these pages.

All this will also mean that interdisciplinary, multidisciplinary and trans-disciplinary approaches, designed as a basic culture to defeat the visions of economic market-centric universality, are an imperative for the advancement of the current social transformation of science. Our greatest challenge is taking it as the main feature of our teaching function. Our role as researchers and intellectuals is fundamental to the international workers movement.

Che clearly claimed that in capitalism new economic mechanisms are necessary, and that the road ahead would be long and in this regard he stated in his writings that the political goal, to build the Socialism of the XXI century, was to create finally new men and women, able to support the experiences, defeats, and hopes of the present, and to turn them into the seeds of the new society. On this path, we are now treading.

PART ONE

TOWARDS A CRITIQUE OF BASIC ECONOMIC CATEGORIES

CHAPTER ONE

ECONOMIC THEORY
FROM UTOPIAN SOCIALISM TO MARX[1]

Before Marx

The principle at the base of the political economy works that Marx read in Paris in 1844 – especially of Adam Smith's *An Inquiry into the Nature and Causes of the Wealth of the Nations* (1776) – is that individual happiness depends on society's welfare; the welfare of society grows together with the increase in the nation's wealth; wealth has its foundations in work; work, in fact, is a better account than the natural products, and is at the origin, by right and by fact, of society.

Classical political economy[2] on the one hand put work at the base of human progress; on the other hand, it identified the capitalist system as founded on the private possession of the means of production and on wage labour. It was meant as the only rational and therefore natural economic system. It was necessary to let the natural laws of the economy work. Such a principle, that Smith inherited from the Physiocrats, became the password of economic liberalism. When we let technology work itself out, the progress that it produces necessarily becomes general progress. Just to give an example, "political economy" defends the technical division[3] of labour because in this way there is an increase of

---

[1] About some of the subjects dealt with in this chapter cf. the introduction to Vasapollo, ed., (2002) and Vasapollo (1996); in a more specific way, for schools and thinkers of pre-marxist socialism see Vasapollo's graduation thesis: *Profit Category from Utopian Socialism to Scientific Socialism*, Roma 1980.

[2] The subject-matter of political economy, the causes of national wealth and the laws of its distribution (which echoes its German name: *Nationalökonomie*) changes after the "epistemologic break" of the marginalist school (the works of Jevons, Menger and Walras are published in the 1870's). A classic of economics which fairly reconstructs that period, concentrating above all on the theory of value and of distribution, is Dobb (1998).

[3] There is difference between *technical* division and *social* division of labour. If the latter has always existed and requires the plurality of working activities *within any possible society, starting from the family* – it means that it is a "natural product" of human evolution – the technical division is more recent and exists inside the work process.

productive power, which causes an enrichment of the whole society in a natural way.

David Ricardo draws from Smith the foundations of his economic doctrine. In *Principles of Political Economy* (1817), he carried further Smith's analysis by criticizing its weakest points. Ricardo began his work affirming in an unquestionable way that "the value of goods… depends on the relative amount of work that is necessary for their production".

In an accessible book, Sylos Labini (2005) recently invited his readers to "study again the classics" of political economy, an appreciable exhortation to heterodoxy, given that the outmoded marginalist theory, in all of its variants including neo-institutionalism, is still dominating the field. In his work, Sylos Labini, even without dedicating specific chapters to Marx, is often in dialogue with him, inserting him among the "Classics," together with two other giants of economic thought: Ricardo and Smith. However, the presupposition for an inclusion of Marx between the classics, warns the author, is that we need to set "aside his revolutionary project" (Sylos Labini 2005: 30).[4]

In his *Principles* Ricardo specifies that what determines value is neither the generic cost of production, which includes labour, profit and interests, nor the labour a commodity can buy, but work applied on actual production, the labour fixed in the goods. So he criticizes Smith, reproaching him for having considered valid the labour theory of value only in the primitive times which preceded the appropriation of soil and the accumulation of capital; in this way, the theory does not present a rigorous scientific meaning. Ricardo opposed himself to this, declaring that the intervention of capital does not modify in any way the validity of the value-labour equation; even in pre-capitalistic societies, as well as within bourgeois society, the means of production, which in capitalism are made of capital, intervene in production and affect value in function of the quantity of labour fixed in the capital, which adds itself to the quantity of labour directly applied at the moment of production. Consequently, only labour itself creates value.

---

[4] The operation to deprive Marx of his political relevance is old and today is being renewed also by authors that used to be Marxists and revolutionary militants. In certain academic milieus there is a tendency to give in to adverse ideological pressures marginalizing the political side, which is the true objective of the Marxist critique of political economy: "The understanding of the laws of movement of bourgeois society," in favour of "reductionist" approaches internal to the academy's limbo.

Value, therefore, corresponds to the cost of production, but the cost of production is resolved above all in terms of labour.

The Contributions of the Socialist School

The strength of pre-Marxist socialism consisted mainly in its strong criticism of capitalism, commerce, and the world of industrialization. Therefore, the background of early socialism is industrial society as well as the terrible damages of physical, cultural and moral nature caused by the industrial revolution which are inherent to that kind of development (e.g. children's mass work, working class' life expectation dropped under 25 years, pauperism, degradation, prostitution, etc.).

"Pre-Marxist" socialism started exactly from these damages. From the examination of the world of work and the factory conditions came the realization that the capitalist factory was a break in the history of human labour, reuniting a large number of workers in a single physical occupation place, and simultaneously depriving them of the final result of their work, the goods. The "Pre-Marxists" posed to themselves the problem, which was going to be at the centre of Marx and Engels' discussion, of a reconstitution of the possibility that the workers could be part of the productive process, and eliminate the capital's appropriation of the results of their work. This turned the discussion toward a solution and pointed to the possibility, reachable for all humans, to live within a new social organization, with a fairer sharing of the products coming from a rational production organization, organized communistically or influenced by the collectivity, even when remaining private.

Once the question has been put in these terms, it is possible to have a general idea of a certain differentiation, within the early socialists, on the central issue of private property. Consequently the proposals put forward were different, ranging from the need to eliminate it, reform it or condition it. Some thinkers believed that capitalist society could be reformed; others thought that a transformation could happen only through a revolution, even violent. Many others, on the contrary, had intermediate positions: there were associationists, collectivists, work-organizers, co-operationists; we must not forget also those who preached permanent insurrection, the anarchists. In view of all these various choices, we must identify the points that distinguish all these thinkers.

A first common point is the complete rejection of the bourgeois world and the proposal for a democratic society. It is possible to find in all of the "utopian" socialists a substantial and anti-formal concept of democracy, almost never referred to democratic-liberal political forms. These thinkers want a democracy with direct participation of the people in the political life through the community, associationism, the farms and the manufacturing concerns, etc; a participation that goes beyond even the most advanced liberal-constitutional forms. It often corresponds to a class democracy that expresses itself as a working class dictatorship, refuses the conservative society, and does not even have a contact point with the democratic instances of other various parties.

Passing from English pre-Marxism to the French one, doctrinal differences come immediately to the surface. In the former, we have noticed an accentuated tendency toward economic analysis, and, more than that, a true study of a science, political economy; in the French socialist movement, we do not only find the critics and the developers of Smithian and Ricardian theories, but theorists active in the successive revolutionary waves in France and in popular insurrections. In France, socialism profited from this concern for praxis, the out-and-out revolutionary practice, to the detriment not just of the theory as it is (in fact there were also pure theorists in French proto-socialism), but also of the theoretical development of economic science as the socialist key.

3. The Mystifications of Political Economy according to Marx

Thanks to Marx, the socialist criticism of capitalist society gained a scientific theoretical force, which raised it to a higher level than the one reached by his forerunners.

The first and fundamental mystification of political economy is, according to Marx, the fact that production is taken as an object without analyzing the formation of the relationships between men during production itself, relations that come to represent a determinate form of production and reproduction of the human community. In the Classics, from this conception comes a second mystification, i.e. mistaking a certain kind of economy, a *particular* social form of human reproduction, as *the* economy and society *tout court*. This way, economics does not see that capitalism as an historical achievement, having had a beginning, is likely to have an ending.

Indeed, the historicity of economic-social formations in classical political economy comes to an obliteration. *A fortiori* this is going to be valid in marginalist economics too, which with respect to the Classics will also lose the dynamic aspect in the attempt to describe a simultaneous and static calculation of the balance of the economy, of wages, of distribution, etc., caused by the plurality of the "productive factors". Finally, it is the very absence of historical perspective that allows a process of naturalization of all these capitalist institutions which are acknowledged as given "data," inside which all the problem of optimization of wealth distribution can be solved.

It is manifest how from this point of view the issue of the social transformation is not even thinkable, because it operates as a factor external to economic analysis.[5]

The study of capitalist reality in its place of more advanced development, England, is done by Marx through the works of Engels on the situation of the English workers, and the study of utopian socialists such as Proudhon, Fourier, Owen. It persuades Marx of the incompatibility between the theoretical assumptions of "political economy" and the reality of bourgeois society.

Initially, in the *Economic-philosophical Manuscripts* (1844), Marx studies the results of the coarse analysis which political economy has applied at the modern industrial society. Political economy theorists affirm that the value of goods is given by the work socially needed to produce them, but also at the same time they show how, with his wage, the worker earns only the smallest part of his effort's product. At the same time, wage is the sale price of the worker's performances, which the worker needs to perform, thus accepting, under the mask of a free contract, a slavery which recalls, at least in the contents if not in the form, the ancient age of slavery.

Economists defend technical progress. But if this means an increase in the profit of capitalists, we must also acknowledge that it means low wages for the workers, work in unacceptable conditions, with the risks of unemployment and of endless misery. Moreover, the division of work, reducing the working activity to mechanical operations

---

[5] Anyway, this is not why marginalist economics can be defined scientific and "neutral" in Weberian terms. The initial choice of the marginalist economist is in fact, consciously or not, a value judgement: the assumption of the "capitalist system" as the best one to produce and distribute national wealth. For some reflections on this argument, confront Vasapollo's introduction (Vasapollo, ed., 2002) and Vasapollo (1996).

infinitely repeated, deprives work of any kind of attractive, producing not only health damages to the worker, but even an irredeemable moral dejection.

If the above is true, capitalist society cannot be seen as a world of harmonic relationships, but rather as a place of general war. Workers and capitalists are in conflict over the determination of wages; landlords and industrialist struggle because while the former want to earn the most from the sale of the ground products which are needed for the maintenance of the working class, the industrialists have an interest in keeping wages as low as possible; the small tenants and the big industrialists are in conflict because the laws of competition provoke a concentration of capital and the downfall of the first ones; bankers, financial capital, are in conflict with productive capital, with industrialists, due to the entity of the interests which burden the loans. Unemployed and *paupers* are in contrast with those holding a stable employment to conquer or maintain a form of survival. The "labour-sellers," always and necessarily in excess, are in permanent competition among themselves.

Synthetically, it is possible to affirm that in the 1844 *Manuscripts*, Marx indicated the historicity of production's relationships and perceived the "contradictory" character of capitalist society. In that moment, by the way, he still lacked a Marxian economic theory that could give a reason to these contradictions and could explain the working of capitalist society.

CHAPTER TWO

THE PRODUCTION PROCESS[1]

Capitalist Production and the Marxian Theory of Value

Work has always been a fundamental socio-economic productive activity. Whether it was a hunting, fishing or stock-raising activity, performed in community or in private, it has always been the only activity functional and necessary to the survival of humankind, even if differently valued according to the historical period and the issues of class, race and ethnic group. It was perceivable immediately in the millennia of reproductions of the archaic communities, where all the work spent socially was equal to the work necessary to the reproduction of the community, and generalized surplus labour was inexistent or anyway just occasional. The economies where the surplus is null are called *stationary*. Wherever there is instead a surplus the economic system is called *dynamic*.[2]

Every mode of production is a complex, a totality of relationships that structure the modalities of interrelation between the individuals who compose a certain community.[3]

That is how those relations define how goods and services necessary to the reproduction of a determinate and spatially delimited (the way in which nature is transformed and adapted by man) community are produced. Since man lives in community and not separately (except for the economic Robinsonades, that someone expected to use as valid

---

[1] Also see Vasapollo (1996; ed., 2002).

[2] For a short but useful introduction to such arguments confront Romagnoli (2001; 63 ss.).

[3] "If we consider the bourgeois society in a broad way, the same society, intended as the man in his social relations, always compares as the last result of the social process of production. Everything that has a defined form, as the product, etc., presents itself as nothing but a transitory moment of this process. Conditions and objectifications of this process are themselves, in the same measure, part of it and the individuals are the only subjects, intended as part of a system of mutual relations that they reproduce and produce *ex novo*. This is their peculiar, unceasing movement process, in which they renew themselves and the world of wealth that they create." Marx (translation from the Italian 1997: II, 410–411).

epistemological bases for modern economic theory)[4] the relationships which develop in the human relations' context, intersubjective, are *social relationships*.

Every mode of production has developed its own social relationships, which have defined in the years also the various caste and class issues, "creating" differentiations *ad hoc*, even in pseudo-racial form.

The capitalist mode of production principally differs from the others because it sets man "free" from the preexistent kinds of ties (of blood, of family, of slavery) typical of each previous age. The capitalist mode of production, destroying, even if not completely, the old ways of production and, partly, their juridical inheritances, generates a "revolution" in the social and economic sphere and in legal arrangements, with the consequence that all men are now formally free and equal in front of the law. The worker is not anymore the slave that *must* necessarily work and serve his master, and is not even the farmer *enserffed* in the juridical-territorial sphere of his "lord"; he is now a "free" man, who can sell his labour-power in the market by his own initiative and alienate it at the best bidder. Hence there is no constriction to work, but just *convenience, opportunity, interest*.

Historically, the "liberation" process of men from the old feudal bonds is started from another parallel process, which Marx defined of "original accumulation" (of the capitalist mode of production). It is characterized by a "run" for the privatization of the production means, which are concentrated in the hands of a (relatively) small number of individuals: e.g. the privatization of land ("enclosures"), the progressive destruction of the artisanal practice which deprives the artisans and their apprentices of the instruments necessary to their work, etc.

The privatization of the means of production causes the "despoiling" of the major part of the active (in working terms) population from every concrete (and not formal) possibility to freely work for themselves, not having any access to the production means because these are a private property, not collective like it happened, for example, in many primitive societies. The (potential) worker, expropriated of the production means necessary to his own free, independent and autonomous activity, in the capitalist mode of production possesses only his labour-power (which represents his only commodity which, once sold,

---

[4] For a deep criticism of the foundations of the bourgeois economic "science" of the marginalist school, with particular reference to the "Austrian school," confront Bucharin (1970).

guarantees his survival). On the labour market, the worker sells the only thing that he owns (whose use value is the living work), a fundamental tool for capital, the only one that can produce a surplus value beyond what is necessary to its own reproduction.

Therefore, the worker seems to be free to sell his goods and the capitalist free to purchase what he needs. By the way neither of them is free to do without, respectively, the other one: their production relationship is at the same time *functional* and *adversarial*.

The worker, possessing nothing but his labour-power as survival means, cannot avoid to sell it to capital. On the other side capital cannot avoid to purchase labour-power, since this is the origin of valorization. The worker, in this dialectical connection process, where each pole needs the other one, is *free* and *equal* only in form and not in substance. In fact, in comparison with an employer, he does not have such a contractual force as to afford to choose whether to sell himself or not, when and at which price, etc. The employer always has the purchasing power, which is superior to the selling power (as A. Smith already noticed). The employer, hence, has the formal and substantial freedom, regardless of the relative abundance of working-power supply, to buy.

He has the power to choose, which is denied to the (aspirant) worker. On the power/freedom of choice, which originates from the property of the means of production, is founded the power of the employer in the labour market as well as in the productive process (triple command of the capital over the work, see above).

The formal freedom of the modern worker does not make an element disappear which, substantially, remains common in all of the types of production in which the property of the means of production is separated from the worker. This element is the relation of dependence established between master and worker, between those who holds the power and those who undergoes it.

The capitalist production relationship (that is the capital-labour relation) may well be defined as the heart of the capitalist mode of production because it determines (even if not in a mechanic and linear way) the peculiar *combination* (*Verbindung*[5]) of the workers and the

---

[5] We preferred to translate the German term *Verbindung* as "combination" rather than as "union," as often Marx's translators do. We think that the term "combination" expresses in a more accurate way that process of organization and complementarization of the productive factors which determinates the productive process.

means of production which characterize a specific way of production.[6] The capitalist production process is composed by the union of two processes: the immediate production process and the circulation process.

The immediate production process (IPP) is, in turn, constituted by two processes: a) work; b) valorization.[7] The finality of the IPP is the transformation of the existent use values in new use values, different from the previous, and the conservation of the old use values, so that they can continue to carry on their function. Anyway it does not bring out only use values, but also exchange values.

Moreover:

> [t]he capitalist way of production, considered in his total nexus, that is considered as a reproduction process, does not produce only goods, does not produce only surplus value, but produces and reproduces the whole *capitalist relationship:* on one side the *capitalist,* on the other *the wage-earning worker* (Marx 1989, p.634).

Inside this process we see the immediate contraposition of the social classes of the wage-earners and the capitalists.

In appearance a worker perceives himself (especially in the productive process) in a relation/position of technical-functionalistic kind between man and machine.[8] a relation based on a technical and organizational rationality (of which the manager is just an "executor"). In reality between variable capital and constant capital a social relationship is established (between those who supply living work and those who hold dead work that functionalizes live work for himself). This contraposition does not develop itself between worker and capitalist, but between working class (collective worker) and capitalist (or capitalist class). In the single production units we have on one side a *fraction* of the collective worker, who brings labour-power and

---

[6] "The way of production [...] does not depend much, and surely not directly, from the productive forces as much as from the social relationships of production" (Jaffe 1990:69).

[7] Such distinction, it is good to remark, does not mean the existence of two separate processes (working and valorization): they are just two *different sides* of the unique work process, posed the capitalist production relationship. About this see Vercelli (1973;44 ss.).

[8] While in the first phase of capitalist development, where craftsmanship and manufacture still prevailed, the utensil was in function of man and his "handcrafted" qualities, after machinism's development and the no longer subjective but objective division of work, the machine system starts to be a huge automaton where the workers become functional appendices.

distributes live work, organized according to the cooperation principles, and on the other side the individual capitalist, personification
of capital.

It is in the working process[9] (WPR) that living work is concretely
supplied, substituting *concrete work*[10] (work qualitatively intended).
This process is determined by the way in which the (single) capitalist
organizes his own business, the way he combines the productive factors[11] (among them the workforce) and the way he practically organizes his business' activity.

This is the "place" where the capitalists, the *managers*, exercise their
control and (re)produce the hierarchies internal to the business, that
reverberate in this way inside society (the said triple control of capital
on work).

An analysis of the labour process is hence fundamental if we want to
understand the innovations which are unceasingly introduced in the
technical and management organization of the firm and of the labour-
factor (but not only), and also (it is a consequence) for a proper reading of the social relations of power and subordination which derive
from it.[12]

The WPR is the "technical-organizational" heart of the immediate
production process: there the extractive techniques of surplus labour
are experimented. By the way, it is not "independent". It can be organized in various ways (nowadays we witness the presence of systems like
the nineteenth-century ones, in parallel to the modern ones. Sometimes
these systems are also combined), but it has anyway to be functional
to another process, which determinates the general characteristics:
valorization (the surplus labour productive process, SLPP).

If a capitalist venture has his reason to be in the profits it realizes,
and if the only source of surplus labour is the living work, it is logically

---

[9] The working process is the activity finalized to the production of use values,
transformation for human purpose of the natural elements, condition of the "organic
exchange" between man and nature. It is then, in his simplest relations, condition of
the existence of every human society which cannot be eliminated or modified.

[10] Work must be read in his double composition of *concrete work* and *abstract work*.

[11] The way the immediate relation is structured between living work, machines,
strategies and the tactics of management and control of such relation and of all of them
which result from that, inside the venture.

[12] If the first analysis (e.g. Panzieri) which have "made school" in various parts of
the world, thirty or forty years ago, and the last ones from the late 1980s, it is undisput-
able that the study of the working process in Italy, apart from special cases, has not
been deepened in the dynamics of its transformation, unlike, for example, from the
United States or Great Britain, where accurate analyses are still produced.

consequent that the working process cannot be organized following non-profit criteria, but instead respecting the needs dictated by the valorization process, that *requires* a surplus labour always above zero (W > 0).

While the SLPP is supposed to produce use values, the finality of the WPR is to produce exchange values.

In the SLPP surplus labour is in evidence. The WPR, where the surplus value is more relevant, is finalized to the production of a larger quantity of value than the one that was put in the process (and more than what was necessary to reproduce the work-force). What is in evidence in the WPR is not the concrete work, qualitatively differentiated, but rather the *abstract* one (which is measure of value and consequently of surplus value). *Abstract labour* leaves aside the specific qualities of the concrete or specific labour (the day labourer carries out determined functions and operations that are different from the one of the engineering worker or the construction worker), work is then considered only from a quantitative point of view (as a muscular and intellectual expenditure of energy): it is calculated in hours/time of supplied work.

Abstract work is suitable to be a measure of value[13] for his intrinsic characteristic of *homogeneity*,[14] which can be quantitatively measured without problems, differently from the concrete work where it is always unequal.

With the progress of capitalism, however, abstract work is not only a concept that can be used to analyze the duplicity of the immediate production process and then the values (of use and exchange) of the goods, but it is also a quality that characterizes work as an activity specifically distributed.

---

[13] It was a constant error of a great part of Marxist scholars, who goes back up to Engels (Cf. Weeks 1981: especially Ch. 1), to believe that the value of goods is equivalent to the quantity of work *incorporated* (hours of work) in the goods (embodied labour), value definable *subjectively* and aprioristically, before the realization of the goods on the market. Weeks (1981: 56) remarks instead that value appears only as a price (on this point many contemporary Marxist theorists that studied the problem of value, agree: from Carchedi to Moseley, Laibman, Shaikh, just to mention the main members of different "schools"). The goods' value is just an "average" which can be elaborated *ex post*, defining the *work socially necessary* to produce them.

[14] The lack of homogeneity of the equation members created measurement problems to the early classics (for example Smith): quantity of working hours/ quantity of agricultural output. On this point cfr. Garegnani (1981: 16 ss.).

After the development of machinism (and the incorporation of the living work's functions and of the machines' knowledge, dead work), living work gets to be always more expropriated (subsumption) of his characteristics, specificity, particularity, quality. A consequence of such tendency is that living work is becoming more and more homogenized: for example, labour is often reduced to functions of control similar between them if not equal; think about the new workers called "cognitive," who practice an "immaterial" rather than the manual activity, where the problem solving, data elaboration, etc. abilities are more or less by nature homogenized, not to mention the working tasks typical of the "new services".

Abstract work is not anymore, just a (simply) intangible concept, but it is the result of the capital's needs to use a work-force (by nature) more and more disqualified,[15] less specialized, adaptable.[16]

It is a "trivialization" process, a new dequalified and precarious standardization of work, about which lot of things have been said in the last years, in the sphere of the so called post-Fordist phase. We are testifying some kind of "metaphysicization" of the living work.

Surplus Labour / Surplus Value

It is clear that if we want to analyse concretely the capitalist society and its development, we must abandon the world of the marginalist approaches and turn back to a class analysis.

According to Marx, the wage (social, because it comes from the class) is nothing but the price paid by the capitalist class to the working class for its reproduction as workforce. The wage is a price (monetary expression of value) historically and socially determined. It is now necessary a brief hint of criticism to the generalized conviction that in Marx there has been a theory of the absolute impoverishment of the proletariat, that is the constant fall of the wage, even below the level of

---

[15] More than about a disqualification, Rieser (2004) likes to talk about an "alienated qualification," that is not controlled/controllable by the worker. It is always important anyway to consider that, talking about dequalification, we refer to a *tendency*. Furthermore, we also have to consider that there are two different interpretations of dequalification, not necessarily parallel: the first one in a Smithian sense, as an advanced vilification of the working tasks and loss of professionality; the other one, Marxist, provokes the *superfluity* of the living work expelled from the working process after being substituted by the machines.

[16] Cleaver (2000: 112).

survival. It is important to specify firstly that Marx, while he is talking about the laws of capitalism, refers to *tendencies*, and never to mechanistic laws (like the chemical, biological or physical ones).[17]

Wage comprehends, besides its direct form, also an indirect one, postponed with a multiplicity of components like for example the Christmas bonus, holydays, liquidation, pension, social State services, politic prices and controlled tariffs.

The capitalist purchases labour-power at its value, he pays the worker with a wage barely sufficient for him to buy the means for his subsistence.[18] Whether, as we supposed, the above-mentioned value is produced by four hours of work, this means that, if he has worked for the first four hours, he has already added to the raw material value and to the machines, a surplus value sufficient to cover the means necessary to his survival. If the productive process ended up in this moment, the capitalist will sell the product at a price equal to the costs he met. Anyway, the worker sold himself to the capitalist for a whole day. If, as we previously supposed, the working day lasts nine hours, in the other five hours the worker continues adding value that exceeds what is finalized to buy the means for subsistence. It is, in Marxian terms, surplus value, on which the capitalist takes control just for himself. In other words, in the capitalist production the product of *necessary work* advanced to the worker under the form of salary; the part of unpaid work, the surplus labour, goes to the capitalist in form of surplus value.

Production of surplus value begins, thus, from the extension of work over the limits *necessary* to the reintegration for the capitalist of the wage or price of workforce.

In *Capital* Marx remarks how the capitalist does not obtain this surplus just from the lengthening of the working day: alongside this form of surplus value, that he calls *absolute*, he analyses the *surplus value* that he calls *relative*, because it depends on the introduction of machines, the introduction of technological innovations, the rhythm increment, the reduction of the so-called "dead times," the increase of productivity. New technologies, in fact, enhancing the productivity

---

[17] For example, Marx theorized an impoverishment tendency clearly relative and not absolute (like some sclerotized Marxist proposes).

[18] We are not talking about biological subsistence (even if there are cases, periods and places where the wage remains at this level or even under), but about the historically and socially determined one: that is relative to the comprehensive development of the whole wealth of the society.

of work and shortening the working time necessary to remunerate the wages, increase correspondingly – being understood the length of the working day – the part of surplus value pocketed from the capitalist, and then increases the *surplus value in* respect to the necessary work.

According to what we previously wrote, it results that the value of every good produced inside the capitalist society, may be divided in three parts. The first one represents the value of the raw material, of the used machines and does not suffer *any quantitative variation of value* during the productive cycle, being *constant capital*, which is symbolically represented with a *c*. The second part, the one which incorporates the value of work-power, suffers by his side of an alteration of value, since, besides reproducing the equivalent of its own value, produces also a surplus, that is the surplus value; it is so denominated *variable capital*, represented with a *v*. The third part is the *surplus value* itself, appointed with a *s*.

Therefore we can write the value of a good with the following formula:

$$C + V + S = \text{total value}$$

The capitalist, when he anticipates the wage, he buys, for a certain quantity of time, the work-force of his "employees" who are inserted inside his own factory. The worker, although remaining independent from the capitalist, suffers an expropriation of the property of his workforce: he becomes, in this way, for this period of time, not any longer the owner, but the *bearer* of labour-power. Labour-power is purchased by the capitalist who assumes its command, its availability.

A capitalist does not found an enterprise to allow the workers to survive through his own entrepreneurial activity, i.e. without his personal profit; he does not even found it to satisfy the needs expressed from the market. His activity is just an instrument to help him achieve his only true objective: realize a profit.

The problem, then, is to identify the "source" of the profit. There are theories supporting points of view which explain differently this characteristic of the CWP: someone affirms that all the productive factors (capital, work, production means) produce profits and some other (Marx), starting from the classics of political economy and distinguishing work from work-force, claims that profit has his one and only source in human living work (LW).

LW is the one supplied concretely by the worker (working activity transformer/conservator of use values) inserted in a working process.

According to Marxian theory, then, once the work-force has been acquired, the capitalist can have it at his own disposal according to his exigencies even in a *despotic* way, being its owner.[19] The capitalist is not satisfied of having his quote of LW = NW (NW being Necessary Work), but during the working day (d) he foists workers to supply a quote of LW > NW: such *surplus* of working hours represents the surplus labour (SL).

SL is precisely that part of unpaid LW (only NW is paid) which determines the surplus value[20] (W) representing the form of SL as a value; just like the necessary value (NV) is the form of NW as a value. Only if SL > 0 a capitalist emprise has reason to live.

The capitalist, taking possession of unpaid work, exploits the workers. This is the core of the Marxian theory of exploitation, which does not have anything "humanistic," pietistic or moralistic: it is a scientific theory in the measure in which it is capable to demonstrate the origin of W (generator of profit).

The limit to the working day, besides the physical one (Passing that limit destroys workforce instead of reproducing it!), is determined not *naturally*, but historically and socially from class struggle,[21] which is crystallized in the contractual definition of the maximum schedule of the working day; such limit is fixed by the ability of the working class to lower the maximum legislative limit of working hours and raising the NW quote inside the g.

The absolute SL reacts against this contractual limit, trying to move it upwards: once the limit has been reached, then, it tries to increase the degree of density, reducing all the spare times of the working day,

---

[19] The analysis we are carrying on is settled on a high level of abstraction; it is clear that in the concrete manifestations of the entrepreneurial power and its control on work, they are limited from many physical, juridical, organizational and practical "boundaries," from the general class struggle itself and from the resistance that the workers oppose to the capitalist authority in the factory.

[20] "Surplus value is nothing but the difference between the value created by the worker and the expenses for his maintenance" (Mandel, translated from the Italian edition 1997b; 154).

[21] This means *politically*. Here politics is relevant if it is interpreted in the global meaning of the term (class politics, entrepreneurial organization, industrial conflicts' management, etc., just to give instances close to the issue dealt with here). A worker does not have to work for a hours' quantity = x a day or at week. Wherever, however and whenever work is decided by the emprise together with the Trade Unions. With such system is even possible to work for 74 hours/week. In this case class struggle gave advantage to the European capital.

and by increasing the charge over the worker (increases the time in which LW is distributed). This tendency is typical of the last decades: see the example of Toyotism that, reducing pores and wastes to zero, saves lost working time; it lengthens the effective working day, even if the maximum duration has already been determined. This operation, anyway, meets often with limits of various nature, so the capitalist has to recur to the extraction of relative SL. It operates on productivity thanks to the introduction of new machines and more rational, effective, efficient and *cooperative* organizations of the working process, consequently setting "free" the exceeding workforce.

The increase of productivity involves a higher quantity of output produced by a single working unit (maybe a smaller quantity of workers can be employed) and once generalized the increase of productivity also for the production of goods "inserted" in the survival/reproduction hamper of the workforce.

If we want to establish the measure by which capital has valorized itself, we have to start from the ascertainment that surplus value is generated only by *living work*. Therefore, in the calculation of the capital's valorization degree, we can consider the part of constant capital as equal to zero. To determine the *valorization degree* we can only refer to the product in value realized *ex novo* (v + p). This means that surplus value has to be related with the anticipated variable capital. We obtain the formula of the "rate of surplus value":

$$\text{Rate of surplus value } p_1 = p/v$$

During a part of the working day, the worker realizes, therefore, the value of the means of subsistence for the reproduction of his workforce. This part of the day is defined by Marx "necessary work time," and the work employed in it "necessary work". The labour that the worker employs during the second part of the working day produces nothing but surplus value for the capitalist. This work is called by Marx "surplus value" and the part of the working day during which it is spent, "excessive work time".

Surplus value is determined by the length of the exceeding part of the working day. This is the reason why surplus value behaves towards variable capital just like surplus value behaves towards necessary work.

The rate of surplus value is the exact expression of the "exploitation rate" to which the worker is subjected by the capitalists. Basing on what we wrote before, profit is constituted by nothing but the surplus value itself. Rather, more properly, profit is the phenomenal form of surplus value, that is the result of the capital altogether anticipated. The profit of the capitalist comes from the fact that he has to sell something he did not pay for. Profit consists in the surplus of the goods' value on the price cost, or in the surplus of the total sum of work incorporated in the goods as regards to the quantity of paid work that the goods contain.

The Marxian theory of value (Marx never used the expression "labour-value") is based instead on an objective approach that does not foresee subjective calculations, even those of the individual capitalist. According to Marx, goods' production prices end up coinciding with the prices realized in the market. They always diverge from value, which is a mean and a "point" around which the prices oscillate (going up and down). Hence, there is no coincidence between the goods' value and their market price. The value is a different thing from the goods' price and has nothing to do with the physical quantity of working hours spent from a (group of) worker(s) to realize a product. It points out, instead, just the quantity of time socially necessary to the realization of these goods (of which, *ex post*, the mean value is calculated). Anyway this dimension is fundamental.

But Marx went still beyond, showing how the capitalists' appropriation of workers' unpaid labour was conformable to the internal laws of capitalism.

As a consequence the liberation of the working class from capitalist exploitation is only possible through the overcoming of the capitalist way of production. This deduction had at that time and still has a great importance, because it questions every kind of illusion regarding the solution of the capital-labour contradiction inside the capitalist way of production through reforms, whichever they are. And this is even truer for the laws of general development.

Engels, in his *Anti-Dühring*, maintains that the overcoming of capitalism and the abolition of the private property of the means of production, passed in the workers' hands, will set them free from the domination of the economic-social relations, because in this way they will take conscience of the objective laws, applying them to the interest of the whole society.[22]

---

[22] It is also true that today this issue has to be faced more cautiously. About these points Cf. Carchedi (1987: 2006a).

If the theses we mentioned above are valid we can maintain, with Marx, that

> *profit is not originated in the moment of exchange; it comes from the fact that goods are sold at their proper value* ("the paradox of profit").

Anyway, in the second book of *Capital*, Marx points out in an explicit way that in the cost of production are present all of the elements which constitute its value, paid by the capitalist or for the which he has put on market an equivalent; and, therefore, these product's costs have to be reintegrated to permit to the capital to preserve itself and to reconstitute its original entity. This means that the value of a good is given by the duration of the work that its production needs, and only a single part of this work is paid; by all means, the costs of the goods are instead only that part of work that the capitalist has remunerated.

It is in chapter 9 of the third volume of *Capital* that is traditionally searched Marx's explanation of the formation of a general rate of profit (average rate of profit) and of the transformation of the goods' value in production prices, starting out from the assumption that the production prices are nothing but the prices realized through the mean of the various profit rates of the different productive ambits. Adding such mean to the cost prices sustained by the same productive ambits we have the "classical" definition of production price. Production prices, hence, are based on the existence of a tendential general rate of profit, which is based on the fact that the profit rates of any single productive ambit have already been transformed in many other average rates of profit.

In fact, as Marx explains in the third book of *Capital*, the social conditions of production are taken as things, and the material conditions of production are comprehended as the result of the facts arbitrarily put in existence by the single individuals.

Marx' economic theory, just like the whole Marxian doctrine, is characterized by a clear social nature, by an intrinsic tendency to action and practice, by an intimate bond between theory and praxis. For the Marxists, knowing the world has always meant transforming it. The objective economic laws of capitalist society manifest themselves during the class struggle for the overcoming of the capitalism.

Marx revealed the objective tendency of the capitalist production to a great exploitation of the working class. Such tendency has manifested and still manifests itself during all of capitalist history. The tendency of advanced capitalism is to combine the extraction of absolute and relative SL. Just as absolute W finds boundaries in its extraction, also the increase of relative SL with the introduction of new machines creates problems. An increase of productivity may cause also an increment of real wages in absolute terms[23] (considered that all the working units produce more value).

The productivity increase practices may generate in this way *contradictory effects* on wages. A work productivity increase[24] causes in fact a reduction in the value of work-force (and then in the NW), and consequently the reduction of the wage (at least the relative one); the contradictory effect is the following: if the productivity increases

> "debases value and prices of many luxury products, it develops serial production [...], incorporates in the life minimum a series of new goods [...] on the contrary aims at a growth of the value of work-force" (Mandel, translated from Italian, 1997b: 244).

Social Classes

Social classes have to be defined basing on the relationships that they engage in the production sphere: the criterion of last instance is the juridical one of the *property of the production means* and even more the one of *property of accomplished product* (Bordiga 1980). This criterion, in its essentiality, divides human society in two groups: the first one, owner of production means and of products; the other one, devoid of such property (the property itself, ontologically, is deprivation, negation: exclusion). In the CWP the class that owns the production means and product has the necessity to put these on market and sell them to

---

[23] But this is only possible when: a) the reserve industrial army is limited; b) the Trade Unions organizations reduce or erase the competition between the workers and organize them to demand, with the fight, wage increases (Mandel 1997b: 240–241).

[24] The productivity increase reached through the adoption of new machines (which to be profitable from capital's point of view have to be labour saving and profit increasing), causes a modification in the organic composition of capital (K/v), whereas the component of stable work (K) increases with respect to the component of variable capital (v). The relation is not anyway between material mass of working instruments and number of workers, but between *value* of production means and *price* of the labour-power. (Mandel 1997b: 280) Also Jaffe (1973: 17 and 77ss.) back this thesis: "(the) organic composition of capital, which is a value concept, is often confused with physical-technical 'composition', for example the number of machines for worker in a certain factory, or the constant capital (value) for worker (a non-value concept)".

realize a profit, which after will be, at least partially, invested: the
behavioural model of the capitalist is dynamic.

The engine of survival of this class is accumulation: the proceeds
realized in the market are reinvested (-> capital) in the productive
sphere to start another productive cycle. The capitalist class is not
founded on blood, religion, cultural privileges: property and then capital availability are central.

In opposition to this social class we find the working class, defined
by its exclusion from capital, and the exclusion from the free access to
the production means as well as the finished products: it only gets
in contact with these elements as living work, in the first case, and as
consumer, in the second case[25]. It owns nothing else but the capacity
to work (labour-power). And its survival as a class comes from the sale
of its labour-power (just like capitalist class, for a valorization of its
capital, needs to acquire labour-power and *make it* "work": it is the
only special "productive factor," because it produces more value than
its own value). The working class is divided internally in a productive
"sector" and non-productive (of surplus value) "sector".

After the definition of the fundamental social classes (it is worth
mentioning that the ones which are mentioned above are abstract and
"pure" definitions, which in reality hardly appear like we have described
them), we can indicate the criteria of belonging of a single subject to a
class or the other: the criterion used is the one of the *function* carried
on by the subject in the WPR.

A subject is called capitalist if he carries on the function of the
capital and is owner of the means of production and/or of the finished
products (and hence of capital); instead, he is a worker he who carries
on the function of the collective worker. After the development of
capitalism and of the factory's organizational system, the fundamental duties of the capitalist (co-ordination of the working process,
decisions, direction, control, and then coercion to work) are not carried on by a single subject anymore – the capitalist exactly, who is also

---

[25] Relations with goods and products are connected, in the first case, by the production relations, and in the second case, by the mercantile ones connected on their
own from money. Only passing by the market the worker becomes a consumer and
then he can take possession of the goods which he (as a collective producer) produced,
paying them a higher price because comprehensive of the capitalist profit. In this way
there are two cases of extortion: the first one, with the subtraction of the surplus
labour; the second one, with the extortion of money in superior quantity as regards
to the cost of production of the goods.

entrepreneur and material director of his business – but are executed by a plurality of subjects that are not part of the capitalist class, because they do not own the means of production and the products, but they hold their *possession* and *disposition power*. Anyway they carry on some of the functions of capital (for example direction, decisions not of last instance, control). It is the phenomenon that gave origin to the *middle classes*, often characterized from the mixture of many functions, belonging to the ambit of capital and work. The degree of major presence of the one or the other defines their major closeness to the capitalist class or the working class.

The middle classes, after the restructuration and the introduction of new machines which incorporate the control and management activities (capital functions) previously carried on by them, can be subjected to the disqualification (superfluity) of their workforce: they are victims of what has been called "proletarianization" of the middle class, which is not an issue strictly relative to incomes.

The Usefulness of the Marxian Analysis in the Current Context

The actual situation of the working class is in large part characterized by a discrepancy growing by nature between the real value of the labour power and the real wage obtained. This fact could be explained because of the increase of the needs socially essential to the survival of the workers, also due to an intensification of the work rhythms and of social productivity, with a growth of the material, social and cultural level of the entire society. As a result, the real wage is strongly delayed vis-a-vis the growing social value of the workforce; the total social value continues to lose compared to the quote destined to profit and generally appropriated by capitalists for the remuneration of capital. The menace of unemployment is always hanging on and on the increase. Particularly, the actual coexistence of conjunctural and structural unemployment, the paradigm of flexible accumulation of the post-Fordist era, are caused by the automation of production and intensification of work. All this exerts a substantial influence on the general worsening of the world situation of the working class. The "uncertainty of existence," about which Engels spoke, is continuing to grow. These objective facts are a convincing confirmation of the validity of the Marxian theory of relative impoverishment. The very development of contemporary capitalism reaffirms entirely another fundamental Marxian thesis, that of the intensification of the proletarianization in capitalist society and the increment, even if in different and articulated forms, of subordinate work and wage-earning work.

The socioeconomic issue of work is not simply connected to unemployment, ever more of a structural character, but concerns a series of problems of quanti-qualitative character and the new figures of work, particularly the precarious ones, the denied work and the non-work, which are internal to the mode of production. The problem of work exists by now also for those who hold a job, due to the fact that it is obligatory to always work more and in the worst conditions, without protection, with an absolute social, and also relative to the single worker, wage always smaller and with high levels of mobility and intermittence.

The actual structural crisis of capitalism, that is also a crisis of overproduction and demand caused by an inclusive tendency to contraction of the social wage of the whole working class, is generated by the passage from material accumulation to other forms of accumulation based on *immaterial* capital. The new processes of accumulation are connected to the strong increments of productivity not redistributed and to the tertiarization processes, also with important displacements in the financial rent. This points to how the so-called post-Fordist cycle of the generalized social factory realizes, besides structural unemployment, thousands of forms of atypical and flexible work, that is precarious, that are accompanied anyhow by a strong growth in terms of social wealth, due to significant increments of productivity. But this kind of social wealth is not useful to the labour factor.

In this way, we identify a marginal economy which evolves time after time, proposing new social figures, new subjects who, whether until not many years ago were guaranteed and functional to development, today are instead excluded, made casual, expelled, emarginated, and constitute new areas of poverty on the increase that the actual model propose in partly new forms. In Italy, for example, in the last years it was noticeable a huge increase of the opening of VAT numbers, correspondent to the emersion of new autonomous workers, a new class of small entrepreneurs more than ever caged within the rules and the bonds typical of the regimes of subordination. These are the new figures of the labour market, which are nothing but the result of the choice of capital to expel labour, creating an induced activity of a tertiary kind, badly remunerated, deprived of the contributively charges for social security; this is the product of a generalized recourse to more or less hidden forms of *task work* to be opposed to every form of rigidity in work and in payment. Thus the labour market is made to be ever more flexible and compatible with the system of centrality of the enterprise and of profit, adapting the whole social corps, through the functions of the profit state, to the organization of the generalized social factory.

Today, however, the overwhelmingly major part of the population in the capitalist countries is composed of wage-earning workers, and the salaried work constitutes the basis of capitalism, on a much larger scale than in Marx's times, inside the processes and the dynamics of functioning of the capitalist way of production of all times.

The more recent changes in the structure of the working class itself point out the extreme importance of the "collective" worker category, introduced and analysed in *Capital*. Such category comprehends the workers of material and mental labour that directly participate to the making of a product and are in any way, compared to capital, waged workers, subordinates. In this way, despite the passage from the Fordist to the so-called post-Fordist age, from the mass-worker to the "social worker," from the centrality of the factory to the generalized social factory, from the "blue collar" to the white-collar workers, from material work to the knowledge and intelligence workers, even in the advanced capitalist countries persists and grows the waged work, in forms always more sophisticated and incisive of exploitation.

In contemporary capitalism, the collective character of the labour process becomes more evident with the growth of the socialization of production, going over the so-called "collective worker," assuming the aspect of the large productive complex, with externalizations and delocalization, but anyway with modalities that reunite all the workers in the same ambit of subalternity, coercion and exploitation. The actual tendencies, with the growth of the number of waged workers employed outside the properly called material production, the increase of the employees', flexibles', precarious' time-workers' and atypicals' number, the increment of intellectual work rate or of the fake autonomous worker, do not witness at all to the "deproletarianization" of the labouring class or of the generic working class.

As always, the workers belonging to these new categories, just like the industrial proletariat, are forced to sell their labour-power to the capitalists. Today more than yesterday, labourers and generic workers are menaced by unemployment, after the introduction of automation.

Their wages are at times inferior to the minimal threshold of survival: the differences with that part of privileged workers constituting the "labour aristocracy" are in this way more evident.

Such differences can, however, be useful. The insertion of the fundamental laws of material production inside the sphere of science and culture is a factor that although at first sight may seem improbable can indeed facilitate the overcoming of capitalism.

PART TWO

CATEGORIES AND DYNAMICS OF THE CAPITALIST SYSTEM AND ITS CRISIS

CHAPTER THREE

THE BASICS OF NATIONAL ACCOUNTING[1]

Marxian Categories and their Statistical Translations

As previously discussed, the basic categories of the Marxian analysis can be expressed in terms of value, time and labour: K (constant capital) represents the time of indirect social labour included in the physical inputs of the production process. V (variable capital) is the value (of reproduction) of the time of direct social labour employed in the production of goods. W (surplus value) stands for the time of direct non-wage social labour employed in the same production process of goods. With such categories it is possible to build the basic relations of Marxian analyses: the exploitation rate or surplus value rate W/v which expresses the relation between the time of direct labour, both wage and non-wage, the organic composition of capital K/v, that can also be found as in K/K + v, a formula that expresses the distribution of capital between time of social labour both indirect and direct and the profit rate W/K + v, or relation between finished surplus value and advanced capital. These categories of value are essential in order to establish the dynamics of capitalism. The primary laws and the whole functioning of the capitalist system, in particular competition, concentration and centralization of capital, wage fixation according to the existence of an overpopulation (permanent working) or the tendency to a fall of profit rates, can actually be explained through these categories and relations.

The translation of the categories of value into prices is an important problem. As a matter of fact, value-time as it is, does not have an equivalent accounting expression in the capitalist system, where each economical relation is measured in prices. The categories in value-labour (or value-time) have an equivalent in terms of prices that is not

---

[1] In this Chapter, references to essential works will be frequently made in order to understand the methodological bases of the subject; in particular Alvaro (1999), De Meo (1975), Giannone (1992), Guarini, Tassinari (1996), Samuelson, Nordhaus (1987) and Graziani will provide our reference points.

always clear. This translation of the categories and relations in terms of value into its monetary or prices equivalents started a rich economical literature about the so-called "problem" of the transformation.[2] This subject becomes even more complicated since conventional economics includes a set of notions that are similar to Marx's ones but that still present a substantially different content.

The notion of "capital" is the most important one: in Marx's work it represents a social relation (a relation expressed through the production process of goods/private embezzlement of surplus value) while conventional economics defines it as a polysemic notion that describes

a. money capital;
b. capital goods;
c. productive investment;
d. financial investment;
e. earnings' flow over different periods of production determined by time discount rate, etc.

Besides, conventional economics does not take into account the essential difference drawn by Marxian political economy between activities that produce new value and those which consume the value produced, or to be more precise, between activities that produce surlpus value and those that consume it.

The different perspectives from which Marxian political economy and conventional economics carry on their analysis, enable us to directly use economic statistics in order to investigate the evolution of the process of capitalist accumulation. To do so, an advanced procedure of reprocessing of the statistical indicators, of the aggregates and the macroeconomic functions is required in order to be adapted to those notions and aggregates that are part of Marxian political economy.[3] The practical inability to provide a complete translation of statistical data beginning from Marxian notions compels to often work with

---

[2] Cf. about the issue the work edited by Vasapollo (2002). The classical criticism to the theory of value-labour appears in the 1896 work by Eugen Böhm-Bawerk (1975).

[3] Many authors used the data provided by the National Accounting System and adapted them to a reading with Marxist categories. Eugen S. Varga (1948) wrote an important piece on the subject, as Shigeto Tsuru also did with its *On Reproduction Schemes*, appendix of Paul M. Sweezy (1942), where he analysed the comparability of Marxist categories and Keynesian aggregates. The economist who most moved forward, as far as the reformulation of statistics into Marxist categories is concerned, is Anwar Shaikh (1990), cf. also Shaikh, Tonak (1994).

approximate data, that is values that do not exactly measure what we want, but whose evolution coincides with the one of the reference category.

For the same reason, reading the statistical indicators and the conventional aggregates, from a Marxian point of view, implies re-reading the data in order to read "other things," different from the interpretation that conventional analysts usually give.

Limits of Conventional Neoclassical Economic Concepts

Conventional economic theory, that is the one that interprets reality from the perspective of capital, was introduced at the end of the XIX century when the economic vulgarization's main aim left out the interpretation of the economic dynamics of society in order to become a justification of the existing order. León Walras (1900) (general equilibrium), Alfred Marshall (1920) (partial equilibrium), Vilfredo Pareto (1945) (optimal and efficient equilibrium) and many others' attempted to develop a "positive economy," neutral to the social phenomena and based on the principle of perfect information. This occurred, paradoxically, in the same historical-scientific period (1870–1930) during which the so-called Heisenberg's uncertainty principle was established in physics. Heisenberg's principle states that in observing nature, the act of observing itself disturbs some of the physical properties and therefore never allows an exact knowledge of reality. There is just one bit of relative (possible) information that is always subject to a margin of error.

As a consequence, at the end of the XIX century, economics was turning into an ideology whose aim was to hide beneath a more and more complex mathematical system a simplistic theory that did not contribute to the knowledge of reality.

Only when the Great Depression of the 1920s and 1930s started, academic economists began to feel the need of vindicating the Classical analytical thought.[4]

After the Second World War an eclectic thought imposed itself without giving up the ideological component of economic theory

---

[4] Joseph Alois Schumpeter was the one who better expressed the political and historical dimension of this reasoning. Other authors, such as Micheal Kalecki or Piero Sraffa, provided this kind of neoclassical thought with an historical perspective. John Maynard Keynes will express in his works in the 1930s, a break with vulgar thought.

It looked for some kind of ruling capacity, in order to manage the public intervention in the economic cycle and the long-term structural change. This new dominant orientation, also known as the neoclassical synthesis, implies the control of the evolution of economics as a science, especially in the United States where the academic establishment imposed this new doctrinal conception of economics.

The development of statistical and accounting systems is in this way an attempt to create an economics that is functional to managing capitalism in the mass-consumption and Fordist-Taylorist era.

The Centrality of the Debate on Productive and Unproductive Labour

The development of the social State too depended mainly on the Fordist accumulation model, on the forms and contradictions of wage labour, on growth and on full employment. Its prerequisites were the normalization of a higher number of individuals' wage-labour, that is their transformation into working citizens, leading, this way, to the generalization of the relationship of the Fordist labour process. Nowadays this generalization is limited by the post-fordist accumulation that questions the traditional model of the Social State.

According to this model, social participation of citizens is essentially linked to the status of wage-worker, and from this link sprang the possibility for individuals to plan the capital-labour conflict with the immediate purpose of improving the levels of social justice and welfare. The crisis of the labour-market or of the dominant principle of distribution of activity and income, generates instead a situation where unemployment and the increasing difficulties of living within the society for larger groups of people, can not be settled anymore through adjustments related to the institutional structures connected to *Welfare* and the economic assumptions of expansionary policies. So the Keynesian model has been questioned: the current crisis in the labour market can not be explained believably simply through the relationship between consumption demand and labour demand, and can not be adjusted through an economic and fiscal policy of expansion.

Nowadays wages are increasingly disconnected from productivity, which is mainly addressed to profit. This depends on the post-Fordist separation between the growth of production and that of employment, and on the choice of a financialization of the economy which involves a distribution of income addressed to the accumulation process.

The increasingly unequal redistributive structure of income involves the disappearance of the role of the welfare state, since the State directly operates on the economic system in support of accumulation, and both regulates and control not only the redistribution of income but the whole social structure in order to support profit. The internationalization of financial flows and the development of the process of de-industrialization of Western countries led to a decrease of how economic policies implemented by individual states affect those mechanisms of accumulation that are growing global. In a model of flexible accumulation, the State quits the social protection system as this is only a rigidity and, as such, must be abolished in order to assume the role of Profit State.

So, in a society based on flexible accumulation and on intangible capital resources, communication and knowledge, it is fundamental to think from a material perspective whether the same kind of job may be productive or unproductive, or whether it could be considered as part of the capitalist system of production depending on whether or not it has been organized within the capitalist enterprise system.

At first glance, the concept of productive labour developed in some of Marx's works does not consider workers and employees of the trade and credit sector in this category (Marx 1978a, book II: Ch. VI and Book III, Chs. XVI–XIX). Marx does not consider this labour productive. According to many social scientists, including most of the Marxists, Marx refused to consider this labour productive because it does not produce changes in material things. According to them, this is a trace of the 'materialistic' theories of productive labour.

Referring to the opposition of the "Classical school" to this concept,[5] someone wonders how Marx could make that mistake. Some others criticize the theories that separate "Intellectual" and "material" aspects of labour, adding that these conceptions of Classical political economy had not been subjected by Marx to the critique they deserved, because Marx himself supported those ideas.

Actually, there is not an obvious contradiction in Marx's ideas. He does not give up the concept of productive labour as a labour organized on capitalist principles, regardless of its concrete nature and useful

---

[5] According to the Classical school Marx's concept is tautological: the productive labour, or the labour that creates value, must certainly be represented in "material" things.

results, typical of the capitalist production. But If it is not so, why Marx does not consider the work of sellers and employees organized into a capitalist trade enterprise as productive labour? To answer this question, we must remember that, when Marx wrote about productive labour in many works before *Capital*, he started with the question of productive capital. According to that theory, capital passes through three stages in its reproduction process: money capital, productive capital and capital-goods.

Phases one and three represent "the process of circulation of capital". In this scheme, "productive" capital does not oppose the unproductive one but the capital in the "process of circulation".

Productive capital organizes the process of creating consumer goods in the wider sense. This process includes all labour required for the goods adaptation to consumption, for example, storage, transport, packaging, etc. In the process of circulation, capital organizes the "mere circulation": buying and selling, for example, the transfer of property from the actual transfer of goods. This capital overcomes the friction of the capitalist market system, this friction obeys to the fact that the system is split into individual economic units: it precedes and follows the process of creating consumer goods, although is linked to it indirectly. The "production of capital" and "the circulation of capital" are independent in Marx's system and they are treated separately, although the unity of the whole process of reproduction of capital must not be lost. This is the basis of the distinction between labour used in production and labour used in circulation. But this distinction has nothing to do with a division between "the labour that operates changes in material things" and the labour that does not have this property.

Marx distinguishes between the labour used by "productive capital," or more precisely by capital in the production stage, and the labour used by the capital-goods or capital-money, or more precisely by capital during circulation. Only the first type of labour is "productive," not because it produces material goods, but because it is used by "productive" capital and this is the form of capital at the stage of production: it produces surplus value. The participation of labour in the production of consumer goods is, for Marx, an additional property of the productive nature of labour but not the criterion to determine it. This criterion continues to be the capitalist organization of labour: the productive character of labour is an expression of the productive character of capital.

The rotation of the stages of capital determines the characteristics of labour that is being used. Here Marx claims his idea that in capitalism the driving force of development is capital: its movements determine the movement of the labour subjected to capital.

Thus, according to Marx, a productive labour is any kind of labour organized according to the capitalist process of production or, more precisely, the labour used by "productive" capital, i.e. capital in the production phase. The labour of the seller is not productive because it is contracted by the capital during the circulation phase (thus it does not change the value of use, nor preserves the integrity of deterioration).[6]

It is clear that interpreting the economic categories one way rather than another, includes a system of national accounting entirely different with the representation of different social, economic and productive structures.

National Income Accounting

Bourgeois economics, in its various attempts to understand and "dominate" or "cause" a variety of social phenomena,[7] would be a mere mental unproductive exercise if it had not an "application field" (society) for its theories, and if it could not make use of the data and the tools that provide them, capable to know "the operative field," on which it must act.[8]

A fundamental starting point for developing economic analysis and proposing economic policies is that of *national wealth*, thanks to National Accounting.[9] It is used to calculate the wealth produced *in* a nation and *by* a nation.[10]

---

[6] Because, as we said above, these types of activities (processing, conservation) make productive labour, which will be mostly provided during the work process.

[7] That it "naturalizes" in most cases, often applying to the studies of social phenomena, the same epistemological assumptions, the same methods and the same techniques used by natural sciences.

[8] Alvaro (1999: 28), in this regard, writes: "political economy needs to 'deal' with the observational data continuously, with a measured economic reality and with statistics. That is, with the economic statistics, because without Economic Statistics political economy becomes the study, analysis, development of theoretical models, suitable to describe the functioning of hypothetical economic systems, whose validity is exhausted in the formal verification of internal consistency, as built on the propositions deduced from the behaviour of the unreal and imagined homo economicus."

[9] For a more detailed discussion of the topics discussed in this section see Alvaro (1999).

[10] This distinction underlies the difference between GDP and GNP (Gross National Product).

At the base of National Accounting

> there is the idea that the whole system of production depends, in its functioning, on four [...] large categories of economic agents: households, enterprises, public administration, foreign trade (Cozzi and Zamagni 1995: 78).

Economic Operators

Economic operators are agents-subjects that permit to read the movement of the production and consumption of wealth within a territory. They are defined according to the function they hold in the cycle of production-consumption and according to the use of the goods and services purchased. They are then aggregates of homogeneous economic actors that allow the identification of broad economic movements internal to a country.

If identification and description for households are simple, for an enterprise operator these activities are more complicated. According to the traditional model, enterprises are classified into three economic sectors: agriculture, industry, services. Statistical units of detection are: company or enterprise, local unit, institutions.[11]

There are some specific sectors of the economy that have always been controlled by the state, as they provide strategic and essential services to citizens and businesses. We refer to companies operating in the field of energy, water, telecommunications, transport, etc., not considering public collective consumption, such as care, health, defence, security, education, namely "production of welfare". In these areas, State intervention is a guarantee that everyone have equal access to quality of goods and services produced, which could otherwise be distributed unevenly and not fairly, both in economic terms and in a general social sense.

The crisis of the Fordist model involves the crisis of the Keynesian approach, since the latter represent the most advanced political synthesis of social compromise. Since the early 1980s, a process of downsizing of the public presence in the economy occurred in all capitalist

---

[11] For a discussion of the issues about definition and identification of the economic operators and for a more intense description of the various breakdowns operations within the categories of the operators, see Alvaro (1999: 31–71).

countries, even where the mixed economy was more pronounced. This occurred especially to adapt public administration to the new conditions of international competition. The main reasons adduced were essentially linked more to political-formal reasons than to the real needs of economic and productive efficiency. Therefore, the motivation of making public companies more competitive was necessarily related to bureaucratic controls that did not manage to allow public companies to operate more quickly and innovatively.

The different roles taken by the State in the rules of management of public enterprises has seen the strengthening of the "privatization" process. Thus, there is a consequent reduction of the power of the "state-entrepreneur" and at the same time a forcing of the process of privatization of the *Welfare State*, imposing a narrowing of the characteristics of universalism of the main public performances. It encouraged an increasing the use of private healthcare, education and training with business characteristics, the use of supplementary private pension schemes.

GNP and GDP[12]

The macro-aggregate widely used until a few years ago for the calculation of national wealth is GNP (Gross National Product), whose origins lie in the works by Simon Kuznets (1901–1985). The importance of this concept is the possibility of measuring the *total value of goods and services produced by a country*, and permitting, therefore, quoting Samuelson, Nordhaus (1987: 98) "to measure the performance of an entire economic system."[13]

The GNP is the measure of *the monetary value*[14] produced and read in its dynamic flow: the flow of goods and services, plus investments

---

[12] In the following paragraphs, although quoting some of the introductory works of political economy and national accounting more used in our universities, we will mainly refer to the important school of Economic Statistics of the Faculty of Statistics, University La Sapienza of Rome and to the works by the most important representatives: De Meo (1975) Giannone (1992) and Alvaro (1999).
[13] Of course, people do not live only by eating bread; nor does society live only with the gross national product. But during our path toward the utopia state of opulence where all worries for material wealth will disappear, we need a summary measure of aggregate economic performance (Samuelson, Nordhaus 1987: 98).
[14] The calculation is based on "market prices".

(private) and the costs of public administration (PA). Here is the classic formula for a closed economy:

$$GNP = C + I + G$$

where C stands for private consumption, I for investment and G for government spending, i.e. public consumption. In an open economy we should consider also (XM), where X stands for exports and M for imports. It should be added, though, that I represents gross investments, including depreciation, so the value represented by GNP is altered, or rather it cannot describe well the reality of the "current" wealth of the country. To avoid this, another measure is used, although it is more difficultly determined, because of the scarcity or inaccuracy of data on it: NNP (Net National Product) which is given by private consumption, plus public purchases, plus net investments.

In summary, as Samuelson and Nordhaus (1987: 108) claimed, GNP (and PNN) can be defined as the sum of three main components:

1. Personal spending for goods and services;
2. Investment spending, both domestic investments and net exports;
3. Public spending for goods and services.

Before continuing, a further distinction should be noted: while GNP expresses the total value of economic activity carried inside and outside a given country *by residents*, GDP (Gross Domestic Product) measures the total value of economic activity carried out only *within* the country concerned, either by residents or by non-residents.

Today GDP is widely used than GNP between by orthodox and dominant economists. It is measured in two quite equivalent ways: with the method of product flow and the one of cost flow. The result is always:

$$GDP = C + I + G + X - M$$

corresponding to all the incomes from labour and from capital (including depreciation, rents, interest, dividends, etc..). The equivalence is obtained, therefore, considering generic components of profits (along with wages and pensions); it is a residue that automatically adapts to changes in costs, incomes and other values.

As we have just written, the term of GDP or GNP indicates that the value of the depreciation of capital, i.e. the monetary value of the "reconstruction" or replacement of capital goods consumed in the previous period, is added to the indicator. Therefore, for measuring the net increase in production, we must deduct the depreciation from capital

$$GDP - A = NDP, \text{ or better}$$
$$GNP - A = NNP$$

where NDP stands for net domestic product and PNN for net national product. Net National Product at factor cost is, in terms of remuneration at productive factors, often called "National Income" (NI) in the strict sense. The PNN at FC or NI is the most significant value, which measures the income per person more precisely than GDP per person usually used, because it deducts variations from prices induced by taxes on production, that may vary substantially between countries and between periods, thereby distorting international comparisons.

If from National Income we subtract the amount of dividends not distributed, corporate taxes and social charges (i.e. the portion of surplus value, which remains in NI) we obtain Personal Income (PI), which represents an approximate measure of the spending capacity of the domestic economies, both of the workers and of capitalists.

If from PI we deduce direct taxes we obtain Disposable Income (DI), which measures the potential consumption of households in the consumption goods and luxury goods in a given period. The basic data of National accounting, as said, allow us to identify the major features of the evolution of an economy. For example, we can identify, even with data of GDP, the tendency to stagnation of a capitalist economy, with a lesser and lesser growth (accumulation rate).

Investment as a Central Category of the Capitalist System

To start a criticism of the current theories and economic practices, it is necessary to introduce some basic concepts used by the dominant economic science that became part of our language and daily life. Investments are the engine of the accumulation process of a capitalist economy, which determines the size of the economic process. The relationship between profit and investment connects the two key variables of the short and long term economic dynamics. An investment is done only if there is a profit to be made. The expected gain determines the investment and the investment determines the volume of the obtained production, employment and unemployment.

Accumulation, and not need, is the source of capitalist production. That is why it is possible to find a great waste in market economies: the use made of available resources depends only on the profit that is obtained. The current profits and those expected are the two key indicators of capitalist economy. They are those that define the level of investment and therefore the production of goods. The rate of return addresses both the behaviour of each individual enterprise, as much as that of the majority of enterprises and sectors that constitute and determine the macroeconomic dynamics. This essential idea is expressed with five basic theses:

a. the working of the economy as a whole is closely bound to the volume of investment;
b. the capitalists' amount of investment depends on the expected rate of profit or return that they believe they will get from their investment;
c. the economy of a country is part of the capitalist global economy. The levels of investment, employment and production of the economy of a country depend not only on the investment and national income, but also on the investment and profits of other places in the world;
d. the volume of production and the number of people employed depend in the short term on the total demand for goods and services. The investment is part of the total demand, therefore its dynamics gives rise to oscillations of total demand and fluctuations of production and employment;
e. The demand for labour is always lower than labour supply. This means that unemployment is a permanent feature of the capitalist system.

The volume of production, and therefore of the employed population, depends on the total demand for goods and services in a given period. The model described above implies that the level of final production depends on the level of initial investment. The investment is connected to a demand for goods and services, with a demand for raw materials, and determines the volume of production, namely the supply, which always adjusts to demand.

As usual there are unproductive resources, and the degree to which a one euro investment turns into a one euro of production depends also on the level of use of the productive resources and this will be a determining factor for the rate of economic growth. The lower the level of use, the more it is necessary to invest in order to achieve the same level of economic growth. This level of investment also determines the situation of the labourforce. Unemployment, as we said, is the difference between labour supply and labour demand.

'Orthodox' economists complain that the phenomenon of unemployment is caused by a number of factors: the rigidity of the labour market (due to too strong and "selfish" Trade Unions: take the accusations against Trade Unions by one of the fiercest economic schools, "the Austrian school"); high salaries that are driven down (which are, among other things, a consequence of a great Unions power), social security and welfare systems that are too expensive. Lack of balance in this particular market would, therefore, be caused by exogenous factors. The market then, if left on its own, should be free to follow its own laws, and in the long run would lead to the disappearance of unemployment. The reason why this would happen is simple: the equilibrium price of a commodity X is reached when the demand equals the supply, so the same would happen if the workers accepted the "rules of the game of market," allowing decreases in pay, benefit cuts, etc., in order to let the price of their labour-power go down to the levels of demand. This way the equilibrium would be achieved and unemployment would drop. In such a situation, the only form of unemployment that would remain would be the "natural," "frictional" one, which is necessary and transient since it is caused by the displacement of workers from a job to another and the search for new jobs.

Productive and Unproductive Investment

The use of resources is a very important factor in order to distinguish between the investment that generates new production capacity and the investment addressed only to the production of already existing means of production. Net investment is the one that expands the available means of production, and the actual accumulation is the difference between gross investment and depreciation or amortization of capital.

The efficiency of investment is determined by the volume of investment itself, by the use of the resources that will be invested and by the level of production obtained.

The investment is also financial, and it simply consists of accumulating more money (financial investments: D – D ' without going through M), although, as pointed out, the real investment is has a different, broader, more ambiguous meaning. Investing in stock, in the purchase of shares, gold or housing are activities which do not increase the production capacity of economy: they are just limited to the redistribution of wealth, or are, in this case, devoted to an ever higher share of GDP to profits and not to profits and wages. And in this case, the tools that are able to measure economic activity are absolutely inefficient, because government statistics are not sufficiently highlighting the weight difference between this kind of financial investment and the productive one.

Investment realizes the value of the goods already produced in the past (the purchase of a car, for example) and promotes the creation of new goods, projecting into the future the current decision to invest. Since the private and public consumption varies very slowly, the variation of total demand depends, to a large extent, on the change in investment. The control of the investment is thus transformed into the key variable of the circuit of accumulation.

For this reason, the present resources available for investment are conditioned by yesterday's public and private consumption. So this excess of available resources for investment may come from the outside. Specifically, the basic purpose of structural adjustments (which will be explained later) is to reduce consumption in order to increase the surplus.

In terms of time, it is not certain that investment is produced by domestic savings, as the generally accepted theory claims. Still this is more evident in the so-called globalized world in which we live. If savings are given by income (or even production), minus consumption, it is not sure that by investing tomorrow, we will have to save today. Investment may increase without reducing consumption, thanks to external help.

CHAPTER FOUR

A CRITIQUE OF NATIONAL ACCOUNTING

Some Problems Posed by National Accounting

Since the times of the World War II, the systems of National Accounting started to develop in an articulated way, taking as their objective the knowledge of the trend of the principal macroeconomic aggregations and the effects of economic and social policies.

The socialist system elaborated the balance model of national economy developed in USSR in the 1920s and later transferred to the remaining part of the socialist field and in the COMECON[1] system.

In the countries characterized by free market, the attempts to quantitative representation of the economy go back as far as William Petty (Sandoval Gonzalez, 2004), and later develop with the Physiocrats. Nevertheless, it is at the end of nineteenth century that National Accounting comes into existence.

The principal references lead to Richard Stone. His works gave origin to the normalized system of accounting and acted like a basis for the elaboration of the United Nations system. According to Stone,

> a social accounting system is a practical means to describe what happens inside an economy, in the measure in which it can be expressed in terms of transactions in an ensemble of accounts connected with the double entry principle (Sandoval Gonzalez 2004: 12).

According to this study, the system is composed of four classes of workers: emprises, families, public administration and rest of the world. Each of these produces, consumes and saves money.

Between the pioneer works at the basis of the construction of the National Accounts System (later NCS) it is necessary to mention also the works of the Oslo Group, which organized the discipline around

---

[1] Council of mutual economic assistance, instituted in 1949 by the socialist countries in Oriental Europe (USSR, Albania, Bulgaria, Czechoslovakia, Poland, Romania, Hungary) with the exception of Yugoslavia, In opposition to the Marshall plan and to coordinate the economies of the socialist countries. Later, also Cuba, Mozambique and Vietnam became part of the union, while Albania left in 1962. It was cancelled in 1990.

one hundred or so macro-economic concepts, with a series of equations referring to a coherent outline.

Also the works of W. Leontiev require a particular mention: with his deep knowledge of the balance system in the Soviet Union, he developed the input-output method that is now largely used in many countries; something similar, the inter-sector balance, was realized by the planners of USSR.

The substantial difference between a system and the other is that in the socialist area, the indicative "global social product" centered on the production of goods and services directly tied to the production, circulation-distribution and commercialization of material goods, was devised basing on a particular interpretation of the Marxian schemes.

The first NCS was adopted by the UN in 1953 and was subjected to successive adjustments. In 1989 the approach between the system applied in the socialist area and the one applied by the UN begins; between the two systems deep differences existed. After the "collapse of the wall," this dichotomy disappears, due to the passage of the eastern countries to the market economy.

The principles of National Accounting imply a valuation of the economic activity in a space (a country) and in a determinate period of time (a year). Even if the concepts which are under the macroeconomic accounting base themselves on the theories that identify value and prices, the necessity to reach a certain realism in the measurements permits to identify how after the developed notions, there is an implicit theory of work-value.

In the National Accounting the added value is interpretable realistically as an aggregation of value in the production process, classified in sector-based terms and in global terms. Anyway, a fundamental problem comes from the activities comprehended under the entry "production".

The idea predominates that the distribution and transport activities, which absorb a big portion of waged work, implicate modifications in the goods, and so they have to be added in the value and material production calculations. More controversial is the case of financial and rental (real estate, leasing) activities. These activities do not produce new value, but simply absorb the incomes of the productive sector.

A similar problem is verifiable in public services. Not being work destined to the production of value-capital, some authors think that it is not productive work, and should then be divided from the calculation of (social) added value. In this case, differently from the activities based on the obtainment of an income from a right to property (on stable material active or financial active), we may consider the public dependents as the makers of an activity functional to the process of capitalist reproduction, and for this are indirectly submitted to capital. But not for this they have to be inserted in the productive work category in the Marxist sense.[2]

Productive work in Marxian terms is just the one utilized by capital for its self-valorization; a work of identical content may be productive or unproductive. This depends on a consideration on the nature of work, on the consideration that in concrete, work generates directly surplus value, and valorizes directly the capital, or not. This is independent from the more or less useful character of such work, and expresses itself always as collective work, as "socially combined work capacity" less tied to the forms and content of individual works. In terms of surplus value is productive the work that has for object material or mental transformations of a use value that has changed or has been conserved at the end of the productive process.[3] For a long time, in Marxist circles a "Classical" idea prevailed, due to a fundamental incomprehension of Marx's texts (In truth some of them are not so clear).[4] According to such "Classical" conception, only material work was considered productive, based on the fact that tangible product was obtained from it. Moving from these assumptions, we were deprived for many years of the instruments to read these transformations internal to the CWP (think about the various and heterogeneous sector of "services" [cf. Carchedi 2004], all of which was believed to be non-productive because of "intangibility"). For a critical analysis of this literature r see Guerrero (1990), who indicates the right method from a Marxian point of view, to individuate the productivity of surplus value. It is a *formal*, not material *determination*. It has nothing to do with materiality of work and product. The material aspect simply is not

---

[2] "Functionaries may convert themselves in wage-earners of capital, but not for this reason they become productive workers. [...] The productive worker is directly exchanged for *money as capital*, destined to function as capital and who, as capital, opposes himself to work capacity." (Marx 1985a: 83).

[3] "Produced value and surplus value (in the working process which produces surplus value) are the result of the action of a single category of agents which, through their concrete work, change the material and mental characteristics of objects and work instruments in a different use value, the product one" (Carchedi 1991: 31), about this point cf. also Carchedi (1977; 1987).

[4] This could be better admitted if we consider the nature of many of the Marxist texts, which remained in the form of notebooks, not definitive and not published.

relevant for such aims. What is interesting is the insertion of (salaried) work inside a capitalist organization and its engagement in the sphere of production.

Marxism and the System of National Accounting

For an exact interpretation of Marx' idea, is necessary to understand clearly that the circulation phase of capital does not correspond to a circulation of capital and to a real distribution of products, that is a process of transfer from the hands of the producers to the hands of the consumers, necessarily accompanied by transport services, storing, packing, etc.

The function of circulation of capital consists only in the transfer of property rights from a person to the other: it is then a transformation from a commodity form of value in a money-form or, inversely, a realization of product-value. These are the "circulation expenses, derivatives of the simple changing of form of value, of the ideally considered circulation" (Marx 1966: 120–121). "Here, we refer only to the general character of the circulation expenses which come from a purely formal metamorphosis" (121). Marx clearly demonstrated the following: "general law is that all the circulation expenses which correspond simply to a change of form in the goods, do not add any value to this" (132).

Marx made a distinction between this "formal metamorphosis," which is the essence of the phase of circulation, and the "real function" of the capital-goods (Marx 1978a: 265). Among these real functions Marx included: transportation, storage, "distribution of goods under a distributive form" (Marx 1966: 264), "shipping, transportation, distribution, retail" (276–282). It is necessary to understand that the formal creation of value is the transfer of the ownership of products and merely serves as a vehicle for its implementation and, simultaneously, the real exchange of goods, as they go from some hands to others, to social metabolism. But theoretically the formal completion, the genuine function of capital in the circulation is totally different from those functions mentioned that are essentially real, alien to this capital and have an heterogeneous character.

The work of the commercial employee is to be considered unproductive, only if it serves to the "formal metamorphosis" of value, to its realization, to its ideal transfer of ownership of the product from a person to another. The 'formal metamorphosis' that occurs in the sales department, and which is separated from all the real functions, requires some costs of transportation and work, the accounting, the bookkeeping, the correspondence, etc. This work is unproductive, but, again, it is such because it does not create material goods, but it rather serves the *formal metamorphosis*, the stage of capital's circulation in its pure form.

Despite what Marx rigorously exposed through its analysis, there are evident limits from a contemporary perspective of the issue, nevertheless the essential bases of analysis keep on being valid, taking into account the concept of the real production and reproduction of the capitalist relations of production.

According to what has been said, it is obvious that there is a difference between Marxian National Accounting and the neoclassical analysis. Nevertheless, it is the only tool that currently enables us to get to know some trends of the economic systems.

Though it is of considerable utility, major limits of this system (CNS) have been reported, by supporters and critics, right from the beginning. Major limitations have resulted, for example, from the description of the full development process: issues such as improving the quality of life of the population and the effect on natural resources are left out of the system on purpose.

As part of modern macroeconomics, the CNS assumes a group of well-known, a priori rules that emphasize uncertainty and an infinite number of theoretical hypotheses that place, though not necessarily, their main referential points into reality, although it is argued that the aim, central to the whole project of National Accounting, is to look for the stability of the functioning of macroeconomics and its balanced functioning. On such basis, there are two main ways in literature to collect the results of modern macroeconomics: the classical analysis and the Keynesian one.

The two differ mainly in their assumptions and conclusions and a multiplicity of models and theories that not all cases rely on, on an equal level of recognition and dissemination, but serve as a basis for policies that have structural arrangement and that have been applied throughout the world in recent years.

PART THREE

A CRITIQUE OF ECONOMICS AS APPLIED TO THE STRUCTURE OF MANAGEMENT:THE ENTERPRISE SYSTEM AND THE PUBLIC ADMINISTRATION SYSTEM

CHAPTER FIVE

A CRITICAL THEORY OF THE ENTERPRISE

Business Models and the System of Development

In modern business a system of valuation of the enterprise (the firm, in mainstream accounts) has been established, which, through methods of calculation of the intangible value, takes account, in addition to the material value of its assets, for some aspects such as: organization, inclusion in the markets, networks of relationships or the evaluation of the employees working under contract or commission for the company.

Gallino has compared the modern enterprise to a republic. This image is only partially satisfying, because the weight of decisions is not equally shared between actors (as, at least theoretically, at polling stations of modern democracies), but certainly it is useful to shed light on one of the main aspects of the enterprise, characterized by political relationships, since they are "essentially power-based relationships" (Gallino 2005: 19).

In capitalist enterprises the aim to maximize profits by optimizing effectiveness and efficiency. This would tend to satisfy all stakeholders who are involved, at different levels, in the life and affairs of the enterprise itself.

The categories of direct stakeholders are three: shareholders, managers and workers; but in contexts such as Rhenan and Japanese capitalism, the three classes of stakeholders should be joined by the direct suppliers, banks, customers, financial investors and public administration.

Among the opponents of the enterprise, namely those who have interests contrary to the goals and purposes of a firm, there are the competitors, minority and opposition shareholders, political, social and media hostile forces. We must also bear in mind that the direct stakeholders have benefits in the participation in the results of an enterprise, with which they share profits, purposes and intents. They have the real control of the firm.

In this sense, control should not be understood in legal terms (in fact it is held by the majority shareholders): it is, however, the management control enacted by those who decide the strategies and the extent and the distribution of the economic results achieved.

These tasks are in the power of economic actors that guide the company in fact, establishing and determining, if necessary, the trajectories of strategic planning.

In this determination, which redefines the very enterprise models, the shareholders often become spectators, for the formal control is substantially shared in various ways among all stakeholders. This trend is more present in Anglo-Saxon capitalism, where the *public company* model prevails, creating a managerial capitalism where the reallocation of ownership and control are continuous.

Many scholars[1] identify and distinguish three main models of capitalism according to the rules of enterprise management, the reallocative processes between ownership and control, the choices of each individual country to place itself in a certain area of influence of international capitalism. The first model, characterized by a strong collective and individual competition, is capitalism in the United States. It evolved through the birth of large enterprises, and is characterized by the presence of an efficient management device, with impressive funds, with the prevalence of stock market dominated by large shareholding. This model has been called, for nearly a century, *managerial capitalism*: this term first appeared in a historical research by Berle and Means (1932, 1966), conducted in the United States in the 1930s with the approval of the Council for the Social Sciences at Columbia University of New York. According to these two scholars, the accomplishment of American capitalism, which involved the prevalence of the managers over the business owners, was determined by the natural evolutionary tendency of national capitalism, dominated by large companies.

There were several criticisms of this theory.[2] In particular, some of them deny its validity, arguing that the so-called managerial capitalism

---

[1] See Vasapollo (1996), Martufi, Vasapollo (1993, 2003).

[2] Ferrarotti (2005: 10) takes up the central thesis of managerial revolution and writes: "there is a sensational divorce between power and property. Professional managers have the power without having the property. Shareholder, even the greatest shareholder must delegate the power, is not always able to control the daily or strategic decisions, and is increasingly an absentee owner, a faded and endangered figure.

has not been fully accomplished even in the USA: the most persuasive argument in this regard highlights the fact that managers are normally also shareholders of the companies that they manage, and it is impossible to separate company's interest from private capital interest (Baran, Sweezy 1968).

The model of personal capitalism, especially referred to British capitalism, but in many aspects similar to the American type, is more personal and family based. In England family and non-managerial ownership led to the development of a closed economic and social system that aims to the retention of its privileges. This situation did not favour the growth of an efficient and competitive management system capable of developing the British economy.

Germany, and similarly Japan, instead, have their capitalisms characterized by a community character, in which a company consists in many economic actors who work performing their own roles for a common purpose: long term development. The immediate profit demanded from American stakeholders is replaced by an increase in the long-term value of the enterprise, where immediate gain is smaller but the importance of a longer life of an enterprise is stronger. As above said, the Japanese model of capitalism is similar to German capitalism, being based on the sense of belonging to the "community nation"; for many scholars the current system in these two countries is called Rhenan-Japanese capitalism.

There are some countries whose capitalist models are more interesting than others, because, in addition to representing situations proposed in very large areas, are sometimes characterized by the success and originality of particular models. Among these forms of capitalism it should be interesting to give a special attention to the management systems adopted in United States and Great Britain (*Public Company*), in Japan and Germany (Rhenan and Japanese associated companies) and in Italy (family owned companies).

In Anglo-Saxon capitalism, *Public Companies* are characterized by the fluidity of capital, because investors, in order to minimize risks, tend to hold their stakes for a short time. The predominantly speculative character of investment, aimed at obtaining short-term results, implies that investments which do not produce immediate earnings are still little appreciated.

In general, Anglo-Saxon capitalism is fundamentally based on the financial market, where strong processes of financialization of the economy are realized because finance becomes self-referential.

This is the foundation on which the globalization processes are based, and is better described as *global competition*.

According to this logic, capital moves where it yields more; it is necessary to pursue profit at any cost and any condition, using labour where it costs less, making production where the controls on environmental impact are smaller, absorbing savings and widening the separation processes with the real economy. This generates a reality where the gap between the real economy and finance is increasingly higher and where finance supports the declining trends in the real economy (such as flexibility of wages and reduction of employment).

In conclusion, this capitalism, with its corresponding enterprise system, results in a highly speculative financial economy, prevailing over the needs of production and of the real economy. In this system, globalization means global domination by using speculative capital, expulsion from the market of the enterprises that prove weak in terms of pursuing profit, increase of unemployment and overexploited labour,[3] widening areas where absolute poverty prevails. It is true not just on the borders of imperialism, but also inside, if we consider how large sections of "services" or "immaterial production" or "traditional" material factory production are organized.

In what we can call a "consociational" enterprise, typical of the German and Japanese systems and characterized by the orientation towards the long term increase of value, the strong presence of financial operators among shareholders and the high management, the company as a whole presents a particular structure.

In fact, the so-called "hard core", made up of stable shareholders, who have the largest share of capital, stands out from a multitude of smaller shareholders who own only the portion of capital actually negotiable on the market. Banks, financial investors and those who have strong interests, such as the original owners, possess large sums of capital; in this kind of business there is no possibility for any shareholder to reach an absolute majority position. Consequently, for the development and growth of the company itself, the role of the manager acquires a great importance. The manager's main goal is maximizing the value of the company in an expansionistic view, endeavouring to

---

[3] About the recent changes in labour process and techniques and Taylorization of entire labour sectors that before were irrelevant to so intense exploitation techniques cf. the book edited by Linhart and Moutet (2005).

achieve the optimal mix between company growth, profitability of invested capital and global development.

German capitalism, like the Japanese model, is characterized by the system of "co-management"; among the stakeholders who participate in management, there are also workers, through their Union representatives. In practice, co-responsibility applies through Unions and their presence in the Board of Directors, where employers are consulted about matters related to personnel, and in the Supervisory Board, which appoints the Board of Management. It follows that there is a forced compression of social conflicts and an absence of conflicts inside the company; the sense of belonging and cooperation makes the organization of German company very stable and resilient. Employees who in this context get, in return for a concerted "company and social peace," higher wages and shorter working hours than Anglo-Saxon, demonstrate a greater sense of "loyalty" to the company itself, increasing the power of the German economic system.

In the present-day process of financialization of the economy, communication increasingly takes financial connotations. In the Anglo-Saxon model, oriented to the acquisition and strengthening of shareholders power, the search for resources of venture capital by means of broadening small shareholders; in the Rhenan-Japanese company, instead, financial communication is more oriented to the strengthening and the involvement of external long term financers.[4]

In both models, however, deviant financial communication takes a strong informative social value. Financial information, covering all communication processes that enable to influence directly not only, for instance, the shares price of the company, also lead indirectly all the subjects in a given territory towards the goals and needs of the financialization of the economy. A run-up is carried out, also by the lower classes, to the subscription of shares and bond, to a false and illusory popular shareholding, that makes people "owners" in the very company that exploits their labour extracting surplus value.

These new processes for determining the value of enterprise reflect the social character of production, as Marx argued:

> A commodity is therefore a mysterious thing, simply because in it the social character of men's labour appears to them as an objective character stamped upon the product of that labour; because the relation of the

---

[4] About the social control of deviant communication see Martufi, Vasapollo (2000).

producers to the sum total of their own labour is presented to them as a
social relation, existing not between themselves, but between the products of their labour. (Marx 1867: Book I, Chapter. 1).

In fact, setting a price on relational, organizational or human capital
with a direct reflection in the financial evaluation of the company,
means giving them a wider potential of productivity as a result of the
mere enterprise form, i.e., of the practical process of capital exploitation. Capitalism has transformed the capacity to generate value
(labour-force) and the monetary expression of value (money) into
goods. In our days the social process of production organization, and
the enterprise itself, become commodity, value which is evaluated, an
expression of capitalist social wealth, taking the form of an "immense
accumulation of commodities," which now includes the means of production of goods, social capital and the enterprise.

Consequently, the generalized social factory must be able to reach a
defined long-term strategic position, where it can transfer its brand,
image, and cultural profile to achieve the consent of the public for its
product, conditioning the behaviour of a vast number of consumers.

Carrying out their productive function, companies are increasingly
oriented toward the strategic project of emphasizing skills, human
capital, intangible values of behaviour and, therefore, deviant communication. The latter becomes an intangible strategic resource, essential
for the expansion of a company, the affirmation of its social message
and, consequently, for the processes of flexible accumulation, which
require labour cuts, slowing down the social demand for labour, culture, goods and spare time.

If we add to it the new post-Fordist economic distribution, characterized by the production of services and information rather than the
mere physical distribution of products, we realize that companies offer
the sales area just as a medium of an announced trade war, then, a first
link in the decision chain for customers and the imposition of rules of
market competitiveness within society.

Consumers are induced to look at the product with a different mind:
they are supposed to want to find some new trend, their focus shifts
from a commodity to its content in terms of service and intangible
resources. In this sense, the store distributes services and the communication of a life style as wanted by capitalism, which only later appears
as actual commodities.

Products become true protagonist, because they are proposed as a
point of reference of entrepreneurship on social life. They adapt to the

current trends of capitalism, since they represent not only an object of consumption but a holder of "generalized, shared values," aimed at the processes of flexible accumulation based on intangible capital.

Human and structural intellectual capital is made up of all the knowledge, information and experiences able to create new wealth. It is about elements of human capital and abstraction, new human intangible resources that in recent years are increasingly important in the differentiation strategies needed for global competition. These strategies are carried out because the production processes suffer the effects of all the progress achieved in information, communication and knowledge field.

But, where can the intellectual capital be found inside a company? It is necessary to search among the people in the enterprise system, among structures and customers. So there are three types of intellectual capital: human, structural and customer.

Individual Aspects and Economic Determination of Self-Financing

Entrepreneurial Dynamics, Values and Valuations

Every enterprise model is the result of the historical economic conditions, the traditions and culture of the country in which it operates. Therefore, the aims of each company, namely the creation of economic value, the increase of values through the process of accumulation in its various forms, can be achieved through different ways of strategy implementation and management goals, which change through time because they have to take into account economic, competitive, cultural, technological, socio-political, competition aspects.

The control of a company, the authority of making strategic and operative decisions depends on the different positions that traders assume. Therefore, in a typical control of Public Companies in Anglo-Saxon capitalism, the objectives are determined by the top management, while in the German-Japanese model management has a particular function of mediation and the task of developing and implementing strategies decided by the various components of the company.

In recent years, a gradual evolution in the management systems of companies is taking place to balance and minimize the hardship involved in these models. There is a gradual rapprochement of the two opposite models of Public Companies and consociational enterprises.

While in the United States there is a transition towards a more stable shareholding, in Japan the incidence of share intersections has been reducing and the company participation and direct dependence from the financial market have been widening. The Anglo-Saxon model, although is designed in accordance with much less egalitarian principles, where aggression, individualism, economic Darwinism dominate, has been increasingly spreading, despite the obvious socio-economic injustices that the system involves at the expense of the disadvantaged social classes.

So, a new idea of investment is being accomplished, with a flexible accumulation based on financial characteristics and investments in intangible assets, beyond business dimensions.

If there is a decline in importance of the enterprise, however, there follows an increasing process of economic globalization in the financial sense, with flexible forms of macroeconomic and entrepreneurial accumulation, with important and decisive consequences on the strategic, corporate and sector-based models, adopted to cope with new situations of international capitalist competition.

As a consequence, top managers can never neglect the social and political role that the company plays in the environment in which it operates. Deviated and deviant communication represents, then, a resource that generates other company resources, especially social values. The acts of the communication process must be developed organically in order to increase the accumulation of capital and lead, through information, to the social persuasion in favour of neo-liberal post-Fordism in a framework destructive of local cultures; to socially impose a culture of enterprise efficiency, breaking the class unity of workers through processes of consociational co-optation, in a general social model that makes the whole of society less united and supportive.[5]

The results are clearly evident: making speculative finance means exporting everywhere a financial capitalism that attacks all forms of solidarity in favour of individualism and social economic Darwinism, creating idiosyncrasy for all that is public, for every social relations based on the values not measured by money.

So it is important to choose investments that generate rather than destroy business entrepreneurial value (Copeland, Koller and Murrine 2002: 21–40). In these cases, remuneration on invested capital

---

[5] For details on privatizations and the Welfare State cf. Martufi, Vasapollo (2003).

(capital-gain) is achieved when invested capital is disinvested to a higher value than the original one. But business value is created and spread by maintaining and strengthening links with the environment outside the company; thereby, linking the enterprise micro-system to the environment macro-system becomes increasingly important.

Privatizing to Tackle the Depreciation of Capital[6]

The value of an enterprise always expresses the ability of the company to a) increase the added value in the production process and b) ensure appropriation for capital in the form of profits, added value, or the most part of itself.[7]

Unlike the past, today we are witnessing a diffusion, in small and medium-sized enterprises, of the elements that can act and influence entrepreneurial strategic decisions, like availability of and speculation on financial capital, skilled human resources, homologated intellectual capital, processes of productive relocation and outsourcing of cycle stages in search of lower labour costs, availability of high quality infra-structures and services, enhancement of information, communication and all the resources of intellectual capital.

We witness a new way of developing the mechanisms for accumula-tion, based on financial characteristics, investment in intangible capi-tal and highly skilled human intellectual capital, but also engaged in the seeking of new outlets for productive investment functional to flex-ible accumulation and lean production, and focused on monitoring the international network system. Therefore, the socially spread enter-prise in the regional system, defined as the system of generalized social factory, is an open and dynamic entity which must be able to create, apart from commodity production, additional intangible resource flows, in order to grow and develop. In these flows, information, devi-ant communication and homologated intellectual capital have a key role because they are capable of moving freely, without the barriers of social conditioning.

---

[6] For information about the value in the enterprise and related issues cf. Alvaro, Vasapollo (1999).

[7] Currently, thanks to information technology, technological product and process innovation, the initial investment is quickly recovered, and therefore it must be replaced by another set of investments to increase or at least keep on the one hand the market share and, on the other hand, enterprise value.

To avoid the devaluation of capital, a set of measures has been used, such as foreign exchange transactions, interest rates, privatization, deregulation. The phenomenon of privatization, which has characterized the last two decades, has appeared in various European countries with different methods and intensity, for the needs of different models of international capitalism to bring the labour movement achievements into question, starting from considering the Keynesian economic and social policies of mediation incompatible.

A new role for the State is taking shape: no longer as regulator and mediator of conflicts, but in the form of a state-enterprise, which gradually overthrows the welfare state, destroys with privatizations the role of the national sconomy; a Profit State which spreads throughout society the idea of enterprise compatibility, market competitiveness and profit.

Before explaining the different international approaches to the privatization process, it is necessary to make some general reflections on the arguments put forward to justify the cession of public enterprises by the State, even when they had good levels of economic efficiency, in order to redesign capitalist development and revitalize the accumulation processes in different forms.

Any privatization process has produced negative quantitative and qualitative effects on employment. Nationalizations have often taken place to let workers keep job position in companies that were going through serious crises and were risking to be expelled from the wild and unregulated market. In these cases there was the affirmation of the Keynesian principle of the State as employer and guarantor in conflicts, with a regulated market oriented toward full employment.

We must consider that even when a privatization is successful, there is a repercussion on the reduction of direct and indirect labour costs, injury insurance expenses, ordinary and extraordinary maintenance costs and the expenses to improve the environmental impact of production.

By reducing these costs it is possible to gain, in the transition from public to private, good results that improve the rates of efficiency and the effectiveness indicators. It should not be forgotten that at best, with this transition, we witness mobility and flexibility of labour and of wages, affecting adversely rhythms, condensation and shifts. Moreover, privatization processes have usually caused reduction of guarantees and compression of Unions rights, reaching a complete lack of any form of income and union security and full rights for workers, particularly in countries with lower levels of economic and democratic development.

Efficiency, competitiveness and better profitability, that the transition from a public company to a private one should achieve, are also illusory and disproved by facts, especially because it is very difficult to establish a correlation between the ownership of a company and its efficiency, and furthermore, because the typical indicators of company productivity, efficiency and effectiveness are almost never "transportable," from private to public and vice versa.

There are no precise, fixed rules, economic dogmas. Economics, in particular business management, should be studied in the processes of interaction between internal and external realities, reading the actual links, not the links caused by political-party-business influence, interpreting the enterprise dynamics and the social consequences that develop between the enterprise microsystem and the socio-environmental macrosystem.

Whatever the model of capitalism, the choice of the privatization processes becomes for neoliberalism essential to exalt the free market, in which the speculative financial economy prevails against productive labour. Privatizations are the lifeblood of capitalism and are crucial for bringing out the dominant principles and the forces aimed to earn targets, which never transform themselves in processes of equitable redistribution and general social utility. Balance, stability, profitability pursued by international capitalism, global Profit State, through privatization, proved to be only a process of destabilization of the political, social and environmental balance.

Enterprise Value

For last twenty-five years, the company competitive character has undergone significant changes and it has been necessary, both in the managerial and in academic field, to support and/or replace traditional principles and theories about enterprise activity with new principles and theories able to capture the main aspects of this change. This implies not only an acceleration of the processes of centralization (autonomous accumulation) and concentration (merger of autonomous capital) of capital, but also an implicit qualitative change in the process of internationalization in the present phase of capitalism.

At present, the principle that plays a key role in modern economics is the concept of enterprise value, which is the pivot of the enterprise activity.[8] This is because the economic system and the attitude of its operators have become increasingly competitive and aggressive (challenges, competition, desire for success, etc.). Moreover, next to the market of products and services, a market for control of companies has emerged: the reduction of the deficit and the consequent decrease of debit rates paid on State public debt has produced an enormous amount of resources, which have been poured into the financial market.

Therefore, the number of shareholders has significantly increased, and they are unwilling to tolerate unsatisfactory results, becoming much more involved in the management of company. Moreover, capitals derived from the banking system have increased and are breaking into the markets, especially the American markets. Therefore, modern managers have the new problem of "value management". That is why many scholars have identified a theory of reference for enterprise management: the theory of value creation. This is able to provide guidance to enterprises to interpret the new features of the markets and environment outside the company itself.

The Theory of Value Creation[9]

The theory of value creation is based on the assumption that company long-term survival and developmentare guaranteed only by generating new value. It is essential, therefore, to choose investments that generate rather than destroy enterprise value.[10] "Value creation" implicitly refers to the process of intersectional transfer of value, analysed by Marx in the accumulation patterns, as a result of differences in the organic composition of capital. But they also include the attempt to quantify the ability to modify selling prices through production prices in order to obtain a "commercial rent" in the process of valorisation of products. This ability is at the base of concepts like "competitiveness" or enterprise "value".

---

[8] The enterprise value must be distinguished from the financial revenue of the enterprise, including future revenue, to include all the tangible and intangible assets, collective organization of social work as a new commodity capable of expressing a value (exchange) itself.
[9] For some references see. Alvaro, Vasapollo (1999).
[10] Cf. Copeland, Koller, Murrine (2002: 21–40).

However, on this question there are strong contradictions, because financial markets take in the data of the real economy according to the logic of financial rent. But the financial rent of assets is not necessarily linked to the economic basis of the enterprise, or to its ability to extract surplus value, but only to speculative conditions of a market in which the prices of production are not only market prices directly determined by supply and demand increase.

In this regard, it is necessary to consider that more and more frequently the value of securities traded in financial markets experiences a strong increase, even when the trend of the real economy is negative. For example, in an economic recession it is possible that, because of the stagnation of consumption, inflation decreases and the expectations of a downturn in the official discount rate increase; this promotes the growth of the stock market, although it reflects a negative moment for economy, in which the downturn of the discount rate does not represents a possible economic recovery, but an immediate opportunity for profit.[11] It is important to underline that the trend of the financial markets may differ from the trend of the real economy. Therefore moving from a notion of economic-financial value to a notion of economic–competitive value would be useful. In this way, the concept of value is complete and helps understand the socio-economic function of enterprise.

Increase in the value of economic capital is ensured by the ability to generate long-term positive cash-flow, or a positive economic profitability. When the value of economic capital is created, it is expected to be transferred in the stock exchange (thus being recognized by the market), in order that shareholders can obtain a benefit. In fact, capital gain is the primary goal of shareholders. They are legally the holders of company, so they mind the results, whether they participate or not in the management of company.

The Evaluation of the Enterprise

The development of the theory of value creation has pushed the attention of both academic and management worlds to the methods of the evaluation of the enterprise (business valuation). To evaluate a

---

[11] Another example occurs when the value of the shares of listed companies is increased due to the dismissal of staff, because of the improvement of management results buying these shares is more profitable.

company all its elements must be taken into account, considering the valuation of its economic capital. It can be achieved through the direct and indirect methods of Business valuation.

The first method concerns the valuation expressed by the market. Through this method it is easy to identify the value of companies listed in the Stock Exchange, while for unlisted companies the only form of evaluation is based on the prices actually paid by the company.

However, direct valuation methods are not sufficiently reliable. Indeed, the value traded in market is often influenced by subjective trading situations, temporary and contingent conditions. Furthermore, negotiations that took place on the European (excluding English) Stock Exchanges) concern limited quantities of securities of companies, which represent a small part of their capital. This means that the prices of securities may not be related to the value of control involvement and therefore are not eligible to make an estimate of the economic capital of the enterprise.

There follows the need to look to indirect evaluation methodologies, not based on market data. This valuation method is usually required when necessary:

- to evaluate if a company runs the risk of hostile takeovers;
- to determine selling and purchase prices;
- to determine the quoted price in the stock exchange;
- to resort to a capital increase;
- to decide, when it is appropriate, to increase capital (Calori, n/d; Ubago Vivas, 1990).

Indirect methods are typical procedures to valuate economic capital. They are essentially based on three types of information:

- *Financial*. Cash flows that will be generated by the investment choices;
- *Income*. Income that will be produced by investment choices;
- *Assets*. Current property value of investment decisions.

Using this information, the following indirect valuation methods of economic take their names: financial approach, income approach, asset-based approach.

CHAPTER SIX

THE ENTERPRISE AND THE MICROECONOMICS OF SOCIALISM

The Basic Rules of Operation

Socialism can be politically and economically characterized by a more or less centralized or decentralized feature, allowing different organizations to settle maintaining the same basic principles of system functioning. The relationship between planning centralization and decentralization is a debate that has never been closed. Sometimes the degree of centralization is shown to depend on the development level of the productive forces, so that in underdeveloped countries planning in its early stages should be highly centralized, with very little autonomous production units. On the contrary, where there is a strong development and access to information and communication technologies, the decision-making mechanism permits a greater decentralization in the planning process without any loss of effectiveness (achievement of objectives) nor efficiency (achievement of goals with the minimum cost).

In this sense, we must distinguish between nationalization and socialization of enterprises; the disappearance of the private means of production does not imply the immediate socialization of the means of production themselves.

In fact, the "state or public ownership" does not guarantee the control by the workers on their labour, and if democratization of economic relations is not achieved, workers will find themselves in a situation of alienation vis-a-vis the product of their work, like under capitalism. State ownership does not guarantee socialism. It implies only a process of centralization in a single legal economic entity of several capitals that pass from a variety of owners and co-owners to a single subject.

Only when there is social control over the production process, when the means of production are owned by the production units themselves and the space around them, and taking decisions about investments and technological changes is socially shared, than it is possible to refer to the autonomy of production units. It may be joined or not by the corresponding legal form that will guarantee the status of "legal subject" (Bettelheim 1993: 101–110). When there is the passage to the socialization of the economic process, microeconomics acquires more importance. At this stage the planning must articulate macroeconomic decisions of production with microeconomic decisions concerning the organization of the process of labour and consumption decisions.

The first major difference between capitalism and socialism refers to the decisions on prices: prices in capitalism, as we said, are established by a microeconomic process, fragmented in companies and sectors. They determine the rules of distribution, the structures of costs and the possible levels of differentiation of profits, and are expressed in the form of market price. On the contrary, in socialism we talk of macro-economic production prices which express the time of social work relative to various productions.

This situation implies a strong change in enterprise accounting. In socialism, the financial elements of the accounting analysis lose importance in favour of technical and real criteria, allowing a development of *physical accounting in terms of working time*, directly and indirectly calculated. It does not concern prices, but an accounting of the links between the units: the accounting of aggregation of production units becomes a big map of social accounting. The accounting techniques are subjected to a radical change. Double-entry bookkeeping leaves its place to input-output microeconomic tables.

The other elements that experience a significant mutation in socialism are the contents and the form of microeconomic utility functions. Socialism maintains the possibility to distribute time between leisure and work, and is also organized to gradually expand the choices of the population, because this is the goal of productivity increase.[1]

---

[1] In his *Critique of Gotha Program* (1875) Marx wrote: Within the co-operative society based on common ownership of the means of production, the producers do not exchange their products; just as little does the labour employed on the products appear here as the value of these products, as a material quality possessed by them, since now, in contrast to capitalist society, individual labour no longer exists in an indirect fashion but directly as a component part of total labour. The phrase "proceeds of labour," objectionable also today on account of its ambiguity, thus loses all meaning. (...) What we have to deal with here is a communist society, not as it has developed on its own foundations, but, on the contrary, just as it emerges from capitalist society; which is thus in every respect, economically, morally, and intellectually, still stamped with the birthmarks of the old society from whose womb it emerges. Accordingly, the individual producer receives back from society – after the deductions have been made – exactly what he gives to it. What he has given to it is his individual quantum of

One of the mistakes of twentieth century socialism was precisely that it ignored this dimension, essential to maintain social motivation and consensus.

In capitalism, the expression of needs is realized after the event, after the distribution of added value is achieved. The limit of needs is determined by the income provided by a person. If such income is zero or nearly zero, even the need for survival is denied. Individual expenses of personal income make good the previous decisions on previous assignment of social labour.

In socialism, by contrast, the expression of needs is converted into an input in the decision-making process of production. Planning can be achieved on the base of individual and collective needs (social, business, environmental, etc.), expressed through appropriate technical procedures.

So, instead of a microeconomic foundation of macroeconomics, as in a system of uncoordinated private decisions, socialism requires a macroeconomic foundation of microeconomics, where prices become endogenous and social decisions determine the decisions of the production units, and the decisions related to the functions of social welfare, joined in the form of aggregate function of social welfare, steer investment decisions.

The above-mentioned elements are only the basic principles or rules of system functioning. The possible forms of social organization of socialist production are several. The recent debate, after the disappearance of Soviet-style socialist governments, testifies to the existence of divergent positions. Starting from the centrality of economic

---

labour. For example, the social working day consists of the sum of the individual hours of work; the individual labour time of the individual producer is the part of the social working day contributed by him, his share in it. He receives a certificate from society that he has furnished such-and-such an amount of labour (after deducting his labour for the common funds); and with this certificate, he draws from the social stock of means of consumption as much as the same amount of labour cost. The same amount of labour which he has given to society in one form, he receives back in another (...) In a higher phase of communist society, after the enslaving subordination of the individual to the division of labour, and therewith also the antithesis between mental and physical labour, has vanished; after labour has become not only a means of life but life's prime want; after the productive forces have also increased with the all-around development of the individual, and all the springs of cooperative wealth flow more abundantly – only then then can the narrow horizon of bourgeois right be crossed in its entirety and society inscribe on its banners: From each according to his ability, to each according to his needs! (http://libcom.org/library/critique-of-the-gotha-program-karl-marx)

democracy (Devine 1988), the models proposed differ substantially, from socialist models based on the socialization of investment maintaining legal and social independence of the enterprises, including private property (Schweickart 1996), to decentralized socialist models, with a planning system built by aggregation from bottom to top (Albert, Hanhel 1991, Albert 2003). Moreover, there are the models that propose a centralized planning accomplished by means of information technology and communication development.[2]

The Double Character of the Process of Socialist Enterprise Governance

An Analysis of the Behaviour of the Socialist Enterprise

The study of public administration, fundamental to understand how the socialist enterprise acts, has assumed a multidisciplinary nature, with a continuous interchange of multiple disciplines (Stillman, 1991), for example:

- from political science it takes the importance of power, politics and public policy;
- from the science of business administration it inherits elements related to management, decision-making and information systems;
- it draws from sociology the approach elements of systems, the importance of organizational theory and the theory of human resources;
- finally, history, economics and psychology introduce the analysis of administrative decisions, economic instruments on public finance, budgeting, fiscal policy and studies on behaviour of actors and groups of public organizations.

Economists have become part of government organisms to give advice on quantitative economic growth neglecting eco-social compatibility, and with this antisocial approach, they pretended to organize everything, from education to health, from social assistance to retirement and trade and military policies.

---

[2] Cockshott, Cottrell (1993). A first presentation of these positions can be found in Arriola (2006).

GNP and GDP numbers have dominated the summits of the Group of Eight, known as G-8.[3] Theoretical and applied economists have excelled compared to their critics and their rivals in other disciplines such as political science, sociology, psychology, law, anthropology, ecology, thermodynamics, chaos systems and theories, and they have supplanted them in public policy; for example with their econometric model on inflation and employment they have caused, introducing restrictive monetary policies and neoliberal financialisation, the unemployment of millions of workers, poverty and hunger for 80% of world population.

The Process of Public Management

There is a recent a tendency to characterize the public management as an articulated multiplicity of processes involved in the economic and social spheres, but articulated with the external projection of politics. In this sphere the external impact of national policies is not evaluated. This is particularly significant in underdeveloped countries, because it conditions their dependence on higher forms of domination of developed capitalism countries.

Public management is the activity realized by a public authority with its own resources, with the aim of realizing concrete, specific and individual projects (Meny, Thoenig 1992). This authority has various means: people, materials, financial credits, which it turn into goods and services able to meet the needs of society in which the management process is carried out.

Other scholars (Robbins, De Cenzo 1996) give emphasis to planning, organization, direction and control as key elements to achieve the goals of public organization through management; for this purpose we must consider that:

a. planning includes objectives, establishes strategies and develops plans to coordinate
b. initiatives;
c. organization determines what is necessary, how and by whom it will be done;

---

[3] The Group of Eight (G8) refers to eight highly industrialized nations, considered as the major powers of capitalist world, that direct the Organization for Cooperation and Economic Development (OECD). This group is composed of: France, Germany, Italy, Great Britain, Japan, United States, Canada, and Russia.

d. management is responsible for directing and motivating all parties involved, choosing the most effective channels of communication and resolving conflicts;

e. monitoring allows control activities, to ensure that they are realized according to plans and to correct any significant deviation.

The Impact of Changes on State Participation

Political-economic changes that have taken place at a global level for the last three decades, have generated another perspective on the public role, and thus a new concept has been invented: the *new public administration*, which results to be inconsistent if it is not supported by the elements of new public management. Nevertheless, the consequences related to the advent of neoliberal model and its socio-political impact identify the potential of business management with that of public management. This innovative version could hide some assumptions and intentions (Barzelay 1993):

a. A trend shown in the public sector in some Western countries, which have transformed the executive of State through the introduction of business management and economic organization techniques.

b. The identification of the new public management as an innovative perspective on the analysis of public administration problems, in which contributions are based on empiricism and the application of administrative traditional values.

c. New public management is considered as a model, a set of principles, policies and techniques for managing the public sector, whose implicit or explicit application is recommended.

New public management, instead of pursuing as objectives the changes in political institutions inside and outside the executive branch, aims at preserving and consolidating political power, and does not provide changes in the institutions that affect its origin, its distribution and forms of legitimacy, as well as the nature of political regime, the relations between State powers, the territorial structure of power and changes in representation systems.

On the other hand, substantial reforms are not focused on the institutional character and role of the State, but are directed to public policies from economics to education, health, building and others fields.

CHAPTER SEVEN

SOCIALIST PUBLIC ADMINISTRATION

The Evolution of the Conceptual Foundations of Public Administration

The administrative activity of a socialist country in the first stage of the transformation of the economy, enhances the transformation of the property of the means of production. For this purpose an intense administrative activity that constitutes an expansion of the pre-existent activity in monopolistic capitalism is required, with the aim of changing the class structure and transform the economic base structure, setting a base democracy in opposition to a bourgeois democracy.

This new government brings with it the unfolding of an administration that can determine the challenges of the new system during the transition period and create the conditions to implement legally the construction of socialism (Garcin 1982).

The economic crisis that broke out in the 1970s, characterized by the last stage of economic stagnation and inflation (combined phenomenon called 'stagflation') strongly hit the capitalist system, although not so deeply as the crises which broke out between 1929 and 1933, but with the same systemic determinants of the financial crises in 2008. It is in these years that the Neoliberal theory came into vogue, put forth by Milton Friedman, based on old doctrines of economic liberalism that have been developing since the 1950s, although they occupied a secondary position during the Keynesian period.

Neoliberal policy,[1] prevailing nowadays, has direct consequences on the public administration. Today there is a strong crisis of the services, which, necessarily, the State must provide to citizens; this results in a disappointment within the so-called democratic societies for their incapacity to solve the increasing population's problems. The poor are

---

[1] For a reconstruction of the transformation processes of public administrations in response to liberal policies and requirements cf. Cassese (2005).

the most affected, but the areas and the classes suffering a decrease in quality of life are increasing.[2]

Neoliberalism makes the State increasingly distant from the interests of the majority of society, and less able to solve problems. Public administrations find themselves split from the social discontent and worse, if we take into account that in many countries, the administration is contaminated by the phenomenon of corruption that corrodes its structures and its credibility.

Reform Processes in Public Management for Socialist Construction

Some scholars[3] talk about the reforms in public administration from two different levels of analysis that are based on the categories of *efficiency and effectiveness*. In connection with efficiency, the low performance of the public administration (in this case we prefer to refer to the operator of public administration or public) is analysed beginning from its high cost, considering the amount of public personnel, the waste of resources and institutional energy and the use of obsolete administrative techniques.

From this analysis, reorganization solutions in the administrative apparatus and the use of modern techniques and methods are recommended to reduce the facilities and staff necessary for its operation. In these actions of cost reduction, State responsibility towards society is usually limited, acting sometimes with apologetic tactics to avoid taking responsibility as State in the face to population.

These two levels of analysis will affect a third level, the crisis of legitimacy, so it can be argued that the lack of credibility in public management generates the need for changes in the public administration, but in turn inefficiency and ineffectiveness lead to further distrust. Thus there is a vicious circle.

The crisis of legitimacy is due to State inability in meeting people's demands and finding solutions to the most pressing problems of

---

[2] As the State withdraws, the development of the so-called 'non-profit sector "is promoted. It is based on the principle of subsidiarity and provides a range of social services previously provided by the PA. The huge difference is that while PA was obliged to provide services according to the principle of the equal quality, in non-profit the provision of services is mandated to voluntary operators and individual initiative.
[3] In *The Search for Government Efficiency* (1986), Downs and Larkey, talk about this question, also taken up by Lane (1995).

society. It results in the crisis of legitimacy of the public administration. Political and economic exchange between the working class and the State is at the origin of the "historic compromise" in the West thanks to the struggles of the labour movement at the origin of the Welfare State. According to this agreement the working class achieves political and legal approval for itself and their interest organizations (Unions), pension and welfare systems, aimed at the availability of free (actually recent studies show that most of "weight" of the Welfare State has been born by its subordinate classes; cf. Shaikh 2003) or a political price services. In return, the working class, through agreements with the historical Trade Unions, ensures a compliance with the rules, a low level of social conflict, softer business relationships, a control of riotous centres, moderate wages: social peace.

When this is broken, the actors of the compromise are hardly able to reward each other, especially when the State, in the crisis of legitimacy, is no longer able to ensure the return to social peace.

We will now analyse the reforms that are being implemented in the public administration in the neoliberal phase in response to the problems of efficiency, effectiveness and the legitimacy crisis (Aucoin 2001).

a) *Reduction of expenditure* is manifested in the rationalization of services, in the reduction of public services, the reduction of the administrative apparatus, the reduction of staff and in avoiding new projects. The analysis for the choice of these measures is carried out only from the efficiency standpoint, considered as balance of resources to obtain more results. This solution, far from resolving problems, exacerbates them, although in many cases the considerable increase in costs in public institutions, mummified by the excess of facilities, inefficiency at management level and not in the labour component is real. This reform will result in an increase of unemployment. Reducing costs is achieved also minimizing the cost of labour: we refer to transformations of labour due to the privatization of public sectors (economic and otherwise) and the outsourcing of functions. Work relationship and employment contracts change and the previously insured guarantees get worse.

b) *Privatization.* This approach has been widely used in Latin American and European countries[4]; the licenses for the delivery of

---

[4] About privatization in Italy and Europe cf. Martufi, Vasapollo (2003). Experiments, resulted as favourable to capital, have been realized in the 90s in Italy with the system of bargaining.

public services are sold to private companies with the aim to reduce costs, especially labour and routine and extraordinary maintenance, so that the State is no longer responsible for some services. In the 1980s and 1990s in all capitalist countries the State sold to private entrepreneurs every type of service (cemeteries, roads, gardens, producing services enterprises): in this way it often sold to other states and multinationals part of its national sovereignty.

c) *Public services only for the most poor?* Some statistics claim that privatization, far from solving the social situation, increases poverty, unemployment, social problems and the most urgent needs of population. As a palliative for this situation new structures that regulate the activity of private enterprises in the public sector are created. The privatization process also involves the introduction of external competence: between public and private (example: health and education) or internal: between different organizations of the public sector. Competence becomes the false characterizing element that keeps some services in the private sphere or in the public one. But what competence? The private competence is oriented towards profit and not towards social needs. So, services to people are governed by the rules of the market (Aucoin 2000: 23).[5]

d) *Sub-contracting and outsourcing.* Subcontract to the private sector for services and products especially inside the administrative (cleaning, computer services)[6] is rife; although it is not new, some services such as the control of the prisons are currently subcontracted with the aim of reducing costs.

e) *Conversion.* It conceals the liberalization or creation of independent state structures, subjected to market pressures. On the other hand, in order to restructure public services, organizations based on the compliance of market objectives, are created; here budget is determined according to economic goals, and not social ones.

f) *Politicization of bureaucracy.* The professionalism of the public service is ignored because it is considered an obstacle to change, so the merits or knowledge gained by staff are not considered and valuated. There is the tendency of some political leaders to appoint

---

[5] We refer to the privatization processes of water that is acting in various parts! In Italy, many municipalities subcontracted aqueducts and water supply networks to private systems. In response many citizens arose in protest movements.

[6] It is very pronounced a process in the private sector where the most modern and large business networks are based on this principle.

managers from the private sector or supporters of their political parties (i.e. spoils system and external consultants). Therefore abetting is favoured, and it carries, among other ills, corruption in the public sector.

g) *Decentralization of the State.* This reform is developed not only in government but also in the economic, social and institutional sphere, so that it reconsiders the role of State, affecting the whole structure of society. Functions are reorganized against the social interest, giving greater possibility of decision and management to local and territorial organisms and sectors. The measures tending to decentralization claim to offer population a greater participation in decisions and thus to reinforce the concept of democracy.[7] However, in order for it to work in all its dimensions, the State must decentralize resources, which seems to be the most critical process.[8]

When the reforms in the public administration are analysed, the focus is on identifying the effort to adopt techniques and processes typical of the private administration. The aim is "to make government as close as possible to business".

The tendency to resort to the methods of the private sector also involves to propose that the public sector are governed by the market mechanisms of supply and demand, accepting the system of prices and consumer's choice to raise the supply, also setting the economic result as a goal to reduce inefficiency. However, with the introduction of market mechanisms in the public administration, the satisfaction of collective needs, the needs accessible to everybody and the achievement of social welfare are put in danger. Assuming techniques and methods of the private sector government lets public administration to be reinvented in key markets. That is conceptually absurd.

For a society that is building socialism, efficiency is the main objective of economic policy, as it is one of its most important potentialities. This statement requires that society makes a better use of its resources, the increase of labour productivity, the achievement of better economic results, but with a high impact of social and environmental

---

[7] In Italy, the law of 8 June 1990 No 142 ("local autonomy") tends toward this direction.

[8] We must not confuse the process of decentralization that involves the passage of power from the higher to the lower level with the decentralization, which refers the creation of regional organizations in which power is maintained by the central level. These two processes can occur in parallel or independently although both are important for the development of the public sector.

compatibility with lower economic and eco-social costs. There will be a positive effect on the financial budget, facilitating participation in international trade and in capital and investment markets, and balancing the negative effect of the actions that may have been adopted and applied by political enemies of the country, threatening national sovereignty.[9]

The efficiency of a society, like the transformations involved, must always be displayed in all the dimensions in which it occurs: at a macroeconomic level, through regulatory processes that promote stability, and ensure the balanced implementation of economic policies; in terms of improvement which will help the increase of efficiency of production process, conceived as the interrelationship of production, distribution and consumption.

Moreover, the determinants of efficiency should not refer only to the reduction in costs and an entrepreneurial profit margin or the reduction of costs as a means to measure it. The manifestation of efficiency should reach the institutional level, through the simplification of the decision-making moment so that the appropriate decisions are taken at the right time to answer situations as quickly and objectively as possible with the necessary regulations, the appropriate structures and the organizations adapted to society demands, i.e. not only in directly economic terms but in relation to an overall social equity.

Finally, it is important to underline that for a society that builds socialism the concept of real efficiency must be closely linked to the quality of final consumption, because failing, qualitatively and quantitatively, to meet the social or individual consumption leads to the waste of resources. As a consequence, efficiency must be analysed in its dual expression, as a minor cost of products favoured by increased productivity and a better growth of satisfaction of population demands. Socioeconomic efficiency is a category on which detailed and comprehensive analysis must be based, to describe the capacity of resources and the conditions able to widen the ability to face external threats on the one hand and to increase economic independence on the other hand.

---

[9] We want to report the experience of Cuba, victim of a blockade by U.S. for fifty years whose adverse impact on the country exceeds 95 billion dollars. Under these conditions it is necessary to wonder how can the efficiency of the Cuban economy be measured.

The Necessity of Establishing Monitoring Systems and Indicators

Results in terms of management, efficiency and effectiveness are obtained only when the leaders of the public service are actively involved in the research and the application in these areas during the development of their functions, putting into practice the measures that contribute to their fulfilment.

Referring to these issues, some scholars (Aucoin 2001) report that pursuing these criteria is an interactive process that must take into account that specifying objectives is not simply a function of management. It is also a function of political leaders to establish and clarify the goals to achieve in each area of politics or the economy.

Identifying a set of indicators of managerial monitoring can be a very effective instrument for the valuation of results of management and their introduction represent a significant step forward for the whole organization.

In the study of public policy an analyst must take into account what is the cycle that a politics undergoes from the moment the problem is defined and structured to the evaluation of politics itself. Policy analysis is research aimed at identifying the right action and involves the whole process of public policy that can be centred on:

a. the external aspects of the government, concerned with the problem, its size, severity, the number of people affected;
b. the behaviour of social actors critical to and with interests in the process;
c. objectives and results, trying to know the adjustments between estimates and actual achievements;
d. the means – human, financial, organizational and technological resources – used to develop politics (Tamayo Sáez, 1997: 282).

Of course, it is important to ensure the efficiency of indicators to measure the result and when it is necessary to make an adjustment, introducing adjustments in their initial information and structure. Then we consider that the system of indicators has to be complete, therefore it should reflect the most important aspects of the objective that has wanted to be achieved and at the appropriate time and allow a clear identification of the importance of each of them.

Moreover, its structure should facilitate the analysis of the results in terms of efficiency, effectiveness, cost-benefit relationship and quality (Ministry of Economy of Spain 1997).

Means and Mechanisms for the Relations between
the State and Economic Policy

State intervention in economy is as old as capitalism, but only during World War I the problem of the control of cycle became to gain relevance. The Neoclassical tradition had forgotten the phenomenon of the cycle and it was only in 1913, with Business Cycle by Mitchell that a social study started. Until then the United States had passed through 30 cycles. Then, some measures began to be applied:

a. The first neutralization measure of the cycle was monetary policy measure, namely the organization of monetary aggregates (M1, M2, M3);
b. Subsequently fiscal policy sprang up, resulting historically in two variants of economic policy: Monetary policy and fiscal policy.

The so-called Great Depression, or crisis of 1929–33, showed that monetary policy alone was not entirely effective as a means against the cycle. In prosperity, the organization of the aggregates money can not alone control the boom; in times of depression, a more liberal monetary policy, is unable to start the recovery.

It is necessary to use other instruments, considered more powerful. Actually it is an illusion to think that the instruments of economic policy are infallible, and it would be schematic to also think that they cannot have any function. Fiscal policy deals with the State organization of public spending, taxes, loans and debt to the State, in order to change the behaviour and choices of other traders. Two major groups of specific instruments of fiscal policy can be established:

a. stabilizing mechanisms;
b. tax variation.

Moreover, there are other instruments that control the so-called movement dynamic of the mechanisms, such as:

a. agricultural subsidies: they increase during depression and decrease in recovery;
b. income taxes: progressive structure that gradually increases according to income[10];

---

[10] There is also the proportional system. While the progressive criterion (progressive taxation) provides a plurality of ascending rates that affect income as it increases, in the proportional system there is only one rate that is applied to all income tax bands.

c. insurance for unemployment: increases when wages increase, becoming reserve to be used during the depression;

d. payments for Social Security: they decrease during recovery when labour increases and increase during depression when labour decreases;

e. transfer payments: interest on debt, payment to elderly, agricultural subsidies, unemployment insurance and social welfare.

These are mechanisms, as established by fiscal policy, which aim at controlling the flow of state resources, adapting them to the needs of each particular moment of the cycle. Clearly, with the changes occurring in the economy, these mechanisms may also change to adapt themselves or to be eliminated, permitting the introduction of other mechanisms more responsive to the needs of the cyclical dynamics of economy. This process goes through the dynamic process of formulation and implementation of economic policies, due to political confrontation and electoral processes, as a result of the political debate.

The Welfare State set in the post-war in Western countries was based on a model that can be summarized as follows: the development of the economy provided employment and job positions; the development progressed regularly, so that the market was able to solve employment request, while State intervened in order to cover the remaining temporary interruptions or marginal conditions of the labourforce and to ensure social peace conditions through forms of "solidarity" when there was a problem in relation to the market, because of temporary unemployment, sickness, old age, training needs.

This model was founded on a social organization based on Fordist full-time male labour, and the availability of women to ensure reproduction activities, where State intervention was merely residual: this method was based on a decisive bargaining power in terms of high conflict power by the labour movement. This model was possible for a far-sighted view by the Conservative and moderate governments, who believed that, since there was not any spontaneity of the system towards full employment, the burden of maintaining the stability of demand and full employment were to be attributed to the State which was entrusted with a function of substitution to private entrepreneurs.

Welfare State ensured that a relationship between economics, politics and society as a project of political governance of crisis tended to define the social pact centred on public debt that supported the old model of State. With the increase of the debt it was inevitable that the problem of the solvency of the Treasury of State emerged and limits were to be placed in this expansion.

The governments of Western countries, which had only partially digested the Keynesian revolution, had to begin to reckon with the question of the block of public spending. But as soon this block was made, from the 1980s, unemployment began to grow dramatically everywhere. The supposed unproductivity of the state created a real political, economic and social redefinition, concealing the true dissipation of resources due to the policy reversal.

The changes due to post-Fordist cycle and flexible accumulation, which also determined the fiscal crisis of the state, ensure that the costs of Welfare are no longer compatible in a system of international high competitiveness, in which there is no space for mediation with the indispensable collective needs. Thus there is a situation of deep crisis in which the State can no longer help the increasingly large mass of unemployed and casually employed; the State can not guarantee a minimum social safety net for all and for the various stages of life, thus is no longer compatible with the modes of capitalist accumulation. It is no longer possible to guarantee a stable employment relationship, supported by an effective supply of basic services and political support to weaker people.

The Profit State operates policy choices within a general project based on a complete reorganization of conflicts and social tensions, restructuring the wild capitalist economic and industrial relations. All this is accomplished through the methods of consensus, spread through a new "consociationalism," that involves the party system, the Trade Unions confederations, business associations, banking and financial institutions and the mass communication system. If "consociationalism" was born and developed in the 1970s, in the next two decades, the co-management and coordination trend of the historical Workers Unions and party organizations finds its highest expression in the neoliberal project founded on the abolishment of the Welfare State and the intense process of privatization.

Although the urgency of reforming Welfare was immediately financial, the neoliberal project contained much more than the intent of fiscal consolidation. Despite repeated attacks, the Welfare survives as a residual symbol of the Keynesian period. The current crisis of the Welfare State is related to a change in the role of the State, since the extraordinary transition phase from industrial to post-industrial that the economy is experiencing demands a more flexible labour market, making the State-form related to the Fordist cycle inappropriate. Changing also the typical role and figure of mass industrial worker leads to an instable position in the labour market, with very little prospects of maintaining that "position" indefinitely. New and more serious problems are added to those of traditional welfare system. In Italy, even the distorted clientelistic-assistance that was created with the national Welfare State is no longer compatible, because of its class favouritism. The growth of services occurred in Italy through a corporatist and political bargaining that has seen the conflict, on one hand, of the individual categories, anxious to improve their condition without regard for the other, and on the other hand, of the political parties aimed to increase their social consensus, resulting in an inegalitarian, corporative nepotism-based welfare system.

Flexible accumulation tends to occur as a progressive end and an actual reduction of benefits provided by Welfare, but especially as a progressive impoverishment of the traditionally protected classes, starting from the whole area of public employment, the craftsmen and small traders, that is those professional classes whose identity and security was guaranteed by presence of the social protection and public services. *Technocentric* solutions developed in the Europe of Maastricht indicate to reform the block of the economic and social forces, that produces, as a consequence, the abandoning of the excluded people and geographic areas more exposed to marginalisation, attempting to spread a rampant and self-centred culture of the market that contributes to create the consent to the neo-liberal idea, so well interpreted not only by the European centre-right governments but also by centre-left or social democratic parties.

The State, in its role as guarantor of social security (in health, education, social security, assistance and protection of the weakest sectors of the population), requires in addition to a balanced economic development also high levels of employment and a tax levying.

In Italy, in the previous Fordist and Taylorist phase of development, with the Keynesian compromise, there was the unification of the labour world in some figures able to represent the whole area of the employees. Today the new flexible accumulation supports, however, a tendency to the division, the fragmentation, the precariousness of labour. The labour market is organized so that division and flexibility are its distinguishing features. The first factor of fragmentation is the establishment of unemployment as a permanent structural mass phenomenon that pushes to the private redefinition of all social life.

In Italy the privatization process begins to strike heavily the Welfare state, focusing on the abolishment of rights universalism and indicating a Welfare State oriented to cover the needs of only the poorest class of population. Thus in Italy the new political and economic consociationalism grew and developed: the neoliberal project of the globalization era, that even in Italy offers tax and economic policies and spending politics, wild privatization processes, the abolition of the Welfare State, political and constitutional reforms, usually with the only condition of maintaining electoral consensus, satisfying special interests related the business world, and a new party politics even more thirsty for power than the previous one, but more compatible with the new patterns of capitalist restructuring. And the new requirements are based not only on the need to consume goods, but above all to consume services, i.e. to make the organization of production related to the outsourcing processes functional and compatible to the adaptation on the new realities of capital.

The future is ever more precarious for workers; the poorest classes will see their direct and indirect wages cut with no serious policy for employment, without any revenue sharing of income, with increasingly strong incentives and concessions to enterprises that counterbalance with the lack of income for most of the citizens.

Even in a reformist and absolutely minimal perspective, the new socialist-inspired economic policies must absolutely aim to cope with structural unemployment, creating new employment opportunities for social and collective benefit, realizing unnecessary commodities, widening the possibilities of women labour, labour to migrants, work for young people, favouring thus also the strengthening of the public social security system. A serious policy must be adopted for a generalized reduction of labour time for an equal wage, including in strongly public and private services, small and micro enterprises, to recognize a minimum *social Income* to unemployed, precarious workers, the retired; to give new impetus to a new, modern and efficient welfare state.

Scientific analysis and policy initiatives must start from establishing rules in contrast with the society of enterprise and the privatization in which the State become not only a guarantor of the balance, a controller. At least an interventionist State is needed, that creates new, different and not marketable jobs, able to implement and regulate the efficiency of the system oriented to the strengthening of a new Welfare State, which guarantees the rights acquired by workers, pensioners, of all citizens, meeting new needs, for a new and more modern system of quality of life.

PART FOUR

A CRITIQUE OF ECONOMICS AS APPLIED TO ECONOMIC
SYSTEMS: REGULATION AND PLANNING

CHAPTER EIGHT

A CRITIQUE OF THE THEORY OF HEGEMONIC LIBERALISM AND THE PARADIGMS OF FINANCIALIZATION

Which Liberalism? Which Market Economy? Which Globalization?

In the 1970s economic growth and market expansion slowed down considerably and in the years that followed the whole world entered a period of structural crisis, that, in spite of small recoveries, was not able to revive accumulation at the necessary rates and the levels necessary to the expansion and remuneration of international capital. From then on the major capitalist countries have exclusively limited themselves to managing the crisis in two-thirds of the globe, inventing new temporary economic-productive and commercial outlets and heading steadily towards a financialization of the economy.

The term "globalization" is now used in current economic lexicon and common language as a sign that economic liberalism tends to be the only development model, which history will not be able to contradict and overcome. It is possible to read the irreversible choice between productive investment in the real economy and processes of exclusively financial speculative investment within the overall logic of the globalization of capitalism.

We witness, in fact, a more and more pronounced gap between the development of the real economy, with its political, economic and social processes, and the choices concerning the financialization of economy. In the latter case, we deal with liberal decision models focused on financial investments that are unrelated to production processes, and pursue a merely speculative logic, and actual dynamics detached from the political economic framework, pursuing the maximization of profits. In this context of "financial bubble," profits are easily made, creating financial and position rents that are a wealth illusion for the country's economy and destroy efficiency and employment. Dislocating the mechanisms of production, financial processes become not only easy sources of wealth for investors, but produce low taxation and property incomes, and often even complete tax avoidance

and evasion[1] Italy is a fertile ground for international financial speculation, granted by a young, asphyxiated, unstable stock exchange, where
the new mercenaries of financial capitalism pursue the illusion of
paper wealth and financial rent.

Liberalism, in other words, has shown to be incapable of offering
a way out of the crisis. It has generated on the contrary new forms
of economic chaos, as a consequence of deregulation and financial
globalization. To understand liberalism and all its implications, it is
necessary to subdivide it into three types:

a. Doctrinal liberalism (Thatcherism)
b. Social-liberalism (Germany, Sweden)
c. Apparent liberalism (Japan, Reagan's US).

Every model of capitalism is based, always and anyway, on the exalta-
tion of the free market in which, although in different forms, speculative
financial economy will prevail against productive labour. But financial
capital, through its monetary flows and its monetary synthesis, in its
aspiration to obtain profits at better conditions exports at the same
time the contradictions of capitalism. For example, the subjective perception of welfare state crisis determines dramatic breaches of confidence in the political classes of a State, and a profound disconnection
from its institutions. Also, there is the fear of losing those privileges
that some middle class social groups have matured, on the perceived
ground that they belong to sectors and activities still included under
the State's social protection.

Privatization of public employment, public services, typical functions
of the State such as education, health, etc., are everywhere generating
phenomena of de-socialization and unification, at least ideally, between
former middle classes and the mass of people who are definitively left
off the circuit of work employment and hold a precarious future.

Clearly, the results derived from the choices of the new post-Fordist
cycle, focusing on a deep privatization of the economy and of social
culture and on a generalized flexibility, become a more general project
leading to a complete reconstruction of conflicts and social tensions.
Economic and industrial relations are based on the logic of a wild
global capitalism, which can no longer accept the Fordist mediation.
Contradictions between market rules and the security of a dignified

---

[1]

life for citizens-workers can be no longer solved starting from automatisms internal to the market and imposed by liberal policies through the mediation spaces of State and Keynesian interventions.

Nowadays, "wild," lawless capitalism is the dominant logic: it follows the simple realization of unscrupulous profit, creating serious social imbalances such as increased unemployment and a generalized low quality of life. The processes of conversion, restructuring and technological innovation are exclusively based on slashing employment, and on the compression of employees earned income: the "best" economic policies are based on increasing profits from tougher job cuts and labour and wages flexibility.

The financialization of the economy, achieved through investments made possible by the surplus of profits derived from not having distributed the productivity gains to the workers, the liberalization of trade and the benefits of the free circulation of goods, have granted to large enterprises a greater diversification of technology and equipment, including a differentiation of supply and customers.

The whole discourse has to be brought back to the logic of the financial bubble that does not lead to a real growth, but to an apparent one based on speculation with easy profits that, through computerized media, allows the instantaneous movement of thousands of billions that destabilize countries, control their economy and politics, stifle any processes of real economic democracy, leading to the neoliberal idea of a *Global Profit State*.

Neoliberal economic policy, focused on the processes of privatization, achieved a macroeconomic framework that highlights recessive trends in many areas, contraction and precarious employment, decrease in real wages, decrease in inflation due to a big drop in demand, a significant increase of poverty and marginalization, high rates of official unemployment and new, widespread hard economic and social conditions.

The above mentioned changes have led companies to develop and adopt decision models geared to maintain and improve their position in the market, trying to "reset and reinvent" the enterprise not only in structure, but also in its working mechanisms and its capacity of conditioning any social structure.

To achieve such transformations, it is necessary to act according to the so-called principle of flexibility, which can be adopted only if the company is able to adapt quickly to changes taking place within and outside the company itself. Talking about enterprise flexibility means essentially the ability of entrepreneurs, top management, enterprise's decision-makers to carry out adaptive business strategies that allow not only to produce different goods and services targeted to different markets, but also to manage the delicate strategic plan of conditioning the whole society to enterprise culture. For this reason more and more immaterial social structures and resources are used, following the principle of minimum cost and maximum benefit and realizing the highest degree of adaptability to the needs of the market, which has also become the market of social life.

Technological flexibility permits, simultaneously, to both increase productivity and create flexibility in production, thus determining a significant contraction in the volume of the labour- force and a decrease in the time needed for production. Labour is not available for everybody and the flexibility of work relationships makes life very precarious and unstable even for those who still hold a more or less permanent job.

So any form of social security or in general of guarantees of the Fordist era is completely eliminated from the productive transformation of the new post-Fordist model of the capitalism of flexible accumulation. The crisis of the labour system has significantly changed the whole society: its consequences have been structural unemployment, the end of the factory as a centre of production (at least in the countries of mature capitalism), the shift to immaterial labour and the increase of forms of subordinated employment with no rules, with a transfer of workers from the world of guaranteed labour to no guarantees at all.

Moreover, the collapse of the Fordist model led to the emergence of new models of flexible accumulation characterized by the increase of product differentiation, namely the process of diversifying products to make them more attractive to a particular target market. The principle that drives this model is based on the fact that, as demand fixes production in relation to models of apparent wild competition, international competition is increasingly based on product quality, labour quality characterized by knowledge resources produced by intangible capital, accompanied by underpaid, outsourced and non regulated labour, and services with a low content of guarantees, and no links between price and quantity produced (typical elements of Fordism).

The Financialization of Economics

Dominant macroeconomics explains that the rate of profit is equal to the rate of interest, because in a balanced economy all activities have the same productivity, the same profits, and also because money would move from one activity to another. The balance determines that the profit rate of production activities will be the same as in financial activities.

If the interest rate is higher than the rate of profit, money will be used not to produce shoes, but for financial assets: in debt or in fixed term deposit accounts.

One of the main characteristics of the economy in the 1980s was the dominance of financial capital. All around the world interest rates were higher than the rates of economic growth. Therefore, at the global level, a part of the surplus went to pay the increasing interest rates. Growth rates in the global economy were reduced by the growth of high interest rates, that is by the dominance of financial capital. This means that the drainage of resources from the productive economy to the financial economy was and still is enormous. This opens, particularly after the so-called sub-primes crisis, a debate in the very decision-making centres themselves of international capitalism about the necessity of a financial reform, because reducing the weight of financial sector is a key factor for a reform of the economic structure.

According to the received wisdom, it appears that the economic system should be closely linked to the financial system and, consequently, capital markets should have an independent life separated from the general economic and social context, because they represents a sort of thermometer of the credibility and efficiency of system-countries and of the whole of international capitalism. If we look at what happens in the daily reality of the market, we can observe that the most common patterns of this received wisdom are denied by the facts.

When everything is left to a blind faith in the laws of the market, without control mechanisms that preserve the collective social interest, the good performance of the stock exchange, financial profits create the conditions for the contraction of productive investment, the negative paths of the real economy that cause high structural unemployment and the increase of social costs in general. Very often there is a wide gap between the trend of the real economy and the size of the capital market. In England, for example, where there is the highest rate of market capitalization, the data of the real economy are discouraging; vice versa, Germany for instance, which has a strong hegemony of the productive economy, at least at the continental level, produces very little results in terms of the development of the stock market. So, a strong capitalization of the stock market does not necessarily provides an efficient and strong development of the real economy: frequently the so called "casino capitalism" rewards to the companies able to cut jobs, reduce the real wages distributed to employees, maximize the flexibility and mobility of workers and their remuneration.

We live in a capitalist system with financial connotations, a capitalism without laws, capable to justify everything with the hypothetical, apparent abilities of self-regulation of the markets.

With the financialization of the economy, exploded at the time of the energy crises of the 1970s, international capitalism has set in a context of increasing degenerative change, in the illusion that the increase in paper and electronic means of payment may be able to create real wealth. The inextricable link between neoliberal globalization and financialization demonstrates the enormous fragility of a capitalist model based on financial speculation, that distances itself from the real economy, in an attempt to solve, or rather hide, its structural crisis.

This is the true meaning of neoliberal globalization, a globalization of financial markets in which the absolute freedom of movement of capital prevails against labour, while the movements of people and goods continue to be subjected to protectionist policies with racial connotations.

In this situation of structural and systemic crisis the debate about radically alternative models of capitalist production becomes even more pressing, and many Marxist researchers start anew the study about the theory and the feasibility of a socialist economy.

CHAPTER NINE

THE OBJECTIVES OF THE SOCIALIST ECONOMIC MODEL

The Transition to Socialism: Different Approaches

The debate over plan and market can be traced back to the beginning of socialism in the Soviet Union. During the period of war communism, decisions were modelled through the direct assignment of the economic resources. Marx and Engels supposed that during socialism work may have also been directly social and that the action of the law of value should not be necessary to determine the economic aspects; this form of regulation was thought to be revolutionary, since it did not use the categories of the capitalist economy.

To accomplish its revolutionary tasks, the transition to capitalism experimented in countries with an unequal economic and political development depends upon the concrete historical conditions. For a thoughtful consideration of such processes, it is instructive to read Nove (1986a: 37) who, writing about the possibility of socialism and about what could a feasible socialism be, proposes to bring deep changes to certain basic concepts of classical marxism. Take for instance the strong critique to the concept of "abundance" (thought to be substantially unrealistic, exception made for some exceptional scientific discovery), which he proposes to substitute with the neoclassical concept of (absolute and relative) "scarcity," more realistic, according to Nove, and useful to economic analysis and to the planning processes. He is peremptory, for example, when he puts in his theoretical model a concept greatly utilized in dominant economics: opportunity cost:

> *being the resources (and time) limited,* everything has an opportunity cost (p.39).

No universal models for the construction of socialism can afford not to be directly connected to the particular situations of the different countries.

The problem is to conciliate the national planning directed by the State with the mechanisms of the market, which are in constant movement, and furthermore, use these mechanisms without letting them become dominant in the motivations and in men's consciences.

The disappearance of the socialist area has made more evident, and compelled to, use of mercantile instruments with the experimentation of forms of mixed economy, without which the enterprises of socialist economies could not survive in the voracious and cruel international market.

Even if the experience shows that it has been necessary to adapt to price and demand oscillations, and to look for funding and, in general, to act pursuant to the legal, commercial and financial rules of market relations, we must bear in mind that the existence of monetary-mercantile relations and the presence of market relations constitute elements that limit the development of the social relations of production in the construction of a socialist society. Moreover, market relationships generate uncertainty in the design of the planning process and the public policies that are associated to it, to the extent that they can act as a barrier against the identification of the objectives of social and economic policies. In this case the guidance role of the government in the management process must always be strategically oriented to the preservation of the basic values and the fundamental aims of the process of socialist construction.

Changes in Socialist Economic Models[1]

The first attempt towards a change in the USSR took place at the beginning of the 1960s, through the development of more sophisticated planning methods proposed by prestigious economists such as Kantorovic, Novozhilov and Strumilin. At that time, the use of computers and mathematical methods, like linear programming, investment tables and sector-based interdependence, were considered to be valid alternatives to the introduction of market mechanisms; but this directive has not had a decisive influence in the USSR. It has reached its most advanced expression and the most favourable results in the DDR (Eastern Germany).

The second attempt towards a change appears in China during the 1960s, developed by Mao Zedong, with a first phase between 1958 and

---

[1] For a deepening of this matter, look at the following texts: Itoh (1995); Novozhilov (1975); Strumilin (1966); Gonzàlez (1997: 2–11); AA. VV. (2002); AA. VV. (2004).

1960 called "The Great Leap Forward," and another from 1966 to 1976, determined by the Cultural revolution. Such last phase was characterized by the political mobilization of the masses for the accomplishment of important economic objectives, the socioeconomic local development at the communities level, the reduction to the minimum of private producers and mercantile relations, and, finally, the attack onto bureaucratic structures and styles, moderated through a high level of political and state control of culture and of the daily life of the citizens.

The third attempt, known as (decentralized) market reform, began in the USSR with the transformations relative to the perfecting of planning, starting from 1965 and lasting until the first half of the 1980s. It melted itself into a combined model which conserved the essential characteristics of a centralized system, but with the intention to tend towards decentralization. This orientation was more accentuated in the socialist countries of Eastern Europe, especially in Poland, Czechoslovakia and Hungary, where it reached its maximum splendour.

It is necessary to refer to the exhaustion of the capabilities of the process of socialist construction in some of these countries, especially in Eastern Europe. The historical conditions which led to the construction of socialism, left their mark over the region and every country which was part of it. The acceleration of the political processes on the thrust of external forces and the underestimation of the historical and national characteristics of such processes, in countries such as for instance Poland and Hungary, led to beginning the socialist construction from imposed conditions, far from the actual capabilities of the country to pursue socialism respecting its internal social-economic characteristics. (AAVV, 1991: 19; AAVV, 2002: 75).

We must also consider the economic wearing out caused by the technological and military race, stimulated by the principal imperial powers and supported by the former USSR, together with the ideological penetration of the capitalist market economies in different spheres of the leadership and in various layers of the populations. Finally, we also have to notice the lack of equalization of the mechanisms of social policies to the levels of development reached by the different countries. All this reasons have prevented the political and economic legitimization of socialism in Oriental Europe.

It is also useful to consider the process of application in the USSR of the so-called *perestrojka* in 1985, which accelerated the decomposition of the mechanism of socialist construction as conceived until that period, deepening the contradictions of the system, favouring a trend which led to the antisocialist tendencies, which eventually caused the construction of the capitalist market economy.

Special Features of Some Economic Planning Models

The Socialist Economy and the Capitalist Economy

The Classical political economists considered the economy as a science which studies the models and processes of formation and distribution of the countries' wealth, while the Neoclassicists emphasized the operational modalities realized by individuals to satisfy their needs, because these actions cause choices functional to the limited means at their disposal. This is the reason for the development of the neoclassical concept of neutrality: the aim of the researcher should be the study of the optimal way, i.e., the more rational and efficient way, to realize that purpose. The observation of reality has always shown the nonexistence of the concept of neutrality with respect to the aims, also because every economic model is by itself the synthetic formulation of an economic theory that in capitalist society necessarily takes after the forms of political-economic-social domination of capital. For this reason the so-called market economy, that is the liberal, and in the present sense "neoliberal" approach, is a systematic structure in which everything is left "to the free initiative of the private individuals in a frame of free competition" with the minimal functions of a state considered to be a necessary damage.

This is, obviously, all in a theoretical sense; a planned economy, often defined as collectivist, is an economic system in which the property of the means of production belongs to the state and the State itself takes the decisions relative to investments, production and the distribution of incomes, that may assume a centralized or decentralized form. For a certain number of years, some economies of the advanced capitalist countries, and in this sense Italy has had a leading role, have applied the so-called mixed economy, in which, also through the assignment of the property of the production means to the privates, the State assumed a role of direction of economic activity through regulative economic and interventionist politics, geared to create employment especially through public enterprises. It is not certainly wrong to conclude that certain problems are similar also in economic systems different in method and in formulation, even allowing that economic problems have a dissimilar importance and various are the solutions.

The fundamental difference between the capitalist economy and the socialist economy, as we have often repeated, is in the field of the objectives. In capitalism, the objective of economic activity is the attainment of maximum profits, under the form of monetary excess or *surplus*. In socialism instead, the objective of the economy is to guarantee the maximum level of welfare to the population. Such fundamental difference is ignored in the greatest part of comparative economy analysis, in spite of its utility in the determination of the rules of economic functioning and in the fixation of the optimum of production and consumption. Maurice Dobb (1972a) shows the incoherence of the attempts to build a theory of social welfare on capitalist bases, pointing out the incompatibility between the maximization of social welfare and the maximization of profits.

Broadly speaking, capitalism works only if the means of production are private property, because only in this way the organization of the production process may be oriented to the maximization of the profits. The competition between capitals determines the efficient and effective assignment of the resources in form of final profitability. The existence of public property enterprises does not modify such overall organization of production, but only if these enterprises accept the accounting criteria (costs and efficiency) proper of the market laws. Therefore, for our aims, whenever the economic activities are subjected to the rules of competition between private capitals, public property is equivalent to a form of private property. In such context, the assessments and fiscal charges represent an income obtained from the workers' and capitalists' profit, and their higher or lesser level, just as their social destiny, does not interfere with the system's principles of functioning.

The degree of property dispersion and the relative number of operators who adopt production decisions influences the functioning of the capitalist economic system, but not its fundamental rules. Also in situations of sector-based monopoly, competition exists in three principal forms: competition between capitals, which channels the investments' flux towards the activities perceived as more profitable; competition between capital and labour, which determines the distribution of the value added between capital's income (profit) and wages; competition between workers, which guarantees the capability of capital to take possession of a substantial part of added value, lowering the wages/productivity relation.

These three forms of competition manifest themselves inside the sectors just as much as between sectors, that is at the level of the economy as a totality. If an economy organizes itself responding to the logic of maximum profit, it cannot substitute such principle without transforming the juridical and social order on which it sustains itself, that is the dominance of private property and wage-earning work.

The differences in basic macroeconomic mechanisms of socialism and capitalism

1. The fundamental characteristics of a socialist economy may be summarized in two principles:

   a. The predominance of collective property of the fundamental and credit-based production means; and
   b. general orientation of the economy to the maximization of social wealth.

   These principles mean that under socialism, macroeconomic decisions are taken before the micro-economic ones, conditioning the decisions of the single productive agents (in capitalism the procedure is inverse). This principle of macroeconomic determination generates three functional characteristics which differentiates socialism from capitalism:

   a. the optimum level of production in socialism is not equal to the optimum level in capitalism;
   b. the investment decisions are based on macroeconomic criteria, while in capitalism the decisions based on macro-economic considerations are more important;
   c. economic calculations are based on production prices and not on market prices, as in capitalism

2. The optimal level of socialist production does not coincide with capitalism in volume or composition. In socialism the optimal level in volume coincides with the maximum, under the restriction of the minimization of the excesses. The investment decisions and the decisions to increase or decrease production have to be articulated in time and in quantity between the sectors both as intermediate consumptions and as final products. On the contrary, according to the capitalist principles of maximum profit, the optimum level of production does not just determine itself increasing the volume of production, but in many occasions also restricting such volume to alter the relation between supply and demand, and

obtain extraordinary profits through an increment of market prices. In fact, the bigger is the degree of property concentration, the further it gets from the potential maximum volume. Waste is a reality of the functioning of capitalism.[2] In particular, there is a massive and permanent waste of human resources, which are kept in situations of unemployment and underemployment. The dissipation of material resources in not strictly socially necessary production; that is, unsold productions[3] is also frequent.

3. Macroeconomic planning exists both in capitalist and in socialist economies. Here are two quotations among those reported by Johansen.

The first one is by the British economist H.D. Dickinson, from 1938. According to his definition, planning is the "taking of fundamental economic decisions – what and how much must be produced, whom has it to be assigned – through the conscious decision of a determined authority, on the basis of a systematic revision of the entire economic system".

In capitalism, planning is limited to the investment decisions realized by the state to provide the social services and the investments in infrastructures. Some private operators realize a micro-economic planning of their activities on their own, which in the case of financial agents and large multinational corporations affect prices and quantities, conditioning the macro-economic balances. Anyway, such planning is realized outside any form of coordination *ex ante* of the operators. It is a private planning, which passes always through the market's check to establish *ex post* its adequacy to the criterion of profitability. Also in the socialist economies, markets accomplish a function, determining some prices and above all contributing to reveal certain variations of demand. As Laibman (2006b) says:

> We will never insist enough on this point: the market ideology does not acquire its preponderance because of the operation of capitalist "ideological apparatus" (the State, the media, the instruction), it is the daily life which distillates it autonomously. This means that

---

[2] The waste of material resources is also caused by the fast obsolescence of the products. Antunes (2006), taking up Meszàros, writes about the *decreasing utilization rate of the use value of goods.*

[3] Bowles, Gordon, Weisskpof (1989) analyse the wastes of the northern American economy, accelerated by the application of the neo-liberal formulas since the 1980s. Sauvy (1972) analyse the planned obsolescence of the products as a normal designing and fabrication system in the capitalism of our times.

it is deceitful to see the ideology "of" market repeated by the left in many erudite texts that confound market with its capitalist historical forms. Such things prevent the comprehension of an essential fact: markets are reality inserted in the society, they evolve and have pre-capitalist, capitalist and post-capitalist forms.

Anyway, inside capitalist reality the basic mechanism for the allocation of the resources is the market, because it is through the market that the private production and investment decisions are ratified as well as the distribution of social work that derives from these decisions. Planning is limited – it does not influence the heart of investment decisions, which concerns installed capability, its utilization and technological change – and being practised only by particular operators, it is fragmentary and defined in the micro-economic level of the entrepreneurial group or the concrete financial entity which implements it. At the centre of such differences there is the process of decision relative to investments: in capitalism, decisions are taken inside the enterprise, and so they form part of the microeconomic functioning of accumulation. The existence of an important portion of investments realized by the public sector, defined at a macro-economic level, does not contradict what we said above, due to its subordinated character, mainly limited to the realization of infrastructures and non mercantile services typical of the public investment in capitalism. At this level, then, the difference between the two systems does not reside much in the dichotomy market/planning, as in the character of planning, which in socialism is coordinated, although it can be centralized as much as decentred. Planning determines the assignation of social work and the investment decisions fundamental for the economy, while market plays a limited and subordinated role. The causal relations, in both of the systems, are described by the following scheme:

– Capitalism: Market (macro) → Planning (micro)
– Socialism: Planning (macro) → Market (micro)

The contents of planning are substantially different between the two systems. In a socialist economy, plans are based on the balance of resources and uses, which are accounted for in material terms. In capitalist economies, physical balances still exist in agricultural accounting. In a socialist economy, on the contrary, material balances can be applied both to agricultural and to industrial activities, to reflect in one single scheme the internal connections of the fundamental processes of enlarged socialist reproduction. Naturally, such balances can be used also for every activity singularly considered.

This means that for a single product, steel for example, we can use a specific material balance:

- Resources: Stocks in the first part of the year – previsions of production – previsions of importation
- Uses: Stocks at the end of the year – previsions of internal consume – detailed for region – detailed for branches of production – exported quantities (Bremond and Geledan,1985).

Prices play a different role in both systems. In a capitalist economy prices are determined once the distribution of the value added between capital and labour has been established, i.e., when we have the average or "normal" rate of profit of the economy. Prices depend on the technical conditions of production and from the input costs.[4] The economic advantages of a sector (higher organic composition of capital, with productivity higher than the sector average) or oligopolistic domination, allow some enterprises to fix a higher rate of profit (the one that conventional economy considers as applied by all of the enterprises and which determines the markup). This facilitates the accumulation of surplus value in enterprises and sectors technologically more advanced and with more oligopolistic power. The procedure of fixing the "market" prices briefly described here has nothing, or not much, to do with Walras' equilibrium theory, whose fixing of prices consists in an auction procedure in the market between supply and demand, which requires a previously realized production with no price.

Two special kinds of prices, wages and interest, express the participation of the producers of added value and of the perceivers of income to the sharing of the spoils. Even if the movements of the relative prices in the long period are conditioned by the relative variations of productivity, in the short period, the market prices are very inadequate signals for the decisional process and they hide more information than they reveal, both with respect to the structure of the market of production, and with respect to the conditions of major or minor sector-based competition in which production develops itself. Since relative prices depend on distribution, the totality of prices may be established only

---

[4] The analytic presentation of this idea can be found in Sraffa (1982), who proposes a determined model. It is obvious that at the same time in which we determine the normal profit, we establish the wage average, through a process that has not much to do with the marginal productivities (that can only express themselves as dynamic limit) and has much to do with the conjunctional and structural conditions of the fight between capital and work.

in a simultaneous form. This shows a contradiction between the capitalist dynamic macro-economy of prices and historical time, which sets a temporal succession and an inter-sector articulation of the flux of goods and work.

The crisis, as an expression of unrealized values (that means of non validated production through the mercantile inter-exchange from the quantity of money expressed through the price) convert themselves in the regular functioning of economy.[5]

In socialism, prices are a direct index of the material costs, reflecting the classical notion of natural prices (Smith, Ricardo) or production prices (Marx). Prices must reflect the contents of direct and non-direct production work with the maximum precision possible.

The difficulty in the simultaneous measurement of the consumption of indirect work (incorporated in the intermediate consumption) is what blocks the realization of the calculations directly in labour-value, and requests a sequential procedure based on index numbers and other technical procedures which allow an approximation of such values under the price form. When the calculations detach themselves from the reference values, they produce sector-based misbalances. Such misbalances are, anyway, strictly technical, tied to the limitations of the measurement practices: So we can define them as "conjunctural". In capitalism, instead, market prices incorporate the structural tendency to the misbalance of accumulation.

The Model of Centralized and Decentralized Planning

This model is characterized by the degree of adoption of the decisions which, at the economy level, is concentrated at the level of the central apparatus of the government and of the state, exception made for the individual ones. These decisions comprehend volume and composition of the investments, of consumption and of foreign exchange; the levels of production and material resources that could guarantee them; prices, aspects and wage increments; basic services and other nonproductive activities. As a factor of economic and accounting coordination, the so-called method "of the balance of material goods," expressed in physical terms, is utilized.

---

[5] Inflation, far from reflecting the structural misbalances between supply and demand, appears to be an instrument of the fight to catch major quotes of the added or exceeding value from the capitalists. See Mandel, Valzer, Jourdain (1970).

The model of decentralized planning starts from the possibility not to consider the market as a general regulator of economic activity (law of value), with the use of the market instruments that will be called to perform specific economic functions inside a general mechanism, regulated by planning.

Consider that the enterprises, starting from an initial endowment of fixed and circulating capitals, organize in autonomous way the productive process, selecting the quantity and the production dynamic, other than the cost structure.

The Reformed Model

In the countries where this model is applied, in major or minimum degree, the necessity to integrate the existent modalities with a bigger use of the monetary-mercantile relations and a more effective entrepreneurial autonomy is recognized. Here are some principles of the model:

a. At a theoretical level, Ota Sik[6] considered that mercantile production in socialism is an objective necessity determined by the possible contradictions of the socialist work, given by the development degree of the productive forces.

b. The problem of decentralization is not only a question of knowledge but also of interests conciliation which cannot be obtained through administrative methods. The model of decentralized management is not an option possible if united to other models, but a necessity inherent to socialist production;

c. Investments had to be financed by the enterprise funds or credits and these took part to the elabouration of the long term plans and projects' selection;

d. Reforms have in reality always been accompanied by strong internal and external imbalances; the remunerations in the enterprises grew without a corresponding productive answer. The internal credit and the budget deficit grew in an uncontrolled way, inflation grew and the volume of importations to satisfy the internal request. According to scholars like Kornai, a big part of the economic advancements came from the so-called second economy (informal sector, private, illicit, *non state*).

---

[6] Czech economist who foresaw the possibility of a construction of socialism in presence of the role of market.

The Flexible Dual Model

The periods of transformation in China (1966–76 with the cultural revolution, 1976–1981, 1984–85 period to which the reform is referred) gradually created a dual model, giving as result three fundamental kinds of enterprise:

a. state enterprises in strategic areas such as energy, transport, tele-communications and in key productions of intermediate goods;
b. the sector of large and medium enterprises, in which only a small percentage of the capability is employed in productions in the frame of national programming, with decisional faculties on the remaining part of the activity which will be regulated by the macro-economic policies;
c. a third sector of small state emprises, of private and collective property, which functioned following market rules.

PART FIVE

A CRITIQUE OF ECONOMICS AS APPLIED TO THE WORLD
SYSTEM: OPEN ECONOMY AND IMPERIALISM

CHAPTER TEN

INTERNATIONAL TRADE AND IMPERIALISM

Long Cycles and the Internationalization of Markets

It is necessary to analyse the misbalances and the inequalities provoked by an unequal capitalist development and by the emersion of new international agreements, of new state communities, of new areas of exchange, of new value areas internal to the actual capitalist polarization connected to the present international division of work and to the consequent productive specialization. Our critique of economics aims to point out in a scientific way the features of the actual phase of the capitalist universalization intended as *global competition*, or as a dimension of the actual phase of imperialism. We are still convinced that one of the specific characteristics of capitalism is the form adopted by imperialism.

Relations of domination existed for a long time, but under capitalism imperialism adopts a substantially economic form. In the recent years, especially as a consequence of the international policies of the *neocon* administration of Bush Jr., in the Anglo-Saxon world many intellectuals organic to the US (and British) establishment support a return to imperialist politics, deemed necessary because of the world-wide chaos produced by the strength of some foes: for instance the ill-famed *rogue States*, on which cf. Chomsky (2001) and Blum (2005) or weak States (Cooper 1996; 2004). In short, imperialist politics does not represent anymore a "dangerous deviation" with respect to peaceful and multilateral international relations, but an added value to the US power. Such views, which have the merit of explaining the strategies and the political-military practices planned by the White House in the last decade, presented in various international geopolitical publications, have obvious limits: they give a partial and "interested" view of imperialism. This is reduced to the mere military aspect, with which the U.S. and their *Coalition of the Willing* seek to solve the international problems of instability and criminality (whether they are real or potential). In short, such (military) imperialism is supposed to be the *answer* of a Western world compelled by international terrorism to save the world.

Before capitalism, the political and economic submission to the empire was a mechanism of wealth appropriation implemented by the imperial forces, but this did not happen systematically, and generally did not modify the basic social structures of the subjected societies.

Under capitalism, on the contrary, imperialistic relations condition form and content of material production in the subjected territories; its socioeconomic structures adapt to the necessities of wealth consumption and capital valorisation by the imperial force. This happens independently from the fact that imperialism includes colonialism, like in the times of the French-British domination of Africa and Asia in the XIX century, or has a post-colonial content, of formal political independence of the dominated territories, like in the period of the imperial domination of the United States.

The necessity of economic imperialism for a correct functioning of capitalism has been analyzed initially by the British labourist economist J.A. Hobson (1902). However, with the Marxist authors of the first part of XX century we got the development of a true theory of imperialism: Kautsky (1898), Hilferding (1910), Luxembourg (1913) and Bucharin (1915).

Lenin (1917) synthesizes all these contributions in the most well known text, *Imperialism, the Highest Phase of Capitalism*, in which he draws the political consequences of the analysis of the imperial dimension of the process of capitalist accumulation.[1]

The fundament of capitalist imperialism consists in the appropriation of the value generated by the workers in the countries dominated by the imperial power.

It is important that we reflect about the strict relationship that ties the dynamic of the long cycles of capitalist reproduction with the course of the internationalization of capital; this gives us the possibility to make some consideration about the actual international situation and its possible tendencies.

The expansion of foreign commerce, with the development of the production regime, is an internal necessity, i.e., its appetite for bigger markets continues its transformation. The processes of goods' exportation and the process of colonial domination of the capitalist centre on its periphery, erect themselves as fundamental characteristics of

---

[1] For an attentive and articulate exam of the argument cf. Vasapollo, Jaffe, Galarza (2005).

capital's internationalization in the conditions of pre-monopolist capitalism. In the long-term dynamics of capitalist development, the first acknowledged long wave of expansion, which goes approximately from 1790 to 1823 and was a phenomenon substantially limited to Great Britain, acted as a scenario for the consolidation of the domination system over the periphery under the British hegemony.

The second wave of expansion, which goes approximately from 1850 to 1873, accompanied by the instauration of the technological mechanized way of production, generated a deep advancement in the development of railway and maritime transport, as well as in the communication sector, letting new countries rapidly join the industrialization process, relying on the foreign commerce. In such way an enlargement of the influence of the peripheral domination of the imperialist centres took place: fundamentally Great Britain, United States of America and Germany. The third cycle of the expansionist wave of the capitalist long cycle, which goes approximately from 1894 to 1914, was interrupted by the First World War and was reactivated between 1920 and 1929. It represents a milestone in the qualitative transformation of the process of internationalization of capital. It breaks up in the sphere of production. The export of capitals sums up with the export of goods as one of the essential aspects of the domination of capital, now transformed from simple industrial capital to monopoly finance capital. This capital export, supported by international monopolies, represents a new phase of the international capitalist division of the labour between rich and poor countries.

This process has been completed with the economic division of the world by the great monopolist aggregates, and the territorial division of the world between the great powers, delineating the existence of a colonial monopoly that enlarged itself gradually from the end of XIX century to the beginning of the XX. In this phase there were hostilities between England, the USA and Germany, above all between the last two, for the world hegemony, because Great Britain could not keep, after 1873, the previous level of development, and was losing its dominating role in innovations, undergoing at the same time a diminution in the growth rates of industrial production.

During this historical phase, the fundamental characteristic of the international capitalist division of labour could be appreciated in the mechanized consolidation of the technological production process in the so-called centre of capitalism. In the periphery, instead, in an important number of countries, the consolidation of phenomena peculiar to backward economies takes place: mono-production, mono-exportation and mono-market, poor and unilateral industrial techno-logical development, phenomena which, through the unequal exchange and the other consequences of internationalization, transform the economy in a world context polarized under the influence of the world domination of capital.

The lengthened shockwave of the fourth long cycle of life of capi-tal, which happens around 1945 and 1973, has its principal scenario in the new accumulation model of the United States, even if Japan and some European countries (especially Germany) are gaining ground. At the end of this period we can notice the consolidation of three imperialist centres. Technologically characterized by the passage from the technological mechanized way of production to the automated one, but with the former still very important, such cycle allows the definitive intensive economic growth of the capitalist centre and favours an internationalization process of the productive capital cycle guided by the transnational enterprises. Such process can be distin-guished not only for the levels of quantitative proliferation of the multinational enterprises, but fundamentally for the fact that these enterprises are deeply interrelated by means of national and transna-tional capitals. This for the first time leads to a conception of capital-ist reproduction as an international process. For all these reasons, this internationalization development stage goes under the name of "transnationalization".

During this phase, the accumulation model is based on the Keynes-ian recipes; new dimension and quality relationships in the capitalist international work division are weaved together.

The structural crisis which provoked the long depressive phase, which starts approximately from 1973–74, even if some hints can be found also in 1971, with the end of the Bretton Wood agreements, con-ditioned a gradual process of economic restructuring which embraced both aspects of the restructuration of the productive relations and aspects of the comprehensive socioeconomic relations, which will con-tinue to acquire international character.

This gradual process of restructuration, which manifested itself in the last decades, constituted the scenario of a transition from the tech-nological mechanized way of production to the automated one, and at the same time the complete manifestation of a new stage of existence of capital's internationalization and of the international capitalist labour division.

The acknowledgment of the objective existence of long alternate accelerated and decelerated waves of development as a normal and regular characteristics of capitalism allows us to realize the emptiness of all the triumphal pro-globalization and pro-externalization claims about capitalism, and allows us to realize that we are living a process of double importance in capitalism's existence: the full development of the imperialist phase, configured by global competition, and simultaneously the formation of the material base for its necessary substitution with a more evolved economic regime.

Simultaneously to these processes, we witness a new phase of the system of contradictions typical of capitalism, in particular of those between wealth and poverty, technological development and unemployment, technological development and the ecosystem, which can be better expressed in terms of conflict (capital-labour, capital-environment, capital-rights) but at the same time in the valorisation of the universalization of the social relations of capitalist production.

It is necessary to point out how the phenomenon of internationalization is enacted through international commerce and the direct and productive foreign investment, through which a certain enterprise acquires the characteristics of a multinational by creating or acquiring production branches in different countries.[2] Direct investments in foreign land (DIF) are pursued practically by those enterprises which want to expand in other countries through the creation of a new productive establishment or acquiring the participation quotes of already existing companies.[3]

It is not by chance that the attention is directed in a specific way at the international dynamics of commerce and investment, whether they are portfolio investments (more closely tied to the financial-speculative aspect), or they are direct foreign investments oriented to

---

[2] Such formula of investment looks after various needs, like "the impossibility to produce sufficient quantities in the origin country, particularly for what concerns the primary sector, for reasons connected to the lack of natural resources; the impossibility to sell sufficient quantities in the destination countries for reasons both connected to the nature of the products and connected to the protective barriers; the possibility to benefit of the compared macroeconomic advantages of the settlement countries, particularly in the developing countries, which generally present low wage costs" (Lafay 1996: 40–41, translated from the Italian edition).

[3] In other words, "such investment is made with the purpose to acquire decisional power in a foreign emprise. It comprehends new plants, fusions, current acquisitions between the mother societies and their foreign branches, and other than that a part of this investment can assume the form of acquisition of quotes of the society capital" (Eurostat 1995; 241 translated from the Italian).

the control of a company (more related to a productive nature). The successive analysis relies on these dimensions of the international economy because they are the ones which more than anything else represent the economic dimension of imperialism.

The Role of International Trade

The conditions of the enlargement of the competition on an international scale are easily visible and material. They are historically identified in the success and diffusion of the informatics and telematics technologies, and in the global diminution of transport cost, which permit an easy movement of commodities and determines the absolute convenience of the delocalization of production in contexts more favourable to capital. (Various Authors, 2003: 11).

It is not only through the movement of the financial interests that we can identify the flux tied to the imperialist relations. International trade transformed itself during the XIX century becoming the system Great Britain privileged to impose to the colonies the mechanisms of international appropriation of value, destroying in the process their productive capacity to favour the English manufacturing exportations, and imposing an international division of labour to the benefit of the capital accumulation of the British enterprises.[4]

In the transition from competitive to monopolist capitalism, from 1876 to World War I, the world industrial production quadruples itself and industrial exchanges triple their volume, while the world population increases of more than 25%.

In this period the increment in international commerce is parallel between the industrialized centre, which exchanges handmade products, and the colonies and dominated countries, which export raw materials.

In the period between the two world wars there is a series of events which affect international trade negatively: monetary crisis, galloping inflation, devaluations, alterations of the international monetary system, the 1929 crisis, the depression of the 1930s, protectionism and the block of international commerce. However, the weight of commerce from the periphery to the centre grows, even if at lower rates than in

---

[4] Cf. over this argument Walter Rodney (1972), who helps us reminding that colonialist capitalism is a result of European and not of northern American imperialism.

the period before the first world war, as a consequence of the necessary supply of the industry of developed countries.

After WWII, colonialist imperialism is substituted by new political and economic relations which allow the old colonies to achieve formal independence, contemporarily to the establishment of new bonds of dependence and domination, weaved by the new dominant power, the United States.

In the new post-colonialist imperialism, the ideology of free commerce has a central role in strengthening the international division of labour of imperialist origin. At the same time, the existence of anti-capitalist revolutionary processes, which subtract a substantial part of the world territory to the dynamic of capitalist accumulation, helps the economic ideology in the invention of a new discourse in the 1950s, quantitative development, as a surreptitious way aimed at the growth and improvement of wealth in the countries of peripheral capitalism.

The failure of the strategies of capitalist development of the periphery was clearer after the crisis which devastated Latin America and Africa during the 1980s.

In parallel, in South East Asia developed, in the context of the Cold War between capitalism and socialism, a regional industrialized pole (in countries like Taiwan, South Korea and Singapore) based on northern American help and on Japanese investments, and on the start of an accelerated accumulation process centred on forms of protective State capitalism, which supplied resources.

The UNCTAD[5] statistics allow us to identify the structural evolution of world trade by regions and groups of countries. The participation in world trade is very unequal; the central countries concentrate the 60–70% of the world commerce, and the peripheral countries around 25–30%, while the socialist countries represent a 10%. The trade between developed countries realizes a 70%, while the exchanges with the periphery represent a 25%, and with socialist countries a 5%. In the decades between 1960–80, even if the value of international trade increases by ten, its volume increases only by three, reflecting a substantial growth of the price of exportable goods, deriving for the major part from the developed countries.

---

[5] See United Nations Conference on Trade and Development (several years).

Since 1980, we witness a restructuration in the international division of labour, in which we do not find any longer a marked specialization for productive sectors. In effect, since 1980 the handmade products represent a growing percentage in all of the peripheral countries, both in those with a sustained development and in those with lesser development.

Between 1980 and 2002 the volume of world trade is increased threefold, as in the previous twenty years, and its value multiplied by 3,1: the unitary value of the world commerce, that is, does not grow. The reason is in the change produced in the international division of labour in the age of the so-called "globalization," started with the 1980s.

In the new international division of labour, space is occupied by the multinational enterprises that can divide the production process delocalizing it with the new technologies which permit the fragmentation of productive processes, to make profit from the cost differences of the labour force. In this way we have a new, true proletariat on a world scale, in strong international and inter-sector[6] competition.

The strong increase of industrial exports of the peripheral countries derives from their insertion in the "world factory" designed by the multinationals, in which the plant localized in the poor countries is the one in the worst shape, which uses more workers, but which contemporarily realizes less added value, with the lowest wages and the highest exploitation rates.

As evidenced by the data of the unitary value of exports, the peripheral countries are the ones which suffer a decrease of the unitary added value in the last years, included the principal manufactures exporters. On the contrary the developed countries, in spite of the dumping[7] prices applied to their agricultural exports, increase the unitary value of their exports with respect to the 1980s.

Such changes in the international division of labour and in the advantages gained through commerce by some countries, make us wonder about the foundations of the theory of international trade, which remains substantially the same enunciated by David Ricardo in 1816, in the VII chapter of his *Principles of Political Economy and Taxation*. Criticizing this theory will permit us to establish the principles of imperialism in matters of international commerce.

---

[6] On this cf. Martufi, Vasapollo (2000a); Casadio, Petras, Vasapollo (2003).

[7] Sale at lower price respect the cost price (subsidized selling prices).

A Critique of the Theory of International Specialization through Trade

The traditional concept of "capital" considers, differently from land and labour, the realized production means. A capital endowment found in many HOS analysis is simply given in quantity; it is apparently about a homogeneous input and often does not consist in production means, because the only productive sectors are sectors of consumption goods. However, a capital endowment is not the same thing as a land endowment, and then the properties of a HOS analysis with a given endowment of capital cannot be the same with a given endowment of land, for the only reason that "capital value" is definable only in terms of relative prices, which are solved within the analysis.

In this way it is not so clear what it means that a country has an endowment of capital of a given value; which unit is used to measure this endowment? Even if these conundrums could be solved, there is no reason for the capital-labour relation of any sector to be inversely proportional to the profit rate; it is not necessary either that between two goods it is the relative price of the more capital intensive to increase, increasing the profit rate.

In other words, two of the primary properties of the HOS analysis, based on land, cannot be transferred by analogy to the version based on a given endowment of capital.[8] Consequently, the HOS theory does not have much to say about the growth of production and commerce which depends on the increment of the investments - capital goods. The HOS theory does not help understand the effect of the behaviour of consumption on trade.

The HOS theory is still the received wisdom in economics to interpret international trade. We must add, however, that many scholars contributed alternative approaches of various degrees of completeness. They go from the so-called theory of availability or the theories of income effect (for example the Linder theory and the Barker theory) to the more well-known theory of the product cycle. This last, created by Hirsch and Vernon, explains how every product realizes its life cycle in three phases:

1. The introductive phase of the new product
2. The phase of development or maturation
3. The phase of standardization or maturity

---

[8] A critical analysis of the neo-classical model in Gerard Destanne de Bernis (1987, ch. I; IV; X).

According to such theory, due to the fact that not all countries have the same possibility of access to technology, they will specialize in the production of a certain kind of goods and will export them, basing on their capability to apply technologies to the creation of new products. Generally, the countries with a high level of industrial and technological development will produce and export goods that are in the first phase of production of their life, that is recently invented products; countries with an intermediate level of industrialization will produce and export goods that are in their second phase of the life cycle, the maturity one; finally, the developing countries will produce and export goods in the third phase, the standardization one.

Despite the theory of product cycle attributing a particular importance to the level of technological knowledge reached by a country to explain its position in the international exchanges, it cannot be used to explain technological gaps and economic backwardness.

CHAPTER ELEVEN

INTERNATIONAL ECONOMIC RELATIONS FROM THE POINT OF VIEW OF THE THEORY OF IMPERIALISM

Marx's Approach

The central point of Marx's economic theory is, as it has been showed so far, the analysis of the tendencies of capitalism, regardless of the will and conscience of men. Marx discovers the internal economic laws on which capital circulation is based and, on this basis, he proves the historical limit of the capitalist system and the inevitability of the success of socialism. Since the conditions are not fully developed, Marx describes the transition to socialism as an historical tendency of capitalist accumulation (Section VII, Chapter XXIV of the first book of *Capital*), and argues that capitalism inevitably leads to the expropriation of the expropriators on a global scale. In Marx's analysis it is possible to identify some key points for interpreting international relations:

a. The continuous centralization of production and capital. As a result the number of business magnates of capital[1] constantly decreases.
b. This process creates "the international character of the capitalist regime".
c. In these historical conditions the monopoly of capital is turned into the engine of the regime of production. The centralization of the means of production and the socialization of labour get to a point where they are incompatible with respect to their capitalist framework.[2]

Since social practice is the criterion by which the accuracy of theoretical principles is measured, new fundamental phenomena that arose within the capitalist system, should be examined.

---

[1] This innovative approach to Marx is recognized even by his honest opponent, Mark Blaug (1995).
[2] It should be noted, however, how socialization is informed by the capitalist parameters.

Although these phenomena do not change the essence of the way production is pursued, it is essential to decipher the 'undergrowth' of new forms that work as scaffolding, a superstructure of the old capitalism, hiding it even more. The Imperialist phase does not expose the essence of capitalism, but makes it more complex and hides it behind a facade that we can call of 'second degree'. The essence of the birth of the monopolist phase is integral part of the mechanism of capitalist accumulation analysed by Marx in section VII of Book One of Capital.[3]

It is important to draw attention to the fact that free competition occurred right from the pre-monopolist capitalism as the antithesis of a monopoly,[4] and that it gave the capitalists, who benefited from a temporary monopoly, the privilege of permanently enjoying extraordinary profits. It is incorrect to say that monopoly is the antithesis of competition.

As Karl Marx himself states, "The monopoly produces competition, the competition creates a monopoly. The monopolists compete with each other, the competitors become monopolists" (Marx 1974: 149).

Formation of Financial Capital 'Kf'

Fictitious capital creates the possibility of merging industrial capital with banking capital under a single, new monopolist unit, since the industrial monopoly capital and the banking monopoly capital become functional forms of existence of finance capital. In the capitalist system, capitals invested in industry and banks cannot absorb or dissolve one another, so they maintain an independent existence within their processes of reproduction and circulation. All this proves that even if finance capital is fictitious, it exists primarily as monopolized financial capital.

The fusion, as a structural union in a single monopoly, is essentially done in terms of fictitious capital, even if its foundation is real capital. Monopolized fictitious capital often relies on securities that are managed by bankers before becoming property of the owners, and banks keep on managing it even after the owner received them. A considerable part of the fictitious capital of industrial monopolies is

---

[3] Cf. Morales (2004b).
[4] Here is recalled that, according to the 'traditional' classification of different types of market, it is divided into: a) competition b) a monopolistic competition; c) oligopoly d) monopoly. *Sub* types b) and c) are called 'imperfect competition' markets.

found in the direct ownership of banks and it becomes part of actual capital.

The combination of a banking monopoly and an industrial monopoly can be obtained without joining them into a new monopolist structure. It is sufficient that there is a tight union validated by financial ties, by a community of big shareholders, by the personal union of management, etc. These are very tight ties and there are levels of subordination, established between the functional forms of finance capital. So they are ties that are based on indirect relations that are both stable and flexible, long-term relations of reliance for the ownership of shares. Lenin, taking into account some of the features of finance capital, observed that it was a particularly flexible and mobile one, but also impersonal and detached from direct production, that lends itself to concentration and can easily be combined through the forms of participation. All these phenomena occur in the transitional period of free-competition capitalism, but still not as dominant forms.

Lenin's Theory of Imperialism

Lenin's theory of imperialism resulted from the need to interpret the new phenomena of the development of capitalism. Lenin developed an intense research that was summarized in his *Philosophical Notes* (1914–1916), in his *Notes on Imperialism* (1915–1916), in his book *Imperialism, the Highest Stage of Capitalism* (1915).

Nowadays, in the midst of the processes of the so-called neoliberal globalization, the underlying structure of changes that have occurred during the 1980s and, more generally, in the last 25 years, in a period of full development of capitalism, after socialism has been defeated in Europe, Marxists are facing a task which is almost similar to the one Lenin himself had to face. It is necessary to read the current events from a scientific alternative perspective rather than from the neoclassical right wing (and left wing) points of view. An updated interpretation of the imperialistic phenomena requires a methodological tool that can be found in Marx's dialectic, but also in Lenin's application of the theoretical principles developed by Marx and Engels, on the monopolist stage of capitalism.[5]

---

[5] Liodakis (2005), in an interesting argument on globalization and imperialism, argues that some of Lenin's theses and some of his methodological settings have been

First of all, Lenin introduced some basic philosophical aspects. Among those concepts, developed in his *Philosophical Notes* and in *Materialism and Empirico-criticism*, there is one that is of great importance in terms of the research on imperialism. It refers to the study and conceptualization of "essence" as a philosophical category. Lenin developed the theory of "levels" or "degrees" of the essence, vital in order to understand what is imperialism or the monopolist stage with respect to capitalism as a way of production and what is a monopoly, a key concept of the new stage, compared to the exploitative essence of capitalism in his new historical period of development. This problem was "solved" by Lenin along the following considerations:

a. Imperialism is, at the beginning, monopolist capitalism, the result of the high level of concentration of production and capital obtained by a small group of major capitalist powers;

b. imperialism is nothing but a superstructure of the old capitalism, so the first does not exist but on the second's structure, it does not deny it mechanically, though it does in its dialectical sense, which means by overcoming or supplementing it in a new and higher historical period of development;

c. therefore, monopoly does not deny competition, but exists on it and with it. It overcomes it and at the same time contains it. Monopoly and competition thus form a dialectical indissoluble unity;

d. monopoly, therefore, does not deny the innermost essence of the way production is achieved, but expresses it on a new level of development; surplus value and the monopoly thus become two levels or degrees of the essence of the way of production;

e. therefore, monopoly is nothing but a second degree economic essence of the form of production, an essence contained in each fundamental economic feature of the new stage.

It is important to make clear what neoliberal globalization currently is, with respect to imperialism: whether it is a completely new moment in imperialism or whether, while presenting us with new phenomena, it is merely a continuation of those trends that were already contained in the imperialist stage (what we have been defining, for many years now, as global competition in the sense of the current configuration of the

---

overcome. He criticizes the excessive emphasis placed on the issue of circulation, mistreating the productive one, and also the special attention to issues related to interstate rivalries, leaving on the background the conflict between capital and labour.

capitalist globalization).[6] It is not difficult to find interpretations that have claimed the term "Imperialism" to be obsolete, since it does not represent any longer the phase that capitalism is currently going through or because, unlike capitalism in the 1980s, the current phase appears to be a regime of production with "human traits," which has eliminated what previously could have been the subject of criticism. These issues will be further discussed later on in this work.

The structure of Lenin's work on imperialism does not resemble that of *Capital*, since the problems studied in it are generally new, and it goes beyond the mere continuation of the study and research on the concept of capitalism. The work was written under the tsarist censorship in order to be divulged, which limited its contents to political conclusions. Yet, it would be a mistake to separate the work of Marx (and Engels) from the work of Lenin: both represent the main body of Marxist research in the field of political economy as a science. Lenin began his research on imperialism starting from Marx's most important scientific discovery from a concrete analytical point of view: the fundamental economic traits that are adopted by capitalism in the new historical phase of its development.

This allows a characterization of this moment as a stage.

The countries involved were England, France, Germany and the United States. As Marx had already supposed, in those countries the concentration and centralization of production and capital had led to the control by a small group of business magnates. The financial oligarchy had usurped and monopolized all of the benefits of the socialization process produced by the historical development of capitalism. In Lenin's work the internationalization of the capitalist cycle, as a result of the process of concentration and centralization of money and production, does not stay within national boundaries, but starts the process of capitalist internationalization; such process expresses very

---

[6] The term 'globalization', unless considered as simply a name, is not reliable. Galbraith says that this is an American invention for hiding the policy of foreign penetration. James Petras (2003), in his recent work, is even more explicit. According to his point of view, we are not facing a symmetric globalization but a form of imperialism which, in its latest variants, takes neo-colonialist features. It should be noted how Petras, unlike many intellectuals, including those of the radical left wing, proposes the imperialist nature of two other geo-political-economic entities: Europe and Japan, in addition to the U.S. Read the first chapter of the aforementioned text. Such theses coincide with what we have been claiming for years (Vasapollo, Casadio, Petras, Veltmeyer 2004; Arriola, Vasapollo 2004, Casadio, Petras, Vasapollo 2003).

clearly the way in which wealth and power are even more concentrated when it comes to the birth of the dominance of monopolies.

This is the movement of the capital accumulation process onto an international level, with such a high degree of concentration of power that it gives rise to a phenomenon of economic differentiation between a financial oligarchy (the apex) and the rest of the bourgeois class. Such a phenomenon has political correlations, which can be briefly analysed as follows. The first and most important feature is the historical tendency of capitalist accumulation. Between the end of the 19th century and the beginning of the 20th century, large-scale production reaches its peak stage, and the exchange creates an internationalization of economic relations and of capital, transforming it. This analysis of internationalization is essential in order to understand the birth and development of the "mechanisms of transition" of cyclical impulses from the centres of developed capitalism towards the rest of the economies of the system.

Lenin necessarily has to evaluate what place capitalism deserves in history, and should not revert to the laws already discovered by Marx. Conversely, he is suggesting that the basic aim is to reveal the influence and the effects exerted on capitalism from the changes occurred in its economy in the late 19th and early 20th centuries, this being the final transition of the whole mode of production to a higher stage of its development: a process in which production did not undergo any changes. It is, therefore, an analysis of new things that occurred after Marx's work, *Capital*, but not from a linear historical perspective. Such a process will not end until capitalism has run out of all its resources for survival. The way in which capitalism will leave the historical scene represents a very important matter and a real challenge for humanity.

Therefore, the contradictions discovered by Marx will not disappear within imperialism but will continue to develop. Also the struggle for the survival of the system of production and the social system as such will keep developing, even at the international scale.

The years between the late 20th and early 21st centuries, after the fall of socialism in Eastern Europe and the USSR, served as confirmation that neither socialism lost its chances of serving as social alternative, nor capitalism has achieved such a success that could turn it into an eternal social regime. Just by observing the huge inequality and those conflicts determined by the current stage of capitalist world development that have now become structural phenomena, the reasons for the necessity of socialism, are still valid, provided that the objective conditions organized the right revolutionary subjectivity.

The U.S. as an Imperialist Economy

In 1894 the United States already occupied the first place in the world, for the volume of its industrial production. In the aftermath of the second World War, that the U.S. won, its economic dominance is supported by a new world order, whose structure remained almost unchanged until September 11 2001.

The economic crisis of 1929–33 was an extraordinary experience for all the capitalist countries, but particularly for the United States, and represented a "watershed" for economic policy. It marked the birth of the "New Deal," which overturned much of the past economic and political beliefs: there was a conversion to the massive interference of the state in the economy. This passage was neither painless nor flat, and had to face the strong opposition of the capitalist class.

Keynesian ideas began to gain ground over the neoclassical economic thought that had been in force until then. Between 1937 and 1939, once the largest economic crisis in the history of capitalism started to be overcome, though it was the war that actually changed the course of the previous economic cycle. From 1945 on, an expansion, for reasons linked to the process of recovery of the capitalist economies torn down by the war, began. It was during the period after 1945, and as early as 1944, that, with the Bretton Woods conference, the United States became the central capitalist power of the (imperialist) system on a global scale.

More than 90% of the goods that could be then marketed could be purchased with U.S. Dollars and thus the dynamics of real trade designated the dollar as the center of the monetary system. The dollar thus occupied a place that allowed it to carry out its monetary and basic financial duties: cash in all currencies; means of payment in the international trade, international resource and form of hoarding.

The Marshall Plan, with which the United States contributed to the financing of the reconstruction of what had been destroyed during the war in Europe, was to improve even further the North American international economic position. The USSR was excluded from the plan, and could not benefit from the United States' interventions. The North American economy kept on producing at its most, both to provide support for the third front and to finance the recovery of its allies' economies. This became a negative paradox for this superpower since, while the allies recovered and also renewed their production system, the American economy continued to produce on the basis of the same technological potential with which they had at the start of the war.

Nevertheless, this situation represented a short-term advantage for the U.S., which started to fade as the Allies completed their recovery process in the mid-1950s.

Meanwhile the United States' only interest was to maintain that economic hegemony that the country had benefited from until the mid 1960s. This is the paradox of the United States' plan to dominate the economy that emerged from the second world conflict. It was a hegemony that, as everything seems to point out, did not respond to the power of the American economy during the twenty years following the Post-war period, but to the almost nonexistent competition that characterized that period, and the weakness resulting from the devastations, caused by the war, of the economies that should have competed with the United States.

Economic Imperialism

Despite the changes, capitalism retains its structural identity and continues to play an historical role in the logic of capitalist global accumulation. The political and economic features and connotations that imperialism already presented during the First World War keep on being valid. Essential economic key features that were defined by Lenin, instead of dissolving, have strengthened. The concentration of production and capital, the domination of the monopolies, capital's export, financial capital and the division of the world into different spheres of economic and political influence continue to grow.

Even the relationship that had already been analysed by Lenin, between imperialism and war is more present than ever.[7]

Neoliberal globalization, the current stage, has emphasized the structural asymmetries within the system and by a small group of imperialist powers, which strengthen their ability to control wealth and to hegemonize trade and financial flows. It has also strengthened imperialist domination and highlighted the submission of peripheral capitalisms, and that of the subaltern classes and groups that represent it all over the world, enhancing the control of the financial oligarchy.

This transnational oligarchy that operates on a global scale controls politics and has almost become a "global government".

---

[7] On such issues see Vasapollo, Casadio, Petras, Veltmeyer (2004); Vasapollo, Jaffe, Galarza (2005).

Imperialism implies, today more than ever, the international organization of markets, of Nation States and of ruling classes, in the fight to overcome its historical limits under the direction of an international bourgeoisie, presided by the most developed capitalist centres, and a tendency towards military and political hegemonization of power by a single, both imperialist and imperial power: the United States of America. However, from an economic and financial point of view and less on the political-military level, we can clearly identify a global competition with at least two other imperialist poles, in addition to that of the US dollar area: the euro area, of the European Union, and that of the Yen or, better, of the new Asiatic currency that is being constituted.

The economic features of imperialism analysed by Lenin between the 19th and 20th centuries, far from disappearing and turning into their opposite, developed to unexpected levels. The first important change occurred with the passage of the supremacy internal to the capitalist system from Great Britain to the United States. This process fully evolved between the First and Second World War. Therefore, the role of leading the economy went from Europe to the U.S.

Hence, the objective conditions for a world economy (markets, production volumes, transportation technologies and distribution) were practically ealized with the end of he Second World War.

After the Second World War, the history of capital was at a controversial turning point: was it necessary to take the world economy to another stage or rather to continue with the system of international relations between nations, which was a hierarchical one and had an hegemonic power?

This was the question that started a major political debate on the structure of the post-war Western World, whose most significant discussion was the new financial and monetary order. As it is well-known, at the end of the debate no world currency was created, but a global order through a national currency was set up: the US dollar, elected as a guide in the international exchanges. This order was given the name of Bretton Woods.[8]

This supremacy of the United States was absolutely hegemonic between 1945 and 1965 (no more than 20 years), although the USSR's possession of nuclear weapons made it relative. Nowadays the U.S,

---

[8] Cf. Vasapollo, Jaffe, Galarza (2005).

has no economic hegemony, but a political-military one. This situation shows that imperialism has a dynamics that no power is able to occupy, as in the case of Great Britain, which was replaced by the United States. The system has no longer accepted a hegemony in economic terms like that of the United States during the 1960s. This means that the capitalist system tolerates political and military supremacy, but does not accept the same level of submission to a single power at an economic level.

This incomplete hegemony, in the present situation of deep crisis, seems to be a condition for the capitalist powers to reopen war scenarios in order to redistribute the world's economy and territory. Everything seems to show that this situation will persist, since none of the capitalist powers can gain supremacy both at the economic and political-military levels, at the same time. Far from representing a problem for the anti-imperialist struggle, this becomes an advantage: the current position the U.S. is in decline.

The intention of the North-American administration to subdue and drag the rest of the capitalist powers to its positions on foreign policy is coming across two big obstacles: on the one hand, economic competition, which tends to tighten, and the danger that this imposition holds for those who cannot see war as the solution to their problems or for those who do not want to bear the costs of the conflicts. This is exactly the dynamics that have recently started to appear: US policy is being questioned by some of its allies. It is telling that only one power, Great Britain, has blindly followed the U.S. until now. The rest of the countries seems to be moving away, since the actions of the U.S. are not appearing successful.

The second most important change of the last few years (from the early 1980s) was the transition from the Fordist-Keynesian stage, which had as its technological foundation the engineering-automobile-petrochemical industry, to the new technological paradigm, which has its foundation in the so-called computer-electronics sector.

Such changes highlight the fact that global competition neither homogenizes nor balances those relationships of interdependence which some expected people to believe in, but leads to a controversial and unbalanced system, intensifying the action of the law of unequal economic and political development. In particular, in South-America the situation has begun to be characterized by a growing opposition to neoliberal globalization and an intensification of the anti-imperialist struggle. The transition to the new technological paradigm did not free the capitalist economy from the problems of the cycle and the economic crisis.

The capitalist economy keeps on having the same behaviour that benefits from the progress of the scientific revolution on the basis of an increase of the working masses' exploitation.

Strategies of Economic Imperialism

Productive Chains

In the last few years, a new concept has been spreading in production: the concept of "vertically integrated production units". This term denotes a set of operations of transformation that allow the production of goods and products in different forms with respect to the Fordist-Taylorist period, finding synergies and affinities between the various stages of production, in order to identify and stimulate the areas subject both to competition and to global competition and with a high value content.

The great industrial and financial capital, once abandoned the old organizational model which provided an "organic" structure of the company including within itself all the phases of production (from the production of *knowhow* and the design, to the assembly line and the cleanup crew), has begun to adopt a policy of outsourcing of various functions and stages of the entire working process, delegated to entrepreneurs who are legally independent, but economically and financially controlled.

The international vertically integrated production units, in particular, have a pyramid-like structure which, through complex relations of participation or commission, allows financial capital to *de facto* manage huge economic, productive and financial groups. The financial control of the parent company ensures the economic, strategic, decisional control/power over the whole group's policies.

The vertically integrated production units are a structure that collects minor capitals that would otherwise be outside the centralizing logic of large oligopolistic capital: scattered, isolated and in hostile competition, risking to perish in vain.[9] In this way they can be regained

---

[9] Compared to their useful and productive function in the logic of a chain. For further technical and industrial analysis among others cf. Breaded, Golinelli (1991).

to the logics and structures of the accumulation of large financial capital. Therefore some real 'integrated structures' of value (the value chain) are created, where the central power is firmly held by financial capital (monopolist and imperialist).

International Zones

In addition to the new planning of the vertically integrated production units, in these last years the development of some kind of industrial districts of international significance has been witnessed: these are national or transnational area clusters of companies integrated with each other into vertically integrated production units. Industrial districts of an international character should not be considered as local national independent systems which are firm and stable, since they go through many internal tensions. Some districts have finished their cycle and disappeared, others have adapted. As with the national local districts, there may then be different types of districts of international significance, depending on the degree of technological advancement of productions, the age of the district, of the nature of the relationships between companies, etc.

However, there is a tendency that seems to unite the various types of districts, which consists in their transformation through the collaboration offered by groups of companies that become a reference and clot point of 'international networks' of enterprises. The companies of the districts are organized vertically in order to operate through external economies that allow to be competitive even when the size is reduced. In this case, the strategic relationships that affect the trade areas are usually outside the district and have a growing transnational character. The company tries to control trading policies through management forms associated between subsidiaries in different countries.

It should be noted that if new players come from the outside, especially if they come from other countries, changes in the shape and functioning of the district can be caused. An example is provided by the acquisitions of companies located in the district by outside firms, also through FDI, especially if these companies are large in size: in this case a concentration process is to be faced. This is a process, which also has an international character that has been planned vertically and can give rise to many problems in a phase of interdependence.

For example, it is difficult to understand what are the boundaries between different vertically integrated production units or between some of their constituent elements, especially since they have a transnational character.

In such cases, the aim of the companies that are part of the vertically integrated production units is not to have ownership control of the largest part of the production cycle, but to secure control of part of it and of the international chain. This happens through the incoming and outgoing flows of the foreign direct investment (FDI) of different countries. So the essential pivot of the chain lies in its "strategic center of gravity," which at the international level means the country where the headquarters of the parent company are located.

It is interesting to analyse the phenomenon of the industrial districts and the international chains in order to monitor the progress and trends of the market in the last decades and to interpret and represent the dynamics of the "relocation" abroad of productive activities (especially manufacturing activities and areas of new technologies, in particular computer science technology).

Patents

A powerful tool of "legal guarantee" of mono/oligopolistic positions is represented by the patent. In a society in which everything needs a patent, logos have turned into a part of people's daily life, so that they are considered symbols just as many others are.[10] This hides the ruthless struggle between capital and constitutes a precise, guaranteed principle of exclusion as effective as a law (also international).

The license assignment agreements, that are effective after a sum of money has been paid, are basically grants of temporary exploitation rights over patents, trademarks etc., and are technological agreements. The sub-supply, subcontract and co-production agreements may be included among the productive kind of agreements.

Of course, the rules on patents have some theoretical limits with respect to the appropriation of goods. To be patentable, knowledge must be characterized by the quality of "novelty" and by the "non

---

[10] On the origins, functions and performative power of the new lifestyles of the logo cf. Klein (2003).

evidence": this allows to distinguish the invention, result of human ability, from the discovery, which may be due to an accident and may be due to the creative activity of nature rather than to that of a person. For these reasons, a machine is patentable, but a new botanical species discovered by a researcher is not.

So the patent nowadays represents a new form (title) of private (intangible) property of the means of production and products.

It allows the company that holds the property title to exercise its control on the idea, the project protected by the constraint of free reproducibility. This should be related to the logical articulation of a process of strategic formulation of deviant nomad communication by the *Profit State*, which needs a critical accumulation of information, followed by phases of operative synthesis and verification in which the operational level of social control is outlined. The moment in which the strategy of control is actuated through the decision-making process of the various institution, also local, displaced all over the territory, has now arrived. That is how the patent means control and capitalist production of the social intelligence.[11]

We can now discuss the most delicate phase of the whole scheme, which implies the means of communication of the strategy of control that must be shared and assimilated by the entire social body, in particular thanks to the communicative intellectual capital that conveys consent in the form of real control of a totalitarian nature. The description of the strategic control of thought, which constitutes the backbone of the activity of the generalized social factory, is determined by the setting of the objectives and the choice between one or more components of the strategy among many possible alternatives. This implies a structural separation between the subjects to be involved and the institutional levels involved, that is the different fashions, central and local, in which the global *Profit State* appears.

Therefore, if the high-level institutions are in charge of the strategic thinking, becoming a role model with respect to the decisions and the actions, the implementation/operational plans are often tactical, and involve the *local institutions*, the sections of the *Profit State* and the business subsystems of the factory which is socially widespread on the territory.[12]

---

[11] For a further study of the issue cf. Martufi, Vasapollo (2000b).
[12] The subject is analysed in detail in Martufi, Vasapollo (1999).

Not Only the US; the Europole in Global Competition

Global competition characterizes this new stage of capitalism that could be summarized as competition and growth without development, with no increase in employment. In the long run, it turns into "absolute impoverishment," and requires the transformation of the bourgeoisie and the middle classes into marginalized social groups.

This phenomenon could be associated with the development of new technologies, especially computer technology and the data transmission devices, which allow increased productivity, declining employment and processes of displacement as we find ourselves in a production context which is less tied to the physical place and territory.

In order to reflect, study and act, it is essential to understand and interpret the data which identify this new phase of capitalist development[13] around the centrality of the international control, a control determined by the role played by new economic subjects of capital, economic corporations subjects and subjects-country, or better said, subject-pole, well defined areas of influence (the dollar area for the pole of the U.S., the euro area for the European Union pole, the Asian area of the yen, etc.).

It is from such analyses that the fundamental phenomena that have led to a territorial redistribution of international control of the process of transformation can be properly interpreted. This happened starting from some characterizations that have become the dynamics of development in the capital-labour relation, whose aim is social control internal to every capitalist country and external collision for the determination of the global domination through the widening of the areas of geo-economic influence of the three major international blocs.

The advantage of the North-American economy over Europe depends on three factors: the control of technology, the flexibility of the system of credit that encourages a more rapid introduction of innovations into the production system and facilitates a greater level of credit, and a controlled and fragmented working class, so that next

---

[13] David Laibman (last 2005) has been developing a comprehensive stage theory of capitalist development based on the principles of historical materialism, a theory aimed at scanning time on high levels of abstraction, that is not linked to the mere empirical, historical, contingent data and that tries to delineate the evolutionary lines of the capitalist development, based on a thorough study of the nature of the way and motion of capitalist production.

to strongly regulated areas (cars, mining, construction, transport) others, especially those that produce workers consumption goods (textiles, nutrition, family services), are fed with an unbroken stream of immigrants who keep wages low and labour time high, which means high level of exploitation and low prices.

The European technological system is unable to articulate public and private investment with the same efficiency as North America, where the public expenditure on innovations (from numerically controlled machine tool, to the internet, through computers or jet engines) occurs in private companies and is quickly transferred to goods of private consumption. The European economic system finds in its financial rigidity its main weakness, as repeatedly shown in many works by J. Arriola (see, among others, Arriola, Vasapollo 2004 and 2005).

The construction of monetary Europe and the economic and social problems related to it, coincide with the Asian crisis.[14]

The international economy was deeply affected by the effects of the severe financial crisis that arose in Southeast Asia. The disorder within foreign exchange markets, which began with the devaluation of the Thai baht, was quickly transmitted to the Philippines, Indonesia and Malaysia, with repercussions on the most robust economies in the region, leading a wave of devaluations, local stock markets crashes and bank failures. The spreading of the crisis from Thailand to other economies in the region highlighted how financial markets, strongly integrated and responsive. While it on the one hand may encourage the efficient allocation of resources, on the other it may enhance the risks of contagion between countries with imbalance factors that are largely common. The experience of South-East Asia also stressed the close interaction between currency and banking crisis and financial globalization, in a post-Fordist context characterized by restrictive monetary policies with consequences on the international level, dominated by a rupture of the previous balances.

Indeed, the disintegration of the Soviet Union and the end of bipolarity have spared a single superpower, the United States, and in addition have tempted the North-American capitalist model to interpret the end of ideologies as an authorization to impose its economic and political force, in a context marked by "unbridled capitalism", in the certainty of its financial and technological superiority.

---

[14] Caracciolo (1997).

The European countries have managed to rebuild a high economic level often in competition with the United States, which initially also promoted the European integration. The member countries convinced themselves of the necessity of constituting a monetary union only after the Fall of 1992, when they saw their first attempt, that had begun in 1978, temporarily destroyed by the financial crisis that affected the whole international context.

The initial hypothesis assumed that through the Monetary Union Europe could manage its own domestic demand, as the U.S. has always done, with an economic integration capable to optimize the best national economic performances, to be exploited on the continental level by limiting the power of Germany.

But the obsessive reference to the German model, which is part of the Maastricht hypothesis, is wrong: Germany is no longer a super-power: the former GDR has proved to be a difficult resource to be managed. The unified Germany came out with larger population and bigger territory than those of the old Federal Republic, but weaker in terms of political balances, economic structure, ability to rule itself and affect the world in terms of geoeconomic hegemony. Such an international influence, with its hegemonic aims of economic blockade, especially of Central-Eastern Europe, must be fulfilled by the European geo-economic pole, under the name of "widening", that is of the annexation to the EU of the former socialist bloc's countries. The term "widening" is very generic and leads to an intensification of the competition and conflicts among countries that wish to join the Union and among the most powerful countries that are already part of it. Within the EU, the most powerful countries are trying to expand their economic and political territories into Central and Eastern Europe, according to their geopolitical priorities and historical and cultural inclinations, strongly determined to affirm the new European pole of international geo-economic nature.

The EU's willingness to be the antagonist pole to the North-American market, in a period when the U.S. economy, though forced and doped, has expanded, tends to significantly exacerbate the geoeconomic war between the two economic blocs, and the crisis that hit the Balkan area and the Middle East area prove it. In Europe, in particular, the activities of direct investment showed a strong acceleration since the mid-1980s, coinciding with the beginning of the economic integration process implemented by the single market with its strong competitive purposes vis-a-vis the United States.

The role of the EU, which is growing more significant, is determined not only by the constitution of the Monetary Union, but also by the very strong acceleration of productive investment oriented to those European countries of the ex-socialist area (which, together with the Mediterranean countries, are actually areas of active European competence). It represents the reason for the political-economic "widening" of Italy into the East which found its concrete accomplishment in the last fifteen years.

Since the Maastricht treaty was signed, the unemployment rate has increased, the economic growth stagnates, the welfare state is facing a crisis all over Europe. The standards of life have gone down, the legitimacy of the political and economic choices, particularly in Italy, is being questioned even if no new, univocal, social-economic and political line has been drawn in Europe. The convergence criteria of the Monetary Union have as their main objective monetary stability and result from a monetarist, neoliberal policy which has as its central target the rate of inflation, looking for financial stability by reducing public deficits of different countries.

So there is much truth in the European monetarist thesis of the external constraint, which imposed, with the Maastricht Treaty, the only way to privatization, monetary policies and structural reform of the *Welfare State*. The citizens keep on being asked for strong sacrifices because of an external constraint, and not in their interests, or to meet their need for better jobs, income and social protection.

The external constraint undermines the legitimacy and the political and economic authority of the single countries since, if the centre of decisions is an uncontrolled, not democratically elected place (see various international institutions), it is not clear, in the long run, what would be the function of the government and of the European Parliament, as well as the unity of Europe itself.[15]

Despite the conflicts of interest, the Euro is a choice made within the dividing geo-economic polar logic ruled by the principles of the financial globalization and global competition. The large continental market ensures for the economic and financial groups of corporations the complete freedom of choice of the different adjustments of the combinations of the production factors, for the implementation of an

---

[15] On the political and economic European construction and its social impact, see, also provided with figures, Arriola, Vasapollo (2004).

integrated production at an international level, with connotations typical of the oligopolistic competition.

Therefore the EU is simultaneously experiencing the transition from the consolidation and definitive affirmation of its own autonomous economic bloc and the internal contradiction of uneven development based on different methods. But the future of the euro is strongly conditioned by the external environment, the financial markets all over the world or the monetary policy of the United States. The euro-hypothesis keeps on taking form and emerge as a tool of trade war, and therefore the U.S. is making efforts to stop it. For the Americans the best kind of Europe has to be sufficiently united but under US control. So they operate in order to make Europe sufficiently divided as to preclude its affirmation as a superpower competitor. The United States, therefore, fear a currency that will promote European exports and threaten the status of the dollar bill as the world reserve currency. The scenario drawn is one of change in the economic stage characterized by the conflict between the US and the EU.

This is why our analysis began with the identification of the methods of development in Europe, considering as central the phenomenology of competition between the US and the EU, but always referring to the labour-capital conflict.

CHAPTER TWELVE

IMPERIALISM AND INTERNATIONAL TRADE IN ACTION

The North-South, but also the East-West Conflict

The main difference between levels of productivity and labour intensity between countries allows the development of the exploitation to which the poor countries are subjected by the rich ones in the context of the world market, since those who are the strongest economically in the exchange, gain a bigger amount of work than the one they deliver. Countries, based on the formal observance of the law of value, operate an uneven mutual exchange which directly influences the processes of development, similarly to what happens with the relation of unequal exchange between labour and capital.

The Neoliberal globalization's peculiarity of being divided into areas of control such as North-South and West-East should not be considered the only peculiarity (think about the role Eastern Europe is playing in the productive relocations of Central European countries, or the dynamics of the Asian variable), as to say its contradictory and uneven nature, which the process of internationalization of productive forces and of social production relations engages under capitalism. The internationalization of capital and production derive from the laws of accumulation and the uneven economic and political development of capitalism, which is something Lenin stated clearly and directly and that remains valid.

With the gradual saturation of the internal market, capital is no longer able to exploit itself. The overproduction of goods on a national scale introduces the need to export them abroad (first stage of capitalism). The excess of not exploitable internal capital implies the need to invest it outside the national borders (this is the essential feature of imperialism emphasized by Lenin [2001: 75-ff.]). The export of capital abroad implies that countries of destination and investment have already entered the capitalist orbit, are capitalist countries and are part of the MPC.[1] The capitalist economy is globalized in order to satisfy its

---

[1] Lenin stated it explicitly. Jaffe (1973) makes this even clearer many times also against Luxemburg's conviction, who believed instead that peripheral countries were out of the MPC.

needs of valorization. The global collision of capitals involves a permanent struggle to be fought at different levels: economic (areas of shared market, access to raw materials), financial (currency areas), legal (patents, international agreements on free trade, protectionism); military (with direct intervention or through intermediaries).

New levels of uneven development of capitalism have been experienced through the processes of integration and economic marginalization of countries, in a global context of capitalist control. To the hegemonic concentration of economic and political power has been opposed the concentration of marginalization and poverty in a number of countries, as a genuine expression of internationalization of the general law of capitalist accumulation.

All data show an increase of the differences between rich and poor countries. This is manifest since in 1960 the gap was 37, in 1992 it had grown to 60 and in 2005 to 74. In the meanwhile 90% of world patents can be found in the developed countries, which collected, over the last five years, more money off the interests paid by the debt than off the amount they send to the Third World in the form of official aid for development: we are now referring to a ratio of 1/6 of every dollar given and received.

Those countries considered poor by the World Bank, that is, those with an average per capita income that amounts to less than one dollar a day and that represent more than half the population of the world, account for 7% of the world's GDP, while the rich countries, with just the 8% of world's population, account for almost 70% of the total 80% of world trade, two thirds of which is held by developed countries (Echevarria 2004).

The struggle to get sources of energy and of raw materials dates back from the past. The first European expeditions were carried out in order to discover territories to exploit and "sources" of wealth that could easily be taken advantage of. We could say, with Jaffe, that colonialism funds and supports the development and survival of the MPC. The worldwide robbery that precedes and goes along with the development of capitalism on a global scale is well-known: "Capitalism has turned into a worldwide system of oppression [...] of the great majority of the world population world by a handful of "advanced" countries"(Lenin 2001: 17 translation from the Italian edition).

The large financial-industrial groups, with the active (political, legal, military) support of "their" own States, are taking over the whole world through their capital, sharing (fighting or not) the entire planet.

The relationships established between imperialist companies and the lower classes of the dominated countries are the foundations of the political relations of a colonial kind that occur between the dominant countries and the colonies. Even Lenin distinguished between colonies and semi-colonies: semi-colonies are formally-politically *independent*, yet economically and financially *dependent*.

We are, therefore, facing an "imperialism without colonies" (Magdoff), which does not mean that the relationship of colonialist exploitation is lacking, but only that modern imperialism is no longer in need to control in a direct, political and exclusively military way the dominated country, but only that it does so (and in a more useful and profitable way for capital itself) through indirect involvement in the socio-economic life of that country.

Jaffe argues, however, that the imperialist policies have basically been "underdeveloping," and have worsened the economic conditions of the countries that are dominated, forcing them to capitalist forms of *guided non-development (relative)*. He writes:

> There relatively was no industrialization of the "underdeveloped" countries. They were left "underdeveloped" by the imperialism (Jaffe 1973: 69).

This is due to the colonialist policies that have limited the industrial field to "primary production," often a "mono-production" (minerals, raw materials, agriculture, subsistence), developing instead the secondary industry in the dominant country's productive system,[2] and that have supported "monoculture" in the agricultural sector which is subject to the monopolies of corporations that have real sovereign powers in the dominated countries ((Mandel 1997b: 741).[3]

Industrial underdevelopment also has visible effects in the countryside, which experiences processes that are opposite to those occurred in mature capitalist countries.

The "pressure on land" (due to inactivity of large sections of population in the industrial sector) leads to a chronic underemployment in rural areas (agricultural overpopulation) that generates an increase of land rent. It follows that the entire social overproduction is "attracted,"

---

[2] So dominated countries have to produce, as colonies, the raw materials that are needed by the central imperialist industry in order to manufacture "secondary" products that will be exported to colonies where this market production sector is absent.

[3] For this reason these countries are also called *company countries*.

captured by land property and usury, that are more profitable in these countries, than most of the industrial sector (Mandel 1997b: 750 ff.).

The sick cycle closes. The *comprador* bourgeoisie in these countries is devoted to the purchase of land, trade, usury (which do not produce wealth[4] but consume it only): goodbye development[5], welcome hefty profits for Western corporations that invest in the primary sector, where they have no rivals, and have plenty of underpaid and overexploited workforce at their disposal. Moreover, the social overproduction that has been won by imperialist corporations mostly comes back in the form of profits.

The profit arising from the relationship of exploitation between imperialist bourgeoisie and the colonial working class, not being reinvested in the country of origin, is not used locally to support development: it is used to counter the potential fall of profit in the imperialist countries, where class struggle has imposed historical compromises between capital and labour to grant to the "central" working class a greater share of direct and indirect wage out of the total value created (even if in the last few decades this relation has been overturned by capital in its own interest, in almost every mature capitalist country).

Unequal and Combined Development

At this point it is clear for all to see that capitalist economic development has not an equal distribution, highlighting huge inequalities and imbalances on a temporal, territorial, sectoral and social levels. Theorists of the dominant economy identify the causes of these imbalances, for example, in the cyclical movement of economy, in the different physical and environmental characteristics of the different territories that can be more or less favorable to production with the identification of core areas of development, semi-peripheral, peripheral and marginal areas as for example, we can identify within the structural imbalances, the so-called "bargaining power" of individual companies, industries or sectors with their related inequalities in rates of development. Even among the so-called social imbalances it is possible to

---

[4] Hence the numerous civil wars aimed at sharing the relatively little wealth of these countries.
[5] The term is here meant in its bourgeois sense. On these issues and on the different interpretations of the concepts of 'growth', 'development' and 'progress' cf. Jaffe (1990), Vasapollo (ed., 2006), Vasapollo (ed., 2008).

identify some problems that "usually" go along with any process of economic development, and are due, for example, to the scarcity of some productive resources or monetary phenomena and to the redistribution of income inequality. What in conventional economics is referred to as asymmetry of development or imbalance, is nothing but the essential character inherent to the capitalist mode of production based on the extortion of surplus value, exploitation and on the class struggle dimension of society development, already well identified by Marx.

In the so-called law of combined and uneven development, the element of inequality is closely related to integration between tasks, production, economic systems: the division of labour is functional to inequality of wages, the expansion of markets depends on the inequality in economic conditions and costs of production.

When deciding what are the essential characteristics of the underdevelopment of the peripheral areas, the most important is the difference in productivity with respect to the single employee in relation to the developed centre, measured as added value per employee. An increase in productivity occurs at a higher rate or in absolute terms that are bigger in the developed countries where there is the highest rate of growth, while in the peripheral countries productivity grows at lower rate.

In this way, if the differences in productivity (measured by each worker in the active population, not per person employed) between the poorest countries and those that are part of the OECD, were 1:44 in 1960, in 2000 they have grown up to 1:58. Even in peripheral countries, or better said, semi-peripheral at a higher level of industrialization and income, the difference in relative productivity has grown bigger in these 40 years, rising from 1:4 to 1:5.5.

If underdevelopment is a low productivity issue and development is a process that is characterized by rapid increases in productivity, then why not increasing the productivity in developing countries at the same speed as in developed countries, including when they have access to modern technology of foreign investment?

The traditional explanation economic theory has to offer is the allocation of factors. It is assumed that the developing countries are characterized by a low endowment of capital and high endowment of labour; so the developing countries, according to this theory, have a prevalence of intensive industries as far as labour and low capital is concerned, so they do not renew capital and have a low rate of productivity.

But this argument is belied by the data of reality. Leontief showed that the exports, in which the U.S., a country that seems to have a high productivity rate, are specialized, are labour intensive, and present a greater labour intensity than many of the products exported from the Third World countries (Leontief 1956). Secondly, supporters of this theory forget that in those Third World countries, in which there is foreign investment, there is the tendency of buying technology and capital-intensive production processes, at least in the industrial sector, with a physical productivity similar to that of developed countries. However, the value measured in production prices continues to be well below the one obtained in production facilities in the developed countries.

Therefore, these differences are conform to one of the most important social relations, that is that between productivity and wage levels, which is impossible to understand along the path of equilibrium theory.

Since the end of World War II, the economic growth of the developed countries is also characterized by wages growing more or less the same way production does. In underdeveloped countries, within the sector that uses modern technology, productivity grows while wages do so much more slowly. The apparent productivity of labour (the value added per employee) is lower in developing countries than in developed ones, because the relation wages/product is lower in the first ones than it is in the second and the unit value of products is also expressed in a lower standard monetary amount. On the other hand the sectorial structure of production differs greatly from centre-countries to peripheral countries. If the characteristic of the industry at the center is the existence of a combination of branches of production of intermediate, final and capital goods, these are normally absent from the partial industrialization of the periphery, or in other cases associated with the export sectors.

As far as the agricultural production is concerned, the model in the developed countries is radically different from that of the underdeveloped countries. For example, in the developed countries the majority of cereals is used for animal consumption, while in underdeveloped countries most of the cereals are for human consumption. The meat and dairy products produce a high added value, while cereals are products with a low added value. The different productive specialization reinforces the differences in the apparent productivity of labour in agricultural activities.

Dealing with the question of unequal exchange means to focus on the sphere of circulation. Logically, if there is an inequality, it must be in the sphere of exchange, that is in the market. If the main inequality between the imperialist "North" and the overexploited "South" consists in this, the problem does not take place in the social relations established within production, but mainly in the sphere of circulation.

A society, a population that manages to obtain the techniques necessary to produce goods that previously had to be purchased, achieves benefits from this direct production[6] because it frees itself from the "yoke" of trade.[7] If the problem, as Mandel points out, does not arise in the early stages of development of the productive forces, when production techniques are relatively simple and reproducible in other social contexts, it appears when the development of techniques and technologies is so advanced that can not be afforded, or copied, by peoples, communities, societies in disadvantaged positions. The fact that trade requires an uneven economic development is not only typical of the MPC but of all historical periods.

It is necessary to reject the theory (shared by many within twentieth-century Marxism) that the development of productive forces, capitalism and worldwide trade make the world homogeneous at certain levels of capitalist production and development.

If according to classical theory the problem of unequal exchange lies in commercial (and political) relationships between dominant and dominated countries, according to Jaffe the problem is right at the heart of the production process of capital: in the labour process.

In the imperialist countries, capital periodically reaches levels of crisis of profitability due to the decrease in the rate of profit. In Western countries for decades the rates of profit in various market sectors have been low (for oligopolistic sectors the question is more vast and complex, see above). According to the capitalist logic, when the rate of profit falls, capital has to migrate to more profitable areas, geographic zones that guarantee higher profit rates in the market sector in crisis. In the colonies, says Jaffe, imperialistic enterprises find convenient economic, political, business and contractual relationships. Colonies, with their convenient tax policies, with complacent laws on

---

[6] If it involves less costs than the ones previously paid for the same goods.
[7] These theories are in radical opposition to the "orthodox" theories on international trade.

environmental standards and on the defence of workers rights, with a labour-force willing to accept any employment and wage (because in a poor country the alternative is hunger), are the place where Western multinationals find their "treasure" of physical and intellectual resources.

The "majority shareholders" of international institutions such as the IMF and the Wprld Bank can legitimize and legally guarantee mere operations of international usury and piracy through pseudo-humanitarian operations, such as international loans. These "Trojan horses" of the dominant countries not only ensure, through specific contract terms, the "free entry" into semi-colonial countries. Also, with the instrument of public debt they guarantee for themselves a fixed annual income, and a conditioning power that, in addition to bending politically and economically such countries, ensures a further transfer[8] of W from the dominated country to the imperialist ones.

Moreover, the colonial relationship does not only assure a super-profit to the investing companies, but also a "benefit" in their motherland; in fact the capitalist enterprises, thanks to the super-profits obtained in the colonies are able to pay to their working class wages higher than they could do without such super-profits.

Jaffe argues that the Western working class is paid for more than it produces. There is a huge return of W from the colonies that is gained by imperialistic enterprises, but also distributed to the working class by their employers. According to Marx's theory of exploitation, the Western working class no longer produces W, but benefits from the SV of others. It participates to capitalist exploitation, its W is not positive but negative (it receives more than it produces).

This socio-economic process also produces clear political effects: the creation of a Western working-class aristocracy involved in a capital-labour compromise, through the consociationalism of the historical left parties and the compatibility of the moderate and pliable dominant Trade Unions with the government, to the benefit of the capitalist imperialist class and the partial advantage of the Western working class.

Imperialist capital ensures social peace and a working class more prone to possible reactionary mass mobilizations, or at least more reluctant to undertake class struggles or strong policy reform actions.

---

[8] In addition to W provided by the overexploitation of the semi-colonies.

We believe that, although Jaffe's theory of W is extremely important, it should be integrated; not all components of the Western working class are "parasitic". Rather, if we take up the Marxian fundamental categories of the collective function of labour and the collective function of capital and base the Marxist analysis of class society on these categories, we can identify the labour aristocracy in that portion of the working class who, although it continues to perform the functions of collective labour, thanks to the development of monopolist capitalism and the imperialist profits, has a range of economic, social, political privileges, granted by a triple material source.

In fact, all the macroeconomic parameters reflect what above said, confirming the neoliberal approach with the same trend of the early 1990s: a strong increase in male and female unemployment rates, and a slow increase in direct and indirect wages (in terms of pay and social benefits) that do not correspond to the equitable redistribution of increments in added value and productivity to capital and labour, leading to a very scarce redistribution toward forms of remuneration to labour.

It is clear that the enterprises, also in mature capitalist countries, made use of benefits that remain in the pockets of entrepreneurs, managers, shareholders, who did not make available at the "social" level some optimal conditions for growth when there were good results. The increase in profits and productivity, in fact, do not correspond to wage increases nor to the qualitative improvement of work conditions, the reduction of working hours, nor to increases in social expenditure (both quantitative and qualitative), nor, finally, to an increase in employment.

In practice, both central, peripheral and semi-peripheral capitalisms continue to gain profits without creating employment opportunities, reconstructing the enterprise structure, to pursue only the perspective of competitiveness based on: processes of productive relocation abroad, employment reductions within the considered countries, over-exploitation of labour with increments in overtime and work rhythms, use of illegal instable labour with few workers rights, flexibility of wages and employment, with cuts to social spending, direct and indirect real wages, with a lesser purchasing power. All this is aimed at determining profits that are not used in productive investment, but to pursue financial speculation and production investment abroad, moving towards countries where it is possible to obtain low cost skilled labour.

Neoliberalism and Unequal Development, even in
Mature Capitalist Countries

We have explained above why in neo-liberal policies there is an emphasis on uneven development, not only in the relatively developed countries and the developing countries, but even within countries of the capitalist centre.

The development of the automated technological production process that must accompany the expansionary phase of the development of capitalism will lead to the transitional consolidation of capitalism, the new level of neoliberal internationalization with implications of military global competition among the imperialist countries, great opportunities of progress in terms of economic efficiency, competitiveness and spread of knowledge; but at the same time, it can not achieve a truly balanced global internationalization of the new technological paradigm, nor the generalized internationalization of normal levels of human development.

The contradictions between wealth and poverty, technological development and unemployment, quantitative growth and the ecosystem, enhancement of capital and marginalization of a large group of countries, are an expression of its weakness and the necessary historical transition of socioeconomic capitalism.

The threat of the explosion of financial crises and of serious trade conflicts now affects both the peripheral countries and the mature capitalist countries. When faced with these phenomena, capitalism has shown a grater steering ability than it was supposed to have. The solution to these serious contradictions already reported during the implementation process of a new model of highly internationalized accumulation is the biggest challenge of capitalism.

The gap between production (industry, services, government) and job requirements has been reformulated with a view only to the development performance of profit, with financial connotations, in which the socio-cultural enhancement of human resources has represented only costs, not a great opportunity to increase the individual and community demands, let alone socio environmental high-sustainable development, or the promotion of activities based on the enhancement of culture and solidarity. All the increases in productivity have not been successfully redistributed. Indeed, as the analysis shows, they are used almost exclusively to remunerate the capital factor, in the form of profits not productively reinvested, which end up to feed "speculative financial bubbles" with easy gain, but no ability to create new and real employment.

To the financial restructuring of the public and private income has not corresponded an adequate strengthening of investment in research, development and innovation, despite this process having been characterized by a strong increase in technological progress, which had, however, the negative implication of a continuous decrease in the level of employment and its insecurity, with the sole purpose of increasing profits by compressing labour costs, the total social wage.

This situation has caused, and causes, the lack of redistribution of productivity increments to the direct and indirect wages of workers, who claim the right to receive such increases through higher pay, or alternatively with reductions in labour time, increases in employment, improvement of the Welfare State, i.e. forms of redistribution of wealth to the employed and unemployed. In the analysis conducted until now, it was possible to verify that this did not happen, that the remuneration of capital was strengthened thus decreasing wages and labour in general. In mature capitalist countries, there are no longer the parameters that ensured the old compromise between capital and labour. Capital gradually undermined (and continues to do so) all the political, economic, social, legal institutions of that Welfare model.

The working class of the mature capitalist countries was deprived of all the guarantees and privileges it enjoyed in last decades. It was decomposed and reorganized in every sector with a purpose: to create new, high profit rates (although the levels reached by colonies are hardly comparable).

This does not mean that the labour aristocracy in countries of mature capitalism (and in colonial countries) has disappeared. It persists but is more elusive: the factors that contribute to structure its material base are multiple and, in particular, in a fragmented working class take a less homogeneous structure.

Imperialism and Financialization in the Current Systemic Crisis

The Productive Fall-Out of Global Competition

The analysis of imperialism would be incomplete if we did not examine in detail the question of the role "played" by finance capital in the advanced capitalist production (CP). If Hilferding thought that, at a certain development level of capitalism, the financial capital alone dominated the political, economic and social scene, Lenin brought the Marxist theory to its origins, against that drift, which brought it to have something in common with Keynesism.

Imperialism is the result of the "combination," the "symbiosis" (Bucharin) of bank capital and industrial capital.

If capitalism is "an immense accumulation of commodities," it is, however, also an "immense collection of funds". The financial power is capable of entering the boards of directors, appoint its own representatives, spread around the world, overcome the national geographic borders, creating trans-national industrial-financial complex (which do not necessarily have a national or supranational base of reference for the defence of their interests).[9] Imperialism is, therefore, the particular conformation of capitalism where financial capital dominates industrial capital, without the disappearance of this last, and represents a solid material basis for old or new speculators and revenues "hunters".[10]

The new post-Fordist phase, with financial features, leads to the dominance of a highly speculative cycle, in which the money invested increases without passing through any intermediary production; in practice there is no transformation of capital into means of production. Financial investment prevails much more than the productive investment, creating speculative "financial bubbles".

Locally, financialization joins a huge increase of inequality of the internal distribution of realized income and wealth, which is less oriented towards labour (in the form of direct and indirect wages), rather moving toward capital in forms of financial surplus, i.e., as a predominant type of compensation in the form of pure financial gain. A consequence of this phenomenon is the risk of a retreat of the Western democracies, a de-socialization, a degeneration of politics and the standardization of the whole society to the logic of profit.

---

[9] See our analysis of currency areas and imperialist clusters in Vasapollo, Casadio, Petras, Veltmeyer (2004) and Vasapollo, Jaffe, Galarza (2005).

[10] We note that, in this regard, Marxist analysis, in recent years, has been getting on, both criticizing the thesis that reduce the ruling financial imperialistic class in a class of parasites and giving them a strategic central role. The members of that class would play the role of strategic agents that have a relevant political function in the management of the enterprise in the wild international market. See La Grassa (2005), who stresses the continuous battle continues inside the ruling class.

The result is a kind of "financial totalitarianism" and the culture of enterprise that, in search of easy financial-speculative and non-productive profits, destabilizes entire areas (see the crisis of Mexico, Brazil, Thailand, Korea, Indonesia, Russia, Argentina), determining processes of political-economic-social instability with consequences that are rendered more critical and violent by the use of ethnic wars, religious fundamentalisms, the disintegration of national unity and a rapid evolving of a more sophisticated use of criminality,[11] all according to the New World Order paradigm.

For many decades, in fact, a worldwide process of great financial movements has taken place, with an inter-bank system that relies on brokers who are spread throughout; the international banks directly carry out most of the functions demanded by individuals and companies with large inter-bank markets that connect local banks and the banks placed in financial centres. In this strong global financial competition context, what has changed in the old concept of globalization (whatever the technology level) is the interconnection of economic phenomena (production, consumption, exchange, increase and centralization of capital, techniques and equipment, new forms of finance, entrepreneurship, competitiveness, new processes of accumulation). These factors tend to the polarization of the most powerful economic hubs (US, EU, Asian hub) of the global economy, through the political use of new processes of financialization of the economy. The new polarized globalization, or rather the modern global competition, brings into play not only the role of the Fordist enterprise and the production process connected to it, but also the international financial and banking systems, real element of innovation in the world economic process.

What is happening is not only the dominance of a new outsourced production system, but also a new financial system, a new accumulation of capital, a "flexible accumulation" of the post-Fordist era, based on the financialization of the economy and the massive use, in terms of accumulation of values, of intangible capital, intangible resources, such as knowledge, information, communication, etc..

---

[11] For the last twenty years a strong link between financialization of the economy and crime has been showed. Take for instance the drug trade and many other illegal trades, such as the arms trade, the illegal market of waste, prostitution and the slave workers market in the so-called submerged economy. They are produced directly to support mechanisms of accumulation, so as to arrive to identify the new concept of "criminal Keynesianism."

International usury has also come up with their international "clearing houses," its regulatory institutions of the various (imperialist) competitive and adversarial powers: for example the IMF, the WB, the WTO, the UN. They represent the vive, although shaky, expressions of the imperialist powers which dictate their agenda, the calendar application, put their vetoes, annihilate any form of opposition – often only verbal – of other unequal "members," write their international law and make it respected as they please.

These instruments are thought to be the warning signs of a single global government run by a single dominant class, where member States have no longer any power and delegate everything to the international "network" of global governance. On the contrary, there is not any single "movement" in or out of these institutions that is not the direct result of the political will of the governments that are involved (in various capacities and with unequal powers) in these institutions. The presence of States is very visible and strong. Indeed, international law has no other legal subject of reference, but the State, sovereign and independent – at least formally.

Systemic Crisis and the Use of Keynesian Variants

Since Marx spoke for the first time about economic crisis, perhaps over a hundred crises have taken place, although with different characteristics, with more or less large deceleration of growth in terms of volume, with more or less large destruction of the labour-force with unemployment and insecurity, with more or less widespread destruction of capital, in particular since financialization has assumed a more central importance. With the important role of finance, the crisis of overproduction and under-consumption explodes in a form not considered in Marx's years, as the bursting of financial bubbles damaging the chances of credit to investment and consumption provokes more significant collapses of real demand that may result, as in the current crisis, in structural and systemic factors. It is not a coincidence that the economic crisis at the end of the 20th century found its solution in the First World War after the "Belle Epoque," in the closing phase of English imperialism. The crisis of the early 1920s found its most apparent manifestation in the outbreak of the financial bubble in 1929 that affected credit capacity and made actual demand fall, and was certainly not solved with the New Deal in 1933, but found definitive solution only with the Second World War, when the era of German dominance expressed in the political-economic features of Nazism closed, and the post-war reconstruction phase was started, centred on the political and economic power of the United States.

The real economy regarded as efficient and in equilibrium can not be separated from the financial economy, because the financial capital and the productive capital join each other in the multinational corporations, the holdings, the interconnections between industrial systems and enterprises of goods and services in general and the banking system, the financial and insurance companies. The financial and productive functions are simply two functions of capital that are increasingly joined in the same economic operator, and also in the mixtures between technical materials and financial speculation activities, made easier and more frequent by deregulation of the financial system.

This is different from affirming, instead, that in trying to end the crisis that has been lasting for 35 years, the international capitalisms have used finance in a super-structural way and also as a speculation substitute to cope with the great difficulty of the processes of accumulation of capital. In this sense there was a prevalence of a relatively autonomous process of speculative finance to offset the insufficient production of surplus value in relation to the overproduction of goods and capital.

With neoliberalism, in the late 1970s, the financial sector and the speculative processes played a key role in economic policy through the financial deregulation, realized by the Reagan and Thatcher governments, which eliminated all restrictions to the movements of capital, realizing in this case a merely financial globalization. The guarantee bank reserves were thus cut, tax heavens increased, there was the proliferation of creative finance and of the opportunity to bet on the stock market not only on the flaws of financial instruments but also on raw materials, exchange rates, food, generating speculation to achieve easy stock profits, and hence influence the determination of prices on oil, wheat, corn, completely oblivious to the fact that those gains meant hunger, misery and destruction for the poor. Any investment opportunities in the real economy is transferred in the apparently more profitable speculative finance, destroying the excess capital for productive purposes.

In order to realize the surplus-value from production in a situation of global competition among companies and currency, monetary and productive areas, through the dynamics of technological innovation of product and process, it is possible to make larger amounts of product with less work than previous technologies afforded and go to the market with competitive lower prices. The increased productivity of labour and capital related to the processes of technological innovation reduces the social labour necessary to obtain the individual product, and that in Marxian terms reduces its value. These processes thus increase the presence of fixed capital in the cycle of production and reduce the necessary labour time, and therefore variable capital is obviously reduced in relative terms with respect to fixed capital. The reduction of required labour, in terms of the relative consequence, reduces the rate of surplus value, that in monetary terms through competitive processes represents the rate of profit on the capital thrown into circulation.

This reduction in the rate of profit due to the overproduction of capitals can be contrasted by destroying or devaluing capital surplus, by reducing surplus value in order to restore the "satisfying" rate of profit. In addition to technological innovation, also the introduction of financial assets, and the power of entrepreneurs of purchasing material and immaterial capital, intermediate goods and services through debt, make the overproduction of capital possible and, through foreign debt, also the overproduction of goods. Clearly, as repeatedly pointed out by Marx, every crisis is manifested as a monetary-financial crisis but the financial element is not the cause of the crisis. This is valid for the current crisis and the 1929 crisis, in which the financial element is an effect and not a cause, which must be sought in the so-called real economy, that is, in the mechanisms of capitalist production.

But the present crisis can be more serious than that of 1929, as it is not sure that the new emerging competitor countries such as China, Russia, India could offset the slump in the U.S. because the United States have a considerable role in world trade, and the important function of their financial market in the global economy, plus over two thirds of the international monetary reserves are in dollars. Moreover, this crisis has an immediate and direct impact on workers in terms of further increase in unemployment. By cutting the direct, indirect, deferred wages and causing the ruin of pension funds, for example, it will increase the mass of the poor with a new strong fall of the middle classes who will join the old poor, homeless people and have their purchasing power increasingly eroded.

That is why we consider it an unresolved structural crisis, extended through the financial deregulation which determined the dominance of fictitious capital but not its exclusivity. Thus we can not claim that this form of capital is a basic element or precursor of the processes of accumulation. In this regard, we could refer to the long cycles of Kondratieff; according to this perspective, after an initial long period of expansion, the post World War II until the early 1970s, a long cycle of crisis can be identified precisely since the early 1970s until now, and in this long crisis capitalisms try to achieve profits mainly through financial speculation. But the particularity is that this crisis is structural and systemic and causes surely the end of the dominance of U.S. capitalism and imperialism, and at the same time announces the terminal phase of the capitalist system itself. This is because the possibility of real accumulation of the system has reached its limit; and because, although in the long period of expansion the Keynesian model and the Keynesian welfare states have let capital increase, the financialization of the economy, the forced privatization, the attacks on the labour rights and costs, the direct and indirect and deferred wages, have not been able to resolve this crisis through the destruction of the value of capital, because it is a systemic crisis.

The financialization of the economy has led not to a solution of the crisis, but to a financial bubble with an unprecedented aggravation of the general economic crisis. The privatization of the economy did not provide solutions, so that today the progressives, the left, as well as the conservatives want to return to an interventionist, governor and employer State, with a Keynesian form, that is not only military based but also constitutes a strong support for companies, banks, insurance enterprises, which at this stage would be doomed to fail without any support to demand in social spending. This form of Keynesianism is called "Keynesianism of the private" or "business Keynesianism". The third attempt to solve the crisis, through a strong attack on and reduction of the labour costs and the general social direct, indirect and deferred wages, did not help solve the crisis because it has led to a general contraction of purchasing power, which has added to the crisis of overproduction the content and the effects of a crisis of under-consumption.

We also must consider, in addiction to it, new phenomena such as the overproduction from exploitation of non renewable resources such as oil, water, food, realizing at the same time the environmental crisis, the food crisis, the energy crisis, the crisis of the rule of law and therefore a widespread systemic crisis.

U.S. Military Imperialism and the Economy:
the Military-Industrial Complex[12]

The Role of the War Economy

The maintenance of asymmetric international economic relations, and particularly of the central imperialist relationship, requires the use of force. Capitalist colonization during the nineteenth century imposed itself by the use of military force and the existence of a clear superiority in this area revealed itself to be fundamental to establish capitalist empires.

The role of the military industry and of military spending, however, goes beyond the simple maintenance of the "secure borders of the empire," because these characteristic already existed in ancient empires. The specificity of capitalism is that military activity is transformed into the central mechanism of the process of capitalist production, being fundamental in the permanent and accelerated innovation process, and in the regulation of business cycle, in a "military Keynesianism" which survives even in the neoliberal era.[13]

Military expenditure carries out two essential functions in North American capitalism: as it is essentially a planned expenditure of the public sector (the Pentagon has been the largest planned economy in the world, even in the era of the USSR), it contributes to oppose the inefficiencies and mismanagement of the market economy. Indeed, through military spending a very important part of the U.S. industrial and service economy is planned. To this planning the spatial distribution of activities, employment, the interconnections between branches, etc., must be added, which make possible the reduction of the impact of the economic cycle in the general level of output.

This fact was one of the discoveries of the virtually planned economy during the Second World War, when the U.S. economy reached the full utilization of productive resources. Later, the war economy contributed to curb recession cycles, promoting the maintenance of

---

[12] About these issues see the fundamental historical book by Baran and Sweezy (1968).
[13] We introduce the basic analytical framework to interpret this phenomenon. To examine the subject see Gabriel Kolko, one of the best analyses of the anatomy of the North American military capital: cf. Kolko (1994, 2006). A specific analysis on the dynamics of the current military imperialism can be found in Casadio, Petras, Vasapollo (2003) and Vasapollo (ed., 2003).

industrial employment and the apparent acceptable levels of growth, measured in terms of GDP.

It is significant that military spending in the United States presents a cyclical profile. It is affected not only by the internal economy but also by the international socio-political situation. But in any case, since the Vietnam War, the cycle presents a very similar profile, with very high spending ceiling and spending plans. The only discrepancy appeared during the years of President Jimmy Carter, when the reduction of military spending was realized in a context of reduction of the U.S. imperialistic power. This important lessons was learned by the next governments.

This political-economic role of military spending explains the consensus about it among U.S. citizens, who support half of the world military spending. But unlike other countries, where this expenditure is usually to pay soldiers, U.S. military spending in the economy creates an industrial sector more dynamic towards the production of arms, acting with the effect of investment of the Keynesian multiplier.

In Europe, where public spending is much higher than in United States, however, most of it is oriented to social services or infrastructure that stimulate much less the local production ability. Thus, although social spending plays a role in regulating the cycle, for example as automatic stabilizers in demand in the case of rising unemployment, it has a smaller structural impact in the production capacity of the European countries.

The U.S. military spending plan has become the main source of productive innovations: from the numerical control machine tool[14] up to the internet, technological change in the last forty years has been determined by technological advances in the military industry. The ability to rely on substantial public funds, with a detailed planning of research activities and results achieved, is the basis of the technological advantages of many branches of U.S. industry that subsequently move to the market competition of private industry. This explains why in U.S. between 60% and 80% of public expenditure in research and development facilities is used for military research, a percentage much higher than the OECD average, which is around 25%.

---

[14] David Noble (1984) shows how the introduction of numerical control in industry, and not other alternative technologies of automation, is the result of a decision by the Airforce, in a joint project with IBM and MIT.

Thus, between imperialism and colonialism of the nineteenth century and North American post-colonial imperialism of the twentieth century, militarism has become the guarantor of imperial power, the political element of capitalist production, configuring a triangle of functions that determines the characteristic of the whole system: the inter-sectoral structure of the U.S. industry, the driving force of technological innovation and the arrangement factor to oppose the business cycle. The United States have produced a military-industrial complex that expresses the common interests between capital and the State, and which the pan-European project of EU aims to reproduce.[15]

We conclude that, increasing the so-called defence budget, military spending is closely linked to the economic interest of a group of major monopolistic companies and the power of an extensive political-military bureaucracy with its collateral groups. This political military bureaucracy generates demand for research, propaganda, training of managers and labour in general, which employs a large elite of intellectuals and technicians financed by the defence budget.

This process has been valid for all the imperialist powers and has been the base of the military industrial complex, as an integral and inseparable part of the political and economic relations of monopolist State capitalism: it was a phenomenon which is not limited to the national level.

The military industry complex is a subsystem of economic-political-military relations, based on the close relationship created between the large military industrial enterprises and the State. This subsystem has also created its own ideological apparatus, that reproduces the ideas of militarism. Its hegemonic centre has been until now in the U.S. and spreads in the world as a multinational subsystem of arms trade, licensing and investments for the joint production of weapons; it relies on military arrangements and the military bases system, training programs and military cooperation, considering as sources for their expansion the underdeveloped countries, which are forced to continuously increase their military spending as subordinate oligarchies support locally the goals of imperialist policy.

These relations have become a necessity in the process of economic, political and ideological reproduction of global imperialism, enhanced,

---

[15] Casadio, Petras, Vasapollo (2003: 81–185 and 257–266). See also Arriola, Vasapollo (2004).

on the threshold of the XXI century, by the military, strategic, regional hegemonic position of the U.S. Today, the danger /threat to world peace is major than the one in the so-called Cold War and of the East-West confrontation.

The merger between banking and industrial monopolies causes their interconnection with the State. This link between State and monopoly generates the phenomenon of a special union between the State and the weapons-producing monopolies, and those monopolies that make production charged to the defence budget or from the budget benefit.

This communion of interests is the guarantee of obtaining the maximum profit, as in a structure of power that achieves to produce its own ideological apparatus. A sector, the arms industry, that enjoys the State privileges, transforms the military economy in a "special segment" which does not follow the same rules applied to the whole national economy.

Imperialism generates militarism, which consolidates the outset of a group of state-military monopolies and military and a large network of relations between the political-military bureaucracy and the monopolistic industry that provides military apparatus. All this, facilitating and intensifying the process of militarization, causes a militarism spiral which is one of the most dynamic and contradictory element of current capitalism.

The development of the military economy produces a permanent trend towards a growing military budget, and a dependence of the economic cycle of the U.S. economy upon arm production and war in general. The so-called production for defence becomes a necessity of the cycle of reproduction of the whole economy, because no other production meets the goals of capitalist production and the continuous increase in profits like defence production.

Lenin had already claimed that the financial oligarchy's interests are opposite to the whole society's goals. Nevertheless, the large group of political-economic-military power goes beyond this definition, because it is a sector within the oligarchy itself, and this sector holds a power which any other sector or social class had never enjoyed, since it is a phenomenon generated by the same development as imperialism. The internationalization of the military industry is not isolated; there are processes of internationalization of capital and production, in addition to the growth of multinational enterprises and the exploitation of capital by the monopolies, that are the most important

producers and traders of goods and are also the most important con-
tractors of their respective governments for the production of armaments. These monopolies have diffused their branches in the other
capitalist powers and between the members of the system, creating a
thick network of interrelationships, which has been used to convert
the military industrial complex in a phenomenon that is not localized
only in the United States. In fact, since the 1950 the influence of this
structure acts in the economy and policy sectors of the major imperialist powers, but with an obvious economic political and technology
supremacy of the United States.

The Transnational Factors of the Military Economy

A series of factors feed the current character of the multinational military industrial complex. Among these the most important are:

a. the broad range of economic and political-military interests of the
    world imperialist powers, particularly of the United States that at
    the end of the twentieth century have strengthened their military
    hegemony;
b. the impact of a wide network of military bases outside the U.S. ter-
    ritory;
c. the existence of an extensive network of alliances and military
    pacts, now strengthened by the opening of NATO to the entry of
    former members of the Warsaw Treaty;
d. the sudden and unprecedented increase in U.S. military budget, fed
    by so-called strategy of "the struggle against terrorism";
e. the enormous expansion of the destructive power of U.S. conven-
    tional military armaments, which tends to change the rules of war,
    so that in order to defend themselves the countries have to use the
    disastrous tactics of terrorism or nuclear weapons;
f. the tendency to develop a nuclear-tactical power, aimed at deter-
    ring Third World countries from fighting against imperialism;
g. the United States started the twenty-first century with an extremely
    aggressive foreign policy, which does not respect the rules of the
    international organizations. The consequence is the spread of the
    worldviews of the most reactionary North American political and
    intellectual sectors.

September 11, 2001 was considered by the U.S. extreme right forces
as the long-awaited opportunity to restore Imperial America, ready
to intervene anywhere and with any justification, as it has happened

in Iraq. The United Nations is paralyzed by the U.S. and has become a means of imposing expansionary policies.

As we have claimed, the military economy is not clearly separated from the rest of the economy, and uses the same mechanisms and instruments that characterize the current global system of capitalist economic relations constituting, in fact, a subset.

What we are describing is a transnationalization, headed while this work is being written by the United States, oriented to increase their military power, both conventional and nuclear; to strengthen their role in the world trade of technological arms; to consolidate the aggression capacity of States such as Israel, which play an important strategic role within a region of particular interest; to increase their capacity of mobilization, without having to depend on alliances.

Korea (1950–1953), Indonesia (1965–1974), the era of Reagan (1981–1989) and now Iraq are occasions for military participation and intervention. South Asia is a demonstration of the rapid growth of the U.S. Empire and the creation of new opportunities for large multinational companies to expand the U.S. empire. The phenomena that push the need for a military industrial growth and do not depend on the operation of the economy to ensure profit, but come from the strategic goal of maintaining the imperial hegemonic power in the world.

The current oligarchy has, like never before, a hold on power, and the most extremist sectors, led by the United States, have led the world to an enormous war that no one can win. This is because the political-military milieux within U.S. society have reached the same position in the political system, of governments, political parties and of the electoral subsystems, with the advantage that the military industrial complex intersects with the three subsystems and has a level of transnationalization that has never been achieved by any other structural component of the U.S. political system.

PART SIX

SCENARIOS FROM THE SYSTEMIC CRISIS AND
THE VALIDITY OF MARX'S SCIENTIFIC ANALYSIS FOR
THE CRITIQUE OF APPLIED ECONOMICS

CHAPTER THIRTEEN

THE POST-FORDIST PARADIGM AND
THE NEW INDUSTRIAL REVOLUTION[1]

On Class Power

Several factors indicate a certain exhaustion of Fordism in the late 1960s (Boyer, Durand 1993). There was the saturation of the market for the products massively introduced at the end of World War II. When the populations of the core countries had all the necessary consumption goods (TV, washing machine, telephone, paid holidays, etc.) a slowdown in sales and in growth occurred.

The potential market, made up of the masses of impoverished peripheral countries, can not consume because their function in the Fordist model of development consisted in working in exchange for subsistence, producing low-cost raw materials and some luxury and consumption goods demanded by the core countries.

It is symptomatic that since the outbreak of the crisis in the early 1970s, only two new products have entered mass consumption in the developed countries: television and the computer, and the productions derived from and related to them. Changes are recorded in the content of products, rather than in the introduction of new products with new features: transistors for chips, steel for plastic, copper for optical fibre.

Another key factor was the redistribution of power within the enterprise from capital to labour. One of the characteristics of the model was the achievement of the "full employment" of the labour-force, even though this characteristic only embraced 20% of the world population and for two decades only, between 1948 and 1968. In fact, during the other two hundred years of capitalism, before and after, there has been no full employment: this phenomenon is an exception. Despite the temporary and spatial limits of the phenomenon, its combination with the strengthening of Unions and the growth of trade

---

[1] About these topics there are frequent references in Vasapollo (1996) and Martufi, Vasapollo (2000b).

facilitated the organization of workers' resistance to the technological changes in progress. This resulted, among others, in the following events (Beaud 1986):

- Increase in the rates of absenteeism;[2]
- Rejection of the assembly line and the numerical control machines;
- Sabotages of the assembly lines and automatic machines;
- Reduction of labour time imposed by the workers.

As a result, the progressive decrease in productivity, together with the rise of wages, caused the consequent reduction of surplus and capital production.

In addiction we must consider the change in the policy framework. The international system took the form of a hierarchy responding to the roles that the different countries played in the international division of labour. In the "pyramid," in the absence of world authorities, a specific country acted as international "judge-arbitrator," but dictated the rules of the game to pursue the specific needs of its capital reproduction.

Since 1871 Germany and the U.S. have challenged the British hegemony that dominated the Earth during the nineteenth century. Therefore, England started to lose its influence in the military (British Army), economic (the textile and steel industry) and financial (the pound) fields. The stability of the 1930s was not replaced by another form of stability. Through various wars, the United States of America (and the dollar) placed themselves at the head of the global economy. These changes implied the passage from a system of gold-pound British power to a dollar-gold U.S. system.

At the end of World War II, the U.S. were the only creditor country, and also did not suffer the disastrous damages undergone by the other allied countries: they had, therefore, the industry and enough money to became the driving force of the development and reconstruction of Europe and the World.

This system worked until Western European and Japanese industry resumed competing with the U.S. industry in the international market. Times have changed and now for the U.S.A. maintaining their military hegemony (war in Korea, Vietnam and Iraq today) costs more than what cost England in the preceding century. Thus, since the late 1960s,

---

[2] For an examination of the phenomenon in Italy see Bianchi, Dugo, Martinelli (1972).

U.S. gold, together with the dollars scattered in the world, does not cover even the fifth part of its due.

This generated the failure of the international monetary system, when President Richard Nixon recognized, in August 1971, that the U.S. could no more guarantee the full convertibility of the dollar to gold, and the international economic system stopped working as it had done up to that time. In 1976, five years later, the IMF admitted that the monetary system no longer existed. Official gold quotation shot up, the controls of exchange rates were eliminated and markets achieved more power in fixing prices and the decisions that marked the beginning of the decline of U.S. financial hegemony.

It is at this time (1978) that the Europeans in order to regulate their trade decided to create the European Monetary System, and subsequently the single currency (1999), to free themselves from the obligation to defend exchange rates from speculative markets and get free from the protection that the USA as a matter of fact exerts on international payments with the reserve function that the dollar still actively holds.

Another factor which influenced the process of crisis is the rise of raw materials prices in 1973. Until that time there were high wage costs and an increasing productivity, coupled with low cost raw materials. In 1973 this situation changed and the increase of commodity prices such as energy (oil), aggravated the crisis of production that had started with the productive slowdown in the late 1960s: and that is how enterprise profits fell down precipitously.

This succession of events was faced by the governments with the usual solutions; severe recessions were experienced and the traditional solutions of increasing public spending were applied to offset the collapse of the economy. But, as it was a long lasting crisis, the rise of expenses with the reduction or slowing down of revenues, ended up into a fiscal crisis of the State.

How Does the Industrial Revolution Continue?

"Like the first, the second industrial revolution changes essentially the source of energy of production and transport. Together with coal and steam, oil and electricity make wheels and machinery work" (Mandel, 1997: 617, translated from the Italian edition).

As a consequence, we can define the industrial revolution as a qualitative process that changes radically the primary energy sources that ensure the reproduction of the entire production process (although the use of "previous" energy sources persisted), causing the growth of new market sectors (for example, the chemical industry, engineering, etc.). However, the industrial revolution is not only a problem of raw materials, for these need, to be exploited, also a new technology that helps "jump" from one previous stage to a qualitatively new one (and it is this quality shift that allows subsequent quantitative improvement).

This process of technical and organizational evolution is not neutral. The technical revolution is premised on the replacement of human labour with labour embodied in the machines.

Technological revolution, therefore, consists in all innovations (continuity in the same technological base) of the radical type (rupture with the continuity) that may involve the new technological systems with direct or indirect consequences, in almost all sectors of activity; it is a change of technological paradigm. We refer, for example to the change from the Keynesian-Fordist phase of capitalism, that existed from the 1930s to the 1970s.

The production of the basic development theorized with Taylor's concept has as its principles labour management and organization:

a. the separation between the conception, planning and control of labour quality and its implementation;
b. the fragmentation and standardization of work;
c. the individual worker's loss of the vision of the entire labour process (Ordonez 2004).

The internal combustion engine, together with electricity, supplied the technological basis to apply the initial forms of advanced mechanization. The crisis of Fordism, in the late 1970s, resulted in a structural crisis of the global economy, making the search by north American economists of new theoretical viewpoints necessary, to overcome the crisis into which the stagflation had left the old theoretical paradigms.

The new industrial cycle and the economic cycle rose from the emergence of electronics and informatics as the new technological basis of the economy. This led to the replacement of the engineering and petrochemicals automobile complex, that is the Fordist Keynesian technology basis of capitalism, with the electronic-computer complex, as a new driving and regenerating force of the social production and capital accumulation. All this is now translated in a new economic dynamism and industrial cycle.

Coming to the structure of national consumption, it should be noted that financial globalization and economic internationalization influenced the economic balance, because the distribution of national income and the consumption demand did not assume the same strategic importance as in the Fordist model. Also the role of the State as economic operator and dispenser of income to production factors changed. The productive change has led to a deconstruction of labour and simultaneously to the crisis of the general system of guarantees.

As we showed previously, in this new economic system public spending is not addressed to a real increase of the national economy in terms of infrastructure and of the efficient production of public services: a society with greater social differentiation is instead realized, where the social protection system in favour of the weaker citizens has been reduced. These groups have been getting bigger, going to include those strata of society that were considered protected until a few years ago (public workers, artisans and traders), thus creating new poverty, new needs, and expanding the area of social outcast.

In particular, for the U.S. economy, the main beneficiary of this new dynamic introduced by the cyclic shift to a new technological paradigm, it has created a phenomenon of economic reactivation, begun in late 1982 (November), until 2000, with only a short-term recession in 1991.

Europe, too, played a key role in the new industrial revolution. The Treaties of Maastricht and Amsterdam[3] are the expression of a policy that establishes the absolute prevalence of the market in the definition and stabilization process of European capitalism, highly imitative of American-Anglo-Saxon model and at the same time competing with it in order to strengthen the European geoeconomic bloc.

But Europe, unlike the United States or Japan or other Asian countries, has not a unique and homogeneous policy of productivity growth, but a series of uneven, qualitatively different models of quantitative growth, which are not necessarily economic and social development models. It is necessary, instead, a policy that actively faces the problems of employment and social protection. The problem of mass unemployment exists everywhere in Europe and it is not just

---

[3] Three excellent books on the class analysis of the European policies of integration are Carchedi (2001), Bonefeld (2001) and Arriola, Vasapollo (2004).

an economic problem, but a structural phenomenon. We are faced with a situation where a full economic recovery cannot reduce the number of unemployed; the quantitative growth of the economy does not mean overall socioeconomic progress nor equal and territorially homogeneous development.

The move towards a new technological paradigm and towards the model of accumulation, which has as its fundamental technological basis the so-called computer-electronics sector, should not lead us to believe that the technological-based system has so changed as to have eliminated the cyclical contradictions and the base of the Fordist-Keynesian cycle. Firstly, capitalism has never been able to standardize its technological base and will not be able to do so, as it feeds on its asymmetries and inequalities in order to survive. This passage to a new cycle of accumulation, which is not Fordist-Keynesian and has the computer-electronics sector as its technological paradigm, is not, at least initially, a phenomenon of the developed capitalist centres nor of the member countries of OECD. Even the "rational core" of Keynesian politics, that is State intervention in the economy, has not gone away. Rather, capitalism progresses on the basis of unequal economic and political development, already examined by Lenin in Imperialism, and keeps the rules of its enterprise system.

The Information Revolution or Third Industrial Revolution

The third industrial revolution, which began to develop in the 1980s, has as its basic component information technology. Although this revolution is considered as "industrial," the conception of industry has changed in the three industrial revolutions: in the first, the workshops were grouped, the machines were already in the factories and the craftsmen were the main workers of the new industrial proletariat; in the second industrial revolution, there was the introduction of the assembly line and scientific labour organization with the controls on time and rhythm. That was the phase of the so-called formal subsumption of labour to capital. Workers, placed in an enterprise organization that they could not control, were nonetheless still able to exert some control over their own work (technical, quality, rhythm).

What we can call hetero-direction was less intense than the one practised after the mechanization development, which deprived the worker of their knowledge and skills, jealously preserved because it represented the power of labour-force resistance subsumed to capital. With the "Taylor revolution," labour will be further stripped and weakened, dominated by the power of capital.

Finally, in the third industrial revolution, which involved the information technologies, there has been the automation processes. From this perspective it is possible to understand cases such as Fiat in the early 1970s, which had no problem in replacing twenty workers with a robot, in the coating phase of the assembly line, because, although robots were much more expensive, they did not go on strike or produced absenteeism (Levidow and Young 1981). In fact, already F. Taylor said that with the scientific labour organization it was necessary to avoid worker's control on the productive process.

Another problem to hold the total control on production process is that all the workers were concentrated in the factory, causing losses to the industry because of strikes and labour and social conflicts. It results in the segmentation and fragmentation of production processes. That is, the long series of assembly lines within a single building became short and dislocated.

Therefore, fragmentation, outsourcing, offshoring are the key of the new production process. Thus there develops a reticular system of integrated enterprises or in a single group or in a chain built on trade commission/supply. Depending on the size and complexity of the entire labour process it can be organized on different levels, so there is a pyramid where the head house turns to their first level suppliers and they in turn commission each "part" of the work process, or individual parts to subcontractors of second, third level, etc. This new structure receives input from the large company, that could be a multinational, and continue level by level, progressively reducing the scale of individual suppliers, until it reaches small or microscopic businesses.

The other element of the third industrial revolution is energy saving. So in vehicles the steel is replaced with plastic in many of their components. Or investment are oriented to research and development.[4]

---

[4] Nowadays, producing one unit of any industrial good demands two fifths of the raw materials needed in 1900. In 1984 to achieve the same production quantities, Japan consumed only 60% of materials first that consumed in 1973. One ton of copper cable can be replaced with 25 kg of optic fibre, which is produced by only about 5% of the energy required to produce copper.

Another dimension of the technological revolution with important consequences in world politics was North American victory in the arms race against the Soviet Union. The U.S. won this race because the resources on armaments are obtained reducing the costs of social benefits, and this process was more acute and brutal in the U.S. than in the USSR. The race served, indirectly, so that the capitalist system functioned in terms of accumulation; and international capital achieved to turn the military effort in a worldwide production of goods and services. Military discoveries were financed with public engagement and the Pentagon was the largest economic planned unit in the world.

One of the most spectacular types of technology is informatics or communication technology. Its entry into the market, since the second half of the twentieth century, led to a change in the rhythms of the innovation processes of the means of production, which once installed (i.e. the dominant technology in a certain period for certain productive tasks) now has a much shorter life. The average life of a computer does not exceed three years, and software is definitely shorter, because a crucial business success is often based on the capacity for technological renewal (Foray 2006: 52).

Almost the whole of this technology has been developed after World War II. It is thanks to the military technology of the Pentagon that electric technology has been replaced by electronics, in a process of technological change in which hegemony is clearly in the U.S.

Every company, in order to compete with a fair degree of efficiency in a context of global competition, must realize a long term planning, adopting strategic plans of and in society, based on optimizing management resources. The process of creating value means wealth production and to achieve this goal, in the current phase of flexible accumulation, it is essential to accumulate resources, tangible and intangible capital to optimize and maintain over time the production cycle, the accumulation of values and the accumulation of social control forms.

So processes of generalized flexibility, derived by the generalized social factory began to be established. This initially posed a problem of adaptation to the large companies, characterized by excessive centralization and the strong rigidity of the production system. The smaller enterprises, however, often with high technology and innovation, were more ready to adopt new information and communicational models, and were able to achieve increased flexibility, wage coercion and various forms of exploitation, traditional or "new". This type of enterprise is more suitable to adapting its structure to the changing demands characteristics of market competition.

In some particular contexts of capitalist development, however, there has been a gradual change in the situation, because while small enterprises could not always cope with the competition with bigger companies, the latter, however, have gradually adapted their structures to the current phase, trying to become more flexible, particularly towards the labour-force, the decentralization and fragmentation of the production cycle, diversifying production and distribution, reaching a kind of district-, sector- and network-based enterprise development. Strong processes of outsourcing and relocation are realized, where communication is a strategic priority, being a strategic resource of abstract capital.[5] The term "resource" in business language means a material or immaterial (tangible or intangible) entity, through which any organization works to achieve its objectives. Assuming this definition, the word "resource" has a broad meaning that involves not only the internal organized system, but also the so-called external environment, for example the market, with which business organizations interact.

Another aspect of this third industrial revolution is the substitution of inorganic raw materials with organic ones (biotechnology and the development of new materials, many of these made up of bacteria to change the conductivity of certain minerals). So information technology and the replacement of inorganic raw materials with organic ones are the two major areas of current research, dynamism and economic accumulation. These changes have many implications in terms of the agrarian question and the bio-banks. A large part of the costs in technology development is carried out to improve productivity and agriculture.

Fordist Enterprises and the Knowledge Economy

The informatics industry is now reaching the so-called "third phase". The first phase is associated with big computers, used only by large companies for administration and accounting. The second phase concerns the last ten-fifteen years, and is distinguished by the great

---

[5] On these topics, will often refer to Martufi, Vasapollo (2000c).

expansion of individual automation with the presence of personal computers, which entered not only the offices but also a large number of people's homes: companies are increasingly more likely to invest in telecommunications and informatics. The third phase, however, is characterized by multimedia information with the presence of new technology that must be constantly updated with methods of co-optation of the various forms of intellectuals. In the final analysis, it is characterized by for the totalitarianism of the strategic deviant communication.

Structural intellectual capital has the task, then, to gather knowledge within the company and to connect people to data, skills, consultants, strategic intangible resources.

Intellectual customers capital is made up of the value of the relation between the enterprises and those who use its services; some appropriate indicators are used to know what is the part of the market captured by the enterprise and how customer demand can be met. Standard intellectual human capital becomes money through the relationship with customers, who are the most valuable capital for the company system. Customer capital is a kind of social consensus for the paradigms of profit.

Integrated communication becomes deviant not because it is a resource of enterprise intangible capital, but because through standard intellectual human capital it creates in society compatible intangible resources, such as continuous interacting knowledge, the image, the ethical and social behaviours of the enterprise, in a nutshell, the "enterprise culture of and in society". The model of integrated deviant communication, produced by the Profit State, conveys deviant culture, letting the various interlocutors measure the enterprise's ability to maintain the right balance between profitability, competitiveness, cost management and imposition of market's ethical-social values on the whole society.

In such a management business culture, information, and therefore knowledge and communication, have a strategic relevance. And the right investment on these resources gives the opportunities to gain competitive permanent advantages for the company, using communication as a image vehicle of business culture. In this culture, the management's creativity that produces new knowledge from knowledge and, developing intangible resources, identifies the procedures to accomplish the flexible accumulation, based on communication and techniques of the production cycle.

Consequently, in the overall strategy of the enterprise the tactical operative decisions are recomposed in cognitive capital, that management must carry, manage and create, in a continuous learning environment designed on flexible accumulation, focused mainly on knowledge and intangible resources.

Thus, in any model of capitalism and business system, the strategic thinking formulates consensus models of decisions about the main activities of the enterprise; and such activities aim at implementing policies consistent with the main priority purposes of the company, based on the imposition of the firm's culture on society. Efficiency, as quantitative relation between input and output, is considered as a short-term indicator: the overall effectiveness is measured by the degree of long-term impact on the external world. Nowadays the evolution of the enterprise – market relation determines success, the efficient and effective development of the enterprise as system of control and social domination.

This type of approach has led to the development of the business model of Japanese capitalism, that has than spread to Western business systems. It is, ultimately, a generalized cultural model, based on the optimization of intangibles recourses, on taking the advantages from the relations with external environment, the concept of cooperation and collaborative spirit: in this sense, the optimization results of business management must be combined with an apparent workers welfare and the general social interest, but always as subservience to the interests of the enterprise culture.

This new social culture and communication is coercive but at the same time is also highly creative and dynamic; it is constantly used to develop, maintain and defend socio-economic constant contacts of apparent mutual satisfaction, using as a vehicle the approved intellectual capital, i.e. resources, intelligences and men in the service of the profit culture, which creates social consensus by rendering the enterprise resources and culture more valuable.

CHAPTER FOURTEEN

SOCIO-PRODUCTIVE CONFIGURATION OF THE KNOWLEDGE ECONOMY[1]

The Knowledge Economy in a Society that Manages Communications

It is evident that information has a very relevant impact on the complex of high structural, productive, economic-financial risks. So, it presents a strong utility also in the production process, where the fall of the reliability of information involves a loss of production or a deterioration of the product quality.

Between 1960 and 1970, especially in Italy, business communication, meant as a set of commercial information (personal selling) developed on the cultural background of the social-economic conditions of that historical-political period. At the end of the 1970s, and in particular during the 1980s, communication assumes the characteristic of deviant strategic resources; deviant because it is exclusively the instrument of the general capitalist interest, but not of the single particular enterprise, in a model of neoliberal totalitarianism focused on information capital.

The changes in the structure of business organization, the adaptation of communication models to the general principle of enterprise flexibility of and in society have serious repercussions on labour organization and on the adaptability of workers to technological innovation, informatics and a communication based on techniques, instruments and models of determination and control of the labourforce, that is, deviant communication as strategic resource of abstract capital.

The principle of social and labour flexibility is applied as a system of social control. But a strict control system can cause evident discomforts and conflicts against the enterprises. It needs to complement the traditional control methods with new alternative means that provide innovative coercive behaviours, oriented to the collabouration and cooperation between the various human resources in the enterprise

---

[1] In this chapter there will be frequent references to Martufi, Vasapollo (1999, 2000b)

and in society. These processes have been widely tested in the "type model" of an integrated factory at FIAT-SATA in Melfi, where a lot of control systems based on language, even electronic, have been realized: we refer, for example, to "Andon" audiovisual communication systems, or the traffic lights that dictate the orders and rhythm of production, or the system of "kanban," where the apparent neutrality of the external requirement to the productive unit hides the enterprise's productive imperative. (see Jib 1998–1999).

Moreover, this approach strongly characterizes the industrial and Trade Unions relations within the enterprise, in which priority is given to the "personalized treatment" with the individual employee (problems of rhythm, permits, breaks, holidays, etc.). Finally, the very structure of the labour process, organized into multiple "micro" companies internal of the mother enterprise, and the dependence of production rewards on the performance of the whole group, facilitate a team spirit that helps horizontal control among the workers.

We witness a conflict of cultures and a flattening of differences between different countries. Everybody drinks Coca Cola or wears jeans, becoming "identical," but the diversity between different social classes gets even deeper, stronger and more penetrating. This situation is useful only to hold and wield the power of capital trough the means of deviant communication. A fundamental component of the new approach to accumulation, through the intangible capital of abstraction; a homologation to the image and culture of the market and of profit, as a unique form of business logic, submitted to the wild capitalist economic interest; a capitalism that dictates the models of cultural-social development, homologates all the intellectuals, neutralizes the political function.

The sociocultural growth of a larger part of population, the modified market conditions, the emergence of more sophisticated informatics and media cause a strong evolution of the concept of communication, considered no longer as a simple process of commercial information transmission, inside and outside, but as an organizational capacity to gain social consensus. A deviant and deviated communication as key factor of the pervasive knowledge system of the post-Fordist generalized social factory, able to finalize knowledge and organizational behaviour as transmission centres of the idea-enterprise to society, through information and decision-making processes that become models of social life.

A flexible organizational structure, in fact, with a strong and determined communicational model already in the strategic phase of planning, promotes harmony and consociational models aimed apparently at participating in the decisions of each component of the company, instead of adopting decisions imposed by a restricted leadership, but still aimed at compressing the conflicts in the labour world and in the unemployment field. This occurs by using, along with traditional media, other instruments, which take into account the wishes of the enterprise, the workers, people outside the production cycle, the customers, that enable the implementation of the decisions imposed on the community to turn it into a set of business interests holders (shareholders, management, suppliers and customers, public administration, workers, all citizens, although differently involved).

Deviant communication thus becomes a means to preserve the interests of the dominant class in society, in the territory, in the socially spread enterprise, in a generalized social factory, in which communication is the evolution phase of information capital, giving up its original priority: the communication with the purpose of the movement of all the ideas, the spread of new cultures, inventions and discoveries.

The integrated strategic deviant communication model is a unified framework of information, knowledge, ideas, decisions, behaviours, that transmits to different social targets the basic elements of the enterprise culture, to affirm the capitalist identity. So the neoliberal enterprise image is defined and managed, by strengthening and enhancing the economic, social and consensus management, focusing on the market laws, where the Profit State's role as pervasive agent is fundamental.

Post-Fordist capitalism is, in fact, a social dynamic system, characterized by a constant technological progress, intangible, capital-based, that expels labour-force, while in the past was functional to material accumulation in order to create new markets, involving the workers in excess. This is no longer valid, because the communication technologies are pervasive and characterized by virtual product as communication is an intangible means and not a produced good.

For the first time a technological leap as that information technology has nothing to do with the dynamic force for social development, but is mainly based on social consensus.

At the same time the growth levels are held without redistributing the produced wealth and guaranteeing development and employment, since there is no compatibility with flexible accumulation, that spreads to and affects social life as a pervasive immaterial force.

Between the strategic planning of the Profit State and the overall nomadic deviant communication strategy, the generalized social factory creates an extraordinary bond. The strategy planning of production and social behaviour becomes the original and primary communicational flow to impose the enterprise culture to society.

In this context, the strategic deviant and deviated communication, realized through the messages of the generalized social factory, becomes the resource of intangible capital for the post-fordist flexible accumulation. All this is oriented to the management of social consensus through the imposition of business culture-image, in a phase of capitalist restructuring focusing on flexible production and accumulation.

Such a form of capital becomes increasingly strategic, because it establishes the new frontier of the flexible accumulation for the entire post-Fordist capitalist system, with the idea of control and exploitation of the social subjects. Deviant behaviour and integrated strategic communication is able to offer to all the subjects, who interact with the socially widespread enterprise system, a unity of purposes, aimed at social control.

The image assumes the role of strategic intangible resource, realized through the nomadic integrated deviant communication: a fundamental resource for the development and success of the socially integrated factory. The image, if properly used, accumulates itself, becoming intangible capital with productive functions for the enterprise and the whole post-Fordist Profit State system, which is oriented to promote new forms of capital accumulation.

It is, ultimately, an image capital as a focal and connecting element of a system of deviant integrated communication models, which converge on it as a set of intangible resources, capital and immaterial accumulation. The "strong product" is represented by social consensus, that shows through the homologation to business competition forms, market culture, meritocratic mechanisms, extreme individualism culture, through the logic of unbridled competition among workers, lower classes, without any conflict with capital.

In this new concept of social advertising – communication aimed at strengthening the market culture, an effective integrated communication, in addition to promote and highlight the distinctive features of each company in relation to the competition, is able to meet the needs of capital, particularly financial capital, and consolidate the overall image of individualistic social welfare.

The total enterprise value depends on the quantification of intangible capital, the increase of values obtained by communication, the quality of immaterial information resources, used and capitalized by the system as a whole. To achieve a high level of consensus, creating and spreading enterprise value, it needs to create and strengthen, in a complex capitalist organization, the functional relationships between all the groups, between all the subjects working in a territory, starting from the single units of the enterprise.

A continuous exchange of ideas, information and knowledge is established to obtain a "peaceful" climate of compatible coexistence and sharing, that involves the workers, the citizens as subjects of work, non-work and denied-work. Everybody is involved in an homologation project to the meritocratic and competitive mechanisms imposed by single enterprises, managed by the financial capital.

Only in recent years the relevance of impulses and the liberty of organizing the enterprise, based on models of close co-responsibility between ownership, management, governmental institutions and workers organizations, has been accentuated. This happened because of the acceptance of negotiations by large Trade Unions, but also because of a different cultural climate, which led the whole society, and therefore also the employees, to give up to demand claims of other target, such as, often, wages.

Society and Immaterial Processes in Knowledge Economies: A Marxist Approach

Only recently in human history people have started to understand certain natural phenomena. The application of technical innovations throughout history was not a new phenomenon, but it has been a constant in the development of society. Marx claimed that historical periods can not be distinguished by the objects they produce, but by the working tools they use, and it is in modern age that the major changes have occurred modifying globally our society.

A lot of authors identify three fundamental periods as major milestones in scientific-technological development. The first relates to the industrial revolution, which caused decisive changes in the transition from craft production to industrial production. This process clearly

defines the identification of two fundamental social classes of capitalism: capitalists and workers. The second period, since the late nineteenth and to the early twentieth century, was characterized by the
massive access to the industrial production, the large use of hydrocar-
bons, by electricity. The last is represented by the third industrial revolution, defined as the "Scientific Technique Revolution" by the Soviet
school, and the new technical-economic paradigm of Western Marxist
thought. In this paradigm the application of scientific technological
progresses is generalized, changing the capitalist accumulation model,
the services and information technologies sphere is made massive, and
communication reaches levels never before suspected in the economic
and social life of the major capitalist nations. This third industrial revolution starts between the 1950s and the early 1960s of the twentieth
century, but takes up major connotation approximately twenty years
later, with a push to use the knowledge for the scientific-technological
development and for the economic-productive configuration of the
post-Fordist flexible accumulation.

Nowadays using terms such as scientific-technical revolution or
technical-economic paradigm, for Marxist economists, corresponds to
the confirmation that the profound social changes can not starts only
from the technological revolution; it needs changes in the ownership
relations so that there is a transformation in the quality of the actually
dominant system of production relations.

It is at this point that the concepts of "knowledge economy" and
"knowledge society" appear, with connected specific elements such as
"immaterial society," "intangible capital resources," "cognitive capital,"
"intellectual capital," "knowledge workers," "immaterial labour, "cognitive workers," etc.

To the knowledge content in the product and in the exports, the
developed countries, representing 20% of humanity, are involved in
more than 90% of the world scientific knowledge creation, while 80%
of the world inhabitants, which belongs to underdeveloped countries,
has a capacity to generate knowledge less than 10%.

While developed countries focus these resources on manufacturing production, the underdeveloped apply them to primary industries. A similar situation takes place in the structure for Research
and Development activities, because in the large high scientific-
technological centres of production and trade and commerce, a very
high percentage is devoted to experimental development, unlike the
underdeveloped countries that invest more resources in basic and
applied research.

Only the mastering and the availability of the newest technology may resolve situations and change structural assets. The problem, from this viewpoint, is that underdeveloped countries hardly have knowledge and technologies – or the investment capacity useful to produce them – to get out of their impasse. As some scholars note, the current scientific and technological revolution is the only one that have recently had a private character: know-how is not an available resource, but is jealously guarded, and the access to it for the countries in need is denied (Curien, Foray 2000).

The originality of the so-called "knowledge society" is that it accelerates the speed of its spread and of its global reach through culture, class and geography until it is getting an expansion and global dominance never seen before in a context of overall social dominance and not limited to the production sphere.

Capitalism will always measure the content of its wealth on working time as a creator of value, to preserve it and achieve its self-improvement. The political economists have the responsibility of analysing the wide dissemination of knowledge and its commercialization, dissecting the methodological and conceptual bases through which value creation passes in the knowledge economy era. It results that when the negotiating of knowledge occurs, the production sold as a commodity is knowledge; knowledge appears here as the final product (patents): the sale of knowledge-product is a commodity, and this product has a value and also a price, which is the result of complex labour.

At this point, there is the contradiction between the transformation from knowledge into value and the value of knowledge as a commodity.

The Marxist theory of labour-value explained more convincingly the significance of knowledge in the creation of value in its present condition only lately: behind the exchange between new technologies, new products and new knowledge there are economic and social relations between subjects in the process of production and services, generating a set of inequalities for the monopolistic domination of the great centres of power. In this international scenario the "knowledge economy" generated a new technoeconomic paradigm.

Recent World Bank reports acknowledge the contribution of knowledge to economic growth, but in the economic tradition, especially in the decades 1950–1960, the mathematical formula that permit to approach this phenomenon had already been understood.

Solow's model demonstrated that a major part of economic growth could not be explained by any traditional production factors; this model showed that technical progress was crucial to explain the dynamics of growth, but simultaneously recognized that it had an exogenous character.

It is not possible to identify a separate field of knowledge from the rest of the productive and service activities. The intangibility of knowledge implicates all spheres of human life, and in particular a restructuring process that brings the importance of knowledge, its application to technological processes and organizational and institutional factors in determining the international competitiveness among countries.

In an economy based on intangible capital resources, the total productivity of factors does not come mainly from traditional factors, but from knowledge.

The central activity of wealth creation is neither the allocation of capital to productive use nor labour.

In these new conditions, the conventional economic theories of the nineteenth and twentieth century, including classical, neoclassical and Keynesian, do not conform to the demands and needs of the production of knowledge; the basic economic resource is not capital nor resources, nor earth, nor labour, but it is knowledge. In this context, the traditional comparative advantages in international economic relations are replaced by competitive advantages, maintaining an exclusive use of knowledge as a competition factor.

The production process involves a physical process of transforming material shape through labour. But it is due to this process that labour becomes the measure of the social value of production, because of the historical capitalist form of social organization of the general production process, i.e. the reproduction process of human social life. And the forms of social organization are a material reality, as real as stones, minerals and organic matter involved in the production process. In reality, there is not a real separation between the production process, which involves the use of organic matter, and the production process of social relations, as reflected in certain interpretations of knowledge's role in the process of capitalist production, which lead to a pre-Marxist conception of material reality.

In his youth, Marx had drawn the critique to philosophical materialism, which limits the objective reality to the processes of nature and reduces the material analysis field of human reality to the natural, physical, chemical or biological, and more recently statisticians aspects. Spiritual aspects, knowledge and social relations are interpreted as epiphenomena, derivations of "natural" processes acting in humans.

But Marx's philosophy overcomes the philosophical dualism that establishes a separation between material and spirit, and applies this double dimension to every phenomenon of nature, even establishing a relationship of the spirit's determination on nature.

In contrast, in historical materialism (Marx and Engels's materialism) the spiritual phenomena, that are generated and perceived through knowledge, are a limited number of phenomena, characterized by their higher-level position with respect to the purely sensual processes. Knowledge is part of the objective reality given by feelings and belongs to the same real field of tangible nature.

Knowledge does not arise spontaneously: it is the result of an individual attitude of intimate reflection about external reality, but it appears in the production of social life as material life. In every historical era, knowledge is seen as determined by the conditions of social development, expressing the purposes and limits of society at the time. That is why knowledge is not only historically determined: it is also determined by class.[2] Knowledge is not neutral but is class-determined.

The Value of Knowledge or Value Originated by Knowledge

The industrialization of knowledge, the control of human energy, human labour thinking, abstraction, carried out by the owners the means of production, is currently the dominant form of the generation of knowledge, and endows them with a power to make social material productive forces dynamic greater than in other stages of the historical development of capitalism.

Any production of goods or services requires a certain amount of knowledge. The problem consists of determining and specifying when knowledge becomes the key component of these processes and becomes vital for the development of new productions of goods and services.

For a first approach to the theme of the knowledge economy from a Marxist theory of labour value standpoint, we need two methodological clarifications. First, for Marx the value of goods is determined by

---

[2] Marx wrote the "Theses on Feuerbach" in a notebook in 1845, at the age of 26, age in which he had already developed the basis of materialist philosophy of history. When Engels published them in 1888, he considered them as "the first document that contains the initial seed of the new conception of the world."

abstract, indistinct, undifferentiated labour: the magnitude of value as the socially necessary amount for the production of particular goods. The human labour that creates value can be: simple labour, which is the labour-force that every person, in the medium term, has in his body, without the need for special education; complex labour, which is the empowered simple labour or multiplied by a small amount of complex labour, and that can amount to a large amount of simple labour.

Therefore, knowledge is a complex labour, that is, empowered simple labour that is included in the process of production, services and in its knowledge, including a high level of productivity and competitiveness. This included knowledge can generate, and in fact generates, product innovation, as well as new technologies and new knowledge. Intellectual labour as a complex labour creates value.

Secondly, labour is the substance of value, but labour itself has no value (it is labour-force that has value): labour creates value.

For a deeper analysis of Marx's idea about the role of knowledge, development of science and technological processes and its application in production as a direct productive force direct, it is necessary to clarify that the study should be organized on the basis of an historically determined society, not society in the abstract, and it refers to capitalist society. Marx's analysis focuses on the historical nature of capitalism, and how the power of capital aims at its destruction and not at its development; that is, its development inevitably leads to its destruction.

At the same extent that the working time is set by capital as the only determining element, the immediate labour and its quantity as determining principle of production disappear. Marx continues explaining how labour is immediately reduced to a small and dependent proportion to the technological application of natural sciences. This analysis enables him to conclude that capital works to the benefit of its own dissolution as the dominant form of production.

Finally, knowledge society, as is a capitalist society, is characterized by having subdued human spiritual activity to the market relations.

And the market value has no other material content than labour-value, the application of human energy, physical and mental, to the production of goods, among which there is now knowledge.

The possibility of patenting knowledge, translating it into private financial profit (e.g. patents on human genome, or certain secretions of plants), is a clear demonstration that the knowledge "economy" is another expression of the market or capitalist economy, that applies a systematic measurement of market profit to knowledge, and does not constitute any exception to the application of the theory of labour-value, which explains precisely how this notion of market profit is built.

At the same time, the knowledge economy cannot be considered as external or alien to the dominant social relation in capitalism (i.e. the capital-labour relationship), determining a new configuration of the labour-capital conflict in the so-called post-Fordist phase.

CHAPTER FIFTEEN

THE DYNAMICS AND IMPLEMENTATION OF ECONOMIC POLICIES IN THE GLOBAL COMPETITION[1]

The System of International Political-Economic Dominance

The profound social and economic changes that have characterized recent decades have greatly influenced the local environment in which each production system has transformed how the entire enterprise is, appears and acts.

At this stage one can witness a globalization of markets, cause and effect of the increased competitiveness and productivity of the economic system as a whole and of the individual traders in particular. The improvement of transport and communications, the progressive demolition of trade barriers, also facilitated by the renewed international political and economic agreements, led to a more direct confrontation among enterprises, that behave as if they were operating in a market without any tie of territorial boundaries. The market, which has become increasingly dynamic and competitive, today seems to present a clear and irreversible trend to become a single market; a market of a global dimension.

Besides the internationalization of the production process, profound changes are recorded in the behavioural patterns underlying the manifestation of the demand for goods and services produced.

In the countries that until not long ago were described as industrialized, and today we prefer to define as the area of advanced, or rather mature capitalism, the consumer has become a far more complex subject than in the past, since the dense network of information available leads to more flexible and multidimensional behaviours, arising from the general context in which information and communication have now assumed a strategic and dominant role.

The new internationalization process has already been proved in markets as a process of global competition for the companies dealing

---

[1] On the subject see Martufi, Vasapollo (2000a), Vasapollo, Casadio, Petras, Veltmeyer (2004).

in the social market (generalization of the post-Fordist kind) in the era of the flexible accumulation. Excluding the circuit of local and traditional consumption, for the vast majority of products now there is no difference in status or perception of domestic products and trans-national products; usually, the products coming from other countries, or for other countries, are treated the same way as domestic products.

Firms now tend to regard the internal market as part of a wider market, divided into many national units: a trans-national market in which to develop global competition in a microeconomic key as competition among companies, and from a macroeconomic perspective as competing geoeconomic poles. The companies, however, are a driving force behind the internationalization, since on the one hand they have dictated the times and forms of the trans-nationality and on the other they have benefited the most from it.

The development of internationalization is connected with the crisis of Fordism; in fact, the liberalization of domestic markets has a very disruptive effect on the structure of power and the balance of Fordism. On the one hand, companies driven by international competition detach themselves from public protection, while on the other the regulatory power of the State decreases, becoming a global Profit State.[2]

In this sense, neoliberal globalization represents the beginning of a new phase in the history of capitalism, which arises from the end of the national society of mass consumption, which had granted too much power to the working classes to the detriment of the national capitalists, weakening the profit rate and thus generating the conditions for the great crisis of the 1970s.

In practice, internationalization becomes deregulation, in which there is not yet a real and systematic post-Fordist reorganization, but a loss of the old organization to achieve a new functional structure for flexible accumulation. Deregulation in fact consists of a gradual dismantling of the rules, which are identified as rigidities of the system; its largest impact is for instance on the welfare and regulation system typical of the Welfare State. Originally tried in the United States, propagated by an individualistic neo-conservative and liberal and apparently anti-government ideology, they were a pillar of the economic

---

[2] For further analysis see Martufi, Vasapollo (1999).

policy of the Reagan administration (the so-called Reaganomics), aimed at the elimination of constraints (laws and public institutions) and control of private entrepreneurship to ensure the efficiency of the economic system. Today this is the gospel of every neoliberal government.

The post-Fordist prospect must not have less organization; instead it requires a more complex system, which must govern a network of interdependencies much wider than that of the Fordist company. It must also coordinate change, which occurs also on capital resources that have increasingly intangible value.

The alternative proposed is to create a mass consumption society, in order to fragment, on an international basis, the working class which was unified at a national level: for example, a part of the German textile working class is composed of the workers from Singapore and Malaysia of the textile firms in Germany; a part of the working class of the automotive industry in the United States are the Mexican or Argentine workers of Ford, etc.

At the same time the consumption capacity of a fringe the population of the poor countries increases, a minority but enough to make the international trade in products of high added value profitable, as well as the internal marketing of part of the production of multinationals. These new consumers replace those who have become poorer, emerging from the number of demand generators: they appear today, in developed countries, in sufficient numbers so that through unemployment, the industrial reserve army, the workers of those countries can be controlled.

We can speak of four forms of capital: financial capital (better capital-investment), productive capital, «human capital» (workforce) and the one called social capital or better «social human capital», which is the accumulation of knowledge and production practices.

The capital-investment should not be thought of as a single body, but as a separate and hierarchical unit in which the productive capital (including FDI), the commercial capital and the financial capital (i.e. the financial investment), which, compared to the past, has taken on a purely speculative note, are combined.

The productive capitals, specifically foreign direct investment and financial investment, interact with each other to access the money mass that enables them to destabilize the economy, or rather to impose in those countries where the productive investment has been oriented the «stability» desired by large geopolitical blocs. The areas with strategic interest, such as Central-Eastern Europe and the Asian area of the former Soviet Union, Eurasia, Latin America, are in fact the battlefield where the two major geo-economic poles (U.S., EU) are fighting their economic war for global control.[3]

This is possible also thanks to interventions in terms of financial internationalization which, using the proceeds of foreign investments on production, are used to launder profits in the West favouring forms of financial speculation leading to easy money.

Productive capital is still subject to State laws; a machine cannot be so easily transported from one place to another. Productive capital moves in an international platform, because multinational firms establish a logic of accumulation that combines their activities in several countries within a single production process.

Human capital, or more precisely the workforce, has even more barriers: not only it has to ask permission at the border, but it also must have a passport, and its transfer costs more than moving a machine. The workforce is moving in an international space with different forms of regulation and enhancement of the workforce.

For its part the capital, the accumulation of knowledge and experience, the know-how, the production culture, are almost strictly national and often even regional, local (think of the phenomenon of the industrial districts in Italy). Therefore, different economic dynamics cross this planet at very different speeds and barriers.

But currently the only actually existing worldwide market, which has surpassed the limits of the regulation of national states, is the global financial capital market.

As such, neoliberal globalization is an unfinished reality, therefore subject to unpredictable changes in its evolution. There is another dimension of the neoliberal globalization that is instead advancing rapidly: in the ecology field there are regional problems (such as acid rain or air, soil and water pollution), but there also are global problems (such as the phenomenon of the ozone layer, the reduction in biodiversity and the overheating of the atmosphere), whose analysis needs more specific insights than those carried out in his work.[4]

---

[3] About these topics, later in this work, references will be made to Martufi, Vasapollo (2000a); Arriola, Vasapollo (2004, 2005).

[4] For a further analysis on this subject see Martufi, Vasapollo (ed., 2008); Vasapollo (ed., 2008).

The Market of Global Financial Capital

The cause behind the growth of the financial sphere are the flows towards this field of fractions of wealth coming from within the real production and that, before being moulded in different forms and transferred to the financial area, had taken on the characterization of wealth determined by the sphere of real production. These flows are the source of perverse mechanisms of accumulation, which determine economies aimed at the domination of finance capital as tools of the relationship of international competition among geo-economic poles, competition mediated through tradeoffs within the supranational organizations (G8, WB, IMF, OECD, CEI, BIS, UN).

These globalization processes on a financial level simply pursue their own internal logic, tending to maximize their financial returns without a leverage effect on the real economy; financial returns that add up to ever higher industrial profits, due to huge increases in labour productivity. These are increases that, since they do not have social redistribution, have increased the share of wealth allocated to the capital factor mostly in the form of income, taking less and less the form of investment able to create more jobs for the benefit of dividends, interest and capital gains to be devoted to financial speculation or foreign investment in countries with low labour costs and less rights.

The appearance of the structural economic crisis, since the early 1970s, led to the destabilization of the labour markets and of the systems of production. Today there continues to exist a system of movement of people (visas, immigration permits, migration authorities); there continues to exist a system of movement of goods (import and export permits, customs authorities), but there is no international monetary system, there is no world currency, there is no monetary authority to regulate the international circulation of money.

The decision taken in 1980 by Ronald Reagan and Margaret Thatcher's governments to complete the deregulation of the financial system, i.e. the elimination of controls, ensuring the free circulation of financial capitals, has led to the replacement of national governments and central banks authority with decisions that result exclusively from market signals. Only in the financial market the authority is almost absolute. The «almost» is because currencies continue to be national or belonging to a specific area.

So, while the goods of a country have a national market, and if they want to leave the country they must go through the mechanisms of international trade, national currencies have a global market. There is no international trade in currencies, subject to adjustments as every trade, but a global trade of currencies.

Financial globalization was largely due to decision taken by the U.S. to deal with their problems of balance of payments without a real adjustment of their economy, avoiding the pressures of the central banks around the world that the United States would not continue with the current payment of their debts with not convertible paper dollars. Since the U.S. has the ability to attract a large part of the world savings deposited in pension funds and investment funds, in this way they finance the deficit in real transactions with a *surplus* of capital.

This way the U.S. has allowed the creation of a huge world market of currencies, in which money creates more money (DD') without going through a real production. But the problems that occur in these global circuits of currencies are carried over in the circuit of the real economy and cause the crisis of not profitable banking institutions, and of their entire customer base. Legally the IMF cannot act on global currency markets in order to help its setting, because by statute the capital account of the balance of payments is not within its competence, but only of national governments. However, balance cannot be kept in this market in the long term. Being an essentially speculative market, balance is what some people earn, and others lose. But a loss concentrated in one or two agents creates a real imbalance in the global financial market, because it produces a great loss of trust and this imbalance is transported into the real economy. What is unknown is how to ensure that temporary imbalances affecting some of the agents are not transformed into an imbalance of the system. The problem is not that a bank fails, but that the one failing is one of the ten global banks that handle 50% of the total transactions between them. If any of these banks went into a crisis of trust, there would be a global financial catastrophe of unpredictable dimensions.

However, for large investors and multinationals the existence of global financial markets is a great advantage, because they have access to credit not limited by national unavailability.

Tools for 'Economic Interdependence,' i.e., Strategies to Enforce Dependency in Global Competition

In the absence of a radical break with the structure of total economic dependence, countries with a medium level of development (and in

Europe those in the Balkans and the former socialist bloc are a striking example as well as much of Latin America, in particular regarding the trade with the U.S.) and the Third World are forced to develop their industry and their agricultural production so that countries bearers of the multinational companies projects will benefit from it. Jaffe (1973, 1990) argues that the colonial countries have been forced to «develop» in productive sectors not suitable for them. He gives the example of African agriculture that, given the environmental characteristics of this continent, would be the less suitable area for an effective, efficient and profitable development; while it would be much more «natural» to intensify and expand it in areas far more fertile and suitable like the large green plains in Europe. Instead the development dictated by the colonial logic has resulted in the development of industry in forced stages in the North (Europe) and of agriculture in the South (Africa). The result is that the development in more dynamic sectors such as the industrial sector leads to a much higher productivity and the ability to increase productive forces to levels not achieved in other areas instead anchored to physical and natural limitations such as agriculture. This is exacerbating even more the gap between North and South.

For example, many Asian countries have converted their transformation processes; their development is now directly subjected to the requirements of the European and U.S. market. One of the proposals by specialists so that developing countries can reach the developed countries is that of the «scenarios of opportunity». In this proposal it is assumed that the underdeveloped countries placed on the technological frontier can take advantage from the possibilities of the current techno-economic paradigm, i.e. from the reduced training time and from the low cost of sufficiently qualified human resources.

This analysis rejects the theory of the product cycle, whereby underdeveloped countries only receive obsolete technologies that had already exhausted their innovative qualities.

Neo-Schumpeterian theorists of technological change argue that a dynamic view of development might allow, under current conditions, a competitive production in developing countries during the swarm phases in the development of technologies. The foundation of this claim is based on the fact that the life cycles of every innovation are becoming shorter, so innovators must recover their short-term investment, since they are more interested in protecting and selling patents for technology than in maintaining the monopolist control. According to several authors,[5] these countries have advantages on costs. Although this possibility exists, it cannot be ignored that this process occurs during the monopolist phase of capitalism, where competition is not falling, but is more acute in order to maintain extraordinary profits.

For this reason, the neo-Schumpeterian conception, according to which the new technological paradigm has real ability to overcome the North-South gap in its various manifestations, is overly optimistic.

It is the external demand of the two great geo-economic poles (the U.S. and the EU) that models the amplitude and direction of the accumulation process of Asian capital functionally to the paradigm of flexible Western accumulation.

Central and South America, Sub-Saharan Africa, South Asia and Indochina have a weak state productive apparatus, and are still not capable of giving impetus to an autonomous industrialization process and are therefore functional to a proper process of colonization by the two poles, U.S. and EU. In these areas we also find countries which, from the 1970s, have experienced a growth in industry with the combined action of foreign capital and capital controlled by the national bourgeoisie, in which multinational capital has a dominant role, which tried to change the terms of dependency and give a new impetus to the industrialization for the construction of processes of domination also dependent on imports, while maintaining a wage distribution structure that should not allow a growth different from the minimum subsistence levels.

The economic growth of some of these countries is due to the process of technological accumulation and change, which has created a new and solid model of financial and technological dependence from the two major economic blocs, the U.S. and the EU. The reproduction on a large scale of the modern industrial apparatus is based on the import of machinery, equipment and manufacturing.

The high level of imports inherent to this model of growth and the lack of dynamism in the export sector, the relationship of unequal exchange, the dynamics of FDI, the movements of the financial capital, the profits remitted to foreign companies, are some of the elements that create in a matter of decades a macroeconomic imbalance and a continuous trend to deficit in the trade balance, filled with increasingly

---

[5] Cf. also García, Sánchez (1999), topics resumed and articulated even by Efrain Echevarria in some of his works.

frequent recourse to foreign borrowing and an excessive use of foreign capital, as a way to manage the balance of payments.

Economic policy keeps leading to monetarist and neoliberal choices, leaving the root causes of the imbalances in the production structure intact, thus deepening the trade deficit.

Following the directions of the World Bank and the International Monetary Fund, many governments continue to implement policies of «structural reforms» and accelerated trade opening, with privatization of state enterprises and economic deregulation, introducing anti-inflationary policies. The first repercussion is the lowering of real wages, the increase of unemployment, deindustrialization, without real productive investments being financed by national capital, and therefore the expansion of complete dependence from the large economic blocks. With the increase of foreign debt and the use of foreign capital, the profitability of this last and the foreign distribution of profits increases, with a higher imbalance in the export sector. The refinancing of the accumulated debt causes the increase in foreign capital with new capital inflows, which are thought to help stop the recapitalisation. Instead a dependent development continues to be funded, having the illusion of obtaining a durable profit. To maintain the profitability levels, the use of foreign capital and dependence on equipment and facilities is encouraged, workers are exploited, public investment are reduced and restrictive policies are applied, thus falling into a vicious cycle of financial and technological dependency that increases foreign debt and makes the survival of entire populations increasingly difficult.

Under the current conditions, internationalization reaches a much higher degree in its development, helping to move to a new techno-economic paradigm. The whole international trade theory, including one of its oldest proposals, the well known law of the comparative advantages by Ricardo,[6] according to which the trade specialization of the trading countries is based on the relative costs, was discussed and revisited by economists.

The traditional theory of international trade has dominated economic thought for a long time. In the vision of Ricardo comparative advantages ensure that trade will be good for all countries, provided

---

[6] Cf. Orati (2003), for a critique of this theory and other theses about the unequal exchange with neomarxist and Third World origin.

that each country specializes in the production of those goods with lower relative costs, with the exchange depending more on factors productivity than on the allocation of resources; international trade, from this perspective, always generates profits.

The classical and neoclassical models have always been based on a set of restrictive assumptions concerning concrete reality: perfect competition, constants returns to scale, national mobility of factors, identical preferences by consumers, free diffusion of technology. On the other hand the relative benefits, the fundaments of international specialization, arise from the comparison of the sectoral structure of the relative costs between countries, i.e. the comparison of the international sectoral structures.

For several years scientific contributions have been added to the creation of a trade theory including technological factors from a new unorthodox perspective, since the classical and neoclassical models have shown an inability to satisfactorily explain the realities of the past years.

For underdeveloped countries, both the concept of comparative advantages by Ricardo and that of absolute advantage by Smith find an insurmountable barrier in international trade, which limits its development and therefore the levels of competitiveness. These inequalities are also reflected in the comparative dynamic benefits, since the starting points to guarantee infrastructures, continuity of the training processes, endogenous scientific and technological abilities, etc. are limited.

All models agree that this is only possible if the country has access to the «necessary human capital», a very productive term from a capital point of view, increasingly used in scientific literature and in the political lexicon to identify the workforce, or better the productive factor labour, also called, with another not very elegant term, human resources. It is very common to refer to social human capital as the set of characteristics and quality of the people of an organization, i.e. its intangible aspects, like education, training, health, living and work conditions, traditional and acquired knowledge, predisposition for change, etc.

Social human capital is the stock of «useful» knowledge and skills affecting capital. The human capital conception has received strong criticism from Marxist theory; this category separates technical relationships from social relationships, so the socio-political size of the enterprise is ignored and thus the relationship of exploitation of the workforce can be ignored as well.

The growing interdependence of markets and technological innovation have changed all of the local systems for businesses; the benefits coming from the localization in districts, such as cooperation, proximity to markets, fast speed of communication, were not enough to allow an overall advantage to the system.[7]

Technological innovation, global homogenization forced by the needs of the consumers, the reduction of customs barriers and the productive transformation are undoubtedly among the main «official» reasons for this new process, which is now affecting the world market.

The truth is that the international entrepreneur, through multinational companies, foreign trade, foreign direct investments, and the role of chains and international business-networks, is constantly looking for new input markets, and especially for new markets to stock up at a low cost with the human factor, labour, and raw materials, ensuring capital in areas that are known as tax havens.

The generalization of flexible production, with its needs in terms of proximity between those who make the orders and the suppliers of parts, semi-finished products and services, has the same impact on the choice of the location to the detriment of medium development countries, in particular, for example, of those industries in Latin America, the Balkans and eastern Europe where low labour costs are associated with a medium-high level of specialization of labour, including some labour-intensive industries.

These same factors explain the marginalization not only of great part of the developing countries, but especially of the countries of Central-Eastern Europe, Latin America and Mediterranean Africa. The opportunities for the relocation of production towards countries at very low wages, made possible by an almost complete liberalization of trade, are transformed for many countries in Eastern Europe, Latin America and even parts of whole continents (mainly Africa) in an absolute globalized movement of capital, causing a new colonialism in the form of absolute marginalization.

For this reason neither the fall of European socialism, or the technological changes of great significance which took place during the last twenty-five years, have led to any change in the essence of the capitalist system of exploitation in terms of a decreased exploitation of workers, in particular of waged workers, or in terms of variation of

---

[7] A Marxist critique of this conception can be found in Herrera (2004: 136–140).

those neocolonial relationships that have characterized for almost a century the capitalist system of the world economy.

If an increasingly frequent phenomenon, at the microeconomic level in business management and at the macroeconomic level for the main world economies, is that of the productive internationalization, it needs to be clarified that with this term is defined the process that involves the management, on a permanent and stable way, of activities of an economic nature in two or more countries.

It is therefore necessary to make the following point: the productive internationalization is about the real and characteristic aspects of business management and not the financial aspects (holding of shares in companies operating abroad).

When speaking of internationalized enterprises a fundamental distinction should be drawn between horizontal integration, in which case the company controls in different geographical areas numerous manufacturing plants that create the same type of products, and vertical integration; i.e. with the output produced in a facility that is the input for another production unit located in a different geographic area.

When the considered phenomenon involves a large number of companies in the same country with clear guidelines from political-economic choices of the country-system, this process is the result of a macroeconomic approach to productive internationalization, referable to what we called global competition, and is expressed through a combination of causes that can be summarized as follows:

a. acquisition of competitive advantages, in the field of the global comparison among businesses and geo-economic poles, which are determined by the management of international presence;
b. exploitation in new geographic areas of competitive advantage held in the original markets, such as geoeconomic and geopolitics influence;
c. research in foreign areas for conditions which may result in elements of competitive advantage for the company, but especially for the country-system.

Regarding the strategic aspects, this process is expressed mainly through the activation of FDI with structural characteristics over time.

The expansion abroad requires, therefore, that the concerned companies review and adapt their organization to the new system. For this reason it is crucial to maintain a balance between the push towards internationalization and adaptation to the entire local structure in which the companies work. This is achieved through political system conditions. Therefore a primary role is assumed by the proper coordination of the relations of integration among the corporate company, the subsidiaries and the reference country-systems with their economic policies.

An integrated network of relationships between different companies is therefore established through the application of the experience gained locally and the strategic policies imposed by the geoeconomic poles. It is, therefore, a model based on interdependence between the units of the group, which takes on the characteristics of a network based on flexibility and geopolitical control.

The growth of competitive conditions, technological innovation, the decrease of time intervals between the design and trade of the products, the characteristics of financial globalization and global competition meant that very often the national branches came to have much better conditions for growth and efficiency than those of the parent company. This situation has facilitated the transition from the hierarchical model to the so-called network model, with an internal organization with characteristics of a non-hierarchical kind and an internal and external market supportive of this approach.

In the network system the parent company and the subsidiary no longer exist, but there is a fundamental strong interdependence between the various units, which must be able to work together without the specific intervention of the centre. The terms centre and periphery are used in order to emphasize the lack of a leader company that organizes and controls the others.

A kind of «network enterprise» is therefore created, consisting of relationships with partners that are within the country of establishment; this system of partnerships allows the reduction of the capital injections, a better integration into the local environment and to manage national issues. The centralized corporation is replaced by a network extended on a global scale; within this network there are forms of internal partnership (e.g. franchising) and forms of external partnership (such as joint ventures).

Multinational enterprises, however, work in two geographical dimensions: the global and regional dimensions. Among the first are those companies operating in sectors with high technological content (such as IT), while among companies with a regional organization are those that distinguish their activities in regions or macro-areas depending largely on the benefits associated with this distinction (such as the possibility of exploiting the homogeneity of markets, best conditions of taxation and the labour market with professionals with a good level of expertise and low labour costs).

It is important to bear in mind that there are two fundamental organizational criteria: vertical and horizontal. In vertically integrated multinational companies the various stages of production are located in different places depending on the benefits, as described above, that can be found in different areas. Therefore the relationship between the branches depends on how the intermediate products are transferred from one stage to another along the border. In multinational companies horizontally integrated, however, the same stage of production is repeated in another country; the same good is produced both by the parent company and by a foreign branch, therefore having to choose between export and investment procedures.

Since it is the finished product that is sold, creating a subsidiary abroad often serves to circumvent tariffs, tax burdens, administrative barriers and transportation costs, appropriate rules and regulations on labour and to compress as much as possible the costs of labour. Moreover horizontal integration is a way to prevent the entry in the market of other companies for competitive reasons.

Multinational enterprises, however, play a key role in the process of integration, propagation and expansion of trade, always in the interests of a «productive and commercial war» for the economic blocks, particularly at this time of fierce global competition. The various mergers, alliances and productive and commercial agreements, the dynamics of the FDI themselves, in short, the various processes of internationalization in recent years, give an idea of the role played by multinational corporations in the global economic competition for geo-economic poles.

In recent years the proliferation of industrial, banking and trading concentrations has been witnessed in all the countries of advanced capitalism. In essence, it was necessary to implement alliances between companies, which have led to their expansion.

In view of the processes of economic internationalization and the productive relocation processes, in the most important capitalistic poles there are constant mergers, acquisitions and financial and industrial concentrations, which often take the form of national-capitalistic processes in search of competitive space.

It should be remembered that most of the international movements of acquisition and fusion take place in three large global blocs, consisting of the European Union, the United States and Japan, and these are the precise areas where concentrations are formed. This occurs to reshape the role of multinationals in the geopolitical and geo-economic conflicts of global competition. It follows that if acquisitions and mergers of companies have grown considerably in recent years it is also true that, whereas previously these operations occurred mainly in economically developed areas, there has been a growth for some time even in areas with a medium level of development.

The interest of multinational companies towards these countries is due to the fact that these economies have low costs of production and very competitive qualitative and organizational standards; for instance, areas of Asia, Balkans and Central-Eastern Europe.

But if you thereby increase the spread of the global enterprise and role of multinational corporations through international productive relocation, these dynamics of spatial distribution lead to forms and intensive processes of control spreading through strong mechanisms of concentration of ownership.

In almost all cases of concentration of ownership efficiency and competitiveness are invoked, resulting in drastic reductions of staff, outsourcing of phases of the cycle, and this increases illegal, precarious and flexible work, in conditions and usually in forms of redistribution all in favour of profit and deriving from the strong gains in productivity.

Structural Adjustment Programs (SAPs) as Political Strategies of Neoliberal Globalization

Goals, Measures and Interventions through the SAP

Perhaps it was in Latin America and Africa that liberal recipes were applied most decisively, from the time when the debt crisis caused the failure of the more or less Keynesian traditional policies applied until then.

The so-called *structural adjustment programs* (SAPs), together with the *stabilization policies*, are the set of economic policy measures recommended to peripheral countries through international financial organizations. Basically, they are the same diagnosis and recipe book that, under the name of Neoliberalism, are applied to developed countries after the change of the political climate worldwide, with the Conservative victory in the early 1980s. There are three axis in the structural adjustment programs:

a. increased competition in markets: agriculture, industry and world trade;
b. improvement of the responsiveness of factor markets: capital, labour and knowledge;
c. the efficiency of the public sector: regulation, social policies and funding.

Therefore, structural adjustments cover a variety of economic aspects:

a. education and human capital (financial quality);
b. long-term research (role of governments, infrastructure, relationships of the basic research with industry and international cooperation);
c. labour market and labour relations (labour relations systems, connection with the economic activity and reforms);
d. financial system and funding of industry (development of financial markets, funding of industry, international cooperation)
e. agriculture (agricultural policies, imbalances and their treatment);
f. industry (national industrial policies, government and industrial settlement, technological development, support strategies);
g. world trade;
h. public sector;
i. regulation (of competitive industries, natural monopolies);
j. social policies (health, pensions, support for the unemployed);
k. financialization of the public sector (growth, tax burden, reform tax).

The structural adjustment programs cover a wide range of state interventions in the economy, and the commercial and social fields. The SAPs incorporate, at different doses and with different temporary rhythms according to the case, the following policies:

a. trade liberalization;
b. privatization of industries and services;
c. agricultural liberalization (price and quantity);
d. dismantling of regulatory agencies and mechanisms to confer licenses;
e. deregulation of labour markets and «flexibility» of salary;

f. reduction and commodification of social services (mechanisms of shared costs, stricter access criteria to welfare and social assistance, social exclusion of vulnerable groups, competition market with state and public institutions with the privatization of social services such as public hospitals, etc.);
g. less attention to environmental problems;
h. educational reforms aimed at training for employment, instead that at the formation of citizenship and at the strengthening of the cultural bases;
i. family policies that worsen the situation of women and children.

All these elements require a massive government intervention that, by changing the legislative framework, the standards setting and the parameters for implementation, significantly change the implementation space and the prospect for public intervention, now mainly focusing on the enlargement of the scope of market relations in social and economic life.

Monetary Policy

In the mid-1980s, many underdeveloped countries were suffering from hyperinflation crises. In an environment in which changes in price levels are constant, and with a highly unstable condition of the exchange rate, it is impossible to think of endogenous conditions conducive to investment and growth. In this situation the traders, with a high degree of uncertainty about the future interest and exchange rate, were indefinitely postponing their decisions and were inclined to speculate.

As already mentioned, the neoliberal policies identified in the State the operator guilty of introducing economic uncertainty and inflationary conditions in the system. The application of years of lax monetary policies had led to their conversion into the primary disturbance of the economic cycle.

The major monetary emissions completed by the central banks of these countries, with the objective of financing the «inefficient» expenses of State, had produced unsustainable inflation rates, with high nominal interest rates that acted as a disincentive to investments, and steady depreciation of the currency, which in turn discouraged the attraction of foreign capital, steadily decreasing the value of the investment in terms of international currency. Furthermore, the constant depreciation increased the amount of international obligations, factor that increases the pressure on the balance of payments.

The IMF proposes the application of restrictive monetary policies, with monetary emission upper limits and using fixed exchange
rates to achieve specific targets to reduce inflation, and thus begin to
prepare the ground for a strong and sustained phase of economic
expansion.

It is argued that, at first, the proposed measures will lead to unpleas-
ant recessive consequences, but the benefits will begin to be experienced in the medium and long term, primarily through interest rates.
The implementation of monetary emission caps caused a continuous
rise in market interest rates, which reduced investment and therefore
aggregate demand in the short term. But in the medium term, with the
reduction of inflation, produced by the measures taken during the
adjustment, the nominal interest rates began to adjust to the new price
levels, which decreased the scissor between actual and nominal interest rates. The decrease of this scissor resulted, in turn, in an increase in
investment, and therefore in the economic dynamic.

Secondly, the stability of the exchange rate allows the reduction of
inflation to sustainable levels in two forms. The first occurs via the
external trade flows and the second through financial flows. In the first
case, the supported fixed exchange rate encourages the entry of imports
at a lower price than national production, introducing competitive
pressures on industry and forcing it to reduce costs, and therefore the
price level. This mechanism of pressure reinforces the objectives of
commercial liberalization, promoting the disappearance of inefficient
sectors through external competition, thus encouraging the sectoral
movement of resources that reinforce the emerging and competitive
export sector of the country. In the long term the country will take
advantage of the fixed exchange rate, experiencing a steady increases in
international reserves, thanks to the surplus on the trade balance
account generated by the favourable location of the export sector in
the world economy.

In the case of financial flows, the acceptance by the central government to maintain a certain exchange rate generates a degree of confidence in foreign investors, who respond by generating a positive inflow
of capital into the country. This flow of capital, either addressed to FDI
(foreign direct investment) or portfolio investment, will allow a relief
of the country's foreign position, increasing international reserves,
thus providing the ability to pay the foreign debt in the short term. It is
argued that all this will reinforce the confidence of international markets in the adjustment process, which will increase investment flows,

thus improving the prospects for economic growth of the country in the future.

As one can see for the IMF it is well worth sacrificing economic growth in the short term, with the aim of obtaining a reduction of the inflation rate that is compatible with economic growth in the long term. Eventually the implicit aim of these measures is to create a pricing system consistent with the needs of a market economy, which, being free from rules, provides accurate information to economic operators, to lead towards a better use of resources and reach an economic growth.

Consequences of the Application of Neoliberal Policies

The international financial system forces countries to work in environments of low inflation and exchange stability, when the structural and macroeconomic conditions are not capable of promoting these situations.

Why? In general, the countries submit to the adjustments to rebuild their international reserves, and in this way to continue to share the international trade. These reserves were eroded mainly by two facts: constant current deficit and increases in the payment of foreign debt. This means that there are two solutions: one is to achieve increases in revenues through improvements in trade and the other is the reduction in the payment of debt service, both through refinancing outstanding debt, and through default.

As a result of how the debt crisis of the 1980s was managed, the financial component of external imbalance increased to a large extent and was not resolved by trade surpluses or the cancellation of debt, but through the return of the country in default to international capital markets, where they could again borrow as sovereign debtors and in this way refinance their debt, in order to avoid liquidity problems in the short term.

In this way, countries are obliged to always attract bigger masses of capital that make it possible to indefinitely refinance the debt through low inflation policies and stability of exchange, despite the fact that, in the first place, the current account deficit will continue and secondly, the stabilization of these indicators will cause irreparable damage to the production capacity of the country and therefore to the stability of the rest of the main «real» macroeconomic indicators such as growth and employment.

Having said that, the reason why the policies of low inflation and stability are fundamental is clear: because this is the only way in which countries can ensure profit to foreign capital and therefore can stimulate their entry into the country, with the goal to continue financing trade deficits and a rising debt; this creates a vicious cycle of debt and recession, which hinders the application of economic policies that enable the country to be pulled out of the crisis.

This vicious circle directly related to the deregulation and liberalization policies imposed by the structural adjustment instead of allowing to pull the country out of the crisis only create worsened conditions for it.

The first to have this effect are the short-term policies of economic stabilization, more precisely the steep reduction of public spending, the reduction of the money supply and the stability of the exchange rate. The combination of these policies results in a environment of high interest rates and of low profit prospects that not even in the best circumstances would lead to a stable and lasting growth. The reduction of public spending with the aim of controlling inflation causes a contraction in economic activity that reduces the income of the population and thus future consumption, affecting the sector of national production with the addition of a serious general deterioration of the working and social conditions for the poorer sections of the population. At the same time, the contraction of the money supply causes an increase in the interest rate that, although helping to achieve the goal of attracting foreign capital in the short term, allowing to finance the checking account deficit and to reduce inflation rates, inhibits the development of the national productive sector by imposing a prohibitive cost on investment.

Finally, the stabilization of the exchange rate, when operated under conditions of high interest rates, causes an inflow of foreign capital overestimating the exchange rate. This appreciation hits the domestic production in two ways: by imposing a «tax» on exports making them more expensive in relative terms, which hits the export sector, while it reduces the cost of imports, creating an incentive for their consumption. The combination of these two factors thereby increases the original external imbalance, reinforcing the need to increase the entry of capital that allows the funding of the increase of imports.

What international institutions, like the IMF and the WB, do not say is that this stabilization is achieved at the cost of mortgaging the future of the country, because the basic problem remains, namely the trade deficits continue and therefore the only way to sustain the economic situation is to promote the entry of more capital, not only to pay past debts, but also to increase international reserves and thus generate confidence in the exchange rate, maintaining a positive image.

Now it is necessary to explain why the fundamental imbalances remain intact and in what way they become the main obstacle for the stabilization to be translated into economic growth.

The most important cause of trade imbalances is the premature trade liberalization. As Stiglitz points out, it is not possible to be so short-sighted and simply hope that new job opportunities will be created as the jobs created by protectionist barriers are lost, when the economic conditions to make this happen do not exist. Instead liberalization creates suitable conditions to block this process, preventing the natural adjustment mechanisms from operating and allow the return to balance.

Applying trade liberalization liberalizes capital movements, which only produce negative effects on the national productive sector. With the neoliberal policies the entry of capital and the resulting surplus in capital account of the balance of payments lead the exchange rate to cease to be transiently determined by the position in the current section of the balance. In this situation it is therefore natural that the exchange rate does not respond rapidly to the changes in the trade flows or to the changes of economic policy that affect the revenue, but more to financial factors and volatile expectations. This translates into a determent so that the exchange rate can vary and allow the application of the principle of purchasing power parity, while reflecting the differential of productivity and therefore of the existing prices, allowing the attainment of the external balance. Therefore exchange rates, by behaving in this way, not only do not produce convergence between the economies concerned with trade, but on the contrary, lead to divergence. Hence the domestic production must compete in markets with the drawback determined by the initial appreciation of the exchange rate caused by the flows of foreign capital. To these initial drawbacks the high interest rates that impede to borrow for productive purposes need to be added, as well as the rise of taxes made with the objective of increasing government revenues to reduce the deficit, and recessive perspectives in the economy, which depresses even more investment. All this forms a fairly daunting picture for national producers.

It is also necessary to say that in practice the processes of commercial liberalization encourage the specialization in sectors where countries have a competitive but not comparative advantage. This leads to overproduction in the world market, from the countries subject to the adjustment, of commodities or raw materials such as coffee, rubber, etc., causing a drop in the prices of these goods. This trend affects the terms of trade of the countries, worsening them in absolute terms and mainly taking into account the rising of oil prices in recent years and the capital goods imported to equip the export sector. For this reason, this dynamic is incompatible with growth and the long-term external balance.

All the phenomena mentioned, namely reduction of spending, monetary contraction and trade and financial liberalization inevitably lead to a fall in economic activity, if not avoided through an expansion of debt; a growth is produced based on that debt instead of growth in exports, on an endogenous growth compatible with a balance of the principal macroeconomic variables. In such cases the increase in debt only causes a strengthening of the measures for the attraction of capital, which in turn will create an even more unfavourable situation for the country against the creditors when the inevitable moment of collapse will come.

A defender of the adjustment policies could say that the fall in economic activity is good for the country's external balance and therefore contributes to the success of the adjustment itself, thanks mainly to the pressure that this causes on domestic prices, thus encouraging the competitiveness of exports on international markets and the reduction of imports as a result of the fall in income. This adjustment system does not work in economies which introduce the financial liberalization because, as stated, all financial flows exceed by far the flow caused by commercial activity and thus allow the financialization of the deficits; despite the income drops, the imports not only do not diminish, but tend to increase as a result of the low prices.

Therefore, supporting measures to reduce spending and the control over the money supply, in contexts of financial and trade liberalization, the IMF is directly responsible for the economic and social disasters, because on one hand such measures do not hit the fiscal deficit nor the external imbalance and, on the contrary, if the interest rate increases as well as the country's obligations, it becomes impossible to escape the crisis.

The key moment and highlight of the process of collapse of the country is marked by the reduction of the international reserves. This fact affects the investors' confidence in the commitment of the country to maintain the exchange rate stable and the ability to meet its short-term obligations without the need for debt refinancing.

At the end of the cycle the country ends up with more debt, more dependence and thus greater external vulnerability, with a State now rendered unable to meet the basic needs of the majority of the population and a national industry out of business.

So now we should ask ourselves: what lessons can be obtained from the application of structural adjustment plans, what are their major defects that eventually end up becoming the reason for their failure? (Davies 2003: 6, 12).

First, to charge the State and the public policies with the fault of the external imbalances. As stated, the problem is not reducing the public deficit to achieve external balance, which may come to be a necessary but not sufficient condition, but it is to create the conditions that allow the disposal of stocks and finally activate the productive capacity of the country to get in this way positive results in the checking account of the balance of payments. Contrary to what international financial institutions hope, structural reforms that promote the reduction of the economic and productive weight of the state sector do not promote the external balance. And they cannot promote it, because the public sector must play a key role when it comes to promoting national policies to overcome the shortcomings of production.

In reality, with the implementation of the reforms, what is being promoted is the destruction of the productive sectors of the countries that are subjected to them, while creating recessive environments where the protection by the State disappears in the key sectors of the economy. Thus the only solution that remains is the application of an active economic policy which promotes the strengthening of the national productive sector, the economic recovery, and through it seeks an increase in revenue to settle the deficit on the long-term.

Secondly, it becomes necessary to analyze more deeply the fact that currently the public deficit is not responsible for the braking macroeconomic effect, as stated by neoclassical theory; the recessive policies are guilty of the low levels of investment present in many economies undergoing the adjustment. Although the domestic savings as a result of deficit reduction are largely increasing, the investment will not increase in a macroeconomic context which includes high interest rates, caused by the monetary policy and by the prospects of low GDP growth, to reduce public, and in particular, social expenditure.

Thirdly, the economic point of view that identifies the foreign balance with the trade balance and the public balance determined by wages and public spending is now obsolete. In the case of foreign balances, it needs to be stated that the trade balances for some years, and as a result of the financial deregulation policies, have stopped to be the centre of the imbalances as the financial flows in the case of many countries are more than sufficient to finance trade imbalances, thus becoming the core of the international economic relations.

On the other hand, in the case of the public balance, every day the fulfilment of the payment of the foreign debt gains importance in public spending, mainly as a result of high interest rates and debt policies in international markets pursued by the countries subjected to adjustment. In this way the policies initiated to solve the deficit and imbalance problems are not incisive, because they depend on another indicator that in turn responds adversely to the policies applied to affect the income, exacerbating the initial problem: the interest rate.

Fourth, trade and financial liberalization, as implemented by international financial institutions (that is attentive to create the necessary conditions to overcome the structural problems caused by trade deficits, hindering the formation of an endogenous process of accumulation and imposing pressure on countries on an economic structure already deformed by years of dependence and exploitation) is only capable of sacrificing the national economy to foreign capital through intensive privatization processes in strategic sectors, only to end succumbing under its weight.

The attack on the State that took place in Latin America during the 1990s left a legacy that will take at least two generations to be erased. In Latin America, and also in Africa, in the decades preceding the debt crisis the State had a key role both from the point of view of consumption and of investment with its activities in some way it compensating for the shortcomings of the accumulation process, namely the weakness of the national capitalist sector in almost all the countries in the region. Privatizations fundamentally played in favour of transnational capital that is exploiting the best part of the national resources.

As a result, the much abused term dependence of Latin America continues to be the one that best defines the structural situation of the continent, for it is renewed and deepened in a double direction: the increasing transnational control of the processes of national accumulation in Latin America is completed with some States weakened to such an extent that they cannot even carry out the minimum regulatory functions, with regard to the provision of infrastructure and the reduction of the reproduction cost of the workforce (basically health and education).

For these countries the new century begins with the burden of debt that works as a mechanism of forced transmission of the surplus towards the countries of the centre: Africa paid 194,000 million dollars in interest on debt between 2000 and 2006, and the volume of debt remained unchanged. Latin America and the Caribbean, for their part, paying 1,100 million dollars during the same period, increase their volume of debt.[8]

The fact that during the application of structural adjustments the economic policy recommendations are followed based on a theoretical frame, the neoclassical theory, implies the disastrous results which billion of people around the world had to suffer.

Although, in political as well as in economic-productive terms, it seems that a «new revolutionary phase» of capitalism is starting, everything seems to indicate that, particularly in the semi-peripheral areas (e.g. Latin America), a new season of awareness of the people to the fact that capitalism has nothing new to offer is taking place. Therefore, since the events that tried to change the historical period, such as the era that we considered the transition to socialism, it seems that a «reflux» has been created, to then have a «return» that began with the twenty-first century; it is a period of revolutionary changes, of anti-imperialist struggle and of a search for alternatives to capitalism, as well as of proclamations of a new socialism.

---

[8] Source: IMF, "World Economic Outlooks," April 2006.

CHAPTER SIXTEEN

THE NEW COMPOSITION OF THE WORLD OF LABOUR AND THE CONSTRUCTION OF AN ANTI-CAPITALIST SOCIAL BLOC

The Modern Proletariat in the New Capital-Labour Contradiction

The transformation of labour and the change of labour performance over the last twenty-five years have clearly shown how the Taylorist-Fordist organization has been left behind in order to start a phase characterized by the model of flexible accumulation. As repeatedly argued in this work, the process of socio-economic transformation of labour itself determines the guidelines of the current socio-economic context in the new way they present themselves.

Though a convincing and definitive reading of society as it is nowadays cannot yet be well defined, the content of the ongoing economic transformations stress that there might have been a change in the essence of labour, but that there has certainly been one in its organization. The very functions, the economic and social figures that are still subject to study, but that have surely nothing to do with the previous economic and social stages, show some new figures both of society and labour and yet still identify the centrality of wage labour, highlighting the typical constraints of subordination that characterize the capital-labour relation in the classical capitalist way of production.

Economic reality is rapidly and inevitably changing, and it tends to make clearer the line of demarcation between property-capital and a class of workers[1] that is facing a more and more precarious and flexible working and social life, and more and more reduced forms of redistribution of wealth and the same margins of social, political and cultural livability as a whole.

So the analysis of the organization of the production cycle, of the characteristics of the productive and social system, of the relations between international areas, of the economic structure of an individual area, all become crucial in order to identify the new social

---

[1] Antunes (2006), as already quoted, defines it as "the-class-that-lives-on-labour".

determinations through the critical understanding of the new structure and organization of the labour market, imposed by the new processes of capital accumulation.

The development of the Fordist-Keynesian society, of the social capital-labour compromise and the post-war growth of the middle classes have made over the past few decades, many sociologists, economists, political scientists and politicians argue loudly for the end of the working class (identified with the entire class of people who work). From an analysis, which is not done only from a "sociological" or reductive point of view, of the composition/division of the capitalist society, it results that the reality is different.

If the Marxian theory of labour value is valid, so is the theory of one class exploitation over the other, and nowadays the working class still "survives" in those countries with a fully developed capitalism. It is precisely the scientific aspect of the Marxian theory that allows us to go beyond the surface. Nowadays the working class not only keeps on existing but is expanding all over the world. Such an expansion implies diversification, lack of homogeneity of forms, and subjectivity.

If what defines the working class is that it is the social class with no means of production, but above all the class that cannot benefit from the products of its own work (Bordiga 1980), then we can support the thesis of its survival and even "rebirth". The working class can still be seen only as a whole, without opposing each worker to another or promoting various forms of exclusion (based, perhaps, on unfounded criteria of "specific subjectivity" in the new class composition, deemed exclusive of one and not common to the others).

There are at least two fundamental and perceptible characteristics that objectively unite the current world working class: piecework wage, which is now widespread on a global scale in an infinite number of different forms (there is a comeback to the wage system of the nineteenth century), and the growing insecurity of the individual job positions, which involves precarious rights, social security, pension ... and life.

The functions of the subject of work, lack of work, of denied work in the different models of capitalism, are, therefore, different since the point of view that affects and regulates the relations between business and society is also different. It is now prominent the thesis according to which the general interest of the workers has to be the culture of the enterprise, achieved through the role of homologated intellectual capital, in a capitalist mode of production based on the exploitation of wage labour, in the various ways in which it presents itself nowadays.

But it is true that the more labour is capitalized, the more capital and labour that turns into capital develop, and the more living labour opposes itself to such development. The more capital presents itself as the creator of profit, that is the source of wealth regardless of labour, the more living labour is alienated from modern forms of capitalist development. And as Marx emphasizes, the antagonistic determination of labour is inherent in the duality of the laws of the rate of profit. The tendency to an increase of profit is highlighted in the directly exploited living labour, even with its innovation and creativity, but at the same time the tendency to a decrease in the rate of profit identifies the antagonistic will, which is not always organized, of living labour against the power of capital.

By analyzing the contradiction between the basis of bourgeois production (measure of value) and its development, we can made clear how the system itself creates the conditions for its own destruction. For this reason Marx shows that the effective wealth becomes less dependent, does not retain any relation to the time of immediate labour to which its production amounts, but depends, ever more, on the overall state of science and of technology, i.e., on the application of science to production (Marx 1976, Book II: 228).

Under these conditions, labour is, now, not limited to the production process, and the worker's role is to supervise and regulate production. There is a passage from Marx that summarizes his thought and that reflects, at the same time, the tendency of mechanized production as a premise to the birth of new social relations and, therefore, the free development of individuality (Marx 1976, book II: 228–229).

What has been pointed out so far, taking into account the current conditions, confirms the methodological and conceptual basis of Marx's thought for the explanation of the endogenous nature of the scientific-technical progress of capitalism. The axis of Marx's analysis circles the production surplus value, which is the aim of the system.

For Marx, the reduction of the immediate time of labour results from the employment of machines in these new conditions of capitalistic production. As it could be said in modern parlance, it refers to tangible products. In Marx's period did not exist what is now called intangible resources or products (sale of knowledge-goods). Despite all this, Marx gives us an important factor to think about, which confirms that capitalism will always measure the content of its wealth starting from labour time as a creator of value, to preserve it and achieve its self-growth.

Marx's clarification is of the utmost importance in order to under-stand to what extent it is valid, and to express the idea of the value of knowledge or its price. Knowledge, meaning labour which is fixed in a tangible product has no value, neither as price, nor as work. For this reason, referring to what we call, nowadays, the economy of knowl-edge it would be more accurate to say that knowledge creates value and encloses it in the product, but knowledge itself has no value. So the discussion focuses on a situation in which the product that is being sold is knowledge. To Marxist theory the study of knowledge as a crea-tor of value is a major challenge that requires further study.

The widespread development of deviant communication highlights, in the most exasperated way, the nature of the separation, indifference, and loneliness that result from the post Fordist-Taylorist capitalist sys-tem, where the development is functional to individual production, i.e., a falsely autonomous job, to a development that creates, at the same time, unemployment and labour that are more and more servile. The best of communication in this context is the best of de-socializa-tion, especially in the labour market.

In Karl Marx's economic theory, the analysis of technology is pro-jected in the following directions:

a. its impact on the accumulation of capital and the share of profit;
b. technological change, automation and collabourative work;
c. science and the problem of fixed capital.

It follows that the whole movement of the capitalist economy is driven by the exploitation of capital, and, within a context of capital-ist competition, class struggle, the institutional regulations, and the intra-technical and inter-technical adjustments materialize and grow in meaning. The expression "knowledge society" has an ambiguous content. Each knowledge is produced within society which is deter-mined by relations of production that delimit its aims. Therefore, knowledge is not neutral, does not exist in the abstract, as the current unequal distribution of wealth around the world directly derives from the capitalist mode of production, the same thing happens with access to knowledge and its use.

While from an economic, monetary and financial point of view, the post-Fordist cycle shapes some apparent economic and financial cor-respondence between countries, though with great difficulty and by worsening even further the workers' quality of life, it does not grant the homogeneity of the social aspects which require adjustments and real changes in each country.

Structural Unemployment and Precariousness as a Characteristic of the Post-Fordist System

The labour demand which constitutes employment (including self-employment) is determined by the level of investment and by the kind of labour that is required in order to work machines. A feature of the capitalist economy is that the demand for labour is always lower than the labour supply.

Therefore, unemployment is a permanent feature of the functioning of the system. Changes in work activities and in the structure of employment correspond to overall changes in society as an expression of a new phase of capitalist development, and also to specific changes related to a new path in the process of national accumulation. The evolution of the structures of employment in the core countries are dominated by a century-long tendency towards the increase of labour productivity, which is its most specific economic feature.

The different activities of the production, distribution and management process are structurally linked with the aim of achieving productivity gains. This common aspect perseveres nowadays, but takes different forms linked to the particular position of each economy within the global structure.

As the neoliberal globalization process moves forward, the economic borders have to continue reducing, especially those that separate the life and work conditions in some countries from those of others. The unification of the labour market on a global scale will mean, at some point, the equality of conditions for workers all over the world. Probably this will cause further deterioration of conditions of life for workers in developed countries, and a relative improvement of life conditions for workers in developing countries, which are part of the new international division of labour.

The free mobility of the labour-force is just a myth, since capitalism cannot function without coercing workers by using mechanisms such as unemployment, job insecurity, differences in remuneration functional to characterizations that are, in many cases, just a way to differentiate between social statuses, but not a factor actually tied to productivity (a bricklayer and an engineer produce the same amount of work, but the first one earns a much lower salary than the second; the products of a primary school teacher and a high school teacher are the same, but the two get different salaries, a psychologist's degree of studies is the same as a lawyer's, but the lawyer earns a higher income than the first, etc.).

The unification of the labour market cannot be made, in any case, by equating each worker in the world to those workers who live in developed countries, because the consumption levels can not be borne by the resources existing on the planet. Here is another great contradiction of capitalist development; universalized consumerism contradicts the levels of environmental sustainability and resources used. Especially in rich countries, this project could be accomplished only through a real social counter-revolution, that would eliminate any trace of the workers' power within the Nation State. This would be possible by removing democracy in these countries, which is something that could occur only through deep social conflicts, that would then turn into a strong generalization of conflict on a global scale.

Therefore, it is quite unlikely that neoliberal globalization could reach its full development. And here is where another source of contradiction lies, since a system based on emulation and on the promise of rewarding when these reveal their illusory nature, begins to generate mechanisms of resistance which can weaken its ability to reproduce as social hegemonic form.

The three permanent forms of overpopulation, as exposed by Marx in his *Capital*, are very helpful in order to explain the dynamics of current unemployment in fully developed capitalist countries:

a. flowing overpopulation, bound to the ups and downs of the cycles of production, measured by the expulsion and attraction of workers in the production process;
b. latent overpopulation, in the form of working population currently not included in the labour supply, such as overpopulation in rural areas or migrant population;
c. static/stagnant overpopulation, which is part of the working population but characterized by irregular conditions of employment, such as temporary or part-time workers. At current conditions, the static form of overpopulation is rapidly growing in the central countries. Marx describes three groups within this category:

    i. *people able to work*: young, immigrants and in some cases women, who can potentially be part of the demand for labour;
    ii. *orphans and poor children*: this group, which is big in peripheral countries, has become small in developed countries, due to what is left of the universal protection systems. However, the statistics on child labour and on illegal labour show that these two kinds of labour still have a chance of being exploited, as Marx said, especially when there is a need of providing *the*

reserve army of labour with new workers, even when the social conditions are those of the most developed countries;

iii. *persons unable to work, disabled people:* including drug addicts and alcoholics, and ill, disabled people that are usually forced into illegal, servile, irregular labour, because of the absence or of the continuous breaking of the social protection for such weak areas: they represent a high proportion of the total population, whose numbers rise substantially in periods of economic crisis like the current one, showing through the accumulation process the constraint of its genesis. The general and absolute law of capitalist accumulation explains how the reserve army of labour increases, at the same time, both the absolute volume of the working class and the productive force of its labour. As during the expansionary stage of the 1950s and 1960s, the relative volume of the reserve army of labour and the social wealth increased thanks to certain conditions that characterized that period, the same way, nowadays, the reserve army of labour is growing in the central countries thanks to the addition of immigrants to the active local population.

Workforce's costs per unit statistically reflect the relation between changes in productivity and the average wage, and bring also some kind of politically relevant information on the evolution of the correlation of forces. It is possible for one to notice, as far as the six main capitalist countries in the world (United States, Japan, Germany, France, Italy and Great Britain) are concerned, that the rise of labour costs per unit, occurred in the late 1960s and early 1970s were under control. But even so, the recent evolution of the workforce costs per unit reflects, besides the differences in average productivity between the U.S. and Europe, the impossibility to let workers who live in the developed countries bear the cost of generating resources for a new wave of centralization of global wealth.

On the contrary, the relation between the rate of economic growth and the long-term interest rates as a reference for the profit rate of financial capital, show a strong contrast before and after 1980. Before that year, the economy grew at a rate higher than that of the long-term interest rate. This relation was abruptly reversed in the 1980s, i.e. under the aegis of neoliberalism. Since then, the existence of some interest rates which were higher than GDP's growth rates, shows that a bigger part of the social product is moving to financial capital, in a growing centralization of resources in the form of money in this field.

The current problem with labour is not only related to structural unemployment, but also to a series of quantitative / qualitative problems, and problems related to the new figures of work and non-work, to the new dimension of precarious work, and more generally of the precariousness of life. Jobs are a problem also for those who hold one, since people work harder and in more and more precarious conditions, with no protection, lower gain and high levels of mobility and intermittence. This kind of phenomenon is known in the English speaking countries as the *working poor*, that is workers that, despite having a regular contract, get a wage/salary that does not allow them to cross the poverty threshold. Such phenomena are now widespread all over the world. Just think about the many part-time jobs: they are structurally "poor" in terms of income.

The advanced economies of the post-Fordist model which characterized, in particular, the last twenty-five years, gave rise to the phenomenon of *deregulation of labour relations* at high-content of precariousness. This phenomenon is characterized by several distinct aspects of the new cycle of flexible accumulation. For example, the existence of "jobs" that do not allow those who perform them to reach such income levels that could cross the threshold of poverty. Research performed in Europe and the United States constantly emphasize the problem of the new kinds of poverty, social figures that emerge along with that of those who are unemployed, made up of a substantial part of citizens who have an intermittent, precarious job, and are highly mobile. These workers are exposed to the risk of accepting low wages, of prolonging the working day, of accepting moderate forms of generalized piecework wage, and their income is often a daily one and extremely low.

The decentralization and relocation of production, and with it the outsourcing by small and large companies, increase the proportion of enterprise clusters within which the working conditions are not regulated. The relation with the worker is of an individual nature and gives no guarantees. In addition to this, the phenomenon of miniaturization of the enterprise to the form of the individual company is spreading, with the consequent broadening of the field of last-generation self-employment of growing layers of workers who were expelled from the parent company, forced to perform a precarious, deregulated work which is even more subordinate than the one they previously held.

The introduction of the production with a low content of executive labour does not suppress the interests of large capital's groups, as well as those of small enterprises in outsourced, low-wage places of production; but it simply encourages us to look for important bases near the traditional centres of production. These keep on providing the capitalist accumulation with a combination unlikely to be matched, since they present a concentration of creditworthy consumers, who often get high incomes, that is areas of free trade, characterized by production systems marked by specializations that can be exploited for intense processes of outsourcing of parts of the low-added-value, production cycle. These areas are characterized by the complete mobility of goods and capital, and by high flexibility in the forms of labour and wages.

In the last twenty-five years, the slowdown of economic development which caused an increase in unemployment levels made a rise of the level of tax pressure possible. The consequences of this increase were noticed especially by workers, since there was no interest in trying to increase the tax withdrawal over capital, and justifying this attitude by claiming that funds are mobile and converge to countries where the labour cost is very low.

Now, the wages, the social contributions and the social system as a whole are being questioned. Capital dismisses the welfare state, as a compromise and social safety net, and this has been cancelled in order to let the neo-liberal monetarist policy, which is a policy of pure market at lower regulative contents, prevail. The needs of private capital, of the non-reinvested and redistributed wealth, are primarily respected, and the growth of the private company's profit is central to political as well as economic activities. Such a policy implies mass unemployment, job precariousness and the dismantling of the welfare state.

Inside the Crisis of the System: Pulling Together the Threads of the Capital-Labour Conflict at the International Dimension

Handling the crisis of the Fordist-Taylorist model means avoiding a massive devaluation of capital, always creating new financial markets, in a speculative context of financial globalization and intense global competition. In order to prevent the devaluation of capital a set of measures have been taken, such as flexible exchange, high interest rates, privatization, *deregulation*, the attack on workers' wages and on the Welfare State, by breaking down social protection policies and by turning the world of labour into a more precarious condition.

The shrinking of the State is a general reality, especially in social protection and public investment. However, the State renews its functions of legitimacy through democratic processes, that appear as a more appropriate framework for implementing policies of adjustment and stabilization, through the consent of a new section of the ruling class.

Handling the Fordist crisis the way it has been done so far implies some elements of weakness. While on the one hand it emphasizes the dichotomy of the West East system, in addition to the North-South system on the other, it produces within those Western areas with fully developed capitalism some social effects that can lead to the questioning of the political-economic models and of social policies.

We witness a savage capitalism that aims at being a universal model by attacking, without the mediation of other geoeconomic poles, especially Japan and Europe.

Over the past twenty-five years there has been the failure of the socialist experience in Europe. On the basis of this event the neoliberals tried to impose three basic ideas: first, that the failure resulted from socialism losing its battle against the social evolutionary push of capitalism, and second, that the failure corresponded to the success of capitalism as a system and, finally, that the opportunity for socialism to occupy a place in the world faded completely. By considering socialism as the "negative monster," and by holding it responsible for all of mankind's illnesses, people wanted to prove how its failure resulted from its negativity and how the system that survived, capitalism, was to be considered the only salvation.

Despite all this, after a few years it is possible to realize how the failure of real socialism did not solve mankind's problems. The illnesses continued to increase, both in the developed capitalist countries and in other countries. The true meaning of the failure started to become visible when it was clear that what had disappeared was the alternative and balancing pole to the negative impositions of capitalism, and that the so-called "Cold War" stage had been a much calmer and more balanced period.

That is how the imperialist powers, and in particular the United States, began to impose their hegemony, building a more dangerous world, since the control over decisions was held by those who considered war as an instrument of domination.

At the same time, during the 1980s, there was a major transformation in the structure of society, especially in South America. New social and political actors appeared. The urban population, 57.2% of the total, in 1970 rose to 64.9% in 1980, and is currently up to 75%. This huge increase in quantity turned the kind of problems affecting the countries of the subcontinent into a dimension that has not yet been sufficiently intercepted neither by the developed countries, nor by South-American politicians. Environmental pollution of large urban areas, the development of diseases resulting from pollution, together with quick deforestation, are about to show the new political and social centrality of the ecology problem.

Are these changes, that are taking place right now, just trends or cyclical answers? Starting from the analysis of the situation in the United States, it seems that neither its domestic political phenomena, nor the relations that are being carried out in terms of American foreign policy, obey a simple cyclical situation. The first factor to be considered has been analyzed when reference was made to the phenomena of hegemony in the context of current imperialism. Despite the United States clear will to impose their foreign policy, both the areas of domestic policy and foreign political actors, that do not accept American impositions since they did not have satisfactory results, show a conflicting attitude. At the same time, the United States is uncontrollably losing its international prestige due to a set of events ranging from the failure in Iraq and Afghanistan to the social problems highlighted in all their brutality and structural character by the so-called *subprime* crisis and by the overall loss of credibility as the engine of the world economy. The questioning of the current American policies is linked to three different international scenarios: Iraq, Palestine and Latin America.

The events that are taking place in Iraq and the Palestine have a military nature and are conflicts characterized by popular resistance and lack of possibilities to find a solution to them, because in both cases the solutions depend on changes that the United States do not accept. In South America neoliberal policies are being questioned, policies that, starting from the strategic role played by Cuba, are producing changes of governments that gave power to revolutionary movements, or popular governments with a progressive leaning that do not want to submit to the rules of economic imperialism. Various articulated political processes based on self-determination, that are for sure of a democratic-participatory nature, have begun in Venezuela, Brazil, Bolivia, Uruguay, Chile, Ecuador, Nicaragua, etc. The characterization of social and popular movements is now getting more anti-imperialist, and it strengthens and expands following the example and leadership of revolutionary socialist Cuba.

The interests of the United States and of the imperialist powers in general, which aim to produce a phenomenon of restructuring of the neo-colonial system, began to clash with those trends that, at least in South America, move in an opposite direction with respect to the path of participatory democracy, with strong reference to the socialist order of Cuba and Venezuela. In such a perspective, the historical left of Western countries should immediately endeavour to find a solution to the problem of how to politically represent the new social bloc of work and of denied work. There is a need, nowadays, to start over from the "bottom," from the alternative economy and the local production out of the market, from the social contradictions in the territories, in order to raise the offensive strategy of the new international world of labour and denied labour.

The neoliberal globalization model of capitalist development generates new needs but also new exclusions. It is of strategic importance to place at the centre of the debate a comprehensive perspective of a different model of social, self-determined and eco-friendly development in which environmental compatibility, quality of life, the fulfillment of new needs, the centrality of labour and the enhancement of leisure time, together with the strengthening of the welfare state and the redistribution of income and of value, and the socialization of accumulation, of the produced wealth as a whole are strategic. Though it cannot be considered a conclusion, this means building the alternative to capitalism starting at the grassroots level and from Marx's thought.

Therefore, it is not simply about presenting forms of intervention exclusively in terms of the distribution of income but to re-enter, through new instruments, the capital-labour conflict, which in fact, is harder and more diversified than ever before. In order to do so it is necessary to start from the new subjectivity of the capital-labour conflict, by reorganizing the unions around the interests of the world of labour, and their solidarity and strength, which characterized the working class in the 1960s and 1970s. And also to start from the organization at the factory floor level and now, being the factory expanded also within the social context, from the organization of the new movement of workers on the territory and the local alternative economies.

A territory represents the centre to which a significant part of the interests of the community, of class, of those new individuals that work in a social factory, generalized by the territorial systems, converges.

These new individuals are those who create a single unit in an organized body, as if they were a whole made up of interacting parts that have a social characterization since they derive from a productive characterization of the neoliberal reconversion, of the way of production and of socially suggesting the centrality of the company, of profit and of the market.

The *territory*, in the sense of social environment, takes on new class connotations, from the new social and demographic features of the resident population to identify the shape that residential areas assume in terms of space and which social groups characterize them, to define a *different social subjectivity* which was previously a typical feature of the factory with which it identified and organized and that now represents the new class composition derived from the new social factory spread over vast areas of the fully developed capitalist countries. This kind of deep process of transformation must necessarily lead to a reconsideration of the old economic and social categories of the old-school economic policies since they have been outdated by progress, and of the assumptions for an alternative project of intervention, in order to escape capitalism.

PART SEVEN

CAPITAL AGAINST NATURE[1]

_____

[1] Many of the themes treated in this part of the work have also been analysed in the Preface and Conclusion of the book: Vasapollo L., Martufi R. (edited by), *L'ambiente Capitale. Alternative alla globalizzazione contro natura. Cuba investe sull'umanità*, Natura Avventura Edizioni, Roma 2008.

CHAPTER SEVENTEEN

HOW CAPITAL DESTROYS HUMANITY

An 'Unnatural' Globalization of Capital

Capitalist production continues to survive only thanks to the brutal and intensive domination and exploitation of the world's human and natural resources. The frequent environmental disasters that are hitting the planet have made it clear to economists that the classical theory is based on the divinity of the "free market". The world economy is deeply changing: neoliberal globalization, privatization, the liberalization of trade and capital markets have worsened the living standards even in those countries with a fully developed capitalism, and the developing countries are likely to recede even further.

In recent years, after the fall of the Berlin Wall and the end of the Soviet Union, the major economic powers imposed a unipolar globalization first, and then a global competition which, in defining the dictates of the imperialist economy, created an accelerated exploitation of nature and labour, dramatically increasing the alterations caused by a wild, unlimited production, a quantitative development oriented solely by the rules of profit of international capital. The system is based in the first place on the accumulation of wealth and profit by a few, and partly on the excessive growth of the inequalities between rich people and poor people, who are always growing in number.

Everything is therefore subject to the desire of increasing profit. Men, animals, society, nature, everything must submit to the rules of development of capitalist production, and at this particular stage to the dictates of financial speculation.

Each year, the international movements of capital are thirty times bigger than the value of the world trade. The growth of rents and profits had as compensation the decline of direct, indirect and delayed wages. It increased the difference between social classes and the concentration of wealth in the hands of few people. The processes of financialization of the economy allow imperialist countries to purloin bigger amounts of surplus value and to submit to their political-economic wishes the whole world and mankind itself.

The financialization of the economy is one of the major causes of the world economic crisis, or better said, it is a choice by international capital in order to try and overcome the current structural crisis of accumulation, which has lasted for over thirty years, or rather hide it. The process of financialization of the economy generates fictitious wealth, released/disengaged from labour. Yet the development of financial wealth with no real work, seems uncontrollable. The wild market economy, that in the current stage has finance as one of its characterizing aspects, and the increasing inequality between the supply of goods and the real needs of people are the results of a global competition that focuses on capitalist development, on quantitative growth for a few people, without redistributing wealth, with no control and no limits.

The 2001 *Human Development Report* of the United Nations showed that 86% of Gross Domestic Product in the world is owned by the richest fifth part of the total of the world population, as opposed to 1% of the total GDP owned by the poorest fifth part. The income of 609 million people (the inhabitants of the less developed countries) amounts to 169 billion dollars and represents 15% of the assets of the world's top 200 multibillionaires.[2] And nowadays this polarization is even more pronounced.

The so-called globalization has not kept its promise of prosperity and development for the vast majority of the world's population. In addition, "[t]he economy of money does not pay attention the economy of nature."[3]

There have been over the centuries, three main stages: the colonization of countries with the consequent birth of the European colonial empires, the stage of capitalist development that allowed the United States to purloin those that were Europe's colonial markets, and finally neoliberal globalization, that is the new name of capitalist globalization as an hegemonic policy of the rich countries against the poor ones.

The so-called "true development," however, was never achieved; there has only been a quantitative development linked to the history of Western countries, whicht has commercialized the relation between men and nature through the exploitation of human and natural

---

[2] Cf. Latouche (2005).
[3] Nebbia (2002).

resources just to generate profit and rents for a small cluster of capitalaists and rentiers. The current model of neoliberal globalization is merely a continuation of the myth of development defined as the means to allow all people to enjoy a dignified and satisfying existence.

In order to strengthen this system, international capital has created institutions such as the World Trade Organization, the International Monetary Fund and the World Bank, which, according to their inventors, are the main support to the world's united development. These organizations have actually served to put the monopoly of large Western, and especially American companies, at the centre. Crises in Asia and the continuing lack of development in the countries of the so-called Third World have shown however, their true nature: they are submitted to the powerful and did not bring any benefits to those who really needed it.

The WTO has widened the gap between rich and poor countries who find themselves trapped by their enormous foreign debt.

These countries, or rather the whole peripheral and semi-peripheral areas, have turned into "slaves" of large financial capital and the wild market, due to the decrease of public expenditures, of wages, the expropriation and complete commercialization of nature, the exclusion of any obstacle to the intervention of foreign capital in the indebted countries, the devaluations of local currencies, and finally the big privatizations.

The increasing growth of the debt of the countries of the so-called Third World to the big Western powers made it possible both to the World Bank and the IMF to continue asking these countries conditions or imposing structural adjustment programs (in order to obtain new loans or to defer those already existing) in full accordance with the needs of finance-capital and the objectives of reducing costs in large enterprises.

Neoliberalism is an economic model that has further exacerbated inequalities and social injustices. The vaunted increase of GDP with its objectives of consumerism has created, even in fully developed capitalist countries, a quantitative growth with no quality development. It has even caused an attack on the welfare state, an increase in unemployment and labour exploitation as well as an increase in the gap between the rich and the poor.

The unending attack on social guarantees is disguised by a form of celebration of instability, which is presented as opportunities for all workers to acquire new experiences through the normalization of unstable and precarious jobs. Stable jobs are replaced by temporary ones, in the name of flexibility and competitiveness.

The so-called social or tempered model of capitalism is no more compatible with the difficult conditions of capital accumulation. In fact, Rhineland capitalism (although it still is capitalism!) is now replaced by the Anglo-Saxon model of capitalism and is characterized by less social guarantees and lower costs of labour, with the attack on overall conditions and on labour rights.

Globalization, which should have made the miracle of a greater wellbeing and a better hope for life for everyone, has actually increased the problems: out-of-control competitiveness, the exploitation of man and nature have led not only to the destruction of the environment and to growing inequalities between rich and poor people, but also to deep crises of the system, with uncertain economic developments, economic collapses of corporations, of countries, and of entire economic areas.

Neoliberal globalization is essentially a continuation of the expansion of the development and colonization that preceded it. That is why we have defined and studied it as global competition.

Growing inequalities between the world's North and South, the end of the welfare state, the growing debt of the countries of the South to those of the North, the destruction of the environmental resources, are only some of the damages caused by neoliberal globalization.

The Consumer Society and Quantitative Development

In the current capitalist system the large national, financial, transnational enterprises, while pursuing only their own interests, create an uneven development. It is essential to prove that the current capitalist system and those theories that legitimate it are unfair, and lead to poverty, inequalities, and huge problems linked to survival.

Giorgio Nebbia concludes his essay (*Lo sviluppo sostenibile*, Edizioni Cultura della Pace, Firenze 1991) with an important observation:

> It is necessary to start a great movement of liberation in order to eliminate the injustices between human beings and towards nature, a new protest for survival, that can make us move from an ideology of growth to one of development. No one can save us but ourselves, our sense of responsibility towards future generations, towards the "others of the future," which we will never know, but whose life, whose happiness depend on what we will or we will not do tomorrow and in the next

decades. The building of a sustainable development and peace can be won only through a just use of the earth's resources, our one and only common home in the universe, through a global justice for a global Man, [Ernesto Balducci].

Without justice in the use of the common goods of our common home, the planet Earth, there will never be peace.[4]

It should not be forgotten that nowadays more than three quarters of the world population is in conditions of extreme poverty and many people live on less than a dollar per day.

The Northern countries use more than 70% of the total available resources and therefore, in order to let developing countries reach a level of acceptable living conditions, the North of the world should reduce its consumption and waste.

Environmental, economic and people's problems have been exacerbated by the neoliberal globalization and the financialization of the economy has led to a fictitious economic growth. The growth of food production in the last few decades was in no way sufficient to solve the problem of meeting the needs for survival. It is estimated that in 2002–2004 more than 950 million people were officially undernourished, which meant that there had been a significant increase over the last years and the latest data show that these figures have risen further. UN figures tell us that about half of the urban population living in Africa, Asia, Latin America and the Caribbean suffers from diseases related to poor sanitary conditions of water.

Just by re-reading Malthus, who was the first to realize, with his essay, that the resources of the planet were scarce, and by recalling John Stuart Mill's thought, one realizes that the problem of the relationship between population and consumption has to be faced.

For this reason, the increase in world's population over the last few decades has to be taken into account: in 1900 people living on the planet were 1,600 million people, in 2000 the number had risen to 6,000 million. Each year the world population grows by more than 70 million people and in 2025 it is expected that the population will be up to about 7.5 billion. It is clear that the more population grows, the more resources are needed in order to support their needs; considered that the material resources of nature do not increase but rather decrease as the population increases, it can be expected that in the future the

---

[4] Poggio (2003:24).

natural resources will fail to be available both for poor and rich people.

The population growth and the resulting greater demand for goods and technology have led to an excessive exploitation of nature. The WWF has estimated at 1.8 hectares the amount of bio-productive space that is necessary to each person, whereas a U.S. citizen consumes 9.6 hectares and a European citizen 4.5 hectares. It is immediately clear how equality on the planet is still not easily achievable. In addition to this, more than three billion people nowadays live on less than two dollars per day. The so-called "progress" in socioeconomic conditions with its changes in consumption occurred in the northern countries of the world. In such countries the population is growing older and has peculiar needs, which has to be analyzed. In addition to this, there is the ever-increasing number of immigrants that move from poor countries to richer countries.

The United Nations predicts that if the current growth rate continues, the world population by the year 2050 will be up to almost 9 billion people and the number of those who do not have enough water will increase. Up until now the number of people who suffer from diseases related to lack of water is up to about 1.7 billion, but it is expected that in 2025 this number will be up to almost five billion.

All scholars in the world claim that, based on an estimate of water and food reserves, for the next years there is no guarantee, for the world's poorest people, of an appropriate development.

The uncontrolled consumerism of the developed countries, that produce and purchase virtually useless and ephemeral goods, resulted in the fact that the environmental problem, as well as the problem of limited natural resources, were not taken into account.

The pursuit of the maximum profit needs an increasing exploitation of man and nature, and does not consider the principle ratified by the UN World Commission claiming that all men have the right to live in an environment suitable to their health and their welfare.

The awareness by movements, associations and progressives in general of the environmental damage caused by industrial production and the so-called technical progress has occurred only recently, and everybody begins to understand that the unregulated exploitation of nature with the capital rules inevitably leads to disastrous consequences that make humanity the victim of its own deeds.

The exploitation, privatization and commercialization of natural resources result in an increasing polarization of income. The rich are getting richer, the poor increasingly poor. Fifty years of quantitative development have not achieved any improvement in the living standards of the population in the developing countries; in fact, in 1950 they had a per capita income that was only 5.3% of the income of industrialized countries, and in 1998 more than 5 billion people in poor countries had an income of 4.9% compared to the 800,000 million of the rich countries.

In early 2003 a fifth of the richest population owned 86% of the world GDP, compared to 1% of the poor countries, while the three biggest billionaires had an income greater than the total of the 600 million inhabitants of the poorest countries.[5]

Official statistics on illiteracy, poverty and disease, confirm that more than 1 billion people live on less than a dollar a day, more than a billion people cannot use safe drinking water because less than 1% fresh water is available to humans; there were more than 2.5 billion people who cannot use quality toilets; energy resources are still not accessible to everybody and the sector is dominated by fossil fuels that produce seriously harmful waste and air pollution. The world economy is subjected to the variability of the oil market.

The entire world system of welfare and health care is influenced by the choices imposed by the neoliberal model and diseases such as AIDS, malaria and tuberculosis fall heavily on the economic balance of Developing Countries as they are managed by the multinational to their advantage.

This situation makes us realize that we cannot continue to think that this economic system is the right one; we can no longer only think about pursuing the maximum profit, accumulation and environmental and human exploitation. We must begin to consider that all countries have to preserve and put at the centre of development goals, human needs, nature, ecosystems, biological diversity and natural resources. We have to consider the environmental macro-system and not capital, as the determining element of the economy and that the self-determined populations must manage the economy, inverting the present situation in which the capitalist economy determines politics.

The capitalist economy, in fact, reflects a logic of colonization and commercialization of all human relationships.

---

[5] Cf. *Per uno'sviluppo durevole e sostenibile*, ed. by Cristina Rapisarda Sassoon in collabouration with Stefania Anghinelli, Francesca Feller, Daniel Ferrer, 2005, Milan, p. 15.

The markets and its laws involve all spaces, common goods and eve-rything is considered as a process of change necessary for its develop-ment. The world of the early twenty-first century in which exploitation, selfishness, injustice prevail and in which ten million children die each year because of the lack of medicines that cost only a few pennies but who could be saved if the United States and Europe redistributes only a small part of annual expenses for trivial goods, continues to hope for an opportunity for progress.

CHAPTER EIGHTEEN

MARKET 'SUSTAINABLE DEVELOPMENT' IN THE DYNAMICS OF THE QUANTITATIVE DEVELOPMENT OF CAPITAL

What is Sustainable Development? How, Why and for Whom?

The current global competition is the continuation in time of the myth of mercantile development defined as the means to enable all humans to have a dignified and satisfactory existence. Neoliberal globalization and this kind of development cannot be separated from the capitalist production system that is configured as development, as quantitative growth without any redistribution of social wealth, without any real progress.

Mercantile development is essentially the wish of Western countries to dominate the world through market, technology and science, that is, through capitalist production always based on, despite the different contexts of capitalism, exploitation by humans of mankind and nature.

The increasing prevalence of environmental emergencies generated new problems. The question is: how long can natural resources be exploited and how long this quantitative growth model can be carried out?

In order to solve the environmental problem the concept of "sustainable development" has been introduced, following the United Nations' dictates, to meet the needs of the present world without damaging the needs of the future world.

To achieve this goal many measures have been taken by the international community over the years, starting from the Stockholm Declaration in 1972, followed by the Bruntland Report in 1987 (which defines sustainable development as "the development which meets the needs of the present without compromising the ability of future generations to meet their own needs"), until 1992 with the United Nations Conference on Environment and Development, which proclaimed 27 principles on Nations' rights and responsibilities through the "Declaration of Rio".

There were in 1994 the Charter of Aalbborg in Denmark (Charter of European Cities and Towns towards sustainability); in 1996 the Lisboa

Action Plan in Lisboa-Portugal; in 1997 the Kyoto Protocol (with the commitment of industrialized countries to reduce greenhouse gases emissions); and in 1999 during the Third European Conference of Sustainable Cities we had the Appeal *of* Hannover -Germany.

In 2001, with the Sixth Environmental Action Plan for the years 2001–2010, targets were plotted in the environmental, health, nature and biodiversity fields and climate changes; in 2002 there was the UN Conference in South Africa and in 2004 the Fourth European Conference on Sustainable Cities in Denmark.

In 2007 the Fifth European Conference on Sustainable Cities was held in Spain and finally 2007 the 13th UN Conference on climate changes held in Bali Indonesia, during which the means to counteract the effects of climate changes have been devised through the so-called "Road Map" that provides the ability to transfer from rich countries to the developing ones the various technologies to enable the development of clean energy. Finally, there was the FAO Food Summit, which took place later in Rome in June 3–5, 2008.

In 1987 the Bruntland Report defined the concept of sustainable development ("development which meets the needs of the present without compromising the ability of future generations to meet their own needs"), emphasizing the increasingly imperative need to involve all social partners in economic growth.

"Sustainable development" is based on the integration of 10 elements: the environment, the economy, socioculture, social equity, inter-local equity, inter-temporal equity (dimensions of equity), diversity, subsidiarity, partnership, networking and participation (principles of the system). It is a model designed to combine the need for growth, poverty reduction and the protection of ecosystems. But in reality through the concept of "sustainable development" a program compatible to capitalist production was launched which has proved to be the false idea of operating without compromising natural resources: if such a thing were true it would be in conflict with the very laws of free market, of wild capitalism. "Sustainable development" is based on the growth of GDP, which involves a growth in the production of goods, and the consequent enhancement of environmental pollution.

The achievement of quantitative growth even in this logic is seen as necessary to reach the other two goals. Growth implies the increase in quantitative production, but to be credible and balanced, it should be accompanied by literacy, by basic and advanced education, improved health care, and improved living conditions for the entire population, in line with the definitions of the international organizations.

In this context, according to the United Nations definition of 1992: "Sustainable development means improving the quality of human life while living within the capacity of supporting ecosystems" and the definition of ICLEI 1994: Durable and sustainable development is the one that provides environmental, social and economic services to all the inhabitants of a community, without threatening social, natural and built systems operativity from which the supply of such services depends."

The link between this idea of sustainable development and the question of social progress is getting clear. The vast majority of commercialized production activities affects the natural environment and social welfare, adversely conditioning the world population.

The Limits of a Growth Without Progress, Without Self-Determined Sustainable Development

Thus, the bizarre idea of a limitation to growth originates as a false, Western-centric alternative, dangerous for the development of mankind, as if the problems of the disasters of capitalist production could be solved by remaining inside it, without overcoming it. In order to put a brake, for example, to the climate change resulting from these transformations a limitation to the consumption of energy and goods is necessary.

If this limit for consumption is unacceptable to the First World citizens, it is even more so for the poor Third World countries populations (they are over 4.5 billion people) who need "consume" at least the minimum that will allow them to live with dignity (with water, electricity, food, refrigerators, education, health, the need for survival with dignity, etc.).

It is estimated that there are processes of desertification in all continents with the exception of Antarctica; at present, the arid lands are populated by more than two billion people and occupy over 40% of the surface of the Earth.

Third World countries are in a harassment and "slavery" status as compared to the rich countries, and they cannot be expected to act responsibly towards environment.

In the so-called developed countries, where about 1.5 billion people live, the primary and secondary needs are almost always satisfied and the abuse of natural resources creates significant damage to nature. What would happen if the 4.5 billion people living in poverty in the

South of the World began to have the proper quantity and quality of goods needed to meet their needs?

The cuts in social spending, the reduced employment and the reduced aid and subsidies for people in Developing Countries, the very reduction of the Welfare State in European countries, has meant that to the inhabitants of Third World countries living below the poverty line we must add a growing range of people of the northern countries who are excluded from a decent welfare because of unemployment, job and social life insecurity and lack of adequate social protections.

There is another aspect we must consider: what would happen if today an immediate and substantial reduction in the production of goods occurred, which assures millions of workers of a wage? A possible decrease in growth would cause a further injustice to the poor around the world because they would be the first to suffer the consequences.

The continuous attacks on the macro-environment, deforestation without limits, desertification, pollution of water and air added to the miserable conditions in which three quarters of the world's population live, constitute a good example of how this capitalist production system has reached a stage in which it is no longer sustainable. Also, the present capitalist crisis is structural and systemic.

Human beings, with their actions, manipulate the quality and diversification of natural resources and at present the demands are greater that the capacities of natural resources.

In 1972 a book entitled "The Limits to Growth" commissioned by the Club of Rome analyzed the problem of growth without control:

> If the present growth trends in world population, industrialization, pollution, food production, and resource depletion continue unchanged, the limits to growth on this planet will be reached sometime within the next one hundred years. The most probable result will be a rather sudden and uncontrollable decline in both population and industrial capacity. It is possible to alter these growth trends and to establish a condition of ecological and economic stability that is sustainable far into the future. The state of global equilibrium could be designed so that the basic material needs of each person on earth are satisfied and each person has an equal opportunity to realize his individual human potential.[1]

But this situation will not change until the current capitalist production persists; the principles at the base of capitalism do not allow

---

[1] Cf. Meadows, at al, 1972:24

possibilities to reach the maximum profit other than through the exploitation of man and nature without rules.

The current neoliberal model needs a lean, flexible production that minimizes costs and does not take into account the real needs of consumers who are inclined to spend more and more in frivolous and non-useful objects.

The European Union with its program "Environment 2010: Our Future, Our Choice," is trying to draw on paper plans to fight climate change, to preserve the flora, wildlife, environment, health and natural resources, to try to fight desertification, pollution, increased waste, etc. To achieve an equitable development at least the principles of an ecological economy must be considered. While environmental economics is regarded as a specialization of neoclassical economics based on the juxtaposition of economics and ecology concepts, ecological economics discusses its essence, the method, the instruments and even the status of the economics, pulling it out of the isolated exchange values universe in to make it a transdisciplinary discipline.[2]

If rich countries continue to consider cooperation only as a way to make poor countries poorer and dependent, and if they continue to cause wars, how can we talk about sustainable development? What sustainability, for whom?

It is clear then that if poor countries began to have levels of consumption similar to the rich countries, our macro-environment system would undergo disastrous consequences in a few years.

Can we think of denying water, fertilizer, and energy to the poorest people in the world, and thus contribute to worsen the situation of these countries that already count every day thousands of deaths?

The exploitation of natural and human resources for the pursuit of the maximum profit, the increasing aggression to nature and people is merely a new form of conquest and domination, the so-called development, or better development in the sense of basically quantitative growth, with all its negative effects whose measurement is tied to the capitalist production method.

---

[2] Cf.Vasapollo (eds, 2006: 48.)

CHAPTER NINETEEN

CAPITAL DESTROYS AND THEN MEASURES

The Cursed GDP

In the past the uninterrupted production of goods was always regarded as a positive thing, and quantitative growth was considered as a valid indicator to measure the social and national welfare. But now we know that an unconditional increase of commodities in a world already overburdened may affect adversely both the environment and the possibility of production in the future, namely that capitalist development contrasts human survival.

The idea of measuring growth through the value of Gross Domestic Product shows all its evident inefficiencies, because this indicator appears to be increasingly inaccurate, if we think for a well known example that an automobile accident that causes victims increases the value of GDP; this index in fact measures just how value is accumulated and does not make any difference whether this growth is due to economic measures favourable or not to environment, human health, growth of quality living conditions.

The GDP ignores the existing natural wealth; it is thereby incapable of considering the waste and the deterioration of the ecosystem. The use of natural resources is considered only in terms of creating monetary entries of wealth, while ignoring the simultaneous process of natural and social loss concerning natural resources.

Development, environment and social progress should not be classified as antagonistic objectives. The idea that an increase in GDP is a good goal to be pursued for all countries is part of the concept of globalized world typical of the neo-liberal policies and of the values of the world of economics and of capitalist commercialization.

Conceived as a tool for measuring the capacity of the war period, GDP with the years has become a kind of yardstick to measure the welfare of a nation: its growth raises acclaim, its stagnation generates concern. This happens for various reasons, among which the impact on employment. Yet, Simon Kuznets himself, its main creator, has stressed several times the error inherent in the formula "more GDP = More

prosperity." As GDP increases every time there is a transaction economy, its growth inevitably tends to be connected to expenditure which,
in some cases, are a sign of distress rather than welfare such as those
associated, for example, to ecological disasters, the fight against crime
and divorce. Expenses incurred for the remediation of an oil spill, or
for treating a cancer due to pollution, although they help GDP grow,
are symptoms of damage to the environment and to humans. On this
front, even for the bravest of defence lawyers, it is difficult to help the
GDP. Growth of spending on Prozac, while stimulating the GDP does
not imply more happiness.[1]

GDP is the yardstick whereby different countries are measured and
compared, but we must always underline the limits of this indicator,
which are analyzed in many works of the past 20 years. First, GDP
measures all the activities containing a monetary transaction ignoring
all others. For example, if a person has a car accident and faces serious
conditions in the hospital there is still a growth of GDP, and the economy of war and wars of aggression maintains demand and increases
the GDP.

The obsession with the growth of GDP means that all commodity production including the negative ones, are regarded positively.
Another feature of GDP is that in its accounting we find both the damages and the repairs of the environment.

If GDP was calculated taking into account the ecological and
social aspects, its value should be significantly reduced in each country. It follows that it is an illusion to think of sustainable development
(sustainable for whom? Sustainable for the laws of the market) because
each production of goods causes a depletion of natural resources and
has devastating social impacts. The acknowledgement that the monetary indicators, such as the Gross Domestic Product, are not able to
detect the worsening and the impoverishment of resources has led to
several proposals, and to consider alternatives, in order to make cor-
rections to GDP. However, all of them remain inside the compatibility
of a National Accounting System that measure with market quantitative formulas the economic dynamics of the capitalist production.

The pursuit of capitalist countries of the growth of GDP is simply a
"statistical lie" because the increase of GDP is certainly not a qualitative improvement in the level of life of all the citizens. It is clear that

---

[1] Cf. http://www.lavoce.info/news/view.php?cms_pk=927.

GDP is a paradox-index that rewards everything that increases the market, rewarding the rules of the capital society.

The So-Called Alternative Indicators and Environmental Laws. But What "Green Perspective"?

Non-Alternative Macroeconomic Indicators

There has been talk for many years to include in the national accounts the aggregate of the "added disvalue," to measure the negative impact of production on the socio-environmental system correcting GDP, or even of creating new indicators that take into account the degradation of the environment through the examination of the costs due to the introduction of, for instance, catalytic converters for automobiles, the cost of incinerators, etc.

So, several "alternatives" have been developed, such as the Index of Human Development (which is based on the per capita income, the level of education and longevity), the Genuine Progress Indicator, GPI (which is obtained subtracting from the GDP the costs caused by pollution of air, water, etc.), and the Green Gross Domestic Production (which considers environmental degradation, etc.). There are many other examples of "alternative" indicators but the various difficulties and obstacles that accompany the implementation of each indicator have not yet been overcome.

Green Gross Domestic Product (Green GDP) is essentially an indicator that takes into account the environmental consequences of economic development. This indicator, like the so-called added disvalue, however, is very difficult to calculate because it is almost impossible to quantitatively calculate the effects of climate or cultural changes as well as of scientific and economic changes. Sometimes physical indicators are used: an example might be the calculation of the emissions of carbon dioxide per year, or the "Waste per capita".

Another example is the calculation of the Genuine Progress Indcator (GPI), that is the indicator ("index of effective progress"or "index of true / real progress") that measures the growth of the quality of life of a nation. This is a distinction between positive changes (e.g. those services or goods) and expenses negative (i.e. those caused by pollution, crime, by accidents). This indicator differs from the classical Gross Domestic Product that calculates all the costs as positive, because to any monetary transaction does not correspond an increase in welfare.

Specifically, the GPI subtracts social costs associated with pollution, crime and environmental degradation, while it adds to the value of the GDP the value of voluntary labour and labour done within the family. Moreover, it considers the distribution of income, so that the higher is equity, the greater is the value of the GPI, the greater is the availability of leisure the higher is the value of index; and it is considered then the cost of durable goods, infrastructure, etc.

As the GDP per capita results to be a limited and distorted indicator of development, some French scholars have identified a different and adjusted GDP, a human development index, which, taking into account other social factors such as education, health and nutrition, introduces human development as factor to be analyzed for the determination of GDP. The United Nations Development (UNDP) defines human development as "as the process of enlarging the range of people's choices increasing their opportunities for education, health care, income and employment, and covering the full range of human choices from a sound physical environment to economic and political freedoms".[2]

The general objectives of human development to be achieved are: an economic growth for everyone and especially poor people, an improvement in education, basic education, human health and environmental conditions. Human development must, therefore, take into account individual income, level of health and education. For this reason it becomes more and more indispensable to introduce new economic indicators that can account for all economic environmental and natural relations.

A prime example is the Human Development Index that should distinguish the difference between "rich" populations and "poor" people, but always through "Western" and capitalist connotations, in a context that does not consider other civilizations, customs and traditions that create different needs.

The Human Development Report in 2005 shows that this index has been showing quite improved values in recent years with the exception of the countries in Sub-Saharan Africa (mainly due to AIDS) and the countries of Eastern Europe (because of the economy decline). In the first places there obviously are Europe, North America and Oceania.

---

[2] Cf. UNDP, Human Development Report, Oxford University Press, New York, 1992.

Statistical Indicators for Measuring Environmental Impact[3]

Enterprises, carrying out their activities, come into contact with the external environment that influences decisions concerning management. The enterprise is a part of the social system, influences the external environment and is influenced by it, because it plays both an economic and a social role, and therefore should act in a socio-economic perspective, that is in the interests of the interdependence between environmental quality and economic development in order to improve production using the most advanced technologies, respectful of environmental laws and pollution control.

It is clear that even for management processes within a business context the importance of the ecological element increases, because it can be considered as an external force, i.e. as a factor of production, a source of external capital, that acts and influences the performance of the entire production. The evaluation of enterprise's assets and income would be, therefore, now largely conditioned by environmental laws. The environment becomes a strategic resource, a capital factor, as the qualifying medium-long term elements of the enterprise activity must tend to the redefinition of power relations between companies and social actors.

Even in microeconomics, the use of indicators, referred to as good instrument for measuring "sustainable development," is essential to take careful choices between the various possible alternatives, to activate an efficient capitalist enterprise not only from a managerial point of view, but from a total social perspective, in particular in all those circumstances in which the enterprise is ecologically involved and is not able to assess the real situation because the technical data are not easily interpretable.

The enterprise considers it necessary to have the use of management and information means, measuring instruments able to express clearly and precisely the composition of the factors used in production and the impact that the productive activity have on the environment and the social contexts, and to extend this knowledge to all external users who need it, always with the purpose of making profits with an "ethics" that is not really social, nor aimed at a social redistribution of profits.

---

[3] Cf. L. Vasapollo, «Nuovi strumenti statistico-aziendali per la misura della compatibilità sociale d'impresa. Gli indicatori socioambientali dell'attività produttiva», *Finanza Italiana*, year V, n. 11–12, nov.-dic. 1997.

In particular, to cope with these consequences of the enterpreneur-
ial activity on natural heritage, two types of indicators are usually distinguished: environmental impact indicators and environmental
performance indicators. This distinction is made because of the different meaning of the measurement activities of a company relative to its
impact on natural capital; indeed while the activity of an enterprise can
be measured in terms of use resources, emissions, waste products, etc.,
to make a survey of its overall impact on the environment is necessary
to make some subjective valuations, or estimates that establish the
effects caused by production management.

The environmental impact indicators analyze the impact of production on the environment through a determination of physical parameters referred to the production the company deals with, for example,
the greenhouse effect, the level of toxicity for human health, fauna,
flora, etc. These indicators can be calculated from a physical point of
view and in monetary terms. Physical indicators point to the enterprise contribution to the changes in global and local environmental
conditions; they are a further measure of the efficiency of the company
in its resources management. For the construction of these indicators,
the most used method is linking the physical flows to some effects
on human health, ecosystems and the impoverishment of natural
resources. There will be primarily a classification of physical flows on
the basis of their environmental impacts and then a characterization of
these physical flows, taking into account environmental impacts on
the greenhouse effect, the decrease of the ozone layer, the toxicity,
energy, waste, smog, etc. Finally, there is the evaluation itself, essential
in a situation where the results of the impact values contrast each
other; it important know how to compare the results obtained to take
various management decisions.

Monetary indicators, instead, allow the company to measure from
an economic perspective all the variations caused to the natural heritage, estimated in terms of monetization, and allows the addition of the
environment variable to the various economic decision-making processes of the enterprise. The environmental performance indicators
provide the qualitative and quantitative information to help the enterprise make an evaluation of efficiency, effectiveness and consumption
of resources in order to enable the top management to adopt the best
strategies oriented to strengthen as much as possible the pursuit of
environmental objectives, also through a better external communication of results (e.g. to corporate stakeholders).

The use of such indicators in relation to the consumption of raw materials, energy, etc. allows the firm to evaluate its efficiency in environmental resources (process indicators), always in terms of the budget of a capitalist enterprise oriented to profit. The company must, however, be able to evaluate its efficiency in economic and financial terms, and uses for this purpose the eco-financial indicators to correlate the interventions for the environment with the costs of investment and management problems that this entails.

The company also controls its ability to achieve the objectives of environmental performance through the so-called environmental management indicators to continuously measure the degree of compliance with legislation and environmental policies and the degree of integration with other environmental functions.

In summary, these indicators enable the company to pay more attention to environmental policy through a clearer, more specific and sectoral formulation of objectives; they also enable a development of the environmental management system, the improvement of external communication and the control, with a reduction in emissions and their costs of abatement and prevention.

The first consideration that is in order at this point, relative to the use of different management and monitoring means of environmental sustainability, is that the environment is considered as a factor of capitalist production and therefore is still subjected to the laws of capital valorization; in fact, the definition of "Nature Capital" which is the "Environment Capital" is largely used. This is a consequence of a market-based environmental policy that uses both advertising and public relations and often has as an enterprise's primary objective to improve its image. Marketing operators should make consumers responsible, even those less sensitive, through pushes which tends to create motivation in people who do not see an immediate advantage in the adoption of environmental policies. It is necessary that consumers understand the importance of the benefits resulting from the adoption of ecological products, highlighting the personal economic health-related benefits of the so-called "green" products.

It should be stressed, however, that although all the environmental indicators of the enterprise (and especially environmental impact indicators) show a high level of complexity and uncertainty in their construction in terms of scientific validity, their integrated use would allow the enterprise to behave and to guide business decisions towards objectives of economic and socio-environmental sensitivity. It is obvious that the considerations to be made are quite different if the case of a capitalist enterprise is dealt with, for in this case everything is related to obtaining the maximum profit, or with a company in a socialist system, with system logics that are "outside" the market, or rather "not" market-based, in which the achievement of the maximum effect is measured in terms of redistribution and safeguarding socio-environmental interests.

Environmental Laws, Monitoring Tools for Management Analyses

> We live on one planet, connected in a delicate, intricate web of ecological, social, economic and cultural relationships that shape our lives. If we are to achieve sustainable development, we will need to display greater responsibility—for the ecosystems on which all life depends, for each other as a single human community, and for the generations that will follow our own, living tomorrow with the consequences of the decisions we take today.[4]

These words of Kofi Annan at the World Summit on Sustainable Development of 2002 show that there is a shared understanding of the urgency of working out national and international laws aimed at protecting our environment and also of institutions, international organizations and enterprises that have the possibility to transform the current model of development according to the principles of sustainability and solidarity.

The entire management activity of enterprises must preserve, in an environmentally aware perspective, the natural heritage that the company has "loaned" from nature and must manage to increase its overall value, even though doing this determines anyway capital accumulation processes that delineate the usual relationships of social domination. Environmental laws dictated by the legislature or by other sources are legal rules that safeguard these capitalist power relations.

Along with environmental laws there are the so-called voluntary standards or technical specifications adopted by national organizations or by European organizations (European Committee for Standardization or CEN) or international organizations (International Organization for Standardization or ISO) that guide firms to produce taking account of environmental needs.

---

[4] Kofi A. Annan, Secretary-General of the United Nations, Johannesburg, South Africa, 26 August-4 September 2002.

The search for a hypothetical balance between business interests and ecology has led to the introduction in the European Union Countries of some self-regulatory and economic instruments.

The Council Regulation (No. 1836/93) of the European Community introduced in 1993 is a new instrument for management and control called EMAS (Environmental Management and Audit Scheme) which can be adopted voluntarily by organizations (companies, public agencies, etc.) to improve their environmental performance and inform the public and other stakeholders on their data and information on its environmental management. The second version of EMAS (EMAS II) was published by European Communities with Regulation 761/2001, subsequently amended by Regulation 196/2006.[5]

In regard to the "voluntary standards" we must mention the Ecolabel (Regulation EC No. 1980/2000), which is the European label of ecological quality that certifies that the product or service has a lower environmental impact throughout its entire lifecycle. The label is essentially a marketing opportunity because it responds to the increasingly pressing need to realize "clean" products. It is also a preventive strategy because it limits the marketing of products that could cause environmental damage and also because it is a trademark that becomes a guarantee of the environmental quality of the product. The label is also an instrument of certification in order to ensure the necessary transparency to market green products. It is, therefore, a voluntary instrument that provides a higher quality than legal standards. It is important to note that:

The European Eco-lable achieved a record year in Italy in 2007, with an increase in the number of licenses equal to 111% compared to previous year: it has passed from 86 licenses and 1384 products and services at the end of 2006 to 174 licenses and 2,474 products and services in late 2007. 2008 will be a challenging year for APAT and the Committee, because The European Commission has charged Italy with the development of the rules policy for granting the European Eco-label to the product group "Buildings," and some revisions of

---

[5] The objective of EMAS shall be to promote continuous improvements in the environmental performance of organisations by means of:
– the establishment and implementation of environmental management systems by organisations;
– the provision of information on environmental performance and an open dialogue with the public and other interested parties.

product groups including "Paper copies and graphic paper," "tourist accommodation service" and "Camping service".

In particular, the importance of the Ecolabel for buildings should be pointed out. It is an important project that provides an integrated approach to environmental problems related to the construction, use and disposal of buildings within the life cycle. This environmental certification will be voluntary and will be added to the energy mandatory provisions of Legislative Decree 311/2006, which allows citizens to be informed about the consumption of a building.[6]

4. The regulations of the of the International Organization for Standardization 14,000 series provide managerial instruments for organizations that want to put under control its aspects and environmental impacts, thus improving their performance in this field.

It should be noted that all the requirements of ISO 14000 are voluntary. The decision to apply the requirements of ISO 14000 is therefore a strategic decision that the enterprise management chooses to take.

The ISO 14001 is the standard that can be implemented by any type of organization that wishes to achieve an improvement in the performance of their activities through the adoption of an environmental management system; this standard was implemented by the new EMAS Regulation. It was joined, in a progressive approach of the international system to the European scheme, by the subset of ISO14030 standards for the evaluation of environmental performance and by ISO 14063 standard for environmental communication. The subset of ISO 14020 disciplines different types of environmental labels and declarations, standardizing different levels of public information on environmental performance of products and services. From this point of view, the labels and declarations have an important role in sustainable consumption, as they define, credibly and transparently, a boundary that distinguishes the products more compatible with the environment from those less compatible. These are supplemented by the ISO 14040 standard that disciplines the methodology to be applied in the life cycle study.[7]

Within the fifth action program, the European Economic Community Commission, in March 1992, approved a Regulation establishing

---

[6] Cf. APAT – Agency for Environmental Protection and for Technical Services – Section ECOLABEL http://193.206.192.245/giorgio/CrescitaEcolabelItalia2007.pdf.

[7] Cf. Copyright © 2000 Reporting P. http://www.bilanciosociale.it/bilancio_sociale .html.

a voluntary environmental management and audit scheme of with the aim of promoting an improvement of environmental performance in industrial activities.

The Audit, born in Canada in the early 1970s to ensure safety and hygiene in the workplace, was subsequently extended to all issues of environmental safety. This instrument is a systematic, objective and documented evaluation (which occurs periodically) of the business organization operation, with regard to environmental benefits agreeing the enterprises policies with the various environmental policies.[8]

In addition to eco-audit other instruments that help analyze and evaluate the overall impact of the productive activity of a company in the macro-social environment, there are the Social Report and Environment Report.

The instrument that is currently considered, in the accounting and quantity approach, the most valid to give visibility to the questions and the need of information and transparency of the customer is the Social Budget: using a model of reporting on the quantities and quality of the relationship between the company and the representative group of the whole society that aims at outlining a coherent, timely, complete and transparent framework of the complex interdependence between economic and sociopolitical factors, consequent to the choices taken.[9]

The Social Report is a very difficult document to draw because, by taking into account many socio-economic-environmental variables it must meet the information needs of those who have "a stake" in the fate of the company and expect economic and financial returns.

The Social Report must inform the various business areas on the social performance that the company adopts, and secondly steer future decisions based on these. The firm must know how to manage the social consensus through an improvement of its image capable to reconcile the interests of the various subjects of the enterprise. Like the operating budget that must follow the requirements and rules, so the Social Budget should provide "relevant, impartial and clear" information. Each of these main principles is divided into the following postulates, so far as the relevance implies the timeliness, relevance and schedule of information, whereas impartiality concerns with completeness, prudence and acceptability of information and finally

---

[8] Cf. APAT - Agency for Environmental Protection and for Technical Sevizi –http://www.apat.gov.it/site/it-IT/Temi/Mercato_verde/Standards_ISO_14000/.
[9] Cf. Matacena (1984: 131–134).

clearly recalls the postulates of understandable, concise and correct information.[10]

Since the 1970s the problem of accounting for externalities appeared in all its importance, as the enterprises that bear costs for environmental protection in fact are disadvantaged compared to the others, because they present a lower added value; it becomes necessary, in order to achieve a more balanced determination of the operating results, to add in the accountings the item of "environmental costs".

Compared with the Social Report, the Environmental Report deals with a specific part of the enterprise activity, analyzing it with specific parameters and following defined guidelines set by different international organizations such as: CEFIC (Council of European Chemical Industry); PERI (Public Environmental Reporting Initiative); FEEM (Eni Enrico Mattei Foundation).

An Environmental Report must have a structure as close as possible to that of the traditional operating budget with a numeric part number and a descriptive one. It is also necessary to ensure the environmental transparency of the enterprise. Within the company a real new managerial philosophy must arise and consolidate, able to manage resources, production and quality in terms of achievement of profit and value creation.

Even if the impact on the environment can be limited by the measures to reduce the negative effects of pollution, the companies have often tended to avoid controls and enforcement measures by the authorities and to follow only part of the laws to avoid any action against the company, believing that the environmental question causes only additional costs. The Environmental Report must have a structure capable of giving accurate information from an environmental point of view, for like the operating budget it compares the aggregated information permitting some economic and financial assessments on the enterprise's activity. The structure of the Environmental Report must enable an estimate on the development of the relationship between business and environment in order to maximize savings on the "Environmental Capital".

It should be noted that while the yield of financial capital can be measured with elements of the same nature (money with money), in

[10] Cf. Copyright © 2000 Reporting R. P. http://www.bilanciosociale.com/bilancio-ambientale.html.

regard to "environment capital" there is a different situation because the return must be measured in terms of the "value" that the enterprise provides to the community, but what value is it? Certainly it is not the value of the social progress and for society but the value of capital accumulation processes.

CHAPTER TWENTY

'CLEAN' ENERGIES OF CAPITALISM: AGRO-FUELS AND PLANNED CRIMES AGAINST HUMANITY

Producing Energy from Food: the Monstrosity of Growth

"Several agricultural products are used in the production of energy; among the so-called agro-fuels, there are sugar cane, corn, beet, palm oil, rape seeds and other oleaginous crops. Included in this category also are by-products of agriculture and livestock, such as straw, sugar cane waste, leaves, stems and buds, bark, sawdust, pods, dung, and other derivatives from preparing food agricultural products, forestry and animal slaughter. In summary, the biomass is a source of energy locally available that can produce electricity, heat and mechanical energy, like liquid, gaseous or solid fuels, thus contributing to the replacement of fossil fuels and to diversify energy sources".[1]

For example, the agro-fuels are said to be clean and green; this is not true because a ton of palm oil production causes 33 tons of carbon dioxide emissions, which is approximately 10 times more than oil. The destruction of tropical forests to produce ethanol through sugar cane produces 50% more greenhouse gas than using the same quantity of petrol. It is said that agro-fuels will not cause deforestation; also this statement is false if we consider, for example, that in Indonesia the loss of forests is caused by palm oil plantations for biodiesel. Agrofuels are considered to promote rural development; also this is a false myth to debunk: in the Tropics, 100 hectares dedicated to family agriculture offer 35 working positions, while the palm oil and sugar cane only 10, the eucalyptus 2 and soybeans only half. It is even claimed that the agrofuels will cause no more hunger in the world; according to the FAO, food in the world would be enough of feed everyone but poverty, also related to high fuel prices which increase food, does not allow anyone to eat properly; this is a mere utopia, since it is not sure that

---

[1] See the dark side of agrofuels, José Antonio Díaz Duque, deputy National Assembly of People's Power, Deputy Minister, Ministry of Science, Technology and Environment of the Republic of Cuba, Vasapollo, Martufi (a eds, 2008).

increasing the production of agrofuels will find the remedy to the world hunger.[2]

Fidel Castro has been very clear in his discussions about this topic:

> I believe that reducing and moreover recycling all motors that run on electricity and fuel is an elemental and urgent need for all humanity. The tragedy does not lie in reducing those energy costs but in the idea of converting food into fuel. It is known very precisely today that one ton of corn can only produce 413 litres of ethanol on average, according to densities. That is equivalent to 109 gallons. The average price of corn in U.S. ports has risen to $167 per ton. Thus, 320 million tons of corn would be required to produce 35 billion gallons of ethanol. According to FAO figures, the U.S. corn harvest rose to 280.2 million tons in the year 2005. Although the president is talking of producing fuel derived from grass or wood shavings, anyone can understand that these are phrases totally lacking in realism. Let's be clear: 35 billion gallons translates into 35 followed by nine zeros! Afterwards will come beautiful examples of what experienced and well-organized U.S. farmers can achieve in terms of human productivity by hectare: corn converted into ethanol; the chaff from that corn converted into animal feed containing 26% protein; cattle dung used as raw material for gas production. Of course, this is after voluminous investments only within the reach of the most powerful enterprises, in which everything has to be moved on the basis of electricity and fuel consumption. Apply that recipe to the countries of the Third World and you will see that people among the hungry masses of the Earth will no longer eat corn. Or something worse: lend funding to poor countries to produce corn ethanol based on corn or any other food and not a single tree will be left to defend humanity from climate change. Other countries in the rich world are planning to use not only corn but also wheat, sunflower seeds, rapeseed and other foods for fuel production. For the Europeans, for example, it would become a business to import all of the world's soybeans with the aim of reducing the fuel costs for their automobiles and feeding their animals with the chaff from that legume, particularly rich in all types of essential amino acids.[3]

And still Fidel Castro claims:

> All the countries of the world, rich and poor, without any exception, could save millions and millions of dollars in investment and fuel simply by changing all the incandescent light bulbs for fluorescent ones, an exercise that Cuba has carried out in all homes throughout the country.

---

[2] 'The five myths of agrofuels, "Mission Today http://www.trentinosolidarieta source. it/article/articleview/2020/1/156 /.

[3] http://panafricannews.blogspot.com/2007/04/reflections-of-president-fidel -castro.html.

That would provide a breathing space to resist climate change without killing the poor masses through hunger.[4]

From the environmental point of view the mass production of agrofuels becomes more damaging than the pollution problem it is deemed to solve.

Agrofuels are offered both as an alternative to oil and as a means to combat global warming, and for this the major international companies are launching this new market, which is, however, harmful to the nutritional needs of peoples.

The FAO says that in the year between March 2007 and March 2008 there was an increase of approximately 88% in the price of cereals, while fats and oils grew 106%; the World Bank claims that last year and a half the price of cereals rose by 80%.

Agricultural land per capita in developed capitalism is almost twice than for underdeveloped areas: 1.36 acres per person in the North against 0.67 in the South, for the simple fact that in underdeveloped areas live about 80% of the world population. The prices of staple foods have increased greatly in the recent months penalizing even more the poorest communities; for example the price of corn has grown in one year by more than 50%. This increase, however, was not caused by poor production, because in recent years there has been a much higher production than in the last years.

The main causes of rising prices are attributable to the increase of grains used for the production of biofuels, increases in the cost of diesel and fertilizers, increase in the consumption of meat that has led to increased demand for animal feed.

It is not acceptable to deprive of food, land and water the poor communities to sustain the luxuries of the Western world.

Malnutrition today threatens 52.4 million South Americans and Caribbeans, that is 10% of the world population. With the expansion of the areas converted to ethanol production, we run the risk of transforming the so-called "biofuels" in "necrofuels," in predators of human beings.[5]

By inventing the engaging and misleading term biofuel the new monstrous fraud of agrofuels is achieved, namely the capitalist exploitation by multinationals agricultural goods for energy market.

---

[4] http://panafricannews.blogspot.com/2007/04/reflections-of-president-fidel-castro.html.

[5] Cf. Frei Betto, "The necrocombustibili" in http://www.che-fare.org/news/Frei%20Betto%201%20necrocombustibili.html.

Examples of Leadership and Anti-Leadership

Forty Heads of State and Government, more than five thousand delegates representing 181 countries gathered for three days in Rome from 3 to 5 June 2008 in the FAO Food Summit. Among the "hottest" issues to be addressed, there was a debate on agro-fuels, agricultural and trade policies, with clashes that viewed on the one side the Latin American countries and the on the other the United States and the European Union.

The closing Statement of the FAO summit in Rome expressed the need to meet the long-term food crisis that needs the coordinated efforts of the international community. All countries and organizations have taken the commitment to allocate 6.5 billion worth of aid, the World Bank has provided 1.2 billion dollars, the U.S. 1.5 billion, France 1.5 billion over five years, the United Kingdom 590 million dollars and Italy has allocated 190 million euros.

The summit ended with only a simple commitment of the Heads of State and many Ministers to take a vague commitment to eradicate world hunger, without absolutely identifying the political responsibilities of the major Western powers, multinationals, and of the very structural crisis in the capitalist production.

But along with the final statement there was a clear statement of position of some Latin American countries, led by the Cuban Deputy Minister in foreign investment, Orlando Requeijo, that giving reading of the Cuba declaration at the general final assembly of FAO reiterated and reinforced a few key interventions requested the day before by the head of the Cuban delegation Ramon Machado Ventura. In support of these arguments Ecuador added: "Venezuela, Argentina and Cuba are not alone. Many countries disagree."[6]

The Cuban delegation claimed openly that this little but significant result, achieved in the final declaration of the summit, depends on the lack of political will by the mature capitalist countries to make substantial and lasting solutions to a global food crisis which is now strongly linked to an energy and environmental crisis, complaining that the final document does not present references to the impact of protectionist agricultural subsidies, monopolistic control of food distribution, the criminal strategy of using agrofuels as opposed to the use of

---

[6] Cf 2008-06-06 12:53; FAO SUMMIT CLOSED, the final declaration approved; http://www.ansa.it/opencms/export/site/visualizza_fdg.html_77952538.html.

grains to solve the problems of food in the southern hemisphere; and there is not any reference on the fundamental issue of climate change due to patterns of production and consumption imposed by neoliberalism, adding to it the consequences of financial speculation on the rising of food prices.

Delegates from Argentina, Nicaragua, Ecuador, Bolivia and Venezuela supported the position of Cuba. In particular, the FAO Ambassador of the Bolivarian Republic of Venezuela, Gladys Francisca Urbaneja Duran in her speech stressed that the food crisis is not a technical problem but a social and political problem, "it is the proof of damage and the historic ruins of the capitalist model ... All these causes may be summed up in one: the character of goods which is attributed to foods in the current international economic structure represented by the capitalist model of production and consumption, which focuses on the maximization of profit opposed to the collective welfare of peoples and the sustainable natural resources."

For these reasons, the Delegate of Venezuela emphasized, we need to give a strong impetus to ALBA, that is the Bolivarian Alternative of the *Nuestra America* people, in order to counter the logic of capitalism, the logic of profit and global competition, and to propose the immediate creation of a *Fondo Especial Agricola* which collects an agreed percentage of the price of a barrel of oil to finance the mechanization of agriculture, the funding of agriculture technology, to develop food production, thereby determining a true popular sovereignty on food, against the interests of multinational corporations.

The delegation of Cuba, while expressing gratitude for the support received from the majority of the present countries on ending the criminal blockade imposed by the Government of the United States, insists that their country will continue to work in defence of justice, equity solidarity "so that hunger will turn soon into a scourge eradicated from the history of mankind."

These important issues supported by the Cuban and Venezuelan delegations and strongly supported also by Argentina, Bolivia, Ecuador and Nicaragua, were the key ideas of those like us in the CESTES-PROTEO who wanted to promote an alternative summit, with several other research centres and associations and grassroots movements, to directly accuse the current international economic order which increases poverty, inequality and injustice.

In fact while the FAO summit on emergency food was inaugurating, at La Sapienza University of Rome an international meeting took place for an alternative summit "Land, water and energy: politics on common heritage".

During the meeting there was a declaration of support to the open letter in defence of the Amazon signed in Brasilia on April 14, 2008 and sent to President Lula and the Brazilian government; also, a support was expressed to the international campaigns for the indigenous and grassroots movements of South American countries that are fighting for the defence and the socialization of common goods, and to the movements in defence of the processes of participatory democracy and self-determination of the governments of Bolivia, Venezuela, Cuba, Ecuador and to all peoples fighting for their independence.

All speakers highlighted how the food crisis, the energy crisis and the environmental decline are the products of the systemic crisis of capitalist production, that is a model supported by rampant consumerism that, in order to accomplish the profits of multinationals, is causing more and more wars, exploitation, poverty and hunger, and for this reason radical alternatives should be created, also supporting the models under construction of the XXI Century Socialism.

CHAPTER TWENTY-ONE

BRIEF CONCLUSIONS:
THE STRUGGLES OF GRASSROOTS MOVEMENTS AND AN
ECONOMIC SOCIO-ECOLOGICAL POLITICAL THEORY FOR
DEVELOPMENT OUTSIDE THE MARKET

A concept is now clear: our macro-environmental system cannot continue to reproduce itself through the continuous unchecked exploitation of natural resources. The solution, however, cannot be a zero-growth or the stopping of development or the false alternatives like the use of agrofuels that are crimes against humanity.

The worsening of the conditions of the world lower classes, made more acute by the wars necessary for the new arrangements of capitalist development, constitutes a good chance for a renewed international solidarity. Renewed internationalism and militant class movements must no longer be postponed; they are made more necessary by the context of the social "endless war".

The challenges of globalization (unemployment, under-employment, changes in the nature of work, the decline of public services and many others) are social issues that transcend the workplace. Meeting the challenges will require that the labour movement that promotes the interests of all workers, whether organized and unorganized. Trade Unions must reach out of the workplace and into the community by building coalitions with the environmental, community, women's, human rights, farm and other people's organizations.[1]

Giving voice to the environmental and social needs must not lead to a negative impact on the already precarious wage conditions; we are afraid, in fact, that firms, to adapt production to the environmental needs, without touching the shares for profits and annuities, would negatively affect wages, causing a further depletion of the welfare of the poorer classes. It is now essential to stop the unbridled pursuit of profit by establishing minimum global standards regarding the social conditions, environment, labour, which all governments should respect and make respected.[2]

---

[1] Brecher, Costello (2001: 194) translated from the Italian edition.
[2] See Vasapollo (ed., 2006).

Whereas the biological survival of the human species and the social survival are closely linked, in order to allow a balanced and equal growth within society, it may be necessary to overcome the capitalist production model and put into question its economic position in everyday life, as it determines only rules for the unbridled search of profit by capitalists!

The challenge therefore is to pursue a society that goes beyond capital, but at the same time that gives immediate answers to the barbarism which afflicts the everyday lives of the working class.Only in this way it is possible to stop forever and wherever the wars of imperialist aggression and expansion, redistribute wealth to the labour and denied labour world, to join together the concept of development and welfare state and progress; a qualitative and self-determined, strongly social and environmental compatible development, based on the centrality of man and nature.

The present development is only the expression of capitalist civilization, that is characterized by its exclusivity when compared to other civilizations of the world; a quantitative growth that configures the capitalist quantitative development model as the sole perspective of humankind. In the current capitalist system large national, financial, trans-national enterprises, following only their own interests create an uneven development. It is essential to prove that the capitalist system, and the theories that legitimize it, is unjust, and leads to poverty, inequalities, and tragic problems of survival, because according to the capitalist production rules that the conflict with society and nature is determined, through the contradictory dynamic of development of productive forces and relations of production.

That is why we give political and economic attention, without any romantic or nostalgic approach, to the reality of Indigenous-African America because the neoliberal restoration sees its wealth / poverty gap grow larger and larger. The role as economic-productive semi-periphery given to the America of indigenous peoples makes it an area where the centrality of the labour-capital conflict is higher and more direct, and this conflict is wilder without the mediation of the capital-nature, capital-science, capital-democracy and capital–rights contradictions within the dynamics of class conflict.

Socialism of the XXI century is as a consequence filled with real class contents. This formulation, although seems to be generic, finds a concrete content in daily life with the decisive structural reforms introduced by Chávez, Morales, Correa, who, due to their radicalism in form and content, represent with Cuba the revolutionary horizon of Latin America, that is the new global concrete reference for the globalized social struggles for resistance and recovery of the social offensive. And it is essential that these actions have, in their deepest nature, a direction against the logic of capital and the market.

The challenge, therefore, is to pursue a society that goes beyond capital but at the same time, to give immediate answers to the barbarism which afflict the daily lives of the working class.

The question has two faces: the first is the problem of moving from social movements to the implementation of a political organization in a party form, a leadership team and the ability to conduct numerous forms of struggle with the strategic focus not only on anti-imperialism but especially on anti-capitalism, for an alternative to capitalist production, using objective and subjective forms and methods.

Only with a guide and an organized political subjectivity, mass movements can pursue the strengthening of the alternative transformation process, overcoming capitalism. As the means of production belong to the people, Cuba, with all the difficulties and contradictions of a still not-completed socialist process, can propose a different relationship with society, with the macro-environment, because the production is oriented to solve people's needs, possibilities of social redistribution and thus respect and protection of nature.

It is necessary to make a globalization of solidarity among peoples so to adapt to the rules of a qualitative, compatible and sustainable development in social, environmental, human rights, civil and labour terms and that is really effective for all countries, a globalization of human rights. On this basis the Cuban Revolution is working, and despite the major limitations imposed by the imperialist aggression, is developing social and environmental outcomes that are now recognized by all most important international organizations.

Moving along the line of developments in Cuba, Venezuela and Bolivia, the partial reforms can be consolidated, the tactics and struggles for partial demands can turn into real strategies for overcoming capitalism. That is why the socialism in the 21st Century continues to consider as a priority reference Cuba, its revolution, its government, and that is why Chavez's alternative and the Bolivarian revolutions, Evo Morales and the Indians movement *"vivir bien"* have assumed the character of socialist revolutions.

It is necessary, then, to develop from now on alternative theories and social struggles to force the redistribution of income and wealth to

workers, the unemployed, the indigenous nartionalities and communities, and to safeguard environment and health, to promote education, training, social culture and knowledge, developing a new critique
of applied economics capable to give shape to a policy of a non-market
socioecological development, alternative to capitalism, and able to
overcome the human and nature exploitation.

The study and the development of alternative theories from a
critique to applied economics are realized in a socio-ecological political economic sense as support and exchange of experiences with the
international struggle of the workers and the indigenous people; in
an interlacing of the theory and practice of class struggle, where
the capital-nature conflict is intertwined within the dynamics of the
capital-labour conflict, for overcoming the capitalist production model
in the concrete construction of socialist processes of and in the twenty-
first century.

A new development model is necessary in which inequality can
be corrected by good policies for social progress that give voice to
minorities and to the marginalization created by the capitalist production system; that is, a new theory of socio-ecological policy centred on
social and environmental compatibility, wanted and imposed by the
struggles of the class movements for an immediate, profound change.
A possible, necessary, indispensable, undelayable Socialism of the 21st
Century, starting also from a minimum program of major structural
reform, but now! Tomorrow may be too late!

This is one common struggle to win together in order to stop the
causes of this increasingly inhumane capitalist social system, in the
horizon of the construction of a different world, a socialist world.

PART EIGHT

CURRENT TRENDS: FROM QUANTITATIVE GROWTH TO THE STRUCTURAL AND SYSTEMIC CRISIS OF CAPITALIST PRODUCTION

CHAPTER TWENTY-TWO

CAPITALIST ACCUMULATION AND ITS CRISES

The Concept of Crisis

The new model of development emerged during the crisis of the late nineteenth and first third of the twentieth century was applicable in all its dimensions since World War II until 1971, year of the failure of the international monetary system that controlled the capitalist flows of goods and money, announcing the new global crisis of the system. Non-equilibrium is an essential element of the capitalist economy, although the conventional economic theory wants to conceal this fact, and only analyse the issues from a viewpoint of equilibrium. Non-equilibrium acquires its larger dimensions when it appears in the form of economic crisis (in this case, better, imbalance).

A (structural) crisis is different from a (cyclic) recession or a depression when there is a set of malfunctions interacting mutually, reinforcing an unstable behaviour model, that ends up in the grinding to a halt of the development model, the interruption of the regular process of accumulation. Large capitalist crises occur when the conditions of accumulation are less stable and sustained. When it happens, the model of development in all its dimensions is questioned, and the overcoming of crisis demands the new conditions of accumulation, articulated together in a model that revitalizes the system.

The crisis usually appears as a special situation in the system. Nevertheless in the last hundred years three great global crisis have been produced: from 1871 to 1896, from 1921 to 1939 and from 1971 until today. Therefore, during the twentieth century, there have been more years of crisis than years of normal economic activity.

As crises seem to be the norm, we need to explain not why there is crisis, but why in some years there is no crisis.

In structural crises the dynamics of accumulation deteriorates, it is ruined. Obviously, between the periods of crisis, there also were phases of economic oscillations. Thus, during the long crisis in which we are still immersed, the economy improved during the period 1986–1990 and worsened from 1991 to 1994. Since 1996 to 1998 the world economy entered a new phase of expansion, and since 1999–2000 a new recession has began.

Therefore, the crisis marked the end of a phase in capitalist accumulation, and the overcoming of the crisis and the beginning of another new phase in history.

Structural crises are overcome only when the structural blocks that have made them were replaced with new forms of social and economic organization.

The major of the capitalist crisis is undoubtedly that of *generalized overproduction of goods*. It is not to be considered as a crisis due to excessive production of goods compared to the real needs of masses.

There is overproduction in the Marxian sense when there is a (relative) abundance of the goods that does not make them profitable. That is, a sale on the market would not allow the realization of profit. The two aspects of the commodity are, therefore, kept separate: if, as use value, it is necessary for the masses' needs, as exchange value, it is in excess.

Schools of Thought on the Theory of Crisis

Since 1980 a fundamental change has occurred. A new consciousness seemed to seize the leaders of the capitalist world who interpret the structural dimensions of the crisis.

In the late 1970s there were three types of alternatives solutions of the crisis:

a. *The conventional neoclassical and orthodox theories.* They promoted supply-side economics ("Buchanan/Reaganomics or Public Choice theories). According to this approach the crisis is due to the State, its excessive spending. The consequent effect is the decline of the tendency to save and invest. Within these theories, the monetarists, like Milton Friedman and Anne Krueger, consider the Keynesian-inspired policies the cause of the crisis, because a lot of money in circulation implies an increase in inflation and consequently a destruction of the economy. Quite similar is the Austrian school of Friederick von Hayek, that claims that credit in the economy causes inflation (by credit). These currents of thought were held by the opposition parties in Western countries during the period 1973 to 1979. When the Conservatives finally came to power in 1980s, they started applying these ideas to their new economic policies.

b. *The Keynesian theory*. Alain Barrere, James Tobin and John K. Galbraith are some of its representatives. They consider that there is a crisis of organization produced by the system of production and distribution. The Keynesian alternative is to create a new social pact. The crisis is associated with the fact that new theories and the new politicians in power see the working class as a part of the problem, and not the solution, and do not guarantee a rapid increase in return on capital, which can occur by supporting the demand with public policy.

c. *Marxist theory*. Among the different currents there were: (1) *French Marxists*, whose most dynamic members are part of the Regulation school. Alain Lipietz (1983, adviser to Mitterrand, after which he became spokesperson of the French Green Party [Lipietz 1993]). He argues that the crisis is the result of the decline of the laws of profit. According to this theory there was a collapse of the regimes of accumulation, extensive (industrial revolution) as well as intensive (XX century); (2) the *radical current* defended by economists like David Gordon, Samuel Bowles and Thomas Weisskopf (1989) and Bowles and Edwards (1990), who analyze the crisis in terms of power, both social organizations compared to the State, as well as the theme of the power of energy producing countries. Finally, (3) the *current of economic cycles*, discovered in early century by the Russian economist N.A. Kondratieff and defended, among others, by Ernest Mandel (1986b, 1997b) and Wallerstein. Kleinknecht (1982), Bernard Rosier (1975) and Rosier and Dóckes (1983), refer to the existence of large cycles of 50 years in the economics history based on technology. At present the economy goes through a recessive long cycle. In general, these economists theorize an alternative that deal with the replacement of the capitalist system with another one, in which the market is subject to the social logic.

The main weakness of these "theoretical" Marxist economists is that their proposals do not form part of a policy program of any relevant social sector in developed countries.[1]

---

[1] It is not the only case. The radical break between theory and practice is shown as one of the key features of "Western Marxism" by Anderson (1977). It is true that within the category of Western Marxism (Anderson himself, already in his work of 1977, criticizes this definition as unsatisfactory) there are intellectual militants such as Karl Korsch, whose work was closely oriented to the renewal of revolutionary theory and practice.

The Counteroffensive of Capital

With advent of neoliberal-minded neoconservatives to state power in the 1980s, the Keynesians were expelled by the US government; Ronald Reagan succeeded Jimmy Carter and Margaret Thatcher succeeded British Labourists. Since then, capital will show its most dynamic character, namely capital's multinational side, both political and economic. The 1980s in other words witnessed a major counteroffensive of capital against labour in the form of a new world order that freed the 'forces of economic freedom' from the regulatory constraints of the welfare-development state. An agenda of 'structural reforms' and policies of neoliberal globalization were the means to this end. In other words, neoliberalism was deemed to be the most appropriate strategy for solving both the production and fiscal crises of the capitalist state. The most important measures implemented in the 1980s and 1990s to advance this 'structural reform' process were:

a. to cause an international recession, with increases in unemployment and insecurity, to weaken the power of workers and Unions (the so-called politics of flexibility). This measure was completed with the activation of new technologies to automate the production processes, massively reducing the need for labour.
b. to untie the State from any effective social participation, to put it at the service of the recovery of enterprises (politics of "deregulation and competitiveness" "adjustment and "privatization");
c. to reverse the direction of Third World countries' politics. In order to do this, several measures were applied: the *coup d'etat* (Latin America and Africa) in the 1970s, attack against the United Nations system, concentrating power in the Security Council and causing the financial crisis of the organisms more linked to the "New International Economic Order (NIEO), such as UNCTAD (United Nations Conference on Trade and Development), or UNESCO (United Nations Educational, Scientific and Cultural Organization) in the 1980s; technological change that reduces the consumption of certain abundant raw materials in the Third World (energy) and largely replaces them (copper or fiber) and, finally, policies known as "programs of structural adjustment," in the control of the economic policies of the 1980s and 1990s, taking advantage of the crisis of foreign debt which allowed to break the redistributive function of State, strengthening its class character and privatizing

its activities in favour of trans-national capital; continuation of the Cold War with the ideological resumption of the conservative project (move from the defensive struggle from the inside, Welfare State, 'Keynesianism', to the fight offensive inside: postmodernism, new individualism) and burst the space occupied by communism using new media penetration (film, music, TV, video).

Conservative governments proposed to lay the new foundations of the relations between rich and poor. At first the global objective of neoliberalism was the control of OPEC. Then they tried to control the countries that had oil and were not part of OPEC (the oil of the North Sea) with the idea of fragmenting the internal organization of the latter. On the other hand, they proceeded to reorder multilateral institutions (UN and international financial institutions).

Consider also that, particularly in the late 1990s, the companies continued to generate much money which is often poured in financial speculations and in increments of distributed dividends.

This could be explained by a simple reasoning:

a. a record increase of net profits is realized;
b. this did not correspond to significant increases in sales nor in added value;
c. there is a substantial retention of Earnings Before Interest, Taxes, Depreciation and Amortization (EBITDA) and Earning Before Interests and Taxes (EBIT);
d. the value added should be distributed to labour and the capital factor, but the increases in direct nor indirect and deferred salary, nor therefore social wage in its generality are not assigned to labour;
e. a reduction in taxation;
f. finance charges on debt fall as a result of the lower cost of money;
g. the major money flows made by companies are not assigned to investment, disposals of assets are also achieved;
h. for several consecutive years, the distributed dividends were greater than capital increase, achieving a negative budget between dividends and capital increases, penalizing self-financing because the shareholders continue to receive more than they give; and
i. there is a clear improvement of the capital structure of enterprises and the relationship between debt and net assets, reaching much lower values in the recent twelve years, even for the reduced amount of debts taken out with banks in favour of short-term loans made by subsidiaries due to the concentration of financial management.

It is clear that the profits accrued to companies (e.g. in Italy) have remained solely in the pockets of entrepreneurs, managers, shareholders, who did not socialize the optimal conditions for growth of the recent years and in particular, in 1998, the year which saw the best results of the last decade.

The Profit State continues to homage entrepreneurs with favourable conditions and operate exceptional discounts to profit, and this does not involve any improvements in social spending because the enterprises' contribution decreases, nor any increments of investment in the Italian market, nor the reduction of working hours, nor any increments in wages, let alone redistribution to labour, nor have, finally, real, full-time, full salary and full rights employment increased.

The new multinationals are financial groups with industrial dominant features and a unique capability to access the financial markets to place their securities and operate as investors. This change has important implications for the qualitative increment and the financial position of the multinationals that adopted themselves this new form of financial groups and reach higher financial levels with an increasingly important function as operators on the financial markets and exchange rates.

Industrial "network" entities appear, characterized by the multiplication of the minority participants and the linkage of many enterprises related to partner with an often highly unequal economic power. This evolution has had the effect of making the borders of production internationalization more related to important interference processes between profit and financial income. A part of the consequences of globalization is withdrawing surplus of other companies through the transfer of productive values for the benefit of the financial one with increments in income, indisadvantage of profits from direct investments capable of creating jobs.

CHAPTER TWENTY-THREE

THE ECONOMIES' CYCLICAL BEHAVIOUR AFTER WWII

How Do Crises of Underconsumption and Overproduction Arise?

Like other Marxist theoretical models, also capitalist overproduction of goods must be interpreted in terms of values and not merely of physical quantities of produced goods. The permanent struggle between rival capitals involves the development of competitive technologies that permit higher productivity, higher profits and greater production of goods. However, the goods, under capitalism, are produced only if they are sold in the market. They enable the closure of the cycle of capital (re) production, enhancement of the capital, the realization of exchange value. A commodity is not produced just because someone needs it (this identifies only the use value), but because someone who needs it, can buy it, and thus allows the realization of its intrinsic value.

On several occasions Marx, ahead of his own time, criticized these theories. The problem has no solution because the temporary increase in demand, supported by the State in various capacities and in different ways, moves in time, postponing overproduction and repeating it at a higher and sharper level. This is because the temporary valorization of commodities does not stabilize the market at determined production quotas (we should only imagine a stagnation). Instead it stimulates the productive sphere to produce more goods than before.

The crisis of overproduction cannot be eliminated because it is inherent to capitalist production, where capital always pushes beyond the latest (temporary) limit to increase itself. This means more commodities, more capital and the inability to close the cycle of capital (re) production positively.

Cycles and Economic Crises

Between 1945 and 1965 there were important changes in the international economic position of the United States. These transformations were the result of three fundamental factors:

a. the economies ravaged by the war recovered, began to compete and to claim their space in the World economy;
b. the U.S. economy, since the economic crisis of 1969–1971, began to show clear signs of exhaustion of its accumulation model;
c. there was a new technological paradigm that differs from the material base of the Fordist Keynesian cycle during the period after World War II.

Scholars of the capitalist cycle virtually disappeared from North American universities, and when the economy began a process of contraction in the late 1960s, in 1969, neoclassical bourgeois economists did not perceive it. The slowdown persisted in every case, and it created unemployment and falling incomes for millions of people.

The experiences of the periods 1964–65 and 1966–67, during the Vietnam war, when military spending revived the rate of industrial growth impacting on GNP, had deceived many people that the economic crisis could be quickly overcome.

Nevertheless, with the period that began in 1969, for the first time after World War II here was a fall of real economic indicators, not caused by war damage, accompanied by a rapid and continuous increase in prices, a phenomenon that lasted more than a year.

That is how, in the 1970s, the North-American economy's cyclical course started. It had great importance and great impact on the world capitalist economy and in particular on the economy of the United States. We are referring to the 1969–1971 crisis, whose roots can be found back in the 1960s and that damaged the entire capitalist economy which, from then on, depended on the course of the U.S. economy reducing to dust the positive attitude that had prevailed in the academic and official circles of the North-American Government.[1]

The capitalist economy during the 1969–71 crisis began to change one of the aspects that characterized the dynamics of the cycles and crises of the postwar period. While GNP was falling, prices rose and many developed capitalist economies synchronized their stages of the crisis. The cause of these phenomena should be looked for within the process of exhaustion of the processes of dynamization that had been

---

[1] Actually, since 1964 the economy had contracted, but the heavy investment for the Vietnam War helped delaying the crisis that eventually occurred as a recession during 1966–67. For further analysis of this topic cf. Vasapollo, Casadio, Petras, Veltmeyer (2004).

imposed by the Second World War on the world and the U.S. economy, since the war was the spark that started the recovery of world capitalism and of the United States as its main agent.

In the early 1970s, the Japanese and Western-European economy had finished recovering, but despite that the U.S. economy had continued its headlong production rush which had been imposed by the supremacy obtained after the war.

But at the end of the 1970s the resources of dynamization, produced by the war, had been exhausted and it was not accidental that this phenomenon had already shown, with particular strength, in the leading economy, confirming what Karl Marx had demonstrated and Paul Samuelson in 1955 had reaffirmed:

For the democratic nations, the economic cycle represented a challenge: if we do not learn to control depression and success periods better that we had done before WWII, the political structure of our society will be threatened. (Translated from the Italian edition: Samuelson 1955: 320–321).

The economic crisis of 1969–1971 occurred through the same dynamics of the controlled negative process, delayed by the economic policy of senior military personnel in the years between 1964 and 1967. During the 1969–1971 crisis, the economic contradictions caused by the exhaustion of factors that characterized the earlier crises started to show, those crises occurred since 1948 that were temporary economic falls, that is short crises that were not deep and experienced no inflationary pressure.

A fundamental phenomenon, which started to be witnessed within the U.S. economy since the 1969–1971 crisis, was the contradiction between production and consumption: contradiction that worsened throughout the decade as a consequence of the negative effects inflation was having on employees' incomes (Samuelson 1955: 320–321).

It is not difficult to realize that, during the period analyzed, the real income or net income increased slightly less than 50% with respect to the index of productivity, and obviously this situation corresponds to large increases in the amount of surplus value. This did nothing but affect the shrinkage of the foundations of consumer goods mass market, as it had already happened to the U.S. economy.

This situation worsened because of the inflationary process. There was a tendency to identify any increase in prices with inflation, but there have been periods when prices increased without inflation, as in the case of seasonal increases and cyclical increases. But the continuous increases in prices, from the second half of the 1970s on, were mostly inflationary. The great gap between the issue of money and the movement of goods and services was the main cause of the prices upward tendency, therefore it was right, back then, to talk about chronic inflation. Defining any increase in the price setting as inflation makes it easier to hide the true causes, and therefore also the deeper ones, for price increases, which is a common habit of many North American economists who are interested in providing a rather superficial analysis. Despite this, monetary inflation was not the only factor involved in prices increases during the 1970s and 1980s, just like it was not the only political instrument intended to create selective increases. There were also other factors that speeded up and supported the process of price increases as well as contributing to monetary inflation, and that interacted with it, such as:

a. the growing process of monopolization of the North American economy;
b. the militarization of the economy that gave rise, in the 1950s, to the phenomenon of the so-called "military industrial complex";
c. the economic policy of the bourgeois state, with its anti-cyclical policy, during the 1970s;
d. the fall of the dollar, devalued in 1971 and then declared inconvertible in 1972;
e. the tendency of monopolies to self-compensate by means of discounts of the supply, on the basis of the increases in prices;

Because of the crisis of 1969–1971, inflation grew as it had never done before, and continued to rise during the crisis of 1974–1975. This led the phenomenon of inflation to a blind alley. It was not only a money-related issue; there is another phenomenon that can help to understand the meaning inflation had during that period.

In addition to the contemporary decline in production and the increased prices, which created the so-called phenomenon of "stagflation," the path to some special dynamics between higher prices and lower ones, had been cleared. Since 1974, the weight of price increases went from being on businesses shoulders to consumers. This phenomenon occurred when the ghost of recession and rising unemployment caused a rise in selling prices, especially in the monopolist field, in order to compensate in terms of received income, the net reduction of quantities sold.

The International Character of the Capitalist Cycle during the 1970s and Early 1980s

The situation that the U.S. economy went through from the 1970s until the 1980s, cannot be fully understood unless we consider the relationship between the economic crisis that took place in the United States and the global crisis, in which the processes of economic capitalist internationalization played an important role, processes that were defined as "mechanisms of cyclical transmission". A special way in which the "interdependence" between the system's economies can be experienced, but clearly within the phenomena of asymmetry that characterize it.

The development of the internationalization of capitalist relations was determined by a number of phenomena that do nothing but define the internationalization of the cycle of world capital the same way as Marx did in his Book II of *Capital*. According to Marx, industrial capital is nothing but the unity and interrelation of the three cycles: money, commodities, production. By analyzing from an historical perspective both the cycle and the market relations, that is the exchange of goods, those who first develop are the monetary relations, though more slowly than the productive ones that improve thanks to the rise of corporations since they work on production in different countries as if they were components of the same production unit.

So the capitalist economy, as it started to work since the end of the Second World War, becomes industrial capital at an international level. As Marx says, "in its continuity the effective cycle of industrial capital is not made up of the unit of the process of production and circulation, but, without exception, of the union of the three cycles: money capital, productive capital and capital goods" (translated from the Italian edition: Marx 1978, Book II: 92). Financial capital, as a simple interrelation between the industrial capital and the banking one, is a phenomenon that existed before the twentieth century. Corporations themselves are a phenomenon prior to the development of imperialist capitalism.

In the analysis carried out so far, a phenomenon that is relevant in order to understand the current nature of the capitalist cycle needs to be succinctly discussed. Along with the development of the internationalization of capital and production, at an international level and as a result of the same process, emerges after the Second World War what has been called a "mechanisms of cyclic transmission" or

"Transnationalized cycle," and reaches high levels from the beginning of the 1970s on. These are the mechanisms that serve as a base and springboard for the transformation of the capitalist cycle: something that goes beyond the possible impacts that give rise to a simple inter-relationship of national capitalists cycles through the world market, creating the phenomenon of the formation of a "transnational, commanded cycle" within the more general tendency of the formation of a "global industrial cycle".

The cycle synchronization at the stage of crisis between the various capitalist economies manifested itself since it was influenced by a set of "mechanisms of transmission". Among the most important of these were foreign trade, export of capital, corporations, the development of the arms trade, banking, monetary and financial relationships could be mentioned.

These factors' actions explain both the cyclic synchronization with the stages of the crisis that characterized the years 1974–75, and the successive tendency of all the major capitalist economies, for the remaining years of the 1970s, identified by a slow, asymmetric recovery process and with high levels of unemployment and inflation, until 1980, when there occurred a new crisis.

The Role of Foreign Trade in the Transmission of the Cycles

The importance and dynamism of this factor as cyclical impulse transmitter within the capitalist economy rose during the 1970s, despite the increase in protectionism in the period of the crisis. Only in the first quarter of 1978 there was a decrease in imports.

The participation of the U.S. in world trade declined, as the table in the following page shows.

Although the importance of the United States was still significant, its participation to exports, at the end of World War II, decreased in the late 1970s.

It is clear that the powers that had suffered the ravages of war, except for France, did not benefit from a significant improvement, especially England that witnessed a period of decline, while Germany and Japan took on important positions. It is to be noted, however, a much more even participation to trade.

The downside for the U.S. is that the decrease of their share of participation in the world trade exports may be offset in part by the fact that the other competitors are more dependent on their foreign trade than Americans are, as far as economic growth is concerned, a kind of trade that the U.S. is able to affect much more than the rest of the developed capitalist countries. This is even truer, if one considers that the dependence of these countries from foreign sources of energy (primarily oil) is much higher than that of the United States, since they have the world's largest real market: all this becomes a powerful tool of negotiation of the economic aspect of US foreign policy. Furthermore, it should be borne in mind that since the United States represent a big market, often the most important as the major capitalist countries are concerned, the U.S. economic cycle, through foreign trade, continuously affects the cyclical movement of the rest of the economies.

Dependence on Raw Materials, Monetary-Financial Relationship and the Transmission of the Cycle

It is important to highlight the phenomenon of dependence on raw materials of developed capitalist countries with respect to the developing ones. In the early 1970s, the dependence of the United States was much less serious than that of the rest of the imperialist powers. But this situation, that instead of being solved was becoming deeper, affected also U.S. foreign policy, which was trying to keep under control the main producing countries.

The point is that there is North American control over a set of strategic products, which other powers cannot give up on, in order to keep their competitive position at the international level.

This is an important "weapon" the United States can use in order to influence both the policy and the economy of imperialist powers. This is an issue that occupies a special place when it comes to U.S. foreign policy, and has always been a major point of friction between the United States and its partners and competitors.

The privileged position of the United States within the world trade of the period is not to be questioned, even if other countries such as West Germany and especially Japan are strong competitors, especially in the case of Japan, that had managed to penetrate deeply into the U.S. market.

The phenomenon of the transmission cycle of the North American economy towards the world economy was a direct consequence of the situation in which the capitalist world system and the North-American economy in particular, were in at the end of the Second World War. This situation can be schematically summarized as follows:

a. During the war, the U.S. has been the main supplier of European capitalist countries, devastated by war, and its industrial, commercial and financial potential did not suffer, on the contrary it increased;
b. the United States, at the end of the war, counted on their reserves of gold, the largest in the capitalist world;
c. the United States invaded the world market with their products. One had to have dollars to buy many kinds of goods and the U.S. currency began to be considered on the basis of the value of gold itself, affirming itself as a reserve currency;
d. the system named after Bretton Woods outlined, at the international level, U.S. control over the monetary-financial capitalist movement;
e. even if the monetary-financial system that emerged had to be directed by a "basket of currencies," in which the dollar had to be a currency like the others, in practice, the circumstances related to military-political dominance made it possible for the dollar to occupy a central position, compared to that of all other currencies.

It is on the basis of the precedents that have just been mentioned, that it is possible to understand what happened to the capitalist monetary system. The emerging monetary system, after all, represented a step forward towards the organization of the capitalist world's finances, since an organization (that did not exist until then) had been established under the exclusive control of the United States. In fact this system was linked from the beginning to fluctuations of the U.S. economy.

For this reason, the system named after Bretton Woods influenced the rest of the capitalist economies, causing the following problems:

a. The difficulties that the United States' balance of payments had to face, from its trade imbalances to the financing of military adventures, to which they took part after the Second World War, countries like Korea, Vietnam, Africa, and other events that had a decisive influence on global finance;
b. the inflation process, that the U.S. economy experienced during the 1970s, had a major influence on the rest of the capitalists economies;
c. the policy directed by the United States, through the IMF and the World Bank, aimed primarily at preserving the dollar as an instrument of the absolute process of expansion of U.S. financial capital,

it had a great influence especially in 1971, when the dollar was devalued and when, in 1972, its inconvertibility was declared, questioning the monetary system itself that had been named after Bretton Woods in 1944.

Since the beginning of the twentieth century, on the basis of the dominance of monopolies, a relevant growth and development of export capital occurred. During the First World War there already was an export of capital that amounted approximately to 46 billion dollars, with obvious advantages for France and Great Britain. Before the Second World War, the main imperialist powers retained an average export of capital of about 47 billion dollars. Nevertheless, during the postwar period, 1945–1970, the amount of exported capital took an important step forward.

After World War II, the superiority of the U.S. in the process of exporting capital was clear, since it handled more than 50% of export. Between the First and World War II, the United States overdid England in the field of capitalist world economy. Since then, the U.S. is a capitalist model and tries to represent the world of the 20th Century, the same way England did in the 19th Century.

The rest of the developed capitalist powers, despite being backed by their strong economic and industrial potentates, assumed that a major part of their future was tied to that of the United States, for some reasons that are still valid and that, schematically, are as follows:

a. The imperialist powers, especially from a strategic point of view, estimate that their chances of expansion and survival depend on the United States' foreign policy, on its dominance, on the control they hold on Third World countries and on the U.S.' military presence in Europe and other parts of the world, although today there is no justification with respect to the "threat of communism," as it was held during the 1970s and 1980s;[2]
b. the large monopolies of the other imperialist powers receive benefits in terms of military applications, markets, investment opportunities and other privileges, in countries controlled by the United States;

---

[2] This is something so important that the so-called "threat of communism," became, after World War II, the factor of articulation of the United States' foreign policy. The same thing is happening, nowadays, with the embargo, or better the total bloc and continuous acts of sabotage against Cuba, guilty of perpetrating a process of socialist self-determination.

c. while competing for the military markets, the other imperialist powers were not able to dispute with the U.S. for the strategic military position it holds worldwide, rather preferring to accept their position as second class powers.[3]

During the 1970s, there were two more phenomena that played a significant role in the process of internationalization of the U.S. economic cycle and in the trans-nationalization of their cyclical difficulties. These phenomena were the export of capital and transnational companies: two sectors of the capitalist world economy's dynamics on which the U.S. had a great control even after the Second World War, a control it is still keeping.

The Economic Cycle of the 1980s, Macroeconomic Policy and New Technological Paradigms

The years 1974–75 and 1981–84 have been extremely important for the economy and for U.S. society in general. The U.S. has suffered the largest economic crisis since the Second World War, coinciding with, and resulting from, a process of accumulation which began to develop at the end of the post-war period, emphasizing the crisis of the model of accumulation and of the economic Keynesian policy, that had been turned inoperative by "stagflation". Thanks to Ronald Reagan's administration, since 1981, the restructuring of economic policy began. The theoretical estimates were concretized into the rapid and sustained reduction in inflation reducing unemployment and the drastic decrease in the fiscal deficit.

The logic of economic policy would have been addressed towards a policy of monetary tightening that implied a decrease in inflationary pressure and to a tax policy that would encourage an increase in supply, i.e. a combination of "Monetary orthodoxy" and "supply recommendations," taking into account that this sick cycle would have led to a dynamic, sustained process that would have broken the chain characterized by the combination between stagnation and inflation.

The U.S. economy, in particular, was moving to a new technological paradigm, in which the economic policy's aim had to be the direct

---

[3] This does not mean that competition, on this level, does not even exist. The EU works on its arms industries helped by North-American corporations, in order to directly assume supplies for its defence.

stimulus to "effective demand" no more. All this happened because there was a gradual passage from the Fordist-Keynesian cycle, based on the paradigm of the technological metal-mechanics-automotive-petrochemical industries, to a cycle called post-Fordist, which has its technological, dominant foundations on the electronic-information paradigm.

There is no doubt that the U.S. economy is currently dealing with a new, dominant, technological paradigm which is different from the one that served as the basis for the Fordist-Keynesian cycle and that the economy had permanently left behind.

The current challenges that the U.S. economy is facing are not determined by the growth of the GDP. This can be clearly noted thanks to the rates of growth achieved since 2002 but especially since 2004.

The U.S. economy continued to grow between 2003 and 2007, although with a tendency to stagnate and in some cases to recede.

Despite this, the greatest difficulties do not derive from the fall of GDP, but from other factors that, which not having been solved, will keep on having a great impact on economic growth over the subsequent periods.

In this scenario characterized by a deep and unending international crisis of capital, the stand-off between Europe and the U.S. plays a relevant role and is a competition that aims at assigning the domain of Eurasia with geopolitical and geo-economic features implemented mainly through the location of Foreign Direct Investments.

During the last decade of the 20th Century and early in the 21st, the political and economic changes that characterized the international context also affected the European capitalist structure, in particular as far as the foreign political and economic relations are concerned. In the period following the birth of the EU, a fierce economic struggle between the U.S. and EU was witnessed, a struggle for the control over the former socialist countries of Central and Eastern Europe and especially over those countries that belong to the Asian area of the former Soviet Union which are all considered to be of significant strategic interest for the world's political and economic dominance.

Right after the institution of the European currency, fearing that it could strengthen the markets and become an internationally recognized reserve currency, the United States started their attack, drawing huge amounts of European capital through the high U.S. interest rates and through the hypertrophy/growth of a kind of economy financed by money coming from Europe.

While Europe, on the one hand, chose restrictive monetary policy in order to meet the financial criteria of the Maastricht Treaty, which caused unemployment and increased social problems, on the other side it is too weak and fragmented in terms of policy to adequately oppose the superpower of the United States. In addition to this, the monetary policy imposed by the European Central Bank tends to confirm restrictive constraints to various governments, in order to exploit the favorable economic situation, to restore public budgets and to reduce the debt without any expansive intervention in the economy in terms of employment.

Europe is actually aiming at a continuous competition with the growth of the U.S., which focuses on prices stability, stimulating the growth of a kind of economy whose features are the easy, high-value exchange of services, especially in terms of finance, strengthening the processes of financialization and imposing structural reforms that point to the liberalization (i.e. privatization) of the social benefits and the removal of any form of labour market rigidities, i.e. flexibility and job insecurity, enlarged to its utmost.

CHAPTER TWENTY-FOUR

AN ATTEMPT TO OVERCOME THE STRUCTURAL AND SYSTEMATIC CRISIS: THE SOLUTION IS A RADICAL ALTERNATIVE

Some Considerations and Interpretations of Neoliberal Globalization[1]

In the field of international economic relations, Marxist scholars had very little to add: just some indications that keep pace with the international development of capital, Lenin's fundamental analysis of the imperialist era, followed by Baran and Sweezy, and elements of an incomplete construction developed by Emmanuel and Palloix. Other current factors to be considered are the theory of mercantile and international, financial trade, the one on global monetary areas and the analytical elements of a theory of foreign trade which, however contextual to their time could already be found in the works written by classic authors.

According to what has been argued so far and taking into consideration the consequences and the political environment of the ongoing process of neoliberal globalization, it can be asserted that, during the 1970s and 1980s, as a response to the process of structural capitalist crisis which was a significant part of the display of the exhaustion of the capitalist model of accumulation that was established with the post-war period, a phenomenon of economic restructuring in the heart of capitalism started.

This process is essentially characterized by the tendency to substitute and consolidate the form of technological production, mechanized through automation, combined with a process of renewal of the economic mechanism, given the obsolescence of the old Keynesian "recipes" for granting the economic regulation through the State's role as a regulator. In addition to this, there is an intense process of

---

[1] The subjective-planning side of globalization is emphasized by authors such as Hirst and Thompson (1997), who do not recognize it as the destiny of humanity and an irreversible process. Important references, for our work are still Casadio, Petras, Vasapollo (2003); Vasapollo, Casadio, Petras, Veltmeyer (2004); Vasapollo, Jaffe, Galarza (2005); Arriola, Vasapollo (2004).

financialization of the economy, that aims at income rather than prof-its, and productive investments based on technological progress and new objective conditions of development of some productive forces, essentially related to the primacy of electronics, informatics, robotics, new materials and biotechnology, among others scientific conquests.[2]

As repeatedly stated, the process of transformation that affected inter-national markets experienced, among its most direct consequences over the last few years, also a fundamental change in how the produc-tion process works. Smaller companies had to combine with each other in order to allow the change from *local for global* (i.e. domestic products and production, international markets), to *global for global* (i.e. multi-local products and production, global markets).

That is how the "virtual enterprise systems" emerged as systems that can temporarily operate as if they were a single company. We witness the creation of some integrated networks on different levels along the same chain of businesses, consisting of interactive cores divided into groups and subgroups, that affect certain infrastructures (informa-tion systems, management systems, values) and are able to respond creatively to the continuous change of scenery and market. This type of network, where information rather than material goods move, is defined "Halo System".

It must then be considered that the high level of technological and scientific knowledge makes it vital for a close link between each companies' sector of each country, to exist. The development of media and transport, by nullifying the distances between different countries, makes it possible for businesses to consider the international market as a whole, starting a fierce international competition. It is easy to under-stand that, for the capitalist enterprise, competing in a global system, means bearing very high fixed costs, and having to find ways to com-pensate, since the variable costs have no strategic value, especially if, to a fierce international competition, one adds elements such as the remarkable transformation of production processes, which lead to the need to move from a production based on a high use of labour (*labour-intensive*) to an industrial model based on material capital (i.e. plant and equipment, *capital-intensive*) and a high increase in costs addressed to intangible capital, such as information, research and development. It is then necessary to have international partners that can contribute to the compensation of fixed costs and with which to define possible

---

[2] About the issue Cf. in particolar Petras, Veltmeyer (2002).

strategies that allow a maximization of the profitability of the company through the compression of direct and indirect labour costs and the reduction of taxation and tax records.

Driven by the new demands of the valorization of capital, these phenomena, undertaken by corporations, have reached international dimensions and have grown intertwined with many others within the process of the globalization of capital with its related restructuring of international economic relations and the process of conformation of a new international division of capitalist labour.

The actual content of globalization does not depend on the free movement of people, or the free exchange between cultures, or the globalization of exchanges, but only on the operations of capital, both in the form of production and finance.

At the roots of the growth of the financial field there are flows towards this sector of fractions of wealth that have arisen within production and that prior to transfer in different forms and in different countries into the world of finance took the form of wages and salaries, or of earnings of labour. These flows are at the source of perverse mechanisms of accumulation, within which the hunt for national economies aims at the domination of financial capital and belongs to the relationship of international competition between geo-economic poles, mediated by trade-offs within the supranational organizations of financial capital.

The Neoliberal globalization of the markets, as it has been suggested before in the text, is a characterizing feature of the last few decades. Political, economic and cultural institutions have to face, every day, this phenomenon that is causing a disintegration of cultures, of purposes and national economies, also because it has taken on the form of global post-Fordist competition of the era of flexible accumulation.

Even from the perspective of capitalist development there are several legal, social and economic problems related to this phenomenon. First, there is no effective control over the functioning of financial markets, since traders may decide to move large sums of money from one part of the world to another, which means, in a context of deregulation, acting solely in accordance to their needs for profit without any political control or monetary authorities' instruments of intervention.

There are also devastating effects on the model and the production cycle since there is growing demand for skilled resources with a high level of immateriality and flexibility. The weakest stages of the cycle at a low added value are excluded, outsourced, relocated abroad in search of skilled, low-wage, unregulated labour.

The disappearance of the manual worker (which is still to be proven) in fully developed countries does not imply the disappearance of productive work, let alone of the working class (which is composed of productive and unproductive employees).[3] Labour persists. It just changes form (barely) and keeps on being exploited within the same capitalist production.

The great methodological critique that should be applied to the theory of the end of labourism consists in not accounting for the world-economy (a single, integrated MPC), but in reading phenomenally (not even attentively, since the reading is limited) only *some* of the tendencies inherent to fully developed capitalist countries. The economy has been global for centuries and even though there has been a lot of talking about globalization, economists of the "end of labourism" theory de-globalize their analysis for no reason and narrow their minds to their weak, postmodern thinking.

A discourse on capitalist restructuring and on new forms of control of capital over labour, is inconceivable without a correct global insight on the phenomenon. The division of labour is, now more than ever, *international* division of labour.

While the Ford-Taylorist model (or part of it) was exported to the suburbs, the Toyota Production System (TPS), in all its varieties, spread all over those fully developed capitalist countries (but also in the most advanced developing countries) and yet both strategies keep on co-existing in fully developed capitalist countries.

Globalization as an Objective Process

The genesis of globalization lies in capital's international leaning. To think of it simply as a new phenomenon, with no explicit reference to the internationalization of capital, in imperialism's current configuration as global competition, would mean ignoring the dialectic of the economic laws of the system as the correlation between the development of the internationalizing essence and the dynamics of its forms of manifestation.

---

[3] What makes someone a worker or a non-worker are the functions performed within the productive process: that is whether it performs a function of collective worker or that of capital. The plurality of cohabiting functions, for example of collective work and capital, determines what Carchedi (1977) defines the "new middle classes".

The internationalization of capital had to enter, primarily, the field of circulation, a phenomenon that is typical of pre-monopolist capitalism and had to penetrate, later on, into the field of imperialist production. The genesis of the manifestation of capital's essence of internationalization is dialectically linked to the genesis of the manifestation of the international projection of the laws of uneven economic and political, capitalist development (translated from the Italian: Marx 1976, Book I: 505).

This phenomenon is very important from a theoretical, methodological and political point of view, since the laws of internationalization and the uneven economic and political capitalist development are laws that express an opposed action: the internationalizing force tends to equality and the law of uneven economic and political development generates forces that tend to vary, although both effects can not be assessed individually.

The main phenomena that make it possible to concretely base the current formation of a new stage of capitalist globalization and presuppose new forms of manifestation of the essence of the phenomenon of internationalization are, for example:

a. The growing international economic interdependence;
b. the internationalization of the cycle of productive capital, expressed through the segmentation of production in different places all over the planet, just-in-time production and level of goods and capital's international mobility; and
c. standardization, which means homogeneity of goods and demand; common system of weights and measures; technological diffusion in the context of capitalism, called post-Fordist or of Western TPS, characterized by a continuous, quick manufacturing, flexible automation, rapid spread or immediate transmission of large amounts of data over long distances through companies' networks, internet, decreased coefficient of capital per unit of product, etc.

3. On the macroeconomic level, the main phenomena of the current capitalist globalization stage can be summarized in an intense restructuring of the international economic space, in terms of:

a. Financial disintermediation, the process of restructuring financial institutions and international trade;
b. the full development of the world market, together with the internationalization of supply and of competition among producers;

internationalization of demand in many sectors related to investments in advertising and in market at an international level;

c. the structuring of a new international capitalist division of labour,
   that corresponds to the needs of the passage to the automated, technological form of production;

d. high level of concentration of international financial capital conditioned by the completion of the internationalization of the cycle
   of its functional parts and emphasizing, at this stage, the internationalization of the monetary-financial capital cycle and of its form
   of existence *sui generis*: the fictitious capital as a joining of the
   resources of intangible, immaterial capital;

e. strong tendency to the formation of economic blocs, of integration
   processes that characterize this stage as a part of the new phase of
   internationalization, which responds to the contradictions and the
   needs of the enhancement of capital, within a context in which the
   interpenetration of economies combines with the new models of
   efficiency and competitiveness. In such context, the economic policies of self-regulation mechanisms are not enough and, therefore,
   there is the need to improve the economies' chances to succeed
   through a regional, local vision, recurring to the complementary
   processes associated to these mechanisms.

*Globalization as a Subjective Phenomenon: The Political Project of
Neoliberal Globalization turns into Global Competition*

The concept of globalization, which has been identified in our works
as global competition,[4] proves once again to have little heuristic value,
if not to be just mystifying, in the event that one keeps in mind the
development of international trade throughout the world. It is more
and more concentrated, at least relatively, within the opposing geo-
economic-political, imperialist poles in their respective areas of influence (South-America for the U.S., Euro-Mediterranean and "Eurasia"
for the EU, the coastal areas of China for Japan, all of Asia for China
itself) (Martufi, Vasapollo 2000a). The struggles for trade are now com-
monplace. In the last few years they resulted into a considerable number of indirect wars (former Yugoslavia, Afghanistan, Iraq) between

---

[4] Cf. for example Casadio, Petras, Vasapollo (2003); Vasapollo, Casadio, Petras,
Veltmeyer (2004).

the U.S. and the European pole. The (supra) national States play, in this deeply political dialectic, a key role.

The role of political geo-economy is becoming important: direct access to energetic resources and to raw materials grants the autonomy related to other imperialist poles. Geo-economic policies are often dictated by the need to "weaken the opponent"(Lenin 2001: 109) rather than the need to supply directly energetic resources and raw materials or to open new markets (see the Iraqi war led against EU and China's aims in the area, in order to take possession of the supply of oil that is now being used by the Americans).

Within this framework of generalized competition between imperialist poles, there is a matter that has to be considered, a matter that has not been analyzed thoroughly so far, that is the "currency areas" (for example, Dollar, Euro, Yen, Yuan, Islamic banking). The global monetary dominance grants what some call the "seigniorage" (which ultimately results in a transfer of W, surplus value, into one's "cash boxes") and the huge collection of capital from all over the world, in one's own geo-political-monetary space: it is enlightening, in this regard, the constant struggle between Dollar and Euro and the various attempts of U.S. establishment to sabotage the euro project, sometimes through real threats.

As a result of the frequent outbreak of wars (promoted by the "Western front," especially the U.S.) during the "long decade" of the 1990s, but especially as a result of the belligerent acceleration started after 9/11, people began to talk about *imperialism* again, were they powerful politicians or common people. Globalization is supposed to be facing a crisis, or there is, anyway, the need to support it through some "imperial policies," which, due to an anti-globalization, universal competitor, should pave, by force, the way to the construction of new Democratic States (Nation Building) pro-West, granting free movement of goods, capital and Western finance (within a framework of *pax imperialis*, that can create the conditions for a new globalization). Imperialism thus assumes a "violent" connotation, no longer socioeconomic. It all comes down to a military policy, which the West uses to defend itself against the enemy.

But the military dimension is the armed hand of the economic contradictions of imperialism: it is sufficient to take a look at the scenario that develops along with the global macroeconomic framework of the 1990s, characterized, at the same time, by very low GDP growth rates (including countries like Japan, that have played a leading role with

respect to the rest of the world's economies); by an unstable global economic situation, interspersed with monetary and financial slow movements, by increases in investments, particularly financial ones, that go
along with the growth of mass unemployment and its technological
and structural nature, together with the containment of real wages,
with flexibility, job precariousness and medieval working conditions in
many countries where labour is exploited.

This is how the worsening of inequalities of income and living
conditions within the large economic capitalist blocs is determined.
This situation goes along with the marginalization of entire regions of
the world trading system and a more and more intense international
competition. As a consequence to such a major structural crisis, imperialism plays its role as a warmonger (Iraq, Balkans, Afghanistan, Iraq
again, the Middle East, etc.).

The competition between Europe and the U.S., whose goal is to
dominate Eurasia, arises in a much stronger and more decisive way,
characterized by geopolitical and geo-economic features, achieved
with the collabouration of the FDI (foreign direct investment), or with
an intervention in terms of financial globalization. In the case of such
an intervention, through the exploitation of the productive foreign
investment, rents, profits can be recycled in Western areas fostering
forms of financial speculation that makes it easy to earn money and to
"strangle" the weakest economies or those that present an average level
of development, in order to favour financial institutions, particularly
non-banking ones on which the growth of large economic blocs
depends.

These elements must be interpreted as the presupposition of maturity of a major new global regime of accumulation, a flexible accumulation, whose functioning is subject to priorities of private, financial,
and highly concentrated capital in which the EU is trying to play a
relevant role and in open competition with the U.S.

The Proof that Global Competition is the Current Stage of Imperialism

First, it is important to reiterate the need to distinguish, as already
mentioned between globalization as an objective process and its
conversion into a political project, which is a subjective phenomenon:
the neoliberal globalizing and universal discourse. Strictly speaking,
"economic globalization" refers to the process of forming a global

economic system. But if globalization exists as a new trend in the economic process, it cannot be said that the economy is a totally globalized reality or that it is subjected to trends that aim at its globalization.

The economy, in a nutshell, is a *structure of structures* in which economic operators, production systems and exchange systems agree. The key economic operators and workers are, at the same time, consumers. The structure of production companies and distribution facilities are essentially those resulting from the existence of a regulated market, i.e. a market where everything has a price and there is a price for everything, so a unit of measure is needed. Modern economies are monetary economies, therefore, and are determined by a global planning which requires the existence of entrepreneurs and a global labour-force, global prices and a global currency, things that do not exist or are "in progress ... but still do not exist".

The expression "economic globalization," as a *structure*, refers to the existence of a global market, in which free financial capital (money, international loans and credits, foreign investment), trade capital (goods and services) and production capital (through segmentation of production processes and relocation in various countries, the aim is to maximize revenues and reduce costs by using raw materials and cheap labour) circulate.

The problem of how capitalism becomes a way of production and universalizes, is important in order to understand how it needs a higher level of development of productive forces to exist. Despite this, it contradicts the development of productive forces, since it does not generalize it. On the contrary, it keeps the differentiation of the levels of development since it needs it as it is nourished by it. This is the reason why the law of uneven economic and political development of capitalism is a real law.

A second aspect refers to the form of functioning of the capitalist economy, i.e. the "cyclical" nature of capitalist production. This phenomenon needs to be explained through Marx, in particular his book II of *Capital*, when the author defines the law that rules capitalist production, presenting it, starting from commodities. Because of the well-known historical events, Marx could finish only book I of *Capital*, published in 1867 and left to Engels the task of completing the other books of the work in three volumes, published in 1885, two years after Marx's death, and then in 1894, shortly before Engels' death. Some researchers suggest that perhaps Engels changed some things in comparison to Marx's thought, but that he was, essentially, very respectful of Marx's analysis, unraveling it as nobody could have done. In no other of Marx's work, his methodology is so coherently exposed as in *Capital* and in *Theories of Surplus value*, the fourth book. So there is not even the slightest doubt about the fact that if one needs to carry on a further analysis of the problem of globalization, the essential starting point is the study of the circulation of capital, but not because globalization is, in its essence, a phenomenon of circulation, but rather because the movement of capital, through the study of the cycle, is what allows one to see in its dynamics the process that facilitates the understanding of the phenomenon.

Capitalism is generalized on the basis of the birth of two separated markets, one of the means of production and the other one of the labour force. This is based on the separation of the producer from his means and conditions in this process. This highlights the dual nature of all economic categories that Marx handles and that distanced him from the consideration of the fact that capitalism was eternal, the last and ultimate form of social production, as the classics Petty, Smith and Ricardo thought. The labour force, as a set of physical and intellectual skills, that Men have in order to exercise the function of labour, that is the transformation of nature appropriate to its needs, has always existed, but only thanks to capitalism becomes a commodity, as every product, created or not, through market methods.

The phenomena that occur in the process of the so-called "original accumulation" are those that historically give rise to the social conditions of the capitalist production system. This happens only after the birth of capitalism and not before it. A scattered social knowledge existed long before capitalism did, but only it makes the existence of the social sciences as a coherent and complete body of knowledge possible, through the universality of its laws.

As a consequence of the development of the world market and the rise of international monopolies this kind of phenomenon finally comes out of the national borders and becomes universal, subjecting the rest of movements within a global economic context. This process, which is the same in every capitalist country, becomes international on the basis of the trade of commodities.

The increase in relative *surplus* of capital in developed capitalist countries, which results from the concentration and centralization of capital and production, unites this process with the export of capital, establishing stronger economic relations between all regions of the world, in a single global market, the debtor is entwined more tightly to the creditor than the seller is to the buyer. This is how the dominance of international monopolies is set and this process at a global level speeds up. Also a development of productive forces that allows up to unexpected limits, an increase in the trade of goods, the flow of capital and the formation of new areas of production, trade, technology, etc., which had already begun to open up when corporations appeared. The State and its role in economy accelerate this process.

This is a process that takes place on the basis of technological, trading and financial dominance, of a set of main capitalist powers which still continue to dominate. The only exception to this is Japan which became part of this set only after its economic recovery from the Second World War.

The current stage of global competition, that is what has been commonly defined as the so-called phenomenon of globalization, which is also to be defined as neoliberal, should be primarily seen as the logical outcome of the process of internationalization of capital and production. Therefore it is an objective phenomenon that does not depend on the fact that it is presented as a transnational, hegemonic oligarchy, that aims at the restructuring of capitalism on a global scale and aims at the "modernization" of the neo-colonial system which was inaugurated after the Second World War in order to recover from a structural crisis of accumulation that characterizes international capitalism at least since the mid 1970s. Hence one can say that the cycle of social capital is being achieved on a more global scale, albeit through the cycle of capital money, of production capital or capital goods.

The internationalization of space in which these processes are carried out is a relatively new phenomenon, especially as far as the cycle of capital money and the cycle of capital-production is concerned, that before, were confined to a more or less narrow space. Capital goods has established and highlighted, since the origins of capitalism, a cycle that developed in the international area, and that imposed the ways of working and of competition in trade and cash flows, which deeply affected the world, undermining the concepts of independence and sovereignty, as a reaction to bond and integration in order to be stronger and without reacting, involuntarily, to the domain and control.

Precisely, the complexity of this process lies in the fact that nothing about it is voluntary since it occurs under the dominance of the international monopolies, of corporations, and of a set of imperialist powers, led by the United States.

It is not possible to analyze the phenomenon of global competition without considering the problems of the ongoing scientific-technical revolution, which is essentially a restructuring of capitalism that branches off to peripheral areas through "mechanisms of transmission". This is a separate branch as the absorption capacity and the competition that are not beneficial to the periphery at all. These mechanisms of transmission are the export of goods, investments, finance and policies directed by the developed capitalist countries mainly through their corporations. This way also drugs, environment, intellectual property etc., are controlled.

On the other hand, the Keynesian policies are obsolete to try and recover from the structural crisis and the parameters of economic policy change. The productive forces quantitatively modify, adapting themselves in order to reach the supremacy of electronics, information and all processes that expand the physical and intellectual skills of man to unexpected levels in the labour-process. The productive forces are supported by biotechnology, by synthetic raw materials, by new materials, etc. Corporations are means or agents of this process and they hold control and supremacy of international business institutions and also supercontrol of coordinating bodies such as: G-7 (G-8 now formally up to the G-20), the OECD, and even military institutions, such as NATO, etc.

In recent years a series of events of a political and economic nature at the international scale changed the structures of the world market through significant alterations in the relations of global competition, that materialized from the analytical point of view of the economic-productive instrumentation, into an exponential growth in imports, exports and in particular foreign direct investments (FDI).[5]

---

[5] Note that the IMF's Balance of Payments Manual defines as "direct" the investment made to acquire an "effective entry" (or lasting interest) in an enterprise (direct investment enterprise) that operates in a country other than the one where the investor resides. Direct investments take on three main forms: acquisition of shares or other, to the outside business equity (equity), reinvestment of the non-distributed earnings by foreign enterprises, injection of other non-equity capital (intercompany loans). The IMF includes within the group of the direct investment enterprises, only those companies of which the investor acquires at least 10% of the ordinary shares or voting power, though acknowledging the possibility of using additional criteria, required to identify whether there is or not a lasting interest between the investor and the foreign counterpart. The direct investment enterprises are further divided into Associates (consolidated companies which the investor holds up to 49%), subsidiaries (subsidiaries, 50% or more) and branches (branches, 100%). Cf. *Banca d'Italia*

Such processes are due, and are also strongly related, to corporations' activities which responded to the unending changes of the international market linked to technological development and to policies of liberalization, with increased levels of competition and a set of expansive strategies.

This led to a sharp rise in the levels of competition and expansion of large corporations, which through acquisitions and merger transactions across borders created real production networks at an international scale. This is how the true nature of globalization is highlighted, a globalization that is more of a global competition for the international poles, of a geopolitical and geo-economic nature.

The relation between transnational capital and different areas of influence is determined by the international division of labour and, therefore, by the way single national economies are placed with respect to the enlargement and redefinition of the international geo-economic poles.

These dynamics are developed against the weak economies leading to super-profits in favour of financial institutions, in particular not banking ones, on which the growth of existing speculative processes is based. The composition and diversification between the growth rates of fixed capital's formation in the private sector of OECD countries, and that of the value of the amount of financial assets faces us with the most critical dimensions of globalization focused on the financial and speculative nature, as discussed earlier.

The accelerated growth of the financial field was followed, right after, by the liberalization and deregulation of national financial systems, in an international kind of regime where a very large fraction of financial transactions takes place in the close field of the relations between specialized institutions, with no counterpart on either the level of exchange of goods and services, or of productive investment. There are, however, very strong ties of economic and social importance between the sphere of production and that of the delocalized finance.

Financial capital favours short-term financial investment transactions in order to recycle funds and make them available for foreign direct investments, addressed to the production sector, but being then available for financial speculation.

(1998: 101–102) *Relazione Assemblea Generale Ordinaria dei Partecipanti,* held in Rome on May the 5th 1998.

Aspects of the Current World Economic and Financial Scenario in the
Face of the Globalization Myth: The Example of Pension Funds

It should be noted that the value of the world trade is just one third of total world gross product value, which means that two thirds of the product are carried out in national markets and not in a hypothetical global market. The external opening of economies is lower in developed countries than it is in countries with lower levels of development. Foreign investment financed, unevenly, productive transformations, it favoured the increase in export share, it increased productivity and competitiveness, allowing developing countries in different ways to achieve economies of scale through systems of international production.

However, more than 75% of the total flows of the worldwide FDI (Foreign Direct Investment) is put into effect among developed countries and concentrates in very few countries, no more than 15 economies. This phenomenon is limited to the fact that receiving economies' swings forward and backwards are frequently very weak.

This means that economic growth, social protection and employment which are generated through the multiplier effect can be relatively low. Therefore, the strengthening of the financial market of easy profits without productive investment, of financial rents, does not depend only on the attack to direct and indirect wages, but also to delayed salary offset by a deterioration of the living conditions of all workers, whether they are employed or not.

This is the perspective from which the current stage of international capitalism and almost all international organizations should be observed. The international organizations are now subject to the monetarist logic of Welfare State's counter-reform, which is based on the demolition of social, economic and civilization achievements starting from the demolition of the public pension system. The real goal of capital, in this area, is not to classify differently the Welfare State but to bring it down. For example, is not about reforming pensions, but about making them private, by charging workers with high contribution in order to enrich the insurance cartels.

This way the forced logic of the use of funds board is introduced, without considering financial crashes and the negative consequences this had on the real economy, for example, on British and American funds. Just think that pension funds of Anglo-Saxon capitalism (United States and Great Britain) and of capitalism of the Rhine area (Germany and Japan) move enormous sums, which, by circulating in deregulated, uncontrolled markets, where savage capitalism dominates chasing the mere realization of profit, create serious social imbalances in terms of subtraction of resources in the form of real investments from employment, thus increasing unemployment, lowering the quality of life in general, and demolishing collective social guarantees.

Pension funds manage huge amounts of money that move from country to country, chasing investments with a high profitability, moving enormous international interests, seizing every favourable opportunity offered by markets, producing, during the increase phase, high securities prices and impressive falls when there is a widespread uncertainty. This way, pension funds become a destabilizing factor, not only as far as the price of securities is concerned, but also with respect to different countries' economic, social and political structure, which are target to the international financial speculation. It should also be taken into account that a pension fund is established in order to deliver, to a deadline, a benefit in favour of the beneficiary in the form of annuity or liquidation of the capitals value. However, these are financial services provided in the long term in which management decisions should be tied to average-long term investment policies. Institutional investors should, therefore, work predictably among income and outcome flows.

In this work too there is the will to ascribe from a theoretical point of view, to the introduction of pension funds, the ability to stabilize the stock market, though this certainly can not be applied to the Italian market, asphyxiated and still lagging behind other advanced capitalist countries' ones. Moreover, the most authoritative sources from institutions, parties and trade unions state that pension funds should have a stabilizing effect, the ability to allow an extension of public debt's average life, should stimulate the tendency towards saving through a diversification of financial instruments offered to savers, favouring the process of reallocation of companies' property of our production system, thus acting as a vehicle for the diffusion of popular shareholding, of the enlargement of bases of economic democracy. But in other countries, where pension funds are more widespread, countries where financial markets are much more significant and extended than the Italian one, some dramatic social events happened that questioned the funds' structure, revealing its real function and purpose.

The pension fund itself should be characterized by a relatively high riskiness, since it should make medium to long term operations. But reality shows that pursuits of profits gives impulse to the creation of short-term speculative policies and to the investment of funds on the stock market, thus being in opposition to its purpose of a welfare nature that had to be fulfilled, and leading to collapses, with huge consequences on the fund's stability and the general progress of economy, during periods of decline in the stock market.

Experience has, therefore, proved how pension funds had a destabilizing effect on market often accompanied by a rise in stock prices caused by excessive liquidity. Thinking that problems related to the crisis of social security can be solved through the development of private security is crazy. The solution is to be found in the strengthening of the public pension system in an increase in its efficiency, in the search for structural balance between revenues and expenses between ways of financing and kinds of services. The only way this can happen is through the enlargement of the employment base, beginning with policies of reduction in working hours for equal wage and restoration of rights certainty.

As a consequence, savings should be channeled into productive investments that create jobs and wealth to be measured not only in terms of GDP, but also of growth of civilization and humanity, achieving not only production of goods, but also developing employment that can cause significant improvements to every aspect of life, of social relationships and social protection.

The growth of a community's degree of civilization is measured by the ability to ensure collective needs of socio-economic balance, solving the problems of weaker citizens, in order to reduce social tension, not fostering it with the uncertainty for the future. Uncertainty due, for example, to the negative effect of the lack of stable prospects, that the introduction and development of pension funds can cause both from the single worker's point of view and, as it has been said, with respect to the effects on the real economy.

The Relevance of Structural and Systemic Crises

In October, 1929 there was the collapse of world economy in which every industrialized country was involved. The great depression, also known as "Wall Street's Crash" had devastating consequences in all industrialized countries and led to major reductions in incomes but also to a collapse of international trade, agriculture and all types of production.

Many analyses were carried out to explain this serious economic crisis that, starting from the U.S., had spread throughout the world. Galbraith, among others, explained that one of the reasons was, for sure, an incorrect distribution of income, an excess of financial speculation and a bad banking system.

The banking crisis was mainly overproduction of capital, lack of fixed rules, etc. but it mainly was, back then as it is nowadays, a structural crisis, inherent to the production system itself, i.e. a specific characterization of the model of capitalist production.

In the following years there was a global economic recovery during which there were many crises, which had little impact and which were followed by minor recoveries until the crisis was definitely solved.

The Second World War allowed the expression of war economy and of Keynesianism itself, with its military characterization both in terms of support of the demand for war fighting and for the consequent stage of reconstruction. If the crisis is a "normal" event, rather than extraordinary as Keynesians think, inherent to the capitalist way of production in order to destroy capital surplus that jams the mechanisms of accumulation and the growth of the rate of profit, then even the economy of war itself is a "normal" way of supporting the demand, induced or imposed, during periods of fall in consumes or rise in production of goods and capital. This is why economic crises occur repeatedly, as for example, the monetary system crisis of 1992,[6] or the Asian Stocks crisis in 1987 or the Wall Street crisis of 2001 with the consequent stagnation that lasted for many years after. The U.S. currency is becoming weaker compared to the euro, which began its rise against the dollar.

> Developed capitalism aspires to continue plundering the world, as if the world were still able to bear it.[7] (translated from Italian)

Current capitalism is driven by finance and the abandonment of Keynesian policies. Finance is now dominant and the wildest form of liberalism has been applied not only to goods and products but especially to the movement of capital, arousing many doubts in neoliberal economists.

---

[6] In 1992 there was the so-called crisis of the European Monetary System caused by the "international speculation" that attacked first the lira (which suffered from a devaluation) and then the pound.

[7] *Reflections of Comrade Fidel*, "The worst variant," http://www.granma.cu/italiano/2008/octubre/vier31/reflexion.html.

Finance changed its role, from one of support to real economy, to one of support of finance itself. Clearly, to get to this situation of unregulated liberalism of finance, the free movement of capital had to be introduced, a condition that Bretton Wood's monetary system did not admit and that, since a few decades ago, did not even exist.

The current monetary system, that U.S. economists call "Bretton Wood II" is no longer based on the dollar-gold convertibility, but on fluctuating exchange rates and the ever-increasing presence of Asian countries to finance U.S. deficit that grew dramatically and that is causing those failures we are facing nowadays.

Now, after almost 80 years since 1929, we are facing again one of the most serious economic and financial crises that the Western world has ever known. It is important to say that the "earthquake" that shook the international Stock Exchanges from the so-called "Black September" on, according to Paul Samuelson (Nobel prize winning economist) means for economy, what the fall of the Berlin wall meant to communism.

Over the last year the world's Stock Exchanges have lost 41% of their capitalization, amounting to 25.9 trillion (thousands of billions) of dollars. Wall Street paid the highest price: 7 trillion dollars. These numbers are so high that no one is able to even think of them. Let's say that worldwide investors have lost, over the past twelve months, the gross domestic product generated all over the world over seven months.[8] (translated from Italian)

If one takes into account that the world GDP amounts to about 44,000 billion, then it is easy to realize that losses are approximately up to 70% of world GDP. But be careful, because the financial capital, by playing a role in the system of fictitious and non-productive capital, does not produce surplus value, does not generate real wealth and hence the Stock Exchange does not burn wealth, but as if it were a kind of zero-sum game, what is lost by someone, is then won by someone else. Where is the happiness, that globalization should have produced? And where is to be found a paradise that finance capital should have secured?

So, where did it all begin? Surely from the actual manifestations of the structural crisis of accumulation of the early 1970s (first oil shock),

---

[8] http://it.biz.yahoo.com/09102008/92/liquidazione-non-sta-risparmiando-nien -te-nessuno.html. There is frequent reference to writings taken from web pages, given the immediacy of the political-economic events occurring at the time when this work was being finished.

which highlighted the systematic inability to keep "adequate" levels in the rate of surplus value, forcing different capitalisms to try the path of neoliberal globalization, which was then characterized as global competition, focusing, as it has been proven in each of our works, books, articles, at least those written over the last 15 years, on the predominance of finance, therefore that of fictitious capital on productive one, and on the privatization and the demolition of the Welfare State, with its related attack on direct, indirect and delayed wages.

This reflected in outsourcing, delocalization of production, massive use of foreign direct investment, breakdown of the world of labour and attacks on rights, development of precariousness which comes along with structural unemployment, with the so-called flexibility of labour, inherent to all new models of flexible accumulation, up to the wars of expansion and control for oil and raw materials and of flows and composition of "human capital" for the society of post-fordist economy, with a high content of intangible resources and to foster areas of Fordism supported by the new forms of slavery. Here is neo-liberalism, a tendency that, while trying to get out the systemic crisis, uses globalization, that led the world's economy to take on the shape of a virtual, immaterial, paper economy, within a global competition that uses the system of financial estate and location incomes in order to enrich a few people, to strangle the world of labour, with no real prospects for a resolution of the crisis, as shown by the latest ups and downs of "cheerful and creative" finance. The U.S., since the forced though desired closure of Bretton Wood's deals, continued to use loans to finance its large deficit. During the years between 2002 and 2007 over 48% of the net funding of the U.S. current deficit was covered by foreign governments. President Bush's tax policy led to a hole in the financial system of more than 7% of the total GDP, in addition to which there has been a growing indebtedness of American families, which for years have kept on spending more than they actually could.

Until 2006, in the U.S. there has been a dramatic rise in property houses prices that over almost ten years (from 1997 to 2006) increased by over 124%. But this situation was determined mainly by the choice of supporting an asphyxiated demand. The excessive rise in debt of U.S. households is more and more linked to the payment of loans stipulated for the purchase of the house and also to consumer debt.

The American system, in order to support the "inflated" growth of GDP, made it possible for banks to grant credit even to customers called Ninja (No Income, No Job and No Assets), i.e. persons who had no steady job, no assets and no type of financial coverage, but who were paying high rents, often higher than their salary.

This practice gives families with precarious economic conditions the possibility to be allowed a loan in order to purchase a house at very favorable interest rates, at the beginning. Clearly this situation could not last and when families experienced an increase in interest rates and could no longer pay their debts, they had to hand over their property for non-payment of loan installments. This situation went on until a speculative bubble was reached, interest rate. This meant, for the vast majority of Americans who had mortgages at adjustable-rates, they were not able to pay the installments anymore. There were also the collapse of securitized financial instruments and the failures of banks and financial institutions. Here is how the financial crisis destroys excess capital.

The increase of real estate values, however, has experienced a significant slowdown since 2007 due to a disproportionate rise in loans estimated interest rates, making unsecured buyers insolvent, and creating a situation in which many could not pay the loan, starting a series of eminent domains that affected many American families.

In this way we had an economic collapse of the system, which had as the appearing provoking factor the so-called *subprime crisis*, or the collapse of the banks, which granted mortgages to people who could not guarantee their solvency. The mortgage crisis in America got disastrously worst in 2008, and on this year's July there has been an increase of the foreclosure procedures for house owners of more than 170% if compared to July 2007; the numbers are really high and concern about 740.000 house owners who are risking the expropriation of their homes.

The strong increase of the interest rates brought a serious insolvency crisis and the failure of many American families (about 2 million). It is remarkable how in June 2008 a big insolvency percentage of the *subprime* mortgages was registered: for example, more than the 37% of those who stipulated mortgages in 2005 had problems with payments and consequently with solvability. In 2006 the situation got worse and the percentage raised to 40%, registering anyway a light decrease in 2007, stopping at around 29%.

The banks that granted these mortgages of "second category" or *subprime* in the ambit of the "creative" finance game, had the idea of securitizing their mortgage loans; in this way there happened to be an insertion on market of absolutely "insecure" titles, which in many cases, being in a certain way "disguised" because endorsed with the complicity of "trusted" rating agencies, were sold also to the holders of pension funds (hitting in such way also the world of work, diminishing with these practices the whole social salary), who ended up having in their portfolio titles which in substance were "waste paper".

It was not enough even the repeated cuts in the discount rate effectuated by the FED. This hard situation was caused in the U.S., especially by the financial and real estate speculation; in this way can be explained the fact that in the last 20 years the real estate price doubled about every five years; by all means, this is not caused by an effective increase of the building's value, but by the forced increase caused by the speculations. Citizens who requested a mortgage were only for a small part those who bought a first house, being in reality for the major part speculators, often also small speculators after a stroke of luck, who bought with the only purpose of selling back at doubled price after few years. In the US, in July 2007 there were 179,599 house foreclosures with an increase of 9% relative to the month of June 2007 and more than 93% respect 2006; the scenario is hence catastrophic and can be extended also to the European countries.

In 2007 in fact, the fear of an even bigger collapse of the *subprime* mortgages caused an accentuate fall of all the stock exchange index which extended itself also to Europe. After thirty years in which the whole US economy indebted itself ever more, we came to the end of the line.[9] With a world GDP of 44,000 billions, there is a public debt in the US of 11,000 billions of dollars.

The 2007 debt level in the USA was equal to 13,8 trillion dollars, a million more if compared to the previous year, while the debt for person has reached the value of 46,115 dollars, that is 184,460 for a family composed by 4 persons. From 1957 to 2007 the total US debt increased excessively, and especially the stratospheric amount of family debts; this means an economy in irreversible structural crisis which sustains itself fictitiously with finance, internal and external debt, public and private and with military keynesism, the war economy.

After these facts we can finally arrive to the so-called "Black September". The hard crisis, evidenced in appearance by its financial distinguishing features, became more accentuated in the USA and influenced all of the Western stock exchanges.

---

[9] Cf. diagrams on http://mwhodges.home.att.net/nat-debt/debt-nat-b.htm#financial.

Lehman Brothers was one of the biggest protagonists of *subprime* capitalism; we can remember that Freddie and Fannie own by themselves more than a half of the 12,000 billion dollars of mortgages hanging over the houses of the American citizens.

The crack of banking colossus like the first great American bank, Lehman Brothers, and the collapse of all the stock exchanges, forced the US government to "nationalize" Fannie Mae Freddie Mac, transforming the two mortgage colossus in public companies for an indeterminate period.

The plan includes also the government's acquisition of obligations guaranteed by *subprime* mortgages possessed by the societies. The president of the Federal Reserve, Ben Bernanke, diffused a communicate in which shows appreciation for this decision of the Treasury, "which will provide a fundamental sustain to the mortgage markets in this period of unusual uncertainness of the credit market. Fannie and Freddie possess or guarantee more than 5,000 billion dollars in mortgage contracts in the US, about a half of the whole country. In the last four trimesters they suffered losses for 14 billion dollars, and more are going to come in the next months, due to the increase of seized houses, foreclosures and missed payments on the mortgage rates."

The growing increase of the insolvencies over the real estate mortgages exposes the two societies to a risk of huge losses, which may cost tens and tens of billion dollars to the American contributors – the rescue may cost about 100 billion dollars according to several sources – but Paulson underlined how the financial impact of a failure of the two societies may be disastrous for the system. "A failure will cause damage to the American's capability to obtain mortgages for their houses, loans to purchase automobiles and the access to other credit channels" he said.[10]

Other important data to understand the reason of the explosion of the speculative bubble over finance and real estate is represented by the facts that explain how market, starting from the subprime mortgages, later enlarged itself until reaching a total value of paperizations and real estate mortgages USA equal to 531.000 billion dollars, more than ten times bigger than the whole world's GDP.

The actual crisis has more systemic characterizations than the previous stock exchange crisis of 1987 and the dot.com one, or more

---

[10] "Crisi mutui: il Governo Usa nazionalizza Fannie Mae e Freddie Mac," 8 September 2008. Available at: http://www.loccidentale.it/articolo/crisi+mutui%2C+il+governo+usa+nazionalizza+fannie+mae+e+freddie+mac.0057398

properly of the New Economy, in 2001, because in this situation not only the financial instruments and structures are endangered, but the entire working force, specialized and non-specialized, is also damaged, together with the low class and middle-high class, without social shock-absorbers and other kinds of mediation that can save the balance of the system, at least partially, saving the purchase power and the whole social wage. The working population remains often without a home and without a possibility to readjust its debt situation; in addition to this, cracks in the pension funds can be registered and also in this case the citizens are the most damaged, especially those who were forced to invest in the funds that were meant to guarantee their pension.

Anyway, there is another element which characterizes the actual crisis: the extraordinary increase of the price of oil and foodstuffs; since 2007 until the summer of 2008 have been registered increments of the oil price as have never been before, until about 150 dollars for barrel.

It is clear that this increase has not been caused by an increased request of crude, but by speculations directed to a research of a bigger surplus; this happens because these profits are destined principally to the multinationals that export it and not to the enterprises which extract it.

Also, the increase in food prices are caused by speculation; with the pretext of the new alternative energy, the agro-combustibles, we arrived to an endless commerce and exploitation of goods like corn, palm oil, etc., that are basilar for the economies of the poorest countries, with big speculation of a financial character (futures, derivates, etc.) over big quantities of foodstuffs. It is clear that the speculations over energy and foodstuffs represent different manifestations of the financialization of economy, which, through fictitious capital, desperately tries to solve a crisis which has clear systemic characters.

Hence the speculations made with oil and foodstuffs contributed to form that financial bubble that exploded during the final months of 2008.

An acknowledged consequence of this crisis is the collapse of the banks which, being between the principal acquirers of the "garbage" titles, found themselves having in their portfolio more than 750 billion dollars of securitized bonds.

In fact, more than the 40% of the capitalization of the stock exchanges has been lost in 2008; numbers show these facts clearly: almost 26,000 billion dollars, while Wall Street registered a loss of 7,000 billions.

And now another risk for the American economy is coming to sight: the speculative bubble of the credit cards. After having flooded the American for years with offers of credit cards and unlimited credit lines, banks and specialized societies are drastically cutting both of them. The squeeze "is interesting also the consumers who deserve credit and is threatening the banking sector, already in big difficulties, with another wave of massive losses, after an époque in which it gained record earnings with the easy credit business, which it contributed to create". In the first semester of 2008, the societies that offered credit cards, devalued risk credits for 21 billion dollars, because "many clients cannot pay their debt anymore. And with the societies dismissing tens of thousands of workers, according to the analysts the sector is going to suffer losses for other 55 billion in the next year and a half".

Let's consider more closely how (in the following lines we are reporting some intervention dated at the end of October and at the beginning of November 2008) the governments of the various European countries acted in October 2008.

In London, the government, to try to put an end to recession, presented a support plan for the banks of 500 billion pounds, that substantially means a nationalization. In fact Great Britain is running into recession: in the third trimester, the British GDP suffered a contraction of 0.5% superior to what was expected. It is the first time since 1992 that in Great Britain is registered a contraction of the lord product respect the previous trimester. The fall is superior to the esteems of the economists, who expected a -0.2%. Comparing to the same trimester in 2007, the British GDP registered a growth of 0.3%, under the average esteem of a +0.5%, after the +1.5% of the previous trimester. Great Britain is on the road of the recession for the first time since 1991, even if technically we cannot talk of a recessive cycle (two consecutive trimesters of negative growth), considering that in the second trimester the GDP remained the same of the previous trimester. Great Britain is the first of the G7 countries communicating the data regarding the third trimester GDP.(Translated from Italian).[11]

Ireland established a form of total guarantee over the banking deposits for a value of more than 400 billions euro, which is practically equivalent to twice the whole GDP.

In Spain it was announced the birth of a fund of 30 billion euro to guarantee the interbanking market.

---

[11] http://temporeale.libero.it/libero/fdg/2271541.html.

In France it is predicted the birth of a new juridical state structure which can guarantee a help to the endangered banks.

In Germany the government operated the rescue of four banks.

In Russia the president Dmitri Medvedev declared that an extra loan equivalent to 950 billion rubles to the most important banks of the country will be granted.

Iceland, after the crisis, was forced to nationalize the three biggest banks of the country.

In Holland, Belgium and Austria the guarantee over the banking deposits was lifted up to 100.000 euro.

In Italy the government defined a saving fund of twenty billions of euro which will help the endangered credit institutes; the government will have a participation without right of vote and commits itself to input new capital whenever banking capitalizations are insufficient.

Also in Japan new rules were introduced to contrast the effects of the crisis and new measures to help the economy to overcome this moment. New expenses for a value of almost 40 billion euro were added to those introduced in August and this amounted to the total number of 26.900 billions of yen (207 billion euros).

The basic principles of capitalism – private property of the means of production, competitiveness and maximum profit – must be preserved at all costs: for this reason the state and capital's governments protect rich people and enterprises and nationalize, socializing the losses over the workers' head. In first place it is necessary to notice how the solutions utilized to try to block the recession threat is not in line with the neoliberalist concept of the non-involvement of the state in the functioning of economy, because the intervention of governments is trying to recover from the disasters of the free market through huge injections of public money inside the economy, subtracted from social expenditures with a private and enterprise's Keynesism that is companion to war Keynesism; in this way *welfare* is destroyed and social wage is attacked in a historical attempt to make the workers pay the crisis through the *Profit State*, the *warfare*, the *miserable's welfare*.

It is interesting to report what Fidel Castro wrote on this:

> On Monday 13th came the announcement of multimillion funds that the European countries are to inject into the financial market to avoid a collapse. Shares rose with the surprising news. In virtue of the aforementioned agreement, Germany had committed – in the rescue survey – 480 billion euros; France, 360 billion; Holland, 200 billion; Austria and Spain, 100 billion each; and so on until the total reached, with the British

contribution of 1.7 trillion euros which, that day – given that the exchange rate between one and another currency is constantly varying – was equivalent to U.S.$2.2 billion, on top of the $700 billion of the United States…The European capitalist countries, their productive and mercantile capacity saturated, desperately in need of markets to avoid strikes by workers and those specialized in services, depositors who are losing their money and ruined campesinos, are in no position to impose conditions and solutions on the rest of the world. That is being proclaimed by leaders of important emerging countries and of those poor and economically plundered nations who are the victims of unequal terms of trade.[12]

The Radical Alternative Derives from Those Who Do Not and Cannot Pay for the Crisis

Then the question is: who is going to pay the costs of the various rescues operated by the governments?

There seems to be no doubt about the answer. They are going to be the workers, the weaker and more emarginated classes; unemployment will grow, the frailty of work and social living, *welfare* expenses will be cut without considering the discomfort of the families which cannot affording to pay the mortgages over their habitations, and will find themselves with no home.

The OECD reports shows that from January to September 2008 there was a growth of the discrepancy between rich and poor people higher than the one registered in the last two decades: this means that the 10% of Italians has an average income equal to 5,000 dollars (with an OECD mean equal to 7,000 dollars) vis-a-vis a 10% of rich Italians who have an income of 55,000 dollars (superior to the OECD mean).

The income's discrepancy – as written in the report – has grown since 2000 in Canada, Germany, Norway, United States, Italy and Finland, while it has decreased in Great Britain, Mexico, Greece and Australia.

The discrepancy has increased in 2/3 of the countries which are part of the organization, OECD explains, and this happened

Because rich families have reached particularly positive results if compared to the middle class and the families which are on the lowest degrees of the social scale.

---

[12] Cf. www.granma.cu, Reflections of Fidel "The unheard of," October 16, 2009 http://embacu.cubaminrex.cu/default.aspx?tabid=11317.

It has to be pointed out that the 10% of the richest population owns 28% of the total disposable income; and is also important to remember that the rate of child poverty in Italy is 15%, with an OECD mean of 12%.

The current systemic crisis will probably lead to the end of the domination of the United States that will be replaced by new centers of power such as Europe, China, India, some other countries such as Russia, Brazil.

History shows that capitalism has always experienced economic crises, more or less serious, that have always been solved through war.

These crises will lead to the creation of a multipolar system in which the United States must share their power with other nations, which could mean the beginning of a period of tougher competition that will further damage the working class.

This is why the capitalist system has to be overcome, but this is not necessarily and exclusively linked to the action of the downward trend in the rate of profit. This means dealing with the perspective of the immediate end of capitalism, that will cause its "self-destruction "and therefore in a theory of collapse? Not really, since the capitalist system will still find ways of implementing measures in order to make the capitalist way of production survive, but mainly because the transition from a way of production to another, or rather the transition to a socialist society, not only implies the dramatic explosion of objectivity in which the crisis presents itself, but the organized presence of subjectivity for a radical alternative, which may address to paths that lead to the overrunning of the capitalist way of production.

U.S. capitalism will always play an important role, but there will be the end of a political cycle during which the U.S. had stood in a dominant position, compared to other centres of power such as Europe, Russia, China, India, Brazil, which will impose, even if in a more diversified way, new forms of capital's political power which, instead of facing crises of an economic nature, will be facing crisis only if the subjective forces of the working class movement will be able to transform the economic and political crisis into a collapse and into the overcoming of the capitalist production system, turning it into a system of alternative relations.

In this case, this situation could lead to a hope for change for the working and popular classes. The capitalist system has not come to an end, but surely it is going through a negative period, and the working class should take advantage of such a moment in order to assert their rights.

Will there be the creation of a political articulation of social groups and classes around the proposal of alternative development? In the meantime, neoliberalism is beginning to run out of time. Here is how Marx's thought is still valid. Marx's economic theory has always made a clear distinction between the material content of capitalist economy, the progressive tendencies of its development and the reactionary ones, determined by its social being which opposes to labour. We must, however, say that in Europe there is no real class subjectivity, capable of expressing the direction and organization of the world of labour, which can keep on fighting for the radical transformation of the capitalist way of production, as it presents itself nowadays. Perhaps only in Latin America, class organizations of workers are creating a situation that is leading to a process of overcoming the society based on capitalist exploitation.

This is why the methodological structure of Marxist theory allows an interpretation of the economic, social, productive and political structures of contemporary capitalism and allows the new international movement of workers, to build, at the same time, the antagonist alternative.

The purpose of State Control changes its orientation with respect to the classical socialist project of the past century. The forms of struggle against power are now in the hands of workers, of the people, of their processes of self-determination.

In the Western world, in fully developed capitalist countries, where conditions are less favourable to the movements of workers, a tactical process of structural reforms for social change could be initiated, starting from a countertrend minimum plan.[13] For example, the existence of an unfinished capitalism which is dealing with a structural crisis, should be taken advantage of, since it leaves many large holes, forms of production, majorities left out of mass consumption, in order to articulate new forms of production and consumption oriented not to the search for profit, but to solving problems of poverty and marginalization.

The achievement of real economic forms of alternative to the capitalist way of production should focus on supporting these new

---

[13] We are referring to a "minimum plan" for the working-class left wing, in a non-revolutionary stage such as the current one is, at least in fully developed capitalist countries, as it is described in Martufi, Vasapollo (1999, 2003) and Arriola, Vasapollo (2004, 2005).

community and cooperative forms of production and distribution on a "human scale".

What is not easy to understand is that, even from a reformist, absolutely minimal perspective, the new economic policy guidelines must be absolutely aimed at fighting structural unemployment, precariousness, creating new employment opportunities of social and collective utility producing goods, not necessarily mercantile ones, increasing the possibilities for women, immigrants and young people to work. It is essential to apply a serious policy of generalized reduction, both in a sectorial sense and in a territorial one, of working hours for equal pay, which should be exercised also within the tertiary, both public and private, and the small and micro enterprises.

In order to do so, it is important to be able to combine a strong, renewed labour Trade Unionism to a new and modern Trade Unionism of the territory, which claims the social redistribution of wealth by affecting the processes of capital accumulation, starting from a different redistributive tax policy, from which capital can not benefit.

This project has still a dark area that coincides with the articulation of the State, or the role of transnational capital. But the new characteristics and demands of popular sectors are clear, as well as those spaces for implementation which are now open to a new possible cycle of affirmation of participatory, radical democracy since they are focused on the class content of political-economic transformation.

It is time to put on the agenda the ability to support, in not only strictly political terms, but just as well by considering macroeconomic alternatives (in this case, on a global scale), the need for a radically different model of development, capable of generating new and different employment, different wealth at different qualitative connotations and high social compatibility, a different way of producing and of social living. A model of development that aims at the distribution of employment, income and accumulation of social wealth. A mode of social quality development that is, therefore, eco-friendly and inclusive, focused on forms of socialization of accumulation, capable of creating wealth and *distributing value by spreading it socially*. This is likely to happen only starting from a strategy that aims at the interests of the new international movement of the workers.

That is why the analysis of Marx and Marxist theory strengthen those social characterizations that express a strong determination to the fulfillment of a radical transformation of the actual state of things.

BIBLIOGRAPHY

Acocella, N., ed. 1999. *Globalizzazione e Stato sociale*. Bologna: il Mulino.

Adorno, T.W. 1951. *Minima Moralia. Reflexionen aus dem beschädigten Leben*. [Italian translation: *Minima Moralia*. Torino: Einaudi. 1994].

Aglietta, M. 1976. *Régulation et crises du capitalisme: l'expérience des Etats-Unis*. Paris: Calmann-Levy.

Aglietta, M., and G. Lunghini. 2001. *Sul capitalismo contemporaneo*. Torino: Bollati-Boringhieri.

Agostinelli, M. 1997. *Tempo e spazio nell'impresa postfordista*. Rome: Manifestolibri.

Aguilera, E. *et al.* 2001. "*Comentarios críticos sobre el Consenso de Monterrey*," *Bollettino ANEC*. No. 64. La Habana: ANEC.

Albert, M. 1993. *Capitalismo contro capitalismo*. Bologna: il Mulino.

_____. 2003. *Parecon: Life after Capitalism*. London & New York: Verso. [Italian translation: *Il libro dell'economia partecipativa*, Milan: il Saggiatore. 2003].

Albert, M. and R. Hahnel. 1991a. *The political economy of participatory economics*. Princeton: Princeton University Press.

_____. 1991b. *Looking Forward: Participatory Economics for the Twenty-first Century*. Boston: South End Press.

Almond, G. and S. Verba. 1963. *The Civic Culture, Political Attitudes and Democracy in Five Nations*. Princeton: Princeton University Press.

Althusser, L. 1967. *Per Marx*. Rome: Editori Riuniti.

_____. 1972. *Lenin e la filosofia*. Milan: Jaca Book.

Althusser, L. and E. Balibar. 1968. *Il Capitale*. Milan: Feltrinelli.

Alvarez González, E. 2006. "*La planification à moyen et long termes à Cuba: notes pour un débat*," in R. Herrera, ed., *Cuba révolutionnaire. Tome 2. Économie et planification*. Paris: L'Harmattan.

Alvaro, G. 1999. *Contabilità Nazionale e Statistica Economica*. Bari: Cacucci.

Alvaro, G. and L. Vasapollo. 1999. *Economia e Statistica Aziendale. Il processo decisionale del sistema azienda*. Padova: CEDAM.

Amato Muñoz, P. 1954. *Introducción a la Administración Pública*. Book 1. Mexico: Fondo de CulturaEconómica.

Amin, S. 1981. *Class and Nation*. New York: New York University Press.

_____. 1989. *Eurocentrism*. New York: Monthly Review Press.

_____. 2003. *Obsolescent Capitalism*. London: Zed Books.

Amin, S., C. Bettelheim, A. Emmanuel and C. Palloix. 1973. *Imperialismo y Comercio Internacional (el intercambio desigual)*. Madrid: Siglo XXI.

Amin, S., A.G. Frank and H. Jaffe. 1975. *Quale 1984*. Milan: Jaca Book.

Anderson, P. 1977. *Il dibattito nel marxismo occidentale*. Rome/Bari: Laterza.

Ankarloo, D. 2002. "New Institutional Economics and economic history," *Capital & Class*. No. 78.

Ansoff, H.I. 1965. *Corporate strategy*. New York: McGraw-Hill. [Italian translation: *Strategia aziendale*. Milan: Etas Libri. 1991].

Antoniello, D. and L. Vasapollo. 2006. *Eppure il vento soffia ancora. Capitale e movimenti dei lavoratori in italia dal dopoguerra ad oggi*. Milan: Jaca Book.

Antunes, R. 2002. *Addio al lavoro? Metamorfosi del mondo del lavoro nell'età della globalizzazione*. Pisa: Biblioteca Franco Serantini.

_____. 2006. *Il lavoro in trappola. La classe che vive di lavoro*. Milan: Jaca Book.

Antunes, R., J. Petras and H. Veltmeyer. 2005. *Lotte e regimi in America Latina. Un filo rosso con l'Italia di ieri e di oggi*. Milan: Jaca Book.

Aoki, M. 1991. *La microstruttura dell'economia giapponese.* Milan: FrancoAngeli.

Arcelli, M. 1997. *Globalizzazione dei mercati e orizzonti del capitalismo.* Bari: Laterza.

Arrighi, G. 1999. *I cicli sistemici di accumulazione.* Catanzaro: Rubettino.

_____. 2003. *Il lungo XX secolo.* Milan: Saggiatore N.E.T.

Arriola, J. 1992. "*El fracaso de los Programas de Ajuste Estructural en America Latina,*" *Realidad Economico-Social.* Annual V. No. 30, San Salvador.

_____. 1999. "*La Globalización economica; porquè ha aumentado la desigualdad?*" *Iglesia viva.* No. 199. Valencia.

_____. 2001a. "*Globalización e imperialismo: liberalización financiera y asimetría monetaria,*" in J. Arriola and D. Guerriero, eds, *La nueva economía política de la globalización.* Bilbao: UPV/EHU. 2000.

Arriola, J., ed. 1988. *Los Nuevos Países Industrializados.* Madrid: Iepala.

_____. 2001b. *Globalización y sindicalismo.* 3 volumes. Alzira: Editorial Germania.

_____. 2003. "*¿La globalización? ¡El poder!*" *Cuadernos Bakeaz.* No. 57.

_____. 2006. *Derecho a Decidir.* Barcelona: El Viejo Topo.

Arriola, J. and J.V. Aguilar. 1995. *El movimiento sindacal ante la integración centroamericana? De la frágil partecipatión a propuesta del Tratado de Integración Social.* San Josè: FES.

Arriola, J. and A. Garcia Espuche, eds. 2002. *El trabajo ante la crisis ecológica del capitalismo,* in *Trabajo, producción y sostenibilidad.* Barcelona: Colección Urbanitats, Seminaris Urbans VI.

Arriola, J. and L. Vasapollo. 2004. *La dolce maschera dell'Europa.* Milan: Jaca Book. [Spanish translation: *La recomposicion de Europa.* Barcelona: El Viejo Topo / La Habana: Editorial Ciencias Sociales; French translation: *L'Europe masquèe.* León: Parangon.].

_____. 2005. *L'uomo precario nel disordine globale.* Milan: Jaca Book. [Spanish translation: *Flexibles y Precarios.* Barcelona: El Viejo Topo.].

Arrow, K. 1987. *Equilibrio, incertezza, scelta sociale.* Bologna: il Mulino..

Aucoin, P. 2000. *Fundamentos de la Administración y Gestión Pública.* La Habana: Material.

_____. 2001. *La Reforma Administrativa en la Gerencia Pública: paradigmas, principios y péndulos.* La Habana: Centro de estudios "Juan F. Lodola".

Avalos Aguilar, R. 2001. *Propuesta de creación de un sistema de evaluación de la gestión pública por medio de indicadores.* Paper presented at the VI International CLAD Congress On State Reform and Public Administration. Buenos Aires, Argentina.

_____. 2004. *Hacia un nuevo paradigma en la evaluacion de la gestion publica: mecanismos y indicatores institucionales.* Reports presented at the VI and IX Congress of CLAD. Buenos Aires / Madrid: CLAD.

Badaloni, N. 1972. *Per il comunismo. Questioni di teoria.* Torino: Einaudi.

_____. 1975a. *Il marxismo di Gramsci. Dal mito alla ricomposizione politica.* Torino: Einaudi.

_____. 1975b. *Marxismo come storicismo.* Milan: Feltrinelli.

_____. 1980. *Dialettica del capitale.* Rome: Editori Riuniti.

Bagnasco, A. 1999. "*Teoria del Capitale Sociale e Political Economy Comparata,*" *Stato e Mercato.* No. 57.

Bain, J.S. 1968. *Industrial Organization.* New York: Wiley.

Bairoch, P. 1999. *Mythes et paradoxes de l'histoire économique.* Paris: Editions La Découverte.

Baldissera, A. 2003. *La teoria delle crisi economiche da Marx a Sweezy.* Padova: CEDAM.

Ballart, X. 1996. "*Modelos Teóricos para la Práctica de la Evaluación de Programas,*" in Q. Bregué and J. Subirats, eds., *Lecturas de gestión pública.* Madrid: BOE.

Banca d'Italia. Various years. *Relazione Annuale Assemblea Generale Ordinaria dei Partecipanti.* Rome.

Banca d'Italia. 2004. *Manuale della bilancia dei pagamenti e della posizione patrimoniale sull'estero dell'Italia*. Rome: Banca d'Italia.

Banco de España. 2001. *Modificaciones en los cuadros de presentacion de la balanza de pagos*. Madrid: Banco de España. 17 April.

_____. 2004. *Balanza De Pagos Y Posición De Inversión Internacional De España*. Milan: Banco de España.

Baracca, A. 2005. *A volte ritornano: il nucleare*. Milan: Jaca Book.

_____. 2008. *L'Itali atorna al nucleare?* Milan: Jaca Book.

Baran, P.A. 1957. *The Political Economy of Growth*. New York: Monthly Review Press.

Baran, P.A. and P.M. Sweezy. 1962. *Il surplus economico e la teoria marxista dello sviluppo*. Milan: Feltrinelli.

_____. 1968. *Il capitale monopolistico. Saggio sulla struttura economica e sociale americana*. Torino: Einaudi.

Barba Noverti, G., A.M. Falzoni and A. Turrini. 1999. *Italian multinationals and delocalization of production*. Centro Studi Luca D'Agliano. Oxford: University of Oxford. April.

Barbetta, G.P., C. Piga and M. Vivarelli. 1996. *Il fenomeno dei gruppi d'imprese in Italia*. Rome: Mediocredito Centrale.

Barca, F. 1993. "*Allocazione e riallocazione della proprietà e del controllo delle imprese: ostacoli, intermediari e regole*," Temi di discussione del Servizio Studi. (Banca d'Italia). No. 194.

Barca, F. and M. Magnani. 1992. *L'industria tra capitale e lavoro*. Bologna: il Mulino.

Baron, P. 1996. *Business and Its Environment*. London: Prentice Hall.

Barzelay, M. 1993. *Administrative Reform: Concept, Visions and Recent Experience*. Cambridge: Harvard University.

Baykov, A. 1952. *Lo sviluppo del sistema economico sovietico*. Torino: Einaudi.

Baudrillard, J. 1974. *Per una critica dell'economia politica del segno*. Milan: Mazzotta.

Bauman, Z. 1988. *Is there a Postmodern Sociology?*" Theory, Culture and Society. Vol. V. Nos. 2/3.

Beaud, M. 1986. *Histoire du Capitalisme, de 1500 a Nous Jours*. Parigi: Points. [Italian translation: *Storia del capitalismo*. Rome: Edizioni Lavoro. 1984].

Becattini, G. 1998. *Distretti industriali e made in Italy. Le basi socio-economiche dello sviluppoeconomico*. Torino: Bollati Boringhieri.

Becattini, G., ed. 1987. *Mercato e forze locali: il distretto industriale*. Bologna: il Mulino.

Becht, M. 1997a. *Beneficial ownership of listed companies in the United States*. Brussels: ECGN.

_____. 1997b. *Corporate ownership and control: the European experience*. Brussels: ECGN.

Becker, G.S. 1976. *The economic approach to human behaviour*. Chicago: University of Chicago Press.

_____. 1981. *A treatise on the family*. Cambridge: Harvard University Press.

_____. 1993. *Human capital: a theoretical and empirical analysis with special reference to education*. Chicago: University of Chicago Press.

Bellamy Foster, J. 2000. *Marx's Ecology: Materialism and Nature*. New York: Monthly Review Press.

_____. 2002a. *Ecology against Capitalism*. New York: Monthly Review Press.

_____. 2002b. "The Rediscovery of Imperialism," *Monthly Review*, Vol. 54. No. 6.

Bello, W. 2002. *Il futuro incerto. Globalizzazione e nuova resistenza*. Milan: Baldini & Castoldi.

Benassi, M. 1997. "*Gerarchia, Mercati interni e reti: le caratteristiche dei processi di internazionalizzazione delle grandi imprese*," in G. Lorenzoni, ed. *Architettureticolari e processi di internazionalizzazione*. Bologna: il Mulino.

Benassy, J.P. 1982. *The Economics of Market Disequilibrism*. New York: Academic Press.

Benjamin, W. 2000. *L'opera d'arte nell'epoca della sua rispoducibilità tecnica*. Torino: Einaudi.

Berardi, F. 1998. *La nefasta utopia di Potere Operaio*. Rome: DeriveApprodi.

Berle Jr., A.A. and G.C. Means. 1932. *The Modern Corporation and Private Property*. New York: Macmillan. [Italian translation: *Società per azioni e proprietà privata*. Torino: Einaudi. 1966].

Bernini, A.M. 1996. *Intervento statale e privatizzazioni*. Padova: CEDAM.

Bettini, M. 2002. "*Italiani veri, presunti e per metà. Riflessioni antropologiche sulla «Bossi-Fini»,*" *Il Mulino*. Vol. 5. No. 403.

Bettelheim, C. 1969a. *La transizione all'economia socialista*. Milan: Jaca Book.

_____. 1969b. *Problemi teorici e pratici della pianificazione*. Rome: Savelli.

_____. 1970. *Calcolo economico e forma di proprietà*. Milan: Jaca Book.

_____. 1993. *Calculo Económico y Formas de Propiedad*. Madrid: Siglo XX. [Italian transaltion *Calcolo economico e forme di proprietà*. Milan: Jaca Book. 1978; *Calcolo economico e forme di proprietà*. Milan: Mimesis. 2005].

Bettelheim, C. and P. Sweezy. 1971. *Transition to Socialism*. New York: Monthly Review Press.

Beveridge, W. 1944. *Full employment in a free society: a report*. London: Allen & Unwin. [Italian transaltion: *Relazione sull'impiego integrale del lavoro in una società libera*. Torino: Einaudi. 1948].

Bianchi, G., A. Dugo and U. Martinelli. 1972. *Assenteismo orario di lavoro e scioperi nell'industria italiana*. Milan: FrancoAngeli.

Bianchi, M. 1970. *La teoria del valore dai classici a Marx*. Bari: Laterza.

Bianco, M. 1993. "*Il controllo nelle public company,*" in *Temi di discussione del ServizioStudi*. Banca d'Italia. No. 195.

Binmore, K. 1992. *Fun and Games: a Text on Game Theory*. New York: Hearth and Company.

Biscarini, G. 1996. "*Principi e tecniche di internazionalizzazione,*" *Nuova serie*. No. 1.

Blaug, M. 1995. "*Reply,*" in F. Moseley, ed., *Heterodox Economic Theories. True orFalse?* Aldershot-Brookfield: Edward Elgar.

Bleitrach, D., V. Dedaj and M. Góngora Ricardo. 2005. *Cuba es una isla*. Mataró: El Viejo Topo.

Bliss, C. and J. Braga de Macedo J., eds. 1990. *Unity with Diversity in the European Community*. Cambridge: Cambridge University Press.

Blum, W. 2005. *Rogue State, 3rd Edition: A Guide to the World's Only Superpower*. Monroe: Common Courage Press.

von Böhm-Bawerk, E. 1975. "*Karl Marx y la cherencia de sus sistema,*" in R. Hilferding, *Valor y precio de producción*. Buenos Aires: Editorial Tiempo Contemporáneo. [Italian translation: *La conclusione del sistema marxiano*. Milan: Etas Libri. 2002].

Boffito, C. 1968. *Socialismo e mercato in Jugoslavia*. Torino: Einaudi.

Bornstein, M. 1973. *Economia di mercato ed economia pianificata. Un'analisi comparata: teorie e casi*. Milan: Angeli.

Bonefeld, W., ed. 2001. *The Politics of Europe: Monetary Union and Class*. Basingstoke: Palgrave.

Bora, B. 1998. *The role of multinational corporations in globalizing the world economy: evidence from affiliates of US multinational companies*. Handbook of the Globalization in the World Economy. Cheltenham / Northhampton: Amnon Levy-Livermore.

Bordiga, A. 1980. *Proprietà e capitale. Inquadramento nella dottrina marxista dei fenomeni del mondo sociale contemporaneo*. Firenze: Editrice Iskra.

Borisov, O.S., V.A. Zhamin and M.F. Makarova. 1975. *Diccionario de Economia Politica*. Madrid: Akal.

Bornstein, M. 1973. *Economia di mercato ed economia pianificata. Un'analisi comparata: teorie e casi*. Milan: FrancoAngeli.

Boron, A. 1995. *State, Capitalism, and Democracy in Latin America*. Boulder: Lynne Rienner.

_____. 2005. *Empire and Imperialism: A Critical Reading of Michael Hardt and Antonio Negri*. London: Zed Books.

Borrego, O. 2001. *Che, el camino del fuego*. Buenos Aires: Hombre Nuevo.

Borretti, B. 2005. "*La società del rischio*," *PROTEO*. No. 3/05. Rome: CESTES.

von Bortkiewicz, L. 1971. *La teoria economica di Marx e altri saggi su Böhm-Bawerk, Walras e Pareto*. Torino: Einaudi.

Bosco, B. 2000. *Pianificazione e mercato nell'economia cubana contemporanea. Analisi delle innovazioni in un sistema socialista*. Milan: Giuffrè.

Bougnoux, D. 1994. *Sciences de l'information et de la communication*. Paris: Larousse.

Bowles, S. and R. Edwards. 1990. *Introducción a la Economía: competencia, autoritarismo y cambio en las economías capitalistas*. Madrid: Alianza Universidad Textos.

Bowles, S., D.M. Gordon, and T.E. Weisskopf. 1989. *La Economía del Despilfarro*. Madrid: Alianza Universidad Textos.

_____. 1990. *After the Waste Land: a democratic economics for the year 2000*. New York: M.E.Sharpe.

Bowman, E.H. 1980. "A Risk Return Paradox for Strategic Management," *Sloan Management Review*. Spring.

Boyer, R. and J.P. Durand. 1993. *L'après-fordisme*. Paris: Syros.

Boyer, R. and Y. Sayllard, ed. 1995. *Théorie de la régulation l'état des savoirs*. Paris: La Découverte.

von Böhm-Bawerk, E. 1975. "*Karl Marx y la cherencia de sus sistema*," in R. Hilferding, *Valor y precio de producción*. Buenos Aires: Editorial Tiempo Contemporáne. [Italian translation: *La conclusione del sistema marxiano*. Milan: Etas.].

Braverman, H. 1998. *Labour and Monopoly Capital. The Degradation of Work in the Twentieth Century*. New York: Monthly Review Press.

Brecher, J. and T. Costello. 1997. *Contro il capitale globale. Strategie di resistenza*. Milan: Feltrinelli.

Bremond, J. and A. Geledan. 1985. *Diccionario Economico-social*. Barcelona: Vicens Vives.

Breton, P. 1992. *L'Utopie de la Communication. Le mythe du village planetaire*. Paris: LaDécouverte.

Brioschi, F., L. Buzzacchi and G.M. Colombo. 1990. *Gruppi di imprese e mercato finanziario*. Rome: NIS.

Bruni, G. 1990. *Contabilità per l'alta direzione. Il processo informativo funzionale alle decisioni di governo dell'impresa*. Milan: Etas Libri.

Brus, W. 1965. *Il funzionamento dell'economia socialista*. Milan: Feltrinelli.

_____. 1974. *Sistema politico e proprietà sociale nel socialismo*. Rome: Editori Riuniti.

Brzezinski, Z. 1998. *La grande scacchiera*. Milan: Longanesi.

Bucharin, N.I. 1926. *Der Imperialismus und die Akkumulation des Kapitals*. Wein: Verlag für Literatur und Politik. [Italian translation: *L'imperialismo e l'accumulazione del capitale*, Bari: Laterza. 1972].

_____. 1966. *L'economia mondiale e l'imperialismo*. Rome: Samonà e Savelli.

_____. 1970. *L'economia politica del rentier*. Rome: Samonà e Savelli.

_____. 1971. *Economia del periodo di trasformazione*. Milan: Jaca Book.

Buckley, P.J. and M. Casson. 1988. "Models of the Multinational Enterprise," *Journal of International Business Studies*. No. 29.

Bulgarelli, M. and U. Zona. 2004. *Mercenari. Il business della guerra*. Milan: NdA Press.

Butera, F. and E. Invernizzi, eds. 1993. *Il manager a più dimensioni. Progettare e gestire i processi dell'impresa informatizzata*. Milan: FrancoAngeli.

Byé, R. and G.D. De Bernis. 1987. *Relations économiques internationales*. Paris: Daloz.

Caffè, F. 1984. *Lezioni di politica economica.* 4th Edition. Torino: Boringhier.
_____. 1990. *La solitudine del riformista.* Torino: Boringhier.
Cafferata, R. and P. Genco, eds. 1997. *Competitività, informazioni e internazionalizzazione delle piccole medie imprese.* Bologna: il Mulino.
Calori, G. and J. Ubago Vivas. 1990. *Strategie finanziarie d'impresa.* Milan: Ipsoa.
Cammack, P. 2003. "The Governance of Global Capitalism: A New Materialist Perspective," *Historical Materialism.* Vol. 11. No. 2.
Canziani, A. 1979. "*Sull'origine e la formazione del pensiero di Kalecki,*" in *Studi di statistica e di economia in onore di Libero Lenti.* Volume II. Milan: Giuffrè.
Capdevila, G. 2003. *Se Esfuman Metas de Reducción de Pobreza.* Accessed at: http://attac.org/indexes/index.html.
Caprio, L. 1989. *Finanza Aziendale: Le decisioni di investimento nei mercati di capitale.* Torino: UTET.
Caracciolo, L. 1997. *Euro No. Non morire per Maastricht.* Rome/Bari: Laterza.
Carandini, G. 1979. *Lavoro e capitale nella teoria di Marx.* Milan: Mondadori.
_____. 2005. *Un altro Marx: lo scienziato liberato dall'utopia.* Rome/Bari: Laterza.
Cararo, S., M. Casadio, R. Martufi, L. Vasapollo L. and F. Viola. 2002. *La coscienza di Cipputi. EuroBang/3: Inchiesta sul lavoro: soggetti e progetti.* Rome: Mediaprint.
_____. 2001. *No/Made Italy. EuroBang/2: La multinazionale Italia e i lavoratori nella competizione globale,* Mediaprint, Roma.
Carcanholo, R.
1981. *Desarrollo del Capitalismo en Costa Rica,* Editorial Universitaria Centroamericana (EDUCA), San José.
_____. 1982. *Dialéctica de la Mercancía y Teoría del Valor,* EDUCA, San José.
Carchedi, G.
1977. *On the Economic Identification of Social Classes,* Routledge & Kegan Paul, London-Henley-Boston.
_____. 1983. *Problems in Class Analysis. Production, Knowledge, and the Function of Capital.* London / Boston / Melbourne / Henley: Routledge & Kegan Paul.
_____. 1987. *Class Analysis and Social Research.* Oxford: Basil Blackwell.
_____. 1991. *Frontiers of Political Economy.* London-New York: Verso.
_____. 2001. *For Another Europe. A Class Analysis of European Economic Integration.* London / New York: Verso.
_____. 2002. "*L'arte del fare confusione,*" in L. Vasapollo, ed., *Un vecchio falso problema. La trasformazione dei valori in prezzi nel Capitale di Marx.* Castel Madama: Mediaprint.
_____. 2004. "*Società dell'informazione, società dei servizi, o società del capitale? Il sindacato deve scegliere,*" *Proteo.* No. 3.
_____. 2005. "*Tra soggettività e oggettività: l'aristocrazia operaia,*" in Various Authors, *Lavoro contro capitale. Egemonia e politica nell'epoca del conflitto di classe globale.* Rome: Quaderni di Contropiano per la Rete dei Comunisti.
_____. 2006a. *Sullo sviluppo delle forze produttive: lezioni per un futuro socialista.* Report presented at the summit «Il bambino e l'acqua sporca». 13–14 May 2006. Rome: dalla Rete dei Comunisti, Quaderni di Contropiano.
_____. 2006b. "*Il ruolo delle innovazioni tecnologiche nello sviluppo capitalistico. Sulla caduta tendenziale del saggio di profitto,*" *Proteo.* No. 2.
Cardona Acevedo, M., F. Zuluaga Diaz, C.A. Cano Gamboa and C. Gomez Alvis. 2004. *Diferencias y similitudes en las teorias del crecimiento economico.* Accessed at: http://www.eumed.net/cursecon/libreria/2004/mca/mca.htm
Carlo, A. 1979. *Il capitalismo impianificabile.* Naples: Liguori.
_____. 1986. *La società industriale decadente.* Naples: Liguori.
_____. 2000. *Economia potere cultura.* Naples: Liguori.
Caroli, M.G. 2000. *Globalizzazione e localizzazione dell'impresa internazionalizzata.* Milan: Franco Angeli.

Carr, E.H. 1978. *Historia de la Rusia Sovietica. La Revolucion Bolschevique (1917–1923)*. Madrid: Alianza. [Italian translation: *La Rivoluzione bolscevica: 1917–1923*. Torino: Einaudi. 1979].

_____. 1984. *Historia de la Rusia Sovietica. Bases de una Economia Planificada (1926–1929)*. Madrid: Alianza. [Italian translation: *Storia della Russia sovietica*. Volume 4/4: *Le origini della pianificazione sovietica (1926–1929). L'unione Sovietica, il Komintern e il mondo capitalistico*. Torino: Einaudi. 1978].

Carranza J., L. Gutierrez and P. Monreal. 1995. *Cuba. La restructuración de la economía*. Madrid: Iepala.

Carrino, A. 1981. *Stato e filosofia nel marxismo occidentale. Saggio su Karl Korsch*. Naples: Jovene. [Italian translation: *La Rivoluzione bolscevica: 1917–1923*. Torino: Einaudi. 1979].

Casadio, M., J. Petras and L. Vasapollo. 2003. *Clash! Scontro fra potenze. La realtà della globalizzazione*. Milan: Jaca Book.

Cassese, S. 2005. *La nuova Costituzione economica*. Rome/Bari: Laterza.

Castaño, H.

2004. *Ocho puntos críticos para una revalorización metodológica de la Economía Política*, in *La Economía Política Marxista Reflexión para un debate*, Editorial Félix Varela, La Habana.

Castro Ruz, F. 1987. "*Discorso pronunciato nel XX anniversario della caduta del Che*," *Cuba Socialista*. No. 30.

_____. 1999a. *Globalización Neoliberal y crisis económica global*, speeches and declarations, May 1998 to January 1999. La Habana: Oficina de Publicaciones del Consejo de Estado.

_____. 1999b. *Capitalismo actual. Características y contradicciones, neoliberalismo y globalización. Selección temática 1991–1999*. La Habana: Editora Política; Melbourne-New York: Ocean Press.

_____. 2003. "*Discorso di chiusura del V Incontro sulla Globalizzazione e Problemi dello Sviluppo*," *Juventud Rebelde* (Special Edition). 14 February 2003.

Cavalieri, D. 1994. *Corso di economia politica*. Volume II: *Analisi macroeconomica*. Milan: Giuffrè.

Cavazzani, A., L. Fiocco and G. Sivini, eds. 2001. *Melfi in time. Produzione snella e disciplinamento della forza lavoro alla Fiat*. Potenza: Consiglio Regionale della Basilicata.

Caves, R.E. 1996. *Multinational Enterprise and economic Analysis*. Cambridge: Cambridge University Press.

Cazzaniga, G.M. 1981. *Funzione e conflitto*. Naples: Liguori.

Cersosimo, D. 1996. *Lavoro e non lavoro*. Catanzaro: Meridiana Libri.

Chang, H. J. 2002. *Kicking Away the Ladder: Policies and Institutions for Economic Development in Historical Perspective*. London-New York-Delhi: Anthem Press.

_____. 2003. "Kicking Away the Ladder: Neoliberals Rewrite History," *Monthly Review*. Vol. 54, No. 8.

Chick, V. 1986. "The evolution of the banking system and the theory of saving, investment and interest," *Économies et Societés*. Cahiers de l'ISMEA, Série Monnaie et Production. No. 3

Chick, V. and S. Dow. 1988. "A postkeynesian perspective on the relation between banking and regional development," in P. Arestis, ed., *Post-Keynesian Monetary Economics*. Aldershot-Brookfield: Edward Elgar.

Chomsky, N. 1999. *Sulla nostra pelle. Mercato globale o movimento globale?* Milan: Marco Troppa Editore.

_____. 2001. *Egemonia americana e «stati fuorilegge»*. Bari: Edizioni Dedalo.

_____. 2002a. *Anno 501 la conquista continua. L'epopea dell'imperialismo dal genocidio coloniale ai nostri giorni*. Rome: Gamberetti.

_____. 2002b. *I cortili dello zio Sam. Gli obiettivi della politica estera americana dal vecchio al nuovo ordine mondiale*

_____. 2003. *I nuovi mandarini. Gli intellettuali e il potere in America*. Torino: Net.

Chomsky, N. and E.S. Herman. 1988. *Manufacturing Consent. The Political Economy of the Mass Media*. New York: Pantheon. [Italian translation: *La fabbrica del consenso ovvero la politica dei mass media*. Milan: Tropea. 1998].

_____. 2005. *La Washington connection e il fascismo nel Terzo mondo*. Volume 1: *L'economia politica dei diritti umani*. Milan: Baldini e Castaldi.

_____. 2006. *Dopo il cataclisma. L'Indocina del dopoguerra e la ricostruzione dell'ideologia imperiale*. Volume 2: *L'economia politica dei diritti umani*. Milan: Baldini e Castaldi.

Ciocca, P. 1991. *Banca, Finanza, Mercato*. Torino: Einaudi.

Ciufo, A. 2001. *"Ripartire da Marx," Utopia socialista*. No. 2.

Clark, J.B. 1899. *The Distribution of Wealth: A theory of wages, interest and profits*. New York: Macmillan.

Claude, M. 1997. *Cuentas Pendientes y evolución de las cuentas del medio ambiente en América Latina*. Quito: Fundación Latinoamericana.

Cleaver, H. 2000. *Reading* Capital *Politically*. Leeds / Edinburgh / SanFrancisco: Anti/Theses-AK.

CNEL. 1999. *Italia Multinazionale 1998*. VII Bi-annual report. Document No. 17, Rome.

_____. 2000. *Postfordismo e nuova composizione sociale*. Rome.

Cockshott, W.P. 1990. "Application of artificial intelligence Techniques to economic planning," *Future Computer Systems*. Vol. II. No. 4.

Cockshott, W.P. and A. Cottrell. 1989. "Labour value and socialist economic calculation," *Economy and Society*. Vol. 18. February.

_____. 1993. *Towards a New Socialism*. Nottingham: Spokesman.

Coda, V. 1995. *L'orientamento strategico dell'impresa*. Torino: UTET.

Coleman, J.S. 1978. "Social Capital and the Creation of Human Capital," *American Journal of Sociology*. No. 94.

_____. 1990. *Foundations of Social Theory*. Cambridge: Harvard University Press.

Colletti, L. 1969. *Ideologia e società*. Rome/Bari: Laterza.

_____. 1975. "Marxism and the Dialectics," *New Left Review*. No. 93.

_____. 1979. *Tra Marxismo e No*. Rome/Bari: Laterza.

Colletti, L. and C. Napoleoni. 1970. *Il futuro del capitalismo. Crollo o sviluppo?* Rome/Bari: Laterza.

Colombi, F. 1989. *Strategie e Finanza*. Milan: Etas Libri.

Cominotti, R. and S. Mariotti, eds. 1990. *L'Italia Multinazionale*. Milan: Etas Libri.

_____. 1997. *Italia Multinazionale 1996. Tendenze e protagonisti dell'internazionalizzazione*. Milan: FrancoAngeli.

Confindustria. 2000. *Rapporto sulle imprese multinazionali italiane*. Rome.

Cooley, T., ed. 1995. *Frontiers of Business Cycle Research*. Princeton: Princeton University Press.

Cooper, R. 1996. *Post Modern State anche the World Order*. London: Demos.

_____. 2004. *The Breaking of Nations: Order and Chaos in the Twenty-First Century*. New York: Grove Press.

Cooter R., U. Mattei, P.G. Monateri, R. Pardolesi and T. Ulen. 1999. *Il mercato delle regole. Analisi economica del diritto civile*. Bologna: il Mulino.

Copeland, T., T. Koller and J. Murrin. 1991. *Il valore dell'impresa*. Milan: Il Sole 24 ore libri.

_____. 2002. *Avaliação de empresas – valuation: calculando e gerenciando o valor das empresas*. São Pãolo: Pearson Education.

Cottrell, A. and P. Cockshott. 2003. *Economic Planning Computers and Labour Values*. International Conference on the Works of Karl Marx and the Challenges of the 21st Century. La Habana.

Cozzi, T. and S. Zamagni. 1995. *Elementi di economia politica*. Bologna: il Mulino.
Cristaller, W. 1933. *Die Zentraler Orte in Suddentshland*. Jena: Fischer Verlag. [Italian translation: *Le località centrali della Germania meridionale*. Milan: FrancoAngeli. 1980].
Critical Art Ensemble. 1998. *Disobbedienza civile elettronica*. Rome: Castelvecchi.
Crozier, M., S.P. Huntington and J. Watanuki. 1975. *The Crisis of Democracy*. Task Force Report #8. Trilateral Commission. New York: New York University Press.
Dahl, R. 1989. *La democrazia economica*. Bologna: il Mulino.
Dahrendorf, R. 1988. *Per un nuovo liberalismo*. Rome/Bari: Laterza.
_____. 1991. *Riflessioni sulla Rivoluzione in Europa*. Rome/Bari: Laterza.
Dalle Magne, J.L. 1972. *La Politique Economique Bourgeoise*. Paris: Maspero.
Davies, F.R. 2003. *Políticas Nacionales y Crisis Financieras*. Presented at the V Meeting of Economists on Globalization and the Problems of Development. La Habana.
Debord, G. 2002. *La società dello spettacolo*. Milan: Baldini & Castoldi.
De Bruno, S. and M. Gabrielli. 1992. *Capire la finanza*. Milan: Il Sole 24 ore libri.
De Brunhoff, S. 1976. *Marx on Money*. New York: Urizen Books.
_____. 1978. *Capital and Economic Policy*. London: Pluto Press.
De Cecco, M. 1992. *Monete in concorrenza*. Bologna: il Mulino.
_____. 1998. *L'oro di Europa. Monete, economia e politica nei nuovi scenari mondiali*. Rome: Donzelli.
De Giorgi, A. 2000. *Zero Tolleranza. Strategie e pratica della società di controllo*. Rome: Derive Approdi.
Della Volpe, G. 1978. *Rousseau and Marx*. London: Lawrence and Wishart. [Italian edition *Rousseau e Marx*. Rome: Editori Riuniti. 1997].
_____. 1980. *Logic As a Positive Science*. London: NLB. [Italian translation: *Logica come scienza positiva*. Firenze / Messina: D'Anna. 1956].
Deleuze, G., F. Guattari, *et al*. 1997. *Rizoma. Millepiani. Capitalismo e schizofrenia,*. Rome: Castelvecchi.
Delors, J. 1998. *Per l'Europa politica,*" *Europa-Europe*. No. 3.
De Marchi, E., G. La Grassa and M. Turchetto. 1994. *Per una teoria della società capitalistica. La critica dell'economia politica da Marx al marxismo*. Rome: La Nuova Italia Scientifica.
De Meo, G. 1975. *Corso di Statistica Economica*. Rome: Edizioni Ricerche.
Demestz H. and K. Lehn. 1985. "The structure of corporate ownership: causes and consequences," *Journal of Political Economy*. Vol. XCIII. No. 6.
Denis, H. 1973. *Storia del pensiero economico*. Milan: Mondadori.
De Vecchi, N. 1993. *Crisi*. Torino: Bollati Boringhieri.
De Vincenti, C. 1978. *Marx e Sraffa. Note su un dibattito di teoria economica*. Bari: De Donato.
Devine, P.J. 1988. *Democracy and Economic Planning*. Boulder: Westview Press.
_____. 2002. "Participatory planning through negotiated coordination," *Science & Society*. Vol. 66. No.1.
Dicken P. and P. Lloyd. 1993. *Nuove prospettive su spazio e localizzazione*. Milan: FrancoAngeli.
Dierckxsens, W. 1998. "*Por un paradigma alternativo ante un neoliberalismo sin perspectiva,*" *Pasos*. No.76 [Available at: http:// www.dei-cr.org].
_____. 2002. "*Racionalidad alternativa ante una nueva depresión mundial,*" *Pasos*. No. 100 [Available at: http:// www.dei-cr.org].
_____. 2003. "*Il capitalismo transnazionale e la guerra: il movimento sociale per una alternativa,*" in Various Authors, *Il potere delle transnazionali*. Monograph of *Quaderni di Alternatives Sud*. Milan: Edizioni Punto Rosso.
_____. 2004a. "*Otra economía es posible. El futuro del mundo a corto, mediano y largo plazo,*" *Pasos*. No. 112. [Available at: http:// www.dei-cr.org].
_____. 2004b. *Sociedad en la modernidad*. San Josè, Costa Rica: Editorial DEI. [Available at: http://www.dei-cr.org].

Dieterich, H. 2002. *La democrazia partecipativa: el socialismo en el siglo XXI*. Bilbao: Baigorri Argitaletxe.

Dieterich, H., E. Dussel, R. Franco, A. Peters, C. Stahmer and H. Zemelman. 1999. *Fin del capitalismo global. El nuevo proyecto histórico*. Tafalla: Txalaparta.

Dietzgen, J. 1973. *L'Essence du travail intellectuel. Ecrits philosophiques annotés par LENINE (Pièces pour un dossier)*. Paris: Maspéro.

Di Marco, G.A. 2005. *Dalla soggezione all'emancipazione umana. Proletariato, individuo sociale, libera individualità in Karl Marx*. Soveria Mannelli, CZ: Rubbettino.

Dioguardi, G. 1995. *L'impresa nella società del Terzo millennio*. Rome/Bari: Laterza.

Dobb M. 1965. *I salari*. Torino: Einaudi.

_____. 1968. *Argumentos sobre el Socialismo*. Madrid: Ciencia Nueva. [Italian translation: *Le ragioni del socialismo*. Rome: Editori Riuniti. 1975].

_____. 1970a. *Problemi di storia del capitalismo*. Rome: Editori Riuniti.

_____. 1970b. *Socialist Planning: Some Problems*. London: Lawrence & Wishart Ltd.

_____. 1972a. *Economia del Bienestar y Economia del Socialismo*. Madrid: Siglo XXI. [Italian translation: *Economia del benessere ed economia socialista*. Rome: Editori Riuniti. 1975].

_____. 1972b. *El Desarrollo de la Economia Sovietica desde 1917*. Madrid: Tecnos. [Italian translation: *Storia dell'economia sovietica*. Rome: Editori Riuniti. 1972].

_____. 1999. *Storia del pensiero economico. Teorie del valore e della distribuzione da Adam Smith ad oggi*. Rome: Editori Riuniti.

Dobb, M., O. Lange and A. Lerner. 1972. *Teoria economica ed economia socialista*. Milan: Editorial Summa I.

Dockés, P. 1975. *L'internationale du capital*. Paris: Presses Universitaires de France. [Spanish translation: *La internacional del capital*. Caracas: Monte Avila Editorial. 1980].

Domar. E. 1948. "The Problem of Capital Accumulation," *American Economic Review*. No. 39.

_____. 1957. *Essays in the Theory of Economic Growth*. Oxford: Oxford University Press.

_____. 1989. *Capitalism, Socialism and Serfdom*. Cambridge: Cambridge University Press.

Domínguez, M.I. 1994. *Las generaciones y la juventud: una reflexión sobre la sociedad cubana contemporánea*. La Habana: Centro de Investigaciones Psicológicas y Sociológicas.

Donaher, K. 2005. *Dieci ragioni per abolire il Fondo monetario internazionale e la Banca Mondiale*. Como: Ibis.

Dornbush, R. and S. Fisher. 1985. *Macroeconomía*. Milan: McGraw-Hill. [Italian translation: *Macroeconomia*. Bologna: il Mulino. 1990; Milan: McGraw-Hill. 2001].

Drèze, J.H. 1991. *Underemploymente equilibria: essays in theory, econometrics and policy*. Cambridge: Cambridge University Press.

Drucker, P.F. 1974. *Management: Tasks, Responsibilities, Practices*. New York: Harper & Row.

_____. 1988. *The New Realities*. New York: Mandarin.

_____. 1989. *Economia politica e management*. Milan: Etas Libri.

_____. 1993. *Post-Capitalist Society*. New York: HarperCollins.

Dunn, W. 1994. *Public Policy Analysis. An Introduction*. Englewood Cliffs: Prentice Hall.

Dussel, E. 1999. *Un Marx sconosciuto*. Rome: Manifestolibri.

_____. 2004a. *El trabajo vivo fuente creadora del plusvalor* (Dialogue with Christopher Arthur), *Herramienta*. No. 27.

_____. 2004b. *La producción teórica de Marx. Un comentario a los Grundrisse*. Delegáción Coyoacán: Siglo XXI Editores.

_____. 2005. "*Hegel, Schelling e il plusvalore*," in M. Musto, ed., *Sulle tracce di un fantasma. L'opera di Karl Marx tra filologia e filosofia*. Roma: Manifestolibri.

Echevarría, E. 1994. *La verdad sobre Cuba: Nuestras argumentos.* La Habana: EMPES.
_____. 2003a. *Globalización y mercado laboral.* La Habana: Editorial Felix Varela, La Habana.
_____. 2003b. *"La lógica detras del ajuste,"* El Economista de Cuba.
_____. 2004. *"Relación entre la economia politica y la economica,"* Economia y Desarrollo. La Habana.
_____. 2005. *"La deuda externa de Mexico,"* Economia y Desarrollo. La Habana.
Echevarría, K. 2001. *Capital social, cultura organizativa y transversalidad en la gestión pública.* CLAD VI International Congress on *State Reform and Public Administration.* Buenos Aires, 5–9 November.
Eckstein, A. 1971. *Comparisons of Economic Systems.* Berkeley: University of California Press.
Ellman, M. 1979. *Socialist planning.* London: Cambridge University Press.
Elson, D. 1988. "Market Socialism or Socialization of the Market?" *New Left Review.* No. 172.
El Trondi, H. 2007. *Ser capitalista es un mal negocio.* Caracas: Editorial Centro Internacional Miranda.
Engel, E. 1897. *La consummation comme mesure du bienêtre des individus, des familles e des nations.* Paris: Bulletin de l'Istitut International de Statistique.
Engels, F. 1950. *Dialettica della natura.* Rome: Ed. Rinascita.
Espina Prieto. M. 1994. *Reproducción de la estructura socioclasista cubana.* Doctoral Thesis in Sociology. La Habana: Centro de Investigaciones Psicológicas y Sociológicas.
Estall, S. 1983. *La localizzazione industriale. Un'analisi dei fattori che condizionano la localizzazione geografica delle attività produttive.* Milan: Franco Angeli.
Eurispes. _____. 2003. *Rapporto Italia.* Roma.
_____. 2006. *Rapporto Italia.* Roma.
Eurostat. 1995. *Europe in Figures.* Luxemburg: OPOCE.
_____. 1996. *ESSPROS Manual, Population and social conditions, Methods.* Luxemburg.
_____. 1997. *Visione statistica dell'Europa 1986–1996,* Luxemburg.
_____. 1998–99. *Vue statistique sur l'Europe 1987–1997,* Luxemburg.
_____. 1999. *Social protection expenditure and receipts: European Union, Iceland and Norway 1980–1996.* Luxemburg.
Everleni, O. 2004. *Reflexiones sobre economia cubana.* La Habana: Editorial Ciencias Sociales.
Fedeli de Cecco, M. 1982. *Rousseau e il marxismo Italiano nel dopoguerra.* Bologna: Cappelli editore.
Fernández, B. J. 2001. *Teoría del estado y del derecho. Teoría del Estrado.* La Habana: Editorial Félix Varala.
Ferrarotti, F. 2005. *Il capitalismo.* Rome: Newton Compton.
Ferrera, M. 1998. *Modelli di solidarietà.* Bologna: il Mulino.
Fieldhouse, D.K. 1977. *Economía e imperio. La expansión europea 1830–1914.* Madrid: Siglo XXI.
_____. 1984. *Los imperios coloniales desde el siglo XVIII.* Madrid: Siglo XXI.
Figueroa, V. 2004. *"Marxismo y Pensamiento Neoclásico entorno al Enfoque Social de la Inversión,"* in *La Economía Política Marxista Reflexiones para un Debate.* La Havana: Editorial Félix Varela.
Fineschi, R. 2001. *Ripartire da Marx. Processo storico ed economia politica nella teoria del «Capitale».* Naples: La Città del Sole.
_____., ed. 2005. *Karl Marx. Rivisitazioni e prospettive.* Milan: Mimesis.
Fiocco, L. 1975. *Classi e pratiche di classe. L'operaio di fabbrica nell'analisi marxiana delle classi.* Venice: Marsilio.
_____. 1998–99. *"La cellularizzazione della forza lavoro e le forme di resistenza alla Fiat di Melfi,"* Collegamenti Wobbly. Per l'organizzazione diretta di classe. Nos. 6/7.
Fisher, I. 1930. *The theory of interest.* New York: Macmillan.

Fisher, P. 1992. *Rational Expectations in Macroeconomic Models. Advanced studies in Theoretical and Applied Econometrics.* Dordrecht: 26 Kluwer Academic.

Fitoussi, J.P. 1997. *Il dibattito proibito.* Bologna: il Mulino.

FMI, *Relazioni e rapporti.* Washington, D.C.: International Monetary Fund.

_____. 2006. *Prospettive dell'economia mondiale.* Washington, D.C.: International Monetary Fund.

Foà, L. 1965. *Piano e profitto nell'economia sovietica.* Rome: Editori Riuniti.

Foa, V. 1996. *Questo Novecento.* Torino: Einaudi.

Font Mario, F.L. 2002. *"Desarrollo tecnológico, competitividad y ajuste neoliberal, algunas tendencias mundiales en los últimos 20 años,"* in F.L. Font Mario, *Economía Mundial. Los últimos 20 años.* La Habana: Editorial Ciencias Sociales.

Foray, D. 2006. *L'economia della conoscenza.* Bologna: il Mulino.

Forsthoff, E. 1958. *Tratado de Derecho Administrativo.* Madrid: Instituto de Estudios Políticos.

Foucault, M. 1978. *Storia della follia nell'età classica.* Milan: Rizzoli.

_____. 1993. *Sorvegliare e Punire. Nascita della prigione.* Torino: Einaudi.

_____. 1994. *Poteri e strategie. L'assoggettamento di corpi e l'elemento sfuggente.* Milan: Mimesis.

François, G. and H. Mariol. 1929. *Législation coloniale.* Paris: La Rose.

Franks, J. and C. Mayer. 1992. *Corporate control: a synthesis of the international evidence.* London: London Business School and City University Business School.

Frasca, G. 1996. *La scimmia di Dio. L'emozione della guerra mediale.* Genova: Costa & Nolan.

Friedman, M. 1957. *A Theory of the Consumption Function.* Princeton: Princeton University.

_____. 1969. *The optimum quantity of money and other essays.* Chicago: Aldine Publishing Co.

Frisch, R. 1932. *New Methods of Measuring Marginal Utility.* Tübingen: Mohr.

Fukuyama, F. 1995. *Trust: The Social Virtues and the Creation of Prosperity.* New York: The Free Press.

_____. 2003. *La fine della storia e l'ultimo uomo.* Milan: Rizzoli.

Galbraith, J.K. 1967. *The New Industrial State.* Boston: Houghton Mifflin. [Italian translation: *Il nuovo stato industriale.* Torino: Einaudi. 1968].

_____. 2001. *"The Meaning of a War Economy,"* *Challenge,* November-December.

Galindo, W. and J. Malgesini. 1994. *El mundo del trabajo del siglo XXI.* La Habana: Ministro de Educación Superior (ENPES).

Gallino, L. 2003. *La scomparsa dell'Italia industriale.* Torino: Einaudi.

_____. 2005. *L'impresa irresponsabile.* Torino: Einaudi.

Gamba, E. and G. Pala. 1996. *Il programma minimo di classe. Per la prassi dei comunisti in una fase non rivoluzionaria.* Naples: Labouratorio politico.

Gandolfo, G. 1975. *Appunti di Macroeconomia.* Rome: Edizioni Ricerche.

_____. 1986. *Economia Internazionale.* Volumes I and II. Torino: UTET.

Gangart, V. 1976. *El Debate sobre la Industrializacion en la URSS," Critica de la Economia Politica.* No. 1.

García, F. and R. Sánchez. 1999. *"El cambio tecnológico y la concepción de los núcleos duros en la Inserción Internacional de la Economía Cubana," Revista Economia y Desarrollo.* No. 2.

Garcini, H. 1982. *Derecho Administrativo.* La Habana : Editorial Pueblo y Educación.

Garegnani, P. 1960. *Il capitale nelle teorie della distribuzione.* Milan: Giuffrè.

_____. 1981. *Marx e gli economisti classici. Valore e distribuzione nelle teorie del sovrappiù.* Torino: Einaudi.

Garofoli, G. and R. Mazzoni, eds. 1994. *Sistemi produttivi locali: struttura e trasformazione.* Milan: Franco Angeli.

Gates, H. 1995. *Camino al futuro.* Bogotá: McGraw-Hill Interamericana.

Gattei, G., ed. 1995. "*I nuovi meccanismi di finanziamento dell'imperialismo*," in Various Authors, *Il capitalismo reale. USA-Germania-Giappone. I protagonisti del nuovo disordine mondiale*. Naples: Labouratorio politico.

_____. 2002. *Karl Marx e la trasformazione del pluslavoro in profitto*. Castel Madama: Mediaprint.

Georgescu-Roegen, N. 1973. *The entropy law and the economic process*. Cambridge: Cambridge University Press.

Gerratana, V. 1972a. "*Formazione sociale e società di transizione*," *Critica marxista*. No. 1.

_____. 1972b. *Ricerche di storia del marxismo*. Rome: Editori Riuniti.

Ghoshal, S. and C.A. Bartlett. 1990. "The multinational corporation as an interorganizational network," *Academy of management review*. Vol. XV. No. 4.

Giannone, A. 1992. *Sistemi di Contabilità Economica e Sociale*. Padova: CEDAM.

Gianquinto, A. 1976. *Marx e la critica interna alla neoclassica*. Rome: La Goliardica.

Gill, L. 1983. *Économie mondiale et imperialisme*. Montréal: Boréal Express.

Giussani P., F. Moseley and E. Ochoa. 1989. *Prezzi, valori e saggio del profitto. Problemi di teoria economica marxista oggi*. Piacenza: Casa Editrice Vicolo del Pavone.

Glyn, A., A. Hughes, A. Lipietz and A. Singh. 1990. "The Rise and Fall of the Golden Age," in S. Marglin and J. Schor, eds., *The Golden Age of Capitalism*. Oxford: Clarendon Press.

Gobbo, F. 1989. *Distretti e sistemi produttivi alla soglia degli anni '90*. Milan: FrancoAngeli.

Goergen, M., Renneboog L. 1998. *Strong managers and passive institutional investor in the UK*. Brussels: ECGN.

Gomez, J.F. 1989. *Intelectuales y Pueblo*. San Josè Costa Rica: Editorial DEI.

Gomes-Casseres, B. 1997. "Alliance strategies of Small Firms," *Small Business Economics*. No. 9.

González, E. and Pons H. 2001. *Algunas consideraciones sobre el concepto de administración pública en el proceso de construcción del socialismo*. Conference presentation: GESEMAD. La Habana.

González, Gutiérrez, A. 1997. "*Economía y sociedad. Los retos del modelo económico*," *Cuba. Ricerca Económica*. Nos. 3/4.

_____. 2001. *Vigencia de la planificación*," *Cuba: investigación económica*. Vol. VII, No. 4.

_____. 2004. *Planificación Global de la Economía Nacional*. La Habana.

Gorz, A. 1978. *Ecologia e Politica*. Bologna: Cappelli.

_____. 1992. *Capitalismo, Socialismo, Ecologia*. Rome: Manifestolibri SET.

_____. 1992. *Metamorfosi del lavoro.Critica della ragione economica*. Torino: Bollati Boringhieri.

_____. 1998. *Miseria del presente, ricchezza del possibile*. Rome: Manifestolibri.

Gouverner, J. 2002. *Comprender la Economía. Un manual para descubrir la cara oculta de la economía contemporánea*. Louvain-la-Neuve: Diffusion Universitarie.

Grabher G., ed. 1993. *The Embedded Firm. On the socioeconomics of Industrial Networks*. London: Routledge.

Gramsci, A. 1977. *Quaderni del carcere*. Torino: Einaudi.

Grandinetti, R. and E. Rullani. 1996. *Impresa trasnazionale ed economia globale*. Rome: La Nuova Italia Scientifica.

Gray, J. 1797. "The essential principles of the Wealth of Nations, Illustrated in Opposition to the some false doctrines of Dr. A. Smith, and Others," in K. Marx, *Storia delle teorie economiche*. Rome: Newton Compton.

Graziani, A. 1977. *Teoria economica. Macroecnomia*. Naples: Edizioni Scientifiche Italiane.

_____. 1998. *Lo sviluppo dell'economia italiana*. Torino: Bollati Boringhieri.

Graziani, A., and A.M. Nassisi. eds. 1998. *L'economia mondiale in trasformazione*. Rome: Manifestolibri.

Graziano, P. 2006. *"Il governo della paura,"* *PROTEO*. No. 1/06. Rome: CESTES.

Grossman, G. 1960. *Value and Plan*. Berkeley: University of California Press.

_____. 1971. *Sistemi economici comparati*. Bologna: il Mulino.

Grossmann, H. 1971. *Marx, l'economia politica classica e il problema della dinamica*. Rome/Bari: Laterza.

_____. 1976. *Il crollo del capitalismo*. Milan: Jaca Book.

Guadarrama, P. 1996. *"El Núcleo Duro de la Teoría Marxista y su Afectación por la Crisis del Socialismo. Actitudes de la Izquierda Latinoamericana,"* in Various Authors, *El Derrumbe del Modelo Euro-Soviético: Una visión desde Cuba*. La Habana: Editorial Félix Varela.

Guarini, R. and F. Tassinari. 1996. *Statistica economica: problemi e metodi di analisi*. Bologna: il Mulino.

Guatri, L. 1987. *La valutazione delle aziende*. Milan: EGEA. [New Editions: 1990 and 1994].

Guatri, L. and S. Vicari. 1994. *Sistemi d'impresa e capitalismi a confronto*. Milan: EGEA.

Guerrero, D. 1990. *"Cuestiones polémicas en torno a la teoría marxista del trabajo productivo,"* *Politica y Sociedad*. No. 5.

_____. 1992 "Labour, capital and state redistribution. The evolution of net taxes in Spain (1970–1987)," *International Journal of Political Economy*. Vol. 22. No. 3.

Guevara, E. 1964. *"Sobre el sistema presupuestario de financiamento,"* in *Obras 1957–1967*. La Habana: Casa de las Américas. [Italian translation: *A proposito del sistema di finanziamento di bilancio*, in E. Guevara, *L'Economia*. Milan: Baldini and Castoldi Dalai. 1996].

_____. 1970. *"La planificación socialista, su significado,"* in *Obras 1957–1967*. La Habana: Casa de las Américas. [Italian translation: *"La pianificazione socialista e il suo significato,"* in E. Guevara, *L'Economia*. Milan: Baldini and Castoldi Dalai. 1996].

_____. 1976a. *"Consideraciones sobre los Costos de Produccion como Base del Analisis Economico de las Empresas Sujetas a Control Presupuestario,"* in *Obras Escogidas*, Volume 2: *"Fundamentos,"* Madrid.

_____. 1976b. *"El Socialismo y el Hombre en Cuba,"* in *Obras Escogidas*. Volume 2: *"Fundamentos."* Madrid.

_____. 1977. *Escritos y discursos*. La Habana: Editorial Ciencias Sociales.

_____. 1996. *L'economia*. Milan: Baldini & Castoldi.

_____. 2006. *Apuntes criticos a la Economia Politica*. La Habana: Editorial Ciencias Sociales. Hailstones T.J.

_____. 1983. *Viewpoints on Supply-Side Economics*. Richmond: Robert F. Dame Editorial.

Hamel, G., and A. Heene. 1994. *Competence-based Strategic Management*. New York: Wiley.

Haraszti, M. 1981. *A destajo*. Barcelona: Montesinos.

Hardt, M., and A. Negri. 2000. *Empire*. Cambridge: Harvard University Press.

Harnerker, M. 2001. *La Izquierda en los umbrales del siglo XXI*. La Habana: Editorial Ciencias Sociales.

Harrod, R. 1939. "Essay in Dynamic Theory," *The Economic Journal: the Journal of Royal Economic Society*. No. 49. [Italian translation: *Dinamica economica*. Bologna: il Mulino. 1990].

Hart, A. 2001. *Etica, cultura e politica*. La Habana: Centro de Estudiós Martianos.

Harvey, D. 1993. *La crisi della modernità*. Milan: il Saggiatore.

Hawken, P. 1993. *The Ecology of Commerce*. New York: Harper Business.

von Hayek, F. 1945. *The Road to Serfdom*. London: Routledge. [Italian translation: *Verso la schiavitù*. Milan / Rome: Rizzoli. 1948].

_____. 1988. *Conoscenza, mercato, pianificazione*. Bologna: il Mulino..

Henderson, H. 2003. *"Jaque al Imperialismo de los Economistas,"* *Diario La República*. 21 July 2003. Uruguay.

Herman, E.S., Mc Chesney R.W. 1997. *Global Media. The New Missionaries of Corporate Capitalism*. London: Cassel.

Hernández, A. and M. Granadillo. 2003. *Análisis Costo-Beneficio. Dispense*. La Habana: Centro Studi di Economia e Pianificazione "Juan F. Noyola".

Herrera, C.L. 2004. *"Algunas Reflexiones Sobre el capital humano," Economía y Desarrollo*. No. 1.

Herrera, R. (ed.) 2006. *Cuba révolutionnaire. Volume 2: Économie et planification*. Paris: L'Harmattan.

Hilferding, R. 1961. *Il capitale finanziario*. Milan: Feltrinelli.

_____. 1975. *Valor y precio de producción*. Buenos Aires: Editorial Tempo.

Hill, C.H. and G. Jones. 1998. *Strategic Management: An Integrated Approach*. New York: H. Mifflin.

Hinkelammert, F. 1997. *Las armas ideológicas de la muerte*. San Josè, Costa Rica: Editorial DEI.

_____. 1998. *El Grito de Sujeto*. San Josè, Costa Rica: Editorial DEI.

_____. 2001. *Itinerarios de la Razón critica*. San Josè, Costa Rica: Editorial DEI.

Hinkelammert, F. and H. Mora. 2001. *Coordinación social del trabajo, Mercado y reproducción de la vida humana*. San Josè, Costa Rica: Editorial DEI.

Hirst, P. and G. Thompson. 1996. *Capire la globalizzazione*. Rome: Editori Riuniti.

_____. 1997. *La globalizzazione dell'economia*. Rome: Editori Riuniti.

Hobsbawm, E.J. 1972. *Studi di storia del movimento operaio*. Torino: Einaudi. [Spanish translation: *El mundo del trabajo: estudios históricos sobre la formación y evolución de la clase obrera*. Barcelona: Crítica. 1987].

_____. 1985. *"Prefazione,"* in K. Marx, *Forme economiche precapitalistiche*. Rome: Editori Riuniti.

_____. 1987. *L'età degli imperi 1875–1914*. Rome/Bari: Laterza.

_____. 1995. *Il secolo breve*. Milan: Rizzoli.

_____. 1999. *Intervista sul nuovo secolo*. Rome/Bari: Laterza.

_____. 2002. *Anni interessanti. Autobiografia di uno storico*. Milan: Rizzoli.

Hodgskin, T. 1827. "Popular political economy," in K. Marx, *Storia delle teorie economiche*. Vol. 3. Rome: Newton Compton.

_____. 1970. *"Difesa del lavoro contro le pretese del capitale,"* in G. Bianco and E. Grandi, eds., *La tradizione socialista in Inghilterra*. Torino: Einaudi.

Horngreen, C. 1981. *Introduction to Financial Accounting*. Englewood Cliffs: Prentice-Hall.

Houtart, F. 1992. *El campesino como actor*. Managua: Ediciones Nicarao.

_____. 1999. *L'Autre Davos*. (with François Polet). Paris: L'Harmattan.

_____. 2001. *La Tiranía del mercado*. Madrid: Edición Popular.

_____. 2002. *Mercado y Religión*. San José, Costa Rica: DEI.

Huang, D. 1970. *Introducción al uso de la matematica en el anàlisis economico*. Madrid: Siglo XXI.

Huntington, S. 1968. *Political Order in Changing Societies*. New Haven, CT: Yale University Press.

_____. 1993. "The Clash of Civilizations?" *Foreign Affairs*. Vol. 72, No. 3.

Husserl, E. 1954. *La crisi delle scienze europee e la fenomenologia trascendentale*. Milan: il Saggiatore.

Hymer, S. 1976. *The International Operations of National Firms: A Study of Direct Investment*. Cambridge: MIT Press.

Instituto de Filosofía. 1997. *Report of the national scientific project "La sociedad cubana contemporánea, Retos y perspectivas."* La Habana: Instituto de Filosofía.

ISTAT. 1981. *Inti della protezione sociale 1975–79. Aspetti metodologici e prime elabourazioni*, supplement to the *Bollettino Mensile di Statistica*. No. 8.

_____. Various years(a). *Annuario statistico italiano*, Rome.

_____. Various years(b). *Rilevazione trimestrale sulle forze di lavoro*, Rome.

Istituto Affari Internazionali., ed. 1997. *Italia senza Europa?* Milan: FrancoAngeli / Torino: Istituto Bancario San Paolo di Torino – Servizio Studi.
_____. 1998. *Come finanziare l'impresa.* Milan: Il Sole 24 ore libri.
Itami, H. 1988. *Le risorse invisibili.* Milan: Gea-Isedi.
Itoh, M. 1980. *Value and Crises, Essays on Marxian Economics in Japan.* London: Pluto Press.
_____. 1995. *Political Economy for Socialism.* New York: St. Martin's Press.
Jaffe, H. 1973. *Processo capitalista e teoria dell'accumulazione.* Milan: Jaca Book.
_____. 1977. *Marx e il colonialismo.* Milan: Jaca Book.
_____. 1990. *Progresso e nazione, economia ed ecologia.* Milan: Jaca Book.
_____. 2003. *La trappola coloniale oggi.* Milan: Jaca Book.
_____. 2005. "*Non prendetevela solo con il «capitalismo»… prendetevela anche con la «gente»,*" *Proteo.* No. 3.
_____. 2008. *Abbandonare l'imperialismo.* Milan: Jaca Book.
Jessop, B. 1982. *The Capitalist State: Marxist Theories and Methods.* Oxford: Martin Robertson.
Jiménez Gómez, F., H. Pons Duarte, and E. González Paris. 2003. *Gestión Pública: Algunas Definiciones, Conceptos y Aplicaciones.* Publication of the Centro de Estudios de Economía y Planificación (CEEP). La Habana: Ministro de Economía y Planificación.
Johansen, L. 1977–78. *Lectures on Macroeconomic Planning.* Amsterdam: North-Holland.
Judge, G.G., R. Carter Hill, W.E. Griffith, H. Lutkepohl and T.C. Lee. 1988. *Introduction to the theory and practise of econometrics.* New York: Wiley.
Kahn, R. 1931. "The relation of home investment to unemployment," *Economic Journal,* June. [in R. Kahn, *Selected essays on employment and growth.* Cambridge: Cambridge University Press. 1972; Italian translation: *L'occupazione e la crescita.* Torino: Einaudi. 1976].
Kaldor, N. 1965. *Saggi sulla stabilità economica e lo sviluppo.* Torino: Einaudi.
Kalecki, M. 1943. "*Il ciclo economico,*" in Michal Kalecki, ed., *Sulla dinamica dell'economia capitalistica. Saggi scelti 1933–1970.* Torino: Einaudi. 1971.
_____. 1967. *Teoria dello sviluppo economico di un'economia socialista.* Rome: Editori Riuniti.
_____. 1975. *Sulla dinamica dell'economia capitalistica. Saggi scelti 1933–1970.* Torino: Einaudi. 1971.
_____. 1985. *Saggi sulla teoria delle fluttuazioni economiche.* Torino: Rosenberg & Sellier.
Kaser, M. 1972. *Comecon. Problemi di integrazione delle economie pianificate.* Milan: Franco Angeli.
Kaser, M. and J. Zielinski. 1975. *La pianificazione economica nell'Europa orientale.* Milan: Feltrinelli.
Katouzian, H. 1982. *Ideología, Metodo y Economía.* Barcelona: Hermann Blume.
Kautsky, K. 1901–02. "*Krisentheorien,*" *Die Neue Zeit.* [Italian translation: *Teorie delle crisi,* in G. Celata, B. Liverani, eds, *Karl Kautsky.* Firenze: Guaraldi. 1976].
Keynes, J.M. 1931. *Essays in Persuasion.* London: Macmillan.
_____. 1963. *Teoria generale dell'occupazione, dell'interesse e della moneta.* Torino: UTET.
Kim, W.C., P. Hwang and W.P. Burgers. 1993. "Multinationals' Diversification and the Risk Return Trade-off," *Strategic Management Journal.* No. 14.
Klein, N. 2003. *No logo. Economia globale e nuova contestazione.* Milan: Baldini & Castoldi.
Kornai, J. 1992. *The Socialist System. The Political Economy of Communism.* Oxford: Clarendon Press.
Kolko, G. 2006. *The Age of War: The United States confronts the world.* London / Boulder: Lynne Rienner Publishers.

Krugman, P. 1995. *Geografia e commercio internazionale*. Milan: Garzanti.
_____. 1999. *Il ritorno dell'economia della depressione*. Milan: Garzanti.
Krugman, P. and E. Helpman. 1985. *Market Structure and foreign trade*. Cambridge: MIT Press.
Krugman, P. and M. Obstfeld. 1995. *Economía Internacional, teoría y política*. Madrid: McGraw-Hill. [Italian translation: *Economia internazionale*. 2 volumes. Milan: Hoepli. 2003].
Kuhn, T. 1969. *La struttura delle rivoluzioni scientifiche*. Torino: Einaudi.
Kurkdjian, V. 1996. *Produrre all'estero: come internazionalizzare la produzione e gli investimenti*. Milan: Il Sole 24ore libri.
Kydland, F. and E. Prescott. 1982. "Time to Build and Aggregate Fluctuations," *Econometria*. No. 50.
_____. 1988. "The Workweek of Capital and its Cyclical Implications," *Journal of Monetary Economics*. No. 21.
Labriola, A. 1965. *La concezione materialistica della storia*. Rome/Bari: Laterza.
Lahera, P., Eugenio. 2000. "Reforma del estado: un enfoque de políticas públicas," *Revista CLAD Reforma y democracia*. No. 16, Caracas: CLAD.
Lafay, G. 1996. *Capire la globalizzazione*. Bologna: il Mulino.
La Grassa, G. 1975. *Valore e formazione sociale*. Rome: Editori Riuniti.
_____. 2005. *Gli strateghi del capitale. Una teoria del conflitto oltre Marx e Lenin*. Rome: Manifestolibri.
La Grassa, G. and M. Bonzio. 1991. *Il capitalismo lavorativo e la sua ri-mondializzazione*. Milan: FrancoAngeli.
La Grassa, G., F. Soldani and M. Turchetto. 1979. *Quale marxismo in crisi?* Bari: Dedalo.
Lahera, P.E. 2000. "*Reforma del Estado: un enfoque de políticas públicas*," *Revista del CLAD Reforma y Democracia*. No. 16.
Laibman, D. 1976. *Beyond the economic Man: A new Foundation for Microeconomics*. Cambridge: Havard University Press.
_____. 1992. *Value, Technical Change and Crisis: Explorations in Marxist Economic Theory and Capitalist Macrodynamics: A Systematic Introduction*, M E Sharpe IncArmonk NY.
_____. 2005. *Theory and Necessity: The Stadial Foundations of the Present*, in «Science & Society», vol. 69, n. 3.
_____. 2006a. *Deep History: A Study in Social Evolution and Human Potential*. New York: SUNY Press.
_____. 2006b. *Siete Tesis para un Socialismo Pujante en el Siglo XXI*. Barcelona: El Viejo Topo.
Lane, J.E. 1995. *The public sector. Concepts, Models and Approaches*. London: SAGE Publications.
Latouche, S. 1995. *La Megamacchina*. Torino: Bollati Boringhieri.
_____. 2005. *Come sopravvivere allo sviluppo*. Torino: Bollati Boringhieri.
Lazar, A. 2003. "*Le transnazionali, attori contemporanei dello sfruttamento mondializzato*," in Various Authors, *Il potere delle transnazionali*. Monograf of *Quaderni di Alternatives Sud*. Milan: Edizioni Punto Rosso.
Ledesma, J. 2004. *Economía, Teoria y Politica*. Buenos Aires: Pearson-Prentice Hall.
Lemert, E. M. 1981. *Devianza, problemi sociali e forme di controllo*. Milan: Giuffrè.
Lenin, V.I. 1984. *Collected works*. Vol. 24. Moscow: Progress Publishers. [Spanish translation: *Obras completas*. Moscow: Editorial Progreso. September 1913-March 1914].
_____. 1953. *Materialismo ed empiriocriticismo*. Rome: Edizioni Rinascita.
_____. 1963. "*La revolución socialista y el derecho de las naciones a la autodeterminación*," in *Opere complete*. Vol. XXII. La Habana: Editorial Política.
_____. 1970. *Stato e rivoluzione*. Rome: Editori Riuniti.
_____. 1974. *L'imperialismo fase suprema del capitalismo*. Rome: Editori Riuniti.

_____. 1976. *Opere scelte*. Rome: Editori Riuniti.

_____. 2001. *L'imperialismo fase suprema del capitalismo*. Naples: La Città del Sole.

Leontief, W. 1951. *The Structure of American Economy 1919–1939: An Empirical Application of Equilibrium Analysis*. New York: Oxford University Press.

_____. 1953. *Studies in the Structure of American Economy*. New York: Oxford University Press.

_____. 1956. "Factor Proportions and the Structure of American Trade: Further theoretical and empirical analysis," *Review of Economics and Statistics (RES)*.

_____. 1966. *Input-Output Economics*. New York: Oxford University Press. [Spanish translation: *Análisis económico input-output*. Barcelona: Gustavo Gili. 1970; Italian translation: *Teoria economica delle interdipendenze settoriali (input-output)*. Milan: Etas Kompass. 1968].

Levidow, L. and B. Young, eds. 1981. *Science, Technology and the Labour Process: Marxist Studies*. London: CSE Books.

Levy, P. 1994. *L'intelligence collective*. Paris: La Découverte.

Lewis, M. 2000. *The New New Thing*. Casale Monferrato: Edizioni Piemme.

Liberman, M.H. 1965. *Piano e profitto nell'economia sovietica*. Rome: Editori Riuniti. [Spanish translation: *Plan y Beneficio en la Economia Soviética*. Barcelona: Ariel. 1968].

_____. 1982. *El Controlo Economico de la Impresa*. Madrid: Index.

Linder, M. and J. Sensat. 1977. *Anti-Samuelson*. New York: Urizen Books-Dutton.

Linhart, D. and A. Moutet, eds. 2005. *Le travail nous est competé. La construction des normes temporelles du travail*. Paris: La Découverte.

Liodakis G. 2005. "The New Stage of Capitalist Development and the Prospects of Globalization," *Science & Society*. Vol. 69. No. 3.

Lipietz, A. 1983. *Le monde enchanté: de la valeur à l'envol inflationniste*. Paris: La Découverte.

_____. 1993. *Vert espérance: l'avenir de l'ecologie politique*. Paris: La Découverte.

Lippit, V. 2004. "Class Struggle and the Reinvention of American Capitalism in the Second Half of the Twentieth Century," *Review of Radical Political Economics*. Vol. 36. No. 3.

Losch, A. 1940. *Die Raumliche Ordnung der Wirtschaft*. Jena: Editorial Fischer. [English translation: *The Economics of Location*. New Haven: Yale University. 1954].

Lucas, R.E. 1985. *Studies in business-cycles theory*. Cambridge: MIT Press.

_____. 2005. *Cuba crecer desde el conocimiento*. La Habana: Editorial Ciencias Sociales.

Lukács, G. 1981. *Per l'ontologia dell'essere sociale*. Rome: Editori Riuniti.

_____. 1990. *Prolegomeni all'ontologia dell'essere sociale*. Milan: Guerini e associati.

_____. 1991. *Storia e coscienza di classe*. Milan: SugarCo.

Luhmann, N. 1990. *Stato di diritto e sistema sociale*. Naples: Guida.

Lunghini, G. 1995. *L'età dello spreco. Disoccupazione e bisogni sociali*. Torino: Bollati Boringhieri.

_____. 2001. "*I nuovi compiti dello Stato*," in M. Aglietta and G. Lunghini, *Sul capitalismo contemporaneo*. Torino: Bollati Boringhieri.

_____. 2002. "*La parte e il tutto: dilemmi della teoria economica*," *Quaderni di rassegna sindacale-Lavori*. No. 4.

Lunghini, G. and L. Rampa. 1992. *Struttura, interdipendenza e tecnologia nell'economia italiana*. Milan: Franco Angeli.

Luporini, C. 1962. "*Il circolo concreto-astratto-concreto*," *Rinascita*. No. 24.

_____. 1972. "*Marx secondo Marx*," *Critica marxista*. Nos. 2–3.

_____. 1978. "*Critica della politica e critica dell'economia politica*," *Critica marxista*. No. 1.

Luxemburg, R. 1913. *Die Akkumulation des Kapitals. Ein Beitrag zur ökonomischen Erklarung des Imperialismus*. Leipzig.

_____. 1925. *Sozialreform oder Revolution?* [Italian translation: *Riforma sociale o rivoluzione?* in L. Basso, ed., *Scritti politici*. Rome: Editori Riuniti. 1967].

Lydall, H. 1984. *Yugoslav socialism: theory and practice*, Clarendon Press, Oxford.
_____. 1989. *Yugoslavia in crisis*, Claredon Press, Oxford.
Macchiati, A. 1992. *Decisioni finanziarie e mercati dei capitali*. Bologna: il Mulino.
Magdoff, H. and P.M. Sweezy. 1979. *La fine della prosperità in America*. Rome: Editori Riuniti.
Maldonado, T. 1997. *Critica della ragione informatica*. Milan: Feltrinelli.
Malinvaud, E. 1983. *Essai sur la théorie du chomage*. Paris: Calmann-Levy.
Mammarella, G. and P. Cacace. 1998. *Storia e politica dell'UE*. Rome/Bari: Laterza.
_____. 1999. *Le sfide dell'Europa*. Rome/Bari: Laterza.
Mandel, E. 1979. *El Capitalismo Tardio*. Mexico: Editorial Era.
_____. 1986a. *Las ondas largas del desarrollo capitalista: la interpretación marxista*. Mexico and Madrid: Siglo XXI.
_____. 1986b. "In Defense of Socialist Planning," *New Left Review*. No. 159.
_____. 1988. "The Myth of Market Socialism," *New Left Review*. No. 169.
_____. 1997a. *Le troisième âge du capitalisme*. Parigi: Éditions de la Passion.
_____. 1997b. *Trattato marxista di economia*. 2 volumes. Pomezia: Erre emme edizioni.
Mandel, E., J. Valzer and J. Jourdain. "1970. *L'Inflation*," *Critiques de l'Economie Politque*, No. 1. Paris: Maspero.
Mandel, E., I. Wallerstein and A. Kleinknecht, eds. 1982. *New findings in long-wave research*. New York: St. Martin Press.
Mankiw, N.G. and D. Romer. 1991. *New Keynesian Economics*. 2 volumes. Cambridge: MIT Press.
Mansfield, E. 1975. *Microeconomia*. Bologna: il Mulino.
Marcuse, H. 1974. *L'uomo a una dimensione. L'ideologia della società industriale avanzata*. Torino: Einaudi.
Marshall, A. 1920. *Principles of Economics: an introductory text*. Houndmills: MacMillan. [Italian translation: *Principi di economia*. Torino: UTET. 1949].
Martinez, O. 2000. *El neoliberalismo en su Laberinto*, in *Economia Mundial: los ultimos 20 años*. La Habana: Editorial Ciencias Sociales.
_____. 2007. *La compleja muerte del neoliberalismo*. La Habana: Editorial Ciencias Sociales.
Martufi, R. and L. Vasapollo. 1999. *Profit State, redistribuzione dell'accumulazione e Reddito Sociale Minimo*. Naples: La Città del Sole.
_____. 2000a. *EuroBang. La sfida del polo europeo nella competizione globale: inchiesta su lavoro e capitale*. Rome: Mediaprint.
_____. 2000b. *La comunicazione deviante*. Castel Madama: Mediaprint.
_____. 2000c. *Le Pensioni a Fondo*. Castel Madama: Mediaprint.
_____. 2003. *Vizi privati... senza pubbliche virtù*. Castel Madama: Mediaprint.
Marx, K. 1844. *Ökonomisch-philosophische Manuskripte aus dem Jahre 1844*. [Italian translation: *Manoscritti economico-filosofici del 1844*. Torino: Einaudi. 1968].
_____. 1847. *Misère de la philosophie*. [Italian translation: *Miseria della filosofia*. Rome: Editori Riuniti. 1973].
_____. 1891. *Lohnarbeit und Kapital*. [Italian translation: *Lavoro salariato e capitale*. Rome: Editori Riuniti. 1970].
_____. 1867–94. *Das Kapital*, 3 volumes. Hamburg.
_____. 1898. *Value, Price and profit*. [Italian translation: *Salario, prezzo e profitto*. Rome: Editori Riuniti. 1971].
_____. 1956. *Historia crítica de la teoría de la plusvalía*. Buenos Aires: Cartago.
_____. 1958. *Lineamenti fondamentali per la critica dell'economia politica*. Firenze: La Nuova Italia. [New Edition: 1997].
_____. 1963. *Scritti inediti di economia politica*. Rome: Editori Riuniti.
_____. 1966. *El Capital*. La Habana: Editorial Venceremos.
_____. 1968. *Il Capitale*. Rome: Editori Riuniti. [New Edition: 1989].
_____. 1971. *Per la critica dell'economia politica*. Rome: Editori Riuniti.

_____. 1974. *Storia delle teorie economiche*. Rome: Newton Compton.

_____. 1976. *El Capital*. La Habana: Editorial Ciencias Sociales.

_____. 1977. *Storia delle teorie economiche*. Torino: Einaudi.

_____. 1978a. *Il capitale*, 5 volumes. Torino: Einaud.

_____. 1978b. *Manoscritti economico-filosofici*. Torino: Einaudi.

_____. 1985a. *Forme economiche precapitalistiche*. Rome: Editori Riuniti.

_____. 1985b. *El Capital*, Vol. I, Chapter. VI (unedited). Madrid: Delegáción Coyoacán / Siglo XXI.

_____. 1988. *Miseria della filosofia. Risposta alla «Filosofia della miseria» del signor Proudhon*. Rome: Editori Riuniti.

_____. 1989. *Il Capitale*. Vol. I. Rome: Editori Riuniti.

_____. 1993a. *Storia dell'economia politica. Teorie sul plusvalore*. Vol. 3. Rome: Editori Riuniti.

_____. 1993b. *Per la critica dell'economia politica*. Rome: Editori Riuniti.

_____. 1997. *Lineamenti fondamentali della critica dell'economia politica 1857–1858*. Firenze.

_____. 1998. *La questione ebraica. Per la critica della filosofia del diritto di Hegel. Introduzione*. Rome: Editori Riuniti.

Marx, K. and F. Engels. 1972. *Opere complete*. Rome: Editori Riuniti. (*Opere scelte*. Rome: Editori Riuniti. 1974).

_____. 1974. *Obras Escogidas en tres tomos*. Moscow: Editorial Progreso Moscú.

_____. 1985. *The German Ideology*. London: Lawrence and Wishart.

Matacena, A. 1984. *Impresa e ambiente: il bilancio sociale*. Bologna: CLUEB.

Mattelart, A. 1996. *La Mondialisation de la communication*. Paris: PUF.

Mattick, P. 1969. *Marx and Keynes: the Limits of the Mixed Economics*. Boston: Extending Horizons Books. [Italian translation: *Marx e Keynes. I limiti dell'economia mista*, Bari: DeDonato. 1979].

Mazzone, A. 1987a. "*Qualcosa che mai era stato nella storia della terra*," *Nuovi Annali della Facoltà di Magistero*. Messina: Università di Messina. No. 5.

_____. 1987b. "*La temporalità specifica del modo di produzione capitalistico (Ovvero: la «Missione storica del capitale»)*," in G.M. Cazzaniga, D. Losurdo and L. Sichirollo, ed., *Marx e i suoi critici*. Urbino: QuattroVenti.

_____. 2000. "*Idea dello Stato. Autogoverno e tirannide: per un'analisi possibile del potere presente e dei suoi limiti*," in G. Pala, ed., *L'Ostato, ovvero come lo Stato degli inganni sia stato sovrastato*. Naples: La Città del Sole.

_____. 2003. "*Crisi e lotta di classe dopo la «crisi del marxismo»?*" *Proteo*, Nos. 2/3.

_____. 2005a. "*Capitale e lavoro, classi, contraddizioni. Una apologia per l'unità di teoria e prassi*," in L. Vasapollo, ed., *Lavoro contro capitale. Precarietà, sfruttamento, delocalizzazione*. Milan: Jaca Book.

_____. 2005b. "*Lavoro e produzione. Plusvalore e lavoro intellettuale*," *Quaderni di Contropiano per la Rete dei Comunisti*. International Forum, 24 September. Castel Madama: Editorial Print.

Mazzone, A., ed. 2002. *Mega2: Marx ritrovato grazie alla nuova edizione critica*. Castel Madama: Mediaprint.

Mazzone, A. and I. Mazzone Haase. 1962. *Essay Bibliographique Oeuvres de Claude-Henri de Saint-Simon 1802–1825*. Annual of the Giangiacomo Feltrinelli Institute. Milan.

McCann Jr., C. 2004. *Individualism and the Social Order*, Routledge, London.

McNally, D. 1993. *Against the Market. Political Economy, Market Socialism and the Marxist Critique*. London: Verso.

Meek, R.L. 1977. *Marginalism and Marxism*, in *Smith, Marx and After Ten Essays in the Development of Economic Thought*. London: Chapman and Hall.

Meidner, R. 1980. *Capitale senza padrone*. Rome: Edizioni Lavoro.

Meny, I. and J.C. Thoenig. 1992. *Las Políticas Públicas*. Barcelona: Ariel Editorial.

Messori, M. 1978. *Sraffa e la critica dell'economia dopo Marx*. Milan: FrancoAngeli.

Mészáros, I. 2005. *Socialismo o barbarie*. Mexico: Editorial de Paradigmas y Utopias.
_____. 2008. *El desafío y la carga del tiempo historico*. Caracas: Editorial Clacso.
Micocci, A. 2002. *Anti-Hegelian Reading of Economic Theory*. Lewiston: Mellen Press.
_____. 2004a. "Critical Observations on Economics, Taxonomy and Dynamism," *Rethinking Marxism*. Vol XVI. No. 1.
_____. 2004b. "The Philosophy of Economics," *International Journal of Applied Economics and Econometrics*. Vol. XII. No. 1.
_____. 2006a. "*Il Mistero della Speculazione*," *Proteo*. No. 2.
_____. 2006b. "*Homo Faber e centralità del lavoro. Classici e Neoclassici, Liberali e Neoliberisti*," *Proteo*. No. 2.
Miles, L.D. 1961. *Techniques of Value Analysis and Engineering*. New York: McGraw-Hill.
Milios, J., D. Dimoulis and G. Economakis. 2002. *Karl Marx and the Classics. An Essay on Value Crises and the Capitalist Mode of Production*. Burlington: Ashgate.
Mill, J.S. 1998. *Principles of Political Economy*. Oxford: Oxford University Press.
Ministerio de Economía y Planificación. 2000. *Memorias del Seminario Internacional sobre Funciones Básicas de la Planificación y Experiencias Nacionales Exitosas*. La Habana: MINEP.
_____. 2002. *Plano 2003. Instrucciones para la su elaboración*. La Habana.
Ministero dell'Economia di Spagna. 1997. *Intervención General de la Administración del Estado: Guía para la definición de objetivos y la medición en el ámbito público*. Juan F. Noyola. La Habana: Centro de Estudios y Planificación.
von Mises, L. 1929. *Kritik des Interventionismus: Untersuchungen zur Wirtschaftspolitik und Wirtschaftsideologie der Gegenwart*. Jena: Gustav Fischer. [Italian translation: *I fallimenti dello Stato interventista*. Soveria Mannelli, CZ: Rubbettino. 1997].
_____. 1936. *Socialism: an Economic and Sociological Analysis*. London: Jonathan Cape.
Missikoff, M. 1984. *La telematica. Tecnologia, applicazioni e riflessi sociali*. Rome: La Nuova Italia Scientifica.
Monereo, M., M. Riera and G. Valdés., eds. 2000. *Cuba: construyendo futuro. Reestructuración económica y transformaciones sociales*. Barcelona: El Viejo Topo.
Monti, E. and M. Onado. 1989. *Il mercato monetario e finanziario in Italia*. Bologna: il Mulino.
_____. 2004a. "*EUA en el 2004: Economia y eleciones*," *El Economista*. No. 1.
_____. 2004b. "*Economía Política Marxista. Retos del Tercer Milenio*," in Various Authors, *La Economía Política Marxista Reflexiones para un Debate*. La Habana: Editorial FélixValera.
_____. 2005. "*La critica dell'economia politica*," *PROTEO*, 3/05. Rome: CESTES.
_____. 2006. "*Economia di guerra e il complesso industriale bellico*," *Revista PROTEO*. 3/06- 1/07. Rome: CESTES.
Mori, A. and V. Rolli. 1998. "*Investimenti diretti all'estero e commercio: complementari o sostituibili?*" *Temi di Discussione del Servizio Studi*. Banca d'Italia, No. 337.
Morishima, M. 1973. *Marx's Economics*. Cambridge: Cambridge University Press. [Italian translation: *La teoria economica di Marx*. Milan: Isedi. 1974].
_____. 1982. *Why Has Japan «Succeeded»?* Cambridge: Cambridge University Press. [Spanish translation: *¿Por què ha «triunfado» el Japòn?* Barcelona: Editorial Critica. 1984 and Barcelona: Editorial Folio. 1997).
Morrison, A. J. and K. Roth. 1992. "The Regional solution: An Alternative to globalization," in *Transnational Corporation*. No. 1.
Moseley, F. 1991. *The Falling Rate of Profit in the Postwar United States Economy*. London: Macmillan Press.
_____. 1995. *Marx's economic theory: true or false? A Marxian response to Blaug's appraisal*, in F. Moseley, ed., *Heterodox Economic Theories. True or False?* Aldershot-Brookfield: Edward Elgar.

Muñoz, R. 2004. *"Algunas Vicisitudes de la Economia Politica en su Evolucion,"* in Various authors, *La Economía Política Marxista Reflexiones para un debate*. La Habana: Editorial Félix Varela.

Murat, M. and F. Pigliaru. 1990. *"Commercio internazionale,"* in G. Lunghini, ed., *Dizionario di Economia Politica*. Vol. 16: *Commercio internazionale-Valore*. Torino: Bollati Boringhieri.

Musto, M., ed. 2005. *Sulle tracce di un fantasma: l'opera di Karl Marx tra filologia e filosofia*. Rome: Manifestolibri.

Napoleoni, C. 1970. *Smith, Ricardo, Marx, considerazioni sulla storia del pensiero economico*. Torino: Bollati Boringhieri.

_____. 1972. *Lezioni sul capitolo sesto inedito di Marx*. Torino: Bollati Boringhieri.

_____. 1985. *Discorso sull'Economia Politica*. Torino: Bollati Boringhieri.

Nardo, J.M. 1987. *La economía en evolución. Historia y perspectivas de las categorías básicasdel pensamiento económico*. Madrid: Siglo XXI.

Nebbia, G. 2002. *Le merci e i valori. Per una critica ecologica al capitalismo*. Milan: Jaca Book.

von Neumann, J. 1945. "A Model of General Equilibrium Theory," in *Review of Economic Studies*. No. 13.

Noble, D. 1984. *Forces of Production: A Social History of Industrial Automation*. New York: Knopf.

_____. 1993. *Progress Without People: In Defense of Luddism*. Chicago: Charles H. Kerr.

Nora, S. and A. Ming. 1977. *L'informatisation de la societé*. Paris: Seuil.

Nove, A. 1963. *L'economia sovietica*. Milan: Comunità.

_____. 1986a. *L'economia di un socialismo possible*. Rome: Editori Riuniti.

_____. 1986b. *The soviet economic system*. Third Edition. Boston: Unwin Hyman [Spanish translation: *El sistema econòmico soviético*. Madrid: Siglo XXI. 1987].

_____. 1987. "Markets and Socialism," *New Left Review*. No. 161.

_____. 1993. *An Economic History of the USSR 1917–1991*. London: Penguin.

Nove, A. and D.M. Nuti. 1972. *Socialist Economics*. Harmondsworth: Penguin Books.

Novozhilov, V.V. 1969. *La riforma economica nell'URSS*. Rome: Editori Riuniti.

_____. 1975. *La medición de los gastos y sus resultados en una economía socialista*. La Habana: Editorial Ciencias Sociales.

O'Connor, J. 1979. *La crisi fiscale dello Stato*. Torino: Einaudi.

_____. 1997. *Natural Causes: Essays in Ecological Marxism*. New York: The Guilford Press.

_____. 2000. *L'ecomarxismo*. VI Edition. Rome: Datanews.

OECD. 1998a. *Maintaining Prosperity in an Ageing Society*. Paris

_____. 1998b. *Policy Brief No. 3; Les nouvelles orientations de la politique industrielle Prospectives de la science, de la tecnologie et de l'industrie*. Paris.

Ollman, B. 1998. "Market Mystification in Capitalist and Market Socialist Societies," in B. Ollman, ed., *Market Socialism. The Debate Among Socialists*. New York: Routledge.

Onado, M. 1992. *Economia dei sistemi finanziari*. Bologna: il Mulino.

Ormerod, P. 1994. *I limiti della scienza economica*. Torino: Einaudi.

Orati, V. 2003. *Globalizzazione scientificamente infondata. Una nuova teoria per il popolo di Seattle*. Rome: Editori Riuniti.

Ordoñez, S. 2004. *"La nueva fase de desarrollo y el capitalismo del conocimiento,"* *Commercio Exterior*. Vol. 54. No. 1

Owen, R. 1971. *Per una nuova concezione della società e altri scritti*. Rome/Bari: Laterza.

Paganelli, O. 1990. *Valutazione delle aziende*. Torino: UTET.

Pagani, A., ed. 1967. *Il nuovo imprenditore*. Milan: Franco Angeli.

Pala, G. 1981. *Il lavoro e le sue forme economiche prodotto, merce e valore; denaro, capitale e prezzo*. Rome: Edizioni Kappa.

_____. 1982. *L'ultima crisi*. Milan: FrancoAngeli.
_____. 1996. *Il Fondo Monetario Internazionale. Il centro operativo dell'imperialismo transnazionale*. Naples: Labouratorio politico.
_____. 2001. "*Ong: Organizzazioni Non poco Governative. Il braccio disarmante del potere transnazionale*," *La contraddizione*. No. 84.
Palma, G. 1996. *Itinerari di Diritto Amministrativo. Lezioni 1993-1994*. Padova: CEDAM.
Panati, G. and G.M. Golinelli. 1991. *Tecnica Economica Industriale e Commerciale*. Vol. 1. Rome: Nis. [New Edition: 1995].
Pannekoek, A. 1976. *Los consejos obreros*. Buenos Aires: Editorial Proyeccion.
Panzieri, R. 1977. *La ripresa del marxismo leninismo in Italia*. Rome: Nuove Edizioni Operaie.
Papi, F., ed. 1976. *Ideologie nella rivoluzione industriale*. Bologna: Zanichelli.
Pareto, V. 1916. *Trattato di sociologia generale*. 2 volumes. Firenze: Barbera.
_____. 1945. *Manual de economía política*. Buenos Aires: Atalaya. [Italian translation: *Manuale di economia politica*. Milan: Università Bocconi. 2006].
Pasinetti, L. 1977. *Sviluppo economico e distribuzione del reddito*. Bologna: il Mulino.
_____. 1984. *Dinamica strutturale e sviluppo economico*. Torino: UTET.
Patton, C.V. and D.S. Sawicki. 1993. *Basic Methods of Policy Analysis and Planning*. Englewood Cliffs: Prentice-Hall.
Pavitt, K. 1984. "Sectoral Patterns of Technical Change: Towards a Taxonomy and a Theory," *Research Policy*. No. 13.
PCC. 1997. *Risoluzione economica*. V Congress of the Communist Party of, 8-10 October, La Habana: PCC.
Pellicelli, G. 2000. *Economia e direzione delle imprese*. Torino: Giappichelli.
Perlo, V. 1974. *The Unstable Economy, Booms and Recession in the USA since 1945*. New York: Editorial International.
Perri, S. 1997. "*Neovalore e plusvalore*," *Economia politica*, No. 2.
Pesenti, A. 1959. *Lezioni di economia politica*. Rome: Editori Riuniti.
_____. 1969. *Manuale di economia politica*. Rome: Editori Riuniti. [New Edition: 1984].
Petix, L. 1994. *Aspetti tipici di analisi strategica di competizione globale e di finanza internazionale*. Padova: CEDAM.
Petras, J. 2003. *Las colonias del imperialismo*. Lima: Juan Gutemberg Editores.
Petras, J. and H. Veltmeyer. 2002. *La globalizzazione smascherata. L'imperialismo del XXI secolo*. Milan: Jaca Book.
Petty, W. 1899. *Economic writings*. 2 volumes. Cambridge: Cambridge University Press. [Original: New York: Kelley. 1963].
Pianta, M. 1989. *L'economia globale*. Rome: Edizioni Lavoro.
Pietranera, G. 1998. *Il capitalismo monopolistico finanziario*. Naples: Ed. La città del sole.
Pigou, A.C. 1929. *The Economics of Welfare* [Italian translation: *L'economia del benessere*. Torino: UTET. 1960].
Piperno, F. 1997. *Elogio dello spirito pubblico meridionale*. Rome: Manifestolibri.
Pizzorno, A. 1999. "*Perché si paga il benzinaio. Per una teoria del capitale sociale*," *Stato e Mercato*. No. 57.
Platone. 1988. *Opere*. Rome/Bari: Laterza.
Poggio, P.P. 2003. *La crisi ecologica. Origini, rimozioni, significati*. Milan: Jaca Book.
Polanyi, K. 1989. *La Gran Transformación. Crítica del liberalismo económico*. Madrid: Ediciones de la Piqueta.
Pons, H. 2000. *Reflexiones acerca del concepto de política pública*. La Habana: Centro de Estudios de Economía y Planificación.
Pons, H., and E. González. 2001. *Diseño, Análisis y Evaluación de Políticas Públicas: Cuestiones Fundamentales*. La Habana: Centro de Estudios de Economía y Planificación (CEEP).

_____. 2002. *"La Gestión Pública: un acercamiento al concepto socialista,"* Presentation at the workshop "Indicadores de Rendimiento de la Gestión Pública." Matanzas: Universidad de Matanzas.

_____. 2006. *"Alcune considerazioni sul concetto di amministrazione pubblica,"* Revista PROTEO, No. 1/06. Rome: Ed. CESTES.

_____. 2006. *"Ritornare alla pianificazione nell'economia nazionale,"* Revista PROTEO. No. 3/06 - 1/07. Rome: Ed. CESTES.

Ponzio, A. 1997a. *Elogio dell'infunzionale? Critica dell'ideologia della produttività.* Rome: Castelvecchi.

_____. 1997b. *Metodologia della formazione linguistica,* Laterza, Bari.

Porta, P. and P. Saraceno. 1997. "The Mandatory Pension System in Italy," in *Contributi di Ricerca IRS.* No. 35.

Porter, M. 1991. *Il vantaggio competitivo delle nazioni.* Milan: Mondadori.

Pozzolo, A.F. 1997. *Gli effetti della liberalizzazione valutaria sulle transazioni finanziarie dell'Italia,* «Temi di discussione del Servizio Studi» (Banca d'Italia), No. 296, Rome.

Prestipino, G. 1972. *"Concetto logico e concetto storico di «formazione economico-sociale»,"* Critica marxista. No. 4.

_____. 1970. *"L'«antropologia» di Engels e la tematica filosofica dei Grundrisse,"* Critica marxista. No. 5.

PROTEO. 1997–06. Rome: Scientific Journal edited by CESTES and Rappresentanze di Base.

Proudhon, P.J. 1903. *Che cos'è la proprietà?* Firenze: Nerbini.

_____. 1945. *La filosofia della miseria.* Rome: OET.

Pulignano, V. 1997. *Oltre la fabbrica. I rapporti di fornitura nel post-fordismo.* Torino: L'Harmattan.

Putnam, R.D. 1996. *Making Democracy Work: Civic Tradition in Modern Italy.* Princeton: Princeton University Press.

Quesnay, F. 1973. *Il «Tableau économique» e altri scritti di economia.* Milan: Isedi.

Raboy, D. 1982. *Essays in Supply-Side Economics.* Washington: Heritage Foundation.

Ramonet, I. 1998. *Geopolitica del caos.* Trieste: Asterios.

_____. 1999. *La tirannia della comunicazione.* Trieste: Asterios.

Rampini, F. 1994. *Il crack delle nostre pensioni.* Milan: Mondadori.

_____. 1996. *Germanizzazione. Come cambierà l'Italia.* Rome/Bari: Laterza.

Rapisarda Sassoon, C. et al. 2005. *Per uno sviluppo durevole e sostenibile.* Milan: Network Sviluppo Sostenibile.

Regini, M. 2003. *Modelli di capitalismo. Le risposte europee alle sfide della globalizzazione.* Rome/Bari: Laterza.

Renneboog, L. 1999. *Corporate governance system; the role of ownership, external finance and regulation,* Working document No. 133. Brussels: CEPS.

Ricardo, D. 1986. *Principi di economia politica e dell'imposta.* Torino: UTET.

Ricoveri, G., ed. 2006. *Capitalismo, Natura, Socialismo.* Milan: Jaca Book.

Rieser, V. 2004. *"Il lavoro nel capitalismo postfordista,"* La rivista del manifesto. No. 50.

Rifkin, J. 1989. *Guerre del tempo. Il mito dell'efficienza e lo svolgimento dei ritmi naturali.* Milan: Bompian.

_____. 1996. *La fine del lavoro.* Milan: Baldini e Castoldi.

Rispoli, M. 1994. *Le forme di internazionalizzazione delle imprese.* Venice: il Carlo.

_____. 1996. *Ambiente competitivo e contenuti operativi della strategia.* Venice: Cafoscarina.

Robbins, S.P. and D.A. De Cenzo. 1996. *Fundamentos de Administración. Conceptos y Aplicaciones.* Mexico: Prentice Hall.

Robinson, J. 1948. *"Marx e Keynes,"* Critica Economica.

_____. 1959. *Ensayos de Economía Postkeynesiana.* Buenos Aires: Fondo de cultura económica. [Italian translation: *Teoria dell'occupazione e altri saggi.* Milan: Etas Kompass. 1967].

_____. 1969a. *L'accumulazione del capitale*. Milan: Edizioni di Comunità.

_____. 1969b. *Saggi sulla teoria dello sviluppo economico*. Milan: Etas Kompass.

_____. 1981. *Sviluppo e sottosviluppo*. Rome/Bari: Laterza.

Robinson, J., and J. Eatwell. 1973. *An Introduction to Modern Economics*. Maidenhead: McGraw-Hill. (Italian translation: *Le dottrine economiche. Teoria, politica e ideologia*. Milan: Etas. 1979).

Robinson, W. and J. Harris. 2000. "Toward a Global Ruling Class? Globalization and the Transnational Capitalist Class," *Science & Society*. Vol. 64. No. 1.

Rodríguez, José L. (2000). "Nuestro modelo no es el que falló en los ex-socialistas," *El Economista de Cuba*. Sección Esta Isla. Enero – Febrero. La Habana.

Romagnoli, A. 2001. *Introduzione alla economia politica. Problemi, metodologie, teorie*. Bologna: Esculapio.

Roncaglia, A. 1981. *Sraffa e la teoria dei prezzi*. Rome/Bari: Laterza.

_____. 1999. *Lineamenti di Economia Politica*. Rome/Bari: Laterza.

Roncaglia, A. and P. Sylos Labini. 2002. *Il pensiero economico. Temi e protagonisti*. Rome/Bari: Laterza.

Rosdolsky, R. 1970. "*Il significato del Capitale per la ricerca marxista contemporanea*," in V. Fay (Coord.), *Cent'anni dopo il Capitale*. Rome: Samonà e Savelli.

Rosenthal, J. 1998. *The Myth of Dialectics*. London: MacMillan.

Rosier, B. 1975. *Croissance et crise capitalistes*. Paris: PUF.

Rosier, B. and P. Dóckes. 1983. *Rythmes économiques, crises et changement social. Une perspective historique*. Paris: La Découverte / Maspero.

Rouland, N. 1992. *Antropologia giuridica*. Milan: Giuffrè.

Rullani, E. and L. Romano, eds. 1998. *Il postfordismo. Idee per il capitalismo prossimo venturo*. Milan: Etas Libri.

Russell, B. 1997. *Elogio dell'ozio*. Milan: Thea.

Saad-Filho, A., ed. 2002. *Anti-Capitalism: a Marxist Introduction*. London: Pluto Press.

Saad-Filho, A. and D. Johnston, eds. 2005. *Neoliberalism: a Critical Reader*. London: Pluto Press.

Salvioni, D.M. 1992. *Il bilancio d'esercizio nella comunicazione integrata d'impresa*. Torino: Giappichelli.

Samuelson, P. A. 1955. *The Foundations of Economics*. Cambridge: Cambridge University Press.

Samuelson, P. A. and W. D. Nordhaus. 1985. *Economics*. New York: McGraw-Hill. [Italian translation: *Economia*. Bologna: Zanichelli. 1987].

_____. 2001. *Economía*. La Habana: Editorial Félix Varela.

Sánchez, N. R. 2005. *Intervento al 'Seminario sobre Economía Política y pensamiento'*, in *La economía Política Marxista. Reflexiones para Un Debate*. La Habana: Editorial Félix Varela.

Sandoval González, R. 2004. *Contabilidad Nacional*. La Habana: Editorial Félix Varela.

Sargent, J. and R. E. Lucas. 1981. *Rational expectations and econometric practice*. London: G. Allen & Unwin.

Sauvy, A. 1972. *Los Mitos de Nuestro Tempo*. Barcelona: Labour.

Saviano, R. 2006. *Gomorra. Viaggio nell'impero economico e nel sogno di dominio della camorra*. Milan: Mondadori.

Schotter, A. 1997. *Microeconomia*. Torino: Giappichelli.

Schumpeter, J.A. 1934. *The Theory of Economic Developments*. Oxford: Oxford University Press. [Italian translation: *Teoria dello sviluppo economico*. Firenze: Sansoni. 1971]

_____. 1939. *Business cycles*, 2 volumes. McGraw-Hill, New York [Italian translation: *Il processo capitalistico. Cicli economici*. Torino: Bollati Boringhieri. 1977].

_____. 1947. *Capitalism, Socialism and Democracy*. New York: Harper.

_____. 1951. "Imperialism and social classes," in P. Sweezy, ed., *Imperialism and Social Classes*. New York: Augustus M. Kelly. [Italian translation: *Sociologia dell'imperialismo*. Rome / Bari: Laterza. 1972).

_____. 1954. *History of economic analysis*. New York: Oxford University Press. [Italian translation: *Storia della analisi economica*. Torino: Bollati Boringhieri. 1959].

Schweickart, D. 1996. *Against Capitalism*. Boulder: Westview Press. [Spanish translation: *Màs allà del capitalismo*. Santander: Sal Terrae. 1998].

_____. 2004. "Successor System Theory as an Orienting Devise: Trying to Understand China," *Nature, Society, Thought*. XVII, No. 4. pp. 389–413.

Sen, A. 1984. *Resources, Values and Development*. Cambridge: Harvard University Press.

Sereni, E. 1970. *Da Marx a Lenin: la categoria di «formazione economico-sociale»*, *Critica marxista*. Quarterly, No. 4.

Shaikh, A. 1980. "The laws of international exchange," in Nell E.J., ed., *Growth, Profits, and Property: Essays in the Revival of Political Economy*. Cambridge: Cambridge University Press.

_____. 1990. *Valor, Acumulación y Crisis. Ensayos de Economía Política*. Bogotá: Tercer Mundo Editores.

_____. 1999. *Real Exchange Rates and the International Mobility of Capital*, New School for Social Research, Working Paper No. 265. New York: The Jerome Levy Economics Institute of Bard College. Accessed at: http://homepage.newschool .edu/~AShaikh/Levyxrus.pdf

_____. 2003. "Who Pays for the 'Welfare' in the Welfare State? A Multicountry Study," *Social Research*, LXX, No. 2.

_____. 2009: Economic Policy in a Growth Context: A Classical Synthesis of Keynes and Harrod, *Metroeconomica*, Vol. 60, No. 3.

Shaikh A. and E. A. Tonak. 1994. *Measuring the Wealth of Nations. The Political Economy of National Accounts*. Cambridge / New York: Cambridge University Press.

Sklair L. 2001. *The Transnationalist Capitalist Class*. Oxford: Blackwell Publishing.

Sloman, J. 2002. *Elementi di economia*. Bologna: il Mulino.

Smith, A. 1776. *An inquiry into the nature and causes of the wealth of nations*. London: Strahan and Cadell. [Italian translation: *La ricchezza delle nazioni*. Rome: Newton Compton. 1995; *La ricchezza delle nazioni*. 2 volumes. Torino: UTET. 1975].

_____. 1937. *The Wealth of Nations*. New York: the Modern Library.

_____. 1999. *The Wealth of Nations*, 2 volumes. Harmondsworth: Penguin.

Smith, T. 2000. *Technology and Capital in the Age of Lean Production. A Marxian Critique of the 'New Economy.'* New York: State University of New York Press.

Solow, R.T. 1956. "A Contribution to the Theory of Economic Growth," *Quarterly Journal of Economics*. No. 70.

_____. 1957. "Technical Change and the Aggregate Production Function," *Review of Economics and Statistics*, No. 39.

_____. 2000. "*La teoria neoclassica della crescita e della distribuzione*," *Moneta e credito*, No. 54.

Sombrero, M. 1996. *Innovazione tecnologica e relazioni tra imprese*. Rome: La Nuova Italia Scientifica.

Sottile, G. 2004. *Alcune note su capitale e lavoro*. Accessed at: http://www.countdown net.info/archivio/Analisi_storico_politica/338.doc

Spulber, N. 1970. *La strategia sovietica per lo sviluppo economico*. Torino: Einaudi.

Sraffa, P. 1982. *Producción de mercancías por medio de mercancías*. Barcelona: OikosTau. [Italian translation: *Produzione di merci a mezzo di merci*. Torino: Einaudi. 1960 e 1999].

_____. 1986. *Saggi*. Bologna: il Mulino.

Stark, D. 1992. "*Le strategie di privatizzazione nell'Europa Orientale*," *Stato e mercato*, No. 34.

Steedman, I. 1977. *Marx after Sraffa*. London: New Left Books. [Spanish translation, *Marx, Sraffa y el problema de la Transformacion*. Mexico: FCE. 1985).

von Stein, L. 1897. *La scienza della publica amministrazione: compendio del Trattato e del Manuale di scienza della pubblica amministrazione ad uso degli italiani*. Torino: Unione Tipografiche Riunite.

Steindl, J. 1976. *Maturity and Stagnation in American Capitalism*. New York: Monthly Review Press.

Stewart, T.A. 1999. *Il capitale intellettuale*. Milan: Ponte alle Grazie.

Stiglitz J.E. 1988. *Economics of the Public Sector*. New York: Norton.

_____. 2002 *La globalizzazione e i suoi oppositori*. Torino: Einaudi.

Stillman, R. 1990. *Preface to Public Administration. A Search for Themes and Directions*. New York: St. Martin's Press.

Stoner, J. and E. Freeman. 1994. *Administración*. Mexico: Prentice-Hall Hispanoamericana.

Storper, M. 1998. *The resurgence of regional economies ten years later: the region as a Strategic Supply Chain Alignment*. London: Gower.

Strumilin, S. 1966. *Ensayos sobre la economía socialista*. La Habana: Editorial Ciencias Sociales.

Stuart Mill, John. 1998. *Utilitarism*. Oxford / New York: Oxford University Press.

Sweezy, P.M. 1942. *The Theory of Capitalist Development. Principles of Marxian Political Economy*. New York: Oxford University Press. [Italian translation, *La teoria dello sviluppo capitalistico*. Torino: Bollati Boringhieri. 1970].

_____. 1946. "John Maynard Keynes," in *Science and Society*, Fall.

_____. 1962. *Il presente come storia*. Torino: Einaudi.

_____. 1980. *Post-revolutionary Society*. New York: Monthly Review Press.

_____. 1981. *Four Lectures On Marxism*. [Italian translation: *Il marxismo e il futuro. Quattro lezioni*. Torino: Einaudi. 1983].

Sweezy, P.M. and C. Bettelheim. 1971. *On the transition to Socialism*. Monthly Review Press, New York [Spanish translation: *Algunos problemas actuales del socialismo*. Mexico: Siglo XXI. 1976].

Sylos Labini P. 1956. *Oligopolio e progresso tecnico*. Milan: Giuffrè.

_____. 1988. *Saggio sulle classi sociali*. Rome/Bari: Laterza.

_____. 1992. *Elementi di dinamica economica*. Rome/Bari: Laterza.

_____. 1994. *Carlo Marx è tempo di un bilancio*. Rome/Bari: Laterza.

_____. 2002. *L'opera di Giorgio Fuà: concezioni feconde e problemi aperti*, in «Rendiconti dell'Accademia Nazionale dei Lincei», Rome: Classe di scienze morali, XIII, No. 6.

_____. 2004. *Torniamo ai classici. Produttività del lavoro, progresso tecnico e sviluppo economico*. Rome/Bari: Laterza.

Tablada, Pérez C. 1987. *El pensamiento economico de Ernesto Che Guevara*. La Habana: Ediciones Casa de las Americas.

Tamayo, Sáez M. 1997. "*El análisis de las políticas públicas*," in Rafael Bañón and Ernesto Carrillo, eds., *La nueva administración pública*. Madrid: Universidad Alianza Textos.

Tarrow, S. 1996. "Making social Science Work Across space and Time. A Critical Reflection on Robert Putnam's Making Democracy Work," *American Political Science Review*, No. 90.

Taylor, F.W. 1911. *The Principles of Scientific Management*. New York: Harper & Perennial.

Tesauro, F. 2003. *Istituzioni di diritto tributario*, vol. I, *Parte generale*. Torino: UTET.

Thompson, E.P. 1968. *The making of the English working class*. London: Penguin Books.

_____. 1979. *Tradición, revuelta y consciencia de clase: estudios sobre la crisis de la sociedad preindustrial*. Barcelona: Crítica.

Thompson, J. 2001. *Strategic Management*. New York: Thompson Learning.

Tiddi, A. 2002. *Precari. Percorsi di vita tra lavoro e non lavoro*. Rome: DeriveApprodi.

Tinbergen, J. 1939. *Statistical Testing of Business Cycle Theories.* 2 volumes. Geneva: League of Nations.
_____. 1967. *Sviluppo e pianificazione.* Milan: Il Saggiatore.
_____. 1993. *Alla ricerca dell'organizzazione che apprende. L'apprendimento organizzativo nel futuro della formazione continua.* Rome: Edizioni Lavoro.
Tosel, A. 1986. "Sul marxismo italiano degli anni sessanta," in *Critica marxista,* No. 6.
Trevino L. and K. Nelson. 1999. *Managing Business Ethics.* New York: Wiley.
Triana J. 2005. *Cuba crecer desde el conocimiento.* La Habana: Editorial Ciencias Sociales.
Trillo, D. 2002. *Análisis económico y eficiencia del sector público.* Paper presented at the VII CLAD about Public Administration and State Reform, Lisbon, Portugal. 8–11 October.
Tucci, M. 2003. *Programmazione amministrativa e pianificazione del territorio.* Torino: Giappichelli.
UNCTAD–United Nations Conference on Trade and Development. 1991–99. Various years. *Handbook of Statistics.* Geneva.
_____. Various years. *World Investment.* Geneva.
UNDP–United Nations Development Programme. Various years. *Rapporto sullo sviluppo umano.* Torino: Rosenberg & Sellier.
Vaccà, S., and G. Cozzi. 2002. "*Le imprese transnazionali come possibili veicoli di sviluppo economico nell'era della globalizzazione,*" in *Economia e Politica Industriale,* No. 116.
Valdani, E. 1991. *Marketing globale. La gestione strategica dei mercati internazionali.* Milan: Egea.
Valle, A. 2000. "*Porque parece mentira o resulta inconveniente la verdad a veces no se sabe,*" *Política y Cultura.* No. 13.
_____. 2003. *Renta y competencia capitalista: con especial referencia al petróleo,* in Palacios M., Debrott S., eds., *Teoría de la Renta y Recursos Naturales,* Mexico: Universidad Autónoma de Chapingo.
Valli, V. 1974. *Sistemi economici capitalisti e socialisti*: Milan: Cooperativa Editrice Bocconiana.
Vanek, J. 1990. *Crisis and Reform: East and West.* Ithaca: Desktop Published.
Vaneigem, R. 1999. *Trattato del saper vivere ad uso delle giovani generazioni.* Rome: Malatempora.
Varga, E.S. 1948. *Changes in the Economy of Capitalism Resulting from the Second World War.* Washington: Public Affairs Press.
Varian, Hal R. 1990. *Microeconomia.* Venice: Ed. Cafoscarina.
Various Authors. 1991. *Lecciones de Economía Política de la Construcción del Socialismo. Carreras Económicas,* tomo I, Dirección de Marxismo-Leninismo. La Habana: ENPES.
_____. 1996a. *El derrumbe del modelo eurosovietico: una vision desde Cuba,* Colectivo deAutores, coordinado por Ramon Sanchez Noda. La Habana: Editorial Félix Varela.
_____. 1996b. *Stato e diritti nel post-fordismo,* Manifestolibri, Roma.
_____. 1998. *L'Italia s'è desta.* Naples: Edizioni Labouratorio Politico.
_____. 2002. *Economía Política de la Construcción del Socialismo: Fundamentos Generales.* La Habana: Editorial Félix Varela.
_____. 2003. "*Il potere delle transnazionali,*" *Quaderni di Alternatives Sud.* Milan: Edizioni Punto Rosso.
_____. 2004. *La Economía Política Marxista. Reflexiones para un debate.* La Habana: Editorial Félix Varela.
Vasapollo, Luciano. 1993. *Il sistema finanziario. Mercati e prodotti.* Rome: Edizioni Lavoro.
_____. 1996. *Dall'entrapreneur all'imprenditore plurimo. Sulla teoria economica della funzione imprenditoriale.* Padova: Cedam.

_____. 1995. *Sulla localizzazione dell'imprenditorialità in Italia*, in «Temi di Attualità» (Dipartimento di Contabilità Nazionale APS. Rome: Università degli Studi «La Sapienza»). No. 2.

_____. 2004. *Novos Desequilibrios Capitalistas*. São Paulo, Brasil: Ed. Praxis.

_____. 2005. *O Trabalho atipico e a precariedade*. São Paulo, Brasil: Ed. Expressao Popular.

_____. 2007. *Trattato di Economia Applicata*. Milan: Jaca Book.

_____. 2007. *Storia di un capitalismo piccolo piccolo*. Milan: Jaca Book.

Vasapollo, Luciano, ed. 2002. *Un vecchio falso problema. La trasformazione dei valori in prezzi nel Capitale di Marx*. Castel Madama: Mediaprint.

_____. 2003. *Il piano inclinato del capitale. Crisi, competizione globale e guerre*. Milan: Jaca Book.

_____. 2005. *Lavoro contro capitale. Precarietà, sfruttamento, delocalizzazione*. Milan: Jaca Book.

_____. 2006. *L'acqua scarseggia... ma la papera galleggia*. Milan: Jaca Book.

_____. 2008. *Capitale, Natura e Lavoro*. Milan: Jaca Book.

Vasapollo, L., M. Casadio, J. Petras and H. Veltmeyer. 2004. *Competizione globale. Imperialismi e movimenti di resistenza*. Milan: Jaca Book. [Spanish translation: *Imperio con Imperialismo*. La Habana: Ciencias Sociales]

Vasapollo L., E. Echevarria and A. Jam. 2007. *"Che" Guevara economista*. Milan: Jaca Book.

Vasapollo L., H. Jaffe and P. H. Galarza P.H. 2005. *Introduzione alla storia e alla logica dell'imperialismo*. Milan: Jaca Book. [Spanish translation: *Introduccion a la Historia y la logica del Imperialismo*. Barcelona: El Viejo Topo].

Vasapollo L., and R. Martufi, eds. 2008. *L'ambiente Capitale. Alternative alla globalizzazione contro natura. Cuba investe sull'umanità*. Rome: Natura Avventura Edizioni.

Vercelli A. 1973. *Teoria della struttura economica capitalistica. Il metodo di Marx e i fondamenti della critica all'economia politica*. Torino: Fondazione Luigi Einaudi.

Vercelli A., and S. Borghesi. 2007. *La sostenibilità dello sviluppo globale*. Rome: Carocci.

Vicari S. 1989. "Invisible assets e comportamento incrementale," *Finanza, Marketing e Produzione*, n°1. Milan: Università L. Bocconi.

Vincent J.M. 1970. *Scienza e ideologia un secolo dopo il Capitale*, in Fay V., ed., *Cent'anni dopo il Capitale*. Rome: Samonà e Savelli.

Viola F. 1989. *La società astratta*. Rome: Edizioni Associate.

Volpi F. 1999. *Introduzione all'economia dello sviluppo*. Milan: FrancoAngeli.

Vygodskij V. S. 1974. *Introduzione ai «Grundrisse» di Marx*. Firenze: La Nuova Italia.

Wallerstein I. 1999. *Dopo il liberalismo*. Milan: Jaca Book.

_____. 2004. *Il declino dell'America*. Milan: Feltrinelli.

Walras L. 1900. *Éléments d'économie politique pure ou Théorie de la richesse sociale*. Paris: File Rouge.

Weber M. 1922. *Die protestantische Ethik und der Geist des Kapitalismus*, in *Gesammelte Aufsätze zur Religionssoziologie*. Tübingen: Mohr. [Italian translation: *L'etica protestante e lo spirito del capitalismo*, Firenze: Sansoni. 1965].

_____. 1944. *Economía y sociedad*. Mexico: Ed. Fondo de la Cultura.

Weeks, J. 1981. *Capital and Exploitation*. Princeton: Princeton University Press.

_____. 1989. *A Critique of Neoclassical Macroeconomics*. New York: St. Martin's Press.

Wheleen T., and J. Hunger. 1993. *Strategic Management and Business Policy*. New York: Addison Wesley.

Whyte, William F. and Kathleen K. Whyte. 1988. *Making Mondragon: the Growth and Dynamics of the Worker Cooperative Complex*. Ithaca: IRA Press. [*Mondragòn: Màs que una utopia*, Txertoa, San Sebastián].

Wicksell, K. 1901–06. *Forelasningar i nationalekonomi*, 2 volumes. Stockholm-Lund. [Italian translation: *Lezioni di economia politica*. Torino: UTET. 1966].

Wilczynski, J. 1972. *Socialist Economic Development and Reforms*. London: MacMillan.

Wilson, Q. 1980. *The Politics of regulation*. New York: Basic Books.

Wilson, W.J. (ed.) 1983. *Crime and Public Policy* San Francisco: ICS Press.

Wolff, E.N. 1986. *Growth, Accumulation, and Unproductive Activity: An Analysis of the Postwar US Economy.* Cambridge: Cambridge University Press.

World Bank. Various years. *World Development Report.* Washington.

Zamagni, S. 1998. *Lavoro, occupazione, economia civile,* in Caselli L. (ed.), *Ripensare il lavoro.* Bologna: EDB.

Zanotelli, A. 1996. *Leggere l'impero. Il potere fra l'apocalisse e l'Esodo.* Molfetta: Edizioni La Meridiana.

INDEX

accounting, 15, 53, 56, 90, 119,
124, 193, 266, 275–6.
national, 53–71, 266.
accumulation,
autonomous, 85.
capitalist, 4, 8, 9, 16, 18, 20, 26, 45, 54,
64, 82, 104, 109, 123–4, 130, 134–5,
139, 144, 150, 160, 170, 175, 188,
192, 202, 216, 236, 241, 243, 272,
277, 309.
crisis of, 252, 291–6, 319, 326.
Fordist, 56.
flexible, 13, 46, 57, 80–3, 104–5,
112, 171, 192, 194–5, 200, 202,
210, 235, 242, 311, 327.
and globalization, 213, 316.
information, 152, 211–2, 216.
internationalized, 168.
and investment, 63–6.
Keynesian, 132, 171, 190, 306.
material, 47, 199, 257.
national, 232.
original, 32, 318.
patterns, 86, 293, 337.
rate, 63.
shortcomings, 232, 325.
social, 254, 337.
technological, 216, 238.
tempered, 254.
of wealth, 251.
administration,
business, 92.
in Cuba, 15, 21.
in the knowledge economy, 193.
neoconservative, 109.
North American, 148, 211.
public, 60–2, 67, 89, 92, 94, 95–97,
99, 199.
of scarcity, 2, 5.
socialist, 95.
agrarian, 14, 193.
agriculture, 60, 61,193, 215, 224, 279,
283, 324.

Bolivia, 245, 283–4, 287.

capital
abstract, 193, 197.

anti-, 135, 287.
financial, 7, 9, 17, 19, 30, 82–3, 110,
113, 140, 146, 149–50, 170, 173,
201, 211–12, 213–14, 216, 241, 253,
276, 301, 304, 311, 314, 317, 321,
326.
flows, 57, 83, 88, 110, 146, 151, 213,
217, 226, 229–30, 232, 291, 295,
311, 319, 322–3, 327.
-labour contradiction, 11, 42, 56,
110–1, 133, 235–8.
-ist accumulation, 4, 8, 9, 16, 18, 20,
26, 45, 54, 64, 82, 104, 109, 123–4,
130, 134–5, 139, 144, 150, 160, 170,
175, 188, 192, 202, 216, 236, 241,
243, 272, 277, 309.
Castro, Fidel, 1, 280–1, 325, 333–4.
Chávez, Hugo, 286–7.
China, 116, 126, 174, 216, 314–15, 335.
class
capitalist, 7, 14, 27–30, 34, 37, 39–40,
42, 45–8, 144–5, 166, 179, 199,
202, 236, 286.
exploitation, 7, 40, 42–3, 48, 162–3,
166, 200, 236.
ruling, 147, 170, 244.
struggle, 40, 43, 97, 162–3, 166, 238,
287, 288, 336.
working, 7, 27–8, 30, 34, 40, 42–3,
45–48, 97, 153, 162, 166–7, 169,
210–1, 235–6, 241, 246, 286, 287,
293, 312, 335, 336.
communications, 9–10, 14, 60, 126, 194,
197, 209.
competition,
capital, 119–20, 123, 141.
global, 8–9, 12, 61, 78, 81–2, 112,
129, 133–4, 136, 142, 147–9,
153–7.
individual, 76, 118.
labour, 13, 44, 119.
monetary, 7.
and monopolies, 140, 142.
perfect, 3.
consumer, 3, 9–10, 45, 58, 70, 80, 99,
209, 211, 218–19, 240, 243, 253–4,
256, 271, 284, 299–300, 317,
327, 332.

www.ingramcontent.com/pod-product-compliance
Lightning Source LLC
Chambersburg PA
CBHW060021030426
42334CB00019B/2131